The Story of Radio Mind

THE STORY OF RADIO MIND

A Missionary's Journey on Indigenous Land

PAMELA E. KLASSEN

The University of Chicago Press
Chicago and London

The University of Chicago Press, Chicago 60637
The University of Chicago Press, Ltd., London
© 2018 by The University of Chicago
All rights reserved. No part of this book may be used or reproduced in any manner whatsoever without written permission, except in the case of brief quotations in critical articles and reviews. For more information, contact the University of Chicago Press, 1427 East 60th Street, Chicago, IL 60637.
Published 2018
Printed in the United States of America

27 26 25 24 23 22 21 20 19 18   1 2 3 4 5

ISBN-13: 978-0-226-55256-9 (cloth)
ISBN-13: 978-0-226-55273-6 (paper)
ISBN-13: 978-0-226-55287-3 (e-book)
DOI: https://doi.org/10.7208/chicago/9780226552873.001.0001

The University of Chicago Press gratefully acknowledges the generous support of the Anneliese Maier Research Award of the Alexander von Humboldt Foundation toward the publication of this book.

Library of Congress Cataloging-in-Publication Data

Names: Klassen, Pamela E. (Pamela Edith), 1967– author.
Title: The story of radio mind : a missionary's journey on Indigenous land / Pamela E. Klassen.
Description: Chicago ; London : The University of Chicago Press, 2018. | Includes bibliographical references and index.
Identifiers: LCCN 2017049038 | ISBN 9780226552569 (cloth : alk. paper) | ISBN 9780226552736 (pbk. : alk. paper) | ISBN 9780226552873 (e-book)
Subjects: LCSH: DuVernet, Frederick Herbert, 1860–1924. | Missionaries—British Columbia—Biography. | Bishops—British Columbia—Biography. | Church of England in Canada—Bishops—Biography. | British Columbia—Church history—20th century.
Classification: LCC BX5620.D85 K53 2018 | DDC 283.092 [B]—dc23
LC record available at https://lccn.loc.gov/2017049038

♾ This paper meets the requirements of ANSI/NISO Z39.48-1992 (Permanence of Paper).

For Georgia, Isabel, and Magdalene

Contents

Illustrations

Plates (following page 180)

Figures

1
The Medium Is the Medicine

Sitting quietly in a house on Robson Street in downtown Vancouver, the archbishop relaxed his mind and prepared to receive a thought—really just a short word—sent by his daughter, Alice, from more than five hundred miles away. Alice was at their home in Prince Rupert on the Pacific coast, overlooking the Hecate Strait, in a room lined with shelves of books featuring the latest psychology and philosophy of the mind. She focused with rhythmic concentration on transmitting a thought to her father not through prayer but through telepathy. It was the early 1920s, at the dawn of the radio age, and Frederick Du Vernet and his daughter had something to prove: the power of radio mind.

Dangling a metal pendulum from an eight-inch string tied to the end of a long pencil, Frederick stilled his mind and body as he awaited his daughter's word from afar. A sheet of paper lay on the table in front of him, on which was drawn an alphabet spread out like a fan (fig. 1). Alice's mind energy flew south to her father's soul, and his hand vibrated in turn, causing the pendulum to bob back and forth over specific letters on the page, spelling out a simple word: C-O-A-T. According to the "telepathic testimonies" Frederick wrote for church journals, city newspapers, and books published across North America, father and daughter had achieved the unspoken communication of mind to mind across distance. Frederick Du Vernet, archbishop and self-declared scientist, proudly announced to the world that he had proved the "laws" of spiritual communication.[1]

Since 1904, Frederick Du Vernet (fig. 2) had served as the bishop of Caledonia, a more than two-hundred-thousand-square-mile area of the Pacific northwest remapped by the Church of England as one of its Canadian dioceses—a region under a bishop's watch and care. The name Caledonia

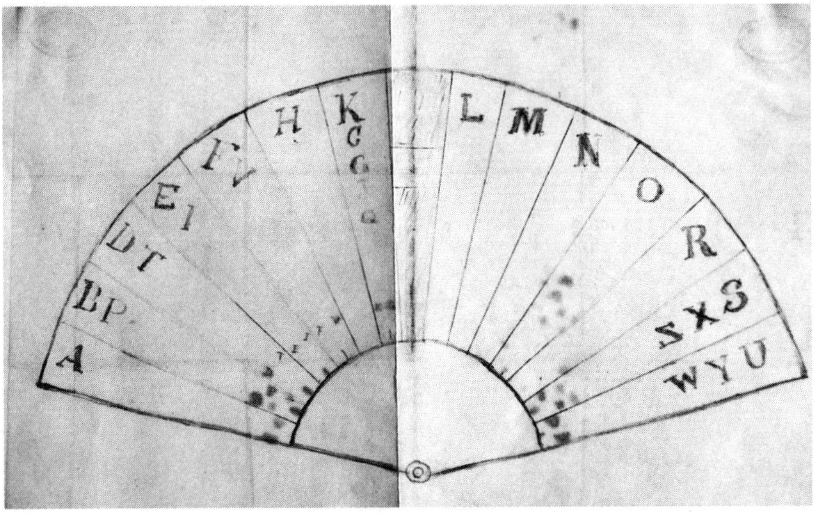

FIGURE 1. Chevreul pendulum chart of Frederick and Alice Du Vernet (ca. 1922). Photograph courtesy of the Diocese of Caledonia Archives.

recalled the Scottish roots of many of the Hudson's Bay Company employees, who were among the first Europeans to live in the region. By 1915, Du Vernet was also the first metropolitan of the Ecclesiastical Province of British Columbia, an even more massive region that aligned with the province of the same name. Undertaking his "scientific experiments" with Alice in his sixties, he wrote with confidence about spiritual energy: "Distance may separate physical brains but not spiritual minds which interpenetrate in the unity of the spirit."[2] A man facing the physical limitations of age and illness after decades of traveling the land and waters by foot, canoe, sailboat, steamer, horseback, and rail, Frederick Du Vernet was journeying to the border of mind and spirit.

Twenty years before Du Vernet wrote about radio mind, the land on which the archbishop's house now stood had been a hill blanketed in cedar, spruce, and cypress trees. The Ts'msyen knew it as Kaien Island, after the foam that hovered over the waters of an intertidal zone abundant with salmon and shellfish, eulachon and herring, seaweed and sea otters. Long before British sailors named Hecate Strait after a Greek goddess of stars and the sea who protected sailors and babies, brought plentiful fish, and calmed storms, the waters surrounding Kaien Island were guarded by other stories of the spirit world.[3]

According to Ts'msyen and Nisga'a oral histories, the land and waters of the region are rich in *spanaxnox*, spirit beings who, as Susan Marsden writes, mark where "space becomes sacred—an opening, or gateway, between the

FIGURE 2. Bishop Frederick Du Vernet, Prince Rupert (ca. 1909). Photograph courtesy of the Prince Rupert City and Regional Archives (P991-72-6156).

human and spirit worlds." Opening up the very possibility of this gateway between worlds is Weeget, also known as Txeemsim, a trickster figure who, disguised as a raven, long ago brought light from the heavens to the dark world of the coast. Tales of the spanaxnox are told in Ts'msyen *adawx*—oral narratives that carry collective weight as the "authorized history of the nation." Similarly, Nisga'a *adaawak*, oral histories that form the basis of collective memory and law both for specific clans and for the Nisga'a more generally, tell of *sbi-nax̱noḵ*, spirit beings who convey lessons. The tales of the spanaxnox are also painted and carved on quartzite and bedrock as petroglyphs, helping mark the territorial boundaries of clans and houses and mapping alliances and conflicts between humans and spirits over the course of millennia.[4]

Its rock blasted away, its trees cut down, its waters turned into one of the deepest harbors on the coast, and its Indigenous people displaced to reserves across the strait, Kaien Island had become by the 1920s Prince Rupert, the coastal terminal of Canada's northern railway line. Du Vernet was well aware that the violent transformation of the land took place without any resolution of what Indigenous nations and settlers both called the "Indian Land Question"; he knew that no treaties had been agreed upon between the two. The Nisga'a had organized an Indian Land Committee to protest the Canadian seizure of their territory, and had traveled to the political centers of Victoria, Ottawa, and London to state their case. Shifting his gaze away from the earthly claims of his Indigenous neighbors—who were often fellow Anglicans—Du Vernet peered at a cosmic realm of universal harmony mediated by radio mind. Just as the rails now conducted settlers and goods to and from this northwestern corner of the continent, so too, insisted Frederick Du Vernet, could the mind send and receive thoughts from afar, broadcasting God's love and energy to heal the world.[5]

Du Vernet lived in a place and time that lucidly reveals the spiritual work of colonial settlement. Coming to the watery home of the Ts'msyen, Nisga'a, Haida, Haisla, and other Indigenous peoples in 1904, Du Vernet was oriented by many different maps: the relatively new map of the Dominion of Canada, founded in 1867, the map of his diocese drawn by the Church of England in Canada (now the Anglican Church of Canada), and surveyors' maps of the land and sea that christened the homes of spanaxnox with names such as "Hecate Strait," "Venn Passage," and "Prince Rupert." He also had a faint understanding of the spiritual maps by which the Ts'msyen and Nisga'a storied their land.

In Du Vernet's version of the story of radio mind, he did not reach the gateway between human and spirit worlds by listening to the adawx of the Ts'msyen or the adaawak of the Nisga'a. Instead, he came to radio mind through reading books written by men who were similarly fascinated by the borders of mind and spirit and who also told stories oriented by the psychic or psychological. These men were renowned scientists and scholars living not at the edges but in the heart of imperial nations, including William James and Josiah Royce of Boston and Henri Bergson and Charles Richet of Paris.

Unlike these luminaries, Frederick Du Vernet lived and traveled in territories that were then often called "Indian Land" by Indigenous peoples and missionaries alike; he met Indigenous people in Anishinaabe territory around the Great Lakes and in the many nations of the northwest coast. His telepathic testimonies were not simply psychic research but also spiritual and colonial exploration. In this, he was not alone. Many Anglicans were among the growing number of early twentieth-century Christians in North America and the British Empire who were finding psychology and psychic research to be fruitful communities of thought. Some turned to alternative religious movements altogether, such as Theosophy or varieties of Spiritualism, but others experimented with new understandings of the spirit while staying within their church.

Missionaries in colonial settings, such as India or British Columbia, often came to their psychic interests through their exposure to the religious and spiritual traditions of the people they were seeking to colonize; they were transformed in the process of living and talking with their desired converts, who had their own theories of mind, body, and spirit. As Gauri Viswanathan described such a dynamic in the context of India, some missionaries grew to "denounce European culture for making its doctrines part of an oppressive system of control, with little or no connection to the spiritual lives of its practitioners." Living in the midst of the Indian Land Question, Du Vernet also came to denounce what "passes as religion" in Christian churches for what he considered to be its utterly outmoded understanding of the spirit.[6]

After more than twenty-five years as a missionary who sought to transform the minds and spirits of Anishinaabeg, Ts'msyen, Nisga'a, and Haida by way of a Christian story, Du Vernet was himself transformed by the ways they understood and mediated spiritual knowledge. In the end, his testimonies about radio mind told a story of cosmic unity that looked quite different from the orthodox narratives of Christian evangelicalism from which he had come and a lot more like the spiritual energies of the land on which he lived.

A Story from the Mouth

"Tell me a story from your mouth, Mama," my daughter would say almost every evening following a bedtime story read from a book. A story from the mouth is not the same as a story from a book—it requires more imagination or feats of recall on the part of the storyteller and holds out the chance of surprise for the listener. With no written script to guide the teller, a story from the mouth is never quite the same story twice. My daughter asked me for a story from my mouth because she wanted some of this unpredictability, but also because she wanted more of me in the story. In turn, she would also get more of herself and her sisters, as I invented stories about squirrels or bunnies or deer sharing the same names as my daughters. While she sometimes groaned as I plotted their animal namesakes into my own version of a morally uplifting fable, my daughter nevertheless listened and asked again the next night for another.

A bedside story from the mouth carries very different emotional resonances than a lecture in a crowded university hall or a video flickering across the internet. Whispering face-to-face or broadcasting coast-to-coast-to-coast, storytellers adjust their message depending on the proximity of their listeners. Not only measured in inches or miles, proximity is also determined by emotional intimacy and ritual protocols of how and by whom stories should be told. Not every story is for sharing with just anybody, as Eden Robinson, a Haisla/Heiltsuk novelist from the northwest coast noted when reflecting on her own writing process: "I knew I couldn't use any of the clan stories—these are owned by either individuals or families and require permission and a feast in order to be published." Such care to protect stories intensified with the arrival of missionaries, according to Haisla elders, since the Haisla "recognized that whatever the missionaries knew about our culture, they tried to suppress."[7] Though shaped by very different protocols than a Haisla clan story, even a story from the mouth told at bedtime has its rules and rituals.

"The truth about stories," novelist Thomas King tells us, "is that that's all that we are." Stories are both "wondrous" and "dangerous"; stories can trap you and release you. King tells what he calls his "native narrative" with a keen awareness "that stories were medicine, that a story told one way could cure, that the same story told another way could injure."[8] Weaving together personal stories of family and friends with political analysis, King also compares Christian and Indigenous creation stories, sizing up Adam with the help of the Trickster. The solitary, omnipotent, and hierarchical God of Genesis, King says, has generated traditions of storytelling very different from the playful and cooperative spirits and animals featured in many Indigenous creation stories.

King goes further to ask, with an ironic innocence, whether "the stories contained within the matrix of Christianity and the complex of nationalism are responsible for the social, political, and economic problems we face? Am I really arguing that the martial and hierarchical nature of Western religion and Western privilege has fostered stories that encourage egotism and self-interest?"[9] Not quite, King answers, but almost. Highlighting the corrosive effects of stereotypical and racist depictions of Indigenous people, while at the same time exemplifying the liberating effects of writing his own native narrative, King makes clear that nations, religions, and people are made out of stories.

Another literary scholar, J. Edward Chamberlin, also reflects on the formative power of stories: "Whether Jew or Arab, Catholic or Protestant, farmer or hunter, black or white, man or woman, we all have stories that hold us in thrall and hold others at bay. What we share is the practice of believing, which we become adept at very early in our lives; and it is this practice that generates the power of stories."[10] The practice of believing. Stories require work; to be a good storyteller one needs practice, and to be a good, or at least a satisfied, listener one needs to believe what one hears, at least momentarily. The practice of belief requires more than just rational assent. It is exercised through all the senses. Stories with the most power make good use of this sensorial overload, hitting you in the gut, tightening your chest to bring you to the edge of tears, and provoking your discerning, calculating mind all at once.

Haunted by the question that he once heard a Gitxsan elder from northern British Columbia put to government officials who were insisting that Gitxsan land was Canadian land—"If this is your land, where are your stories?"—Chamberlin sets out to tell a story of Canada. Turning to his own family stories of his grandfather in Fort Macleod, Alberta, as well as to songs, treaties, poetry, and other genres, Chamberlin contends that stories—and land restitution—must be at the heart of any attempt to take responsibility for and to remedy the ways that North America came to be through the theft of Indigenous lands. Stories can both unite and exclude; they can be shared and they can be protected. Stories must be understood in their paradoxical power, as tales that can create a reality—even a nation—that makes sense to one group of people, but not to another. As creative ways of imagining our world, stories are both make-believe and making believe, they are wondrous and dangerous, and there are always more that can be told.

The Gitxsan elder's question—as passed on by Chamberlin's story—now also haunts me. In response, I tell a story of the life and travels of a man who thought of Canada as his land, from his childhood on the southern border of Quebec overlooking New York State, to his youth and early career in Toronto, to his last twenty years living among the Ts'msyen, Nisga'a, Haida, Gitxsan, and white and Japanese settlers in northwestern British Columbia. Frederick H. Du Vernet, a Toronto-based Anglican priest, missionary, occasional seminary professor, and fledgling photojournalist, eventually became an eminent churchman with many roles to his credit—including first archbishop of British Columbia and cofounder of what would become the Vancouver School of Theology. Along the way, he told stories that claimed Indigenous land as Canadian land. He also told stories that showed he knew quite well that Ojibwe,[11] Nisga'a, and Ts'msyen people had their own stories about their territories, stories that also turned land and people into nations.

Living as a colonial missionary-bishop among Indigenous peoples, both Christians and non-Christians, Du Vernet was a man of many paradoxes. He was an early adopter of such new storytelling technologies as photography and radio, and his embrace of these media also brought him to see human relationships and the world of the spirit in new ways. Convinced of the righteousness of building Canada as a Christian nation, he was also adamant that sending Indigenous children to faraway church residential schools was both dangerous for the children and catastrophic for their parents. By the end of his life, he was a modern mystic of mediation living at the edge of an empire that was still contested by the very Nisga'a, Ts'msyen, and Haida people who had joined his church. His burgeoning interest in psychic research and his experiments with the healing power of what he called radio mind form a story worth telling not only for its curious twists and turns, but also for what it reveals about the practices of believing that brought Canada into being, and maintain it still.

Following Du Vernet's missionary journeys, I traveled to his birthplace in Quebec, to his college and first church posting in Toronto, and to what is now the Kay-Nah-Chi-Wah-Nung Historical Centre run by the Ojibwe of the Rainy River First Nations, a place that he visited in 1898. I also twice made the trip to what he knew as the Diocese of Caledonia in northwestern British Columbia, visiting Prince Rupert and the Cathedral Church of St. Andrew's, the Nisga'a Nation, the Ts'msyen Metlakatla First Nation, and Haida Gwaii. Walking in those places and speaking with the people who live there now has made it possible for me to imagine his life in ways that books and archives never could have on their own.

The story of radio mind that I have come to tell examines the very mechanisms and media—in this case, photography, the printing press, maps, and radio—that enabled the spiritual invention of the Canadian nation. The means by which we tell our stories shape our relationships, our ethics, and our emotions. If stories are medicine that can both cure and injure, part of what gives them this power is the medium by which they are told. A totem pole and the paper that comes out of a printing press both tell stories. The labor and skills required to carve a story into cedar or to forge a press out of iron, however, demand very different kinds of natural resources, social organization, technological know-how, interpretive wisdom, and modes of preservation.

To borrow from philosopher Simone de Beauvoir, a medium is not born but made. The making of a medium occurs through ongoing processes of collective human labor: the original casting and assembling of a printing press, let's say, and its use, maintenance, and repair. In the midst of all this labor, the relationships people have with their preferred media and with each other through their media—whether totem poles, printing presses, or cell phones—can take on spiritual, therapeutic, or even traumatic contours. The medium may be the message, in the famous dictum of Marshall McLuhan, but the medium is also the medicine that can cure and injure.[12]

The making of both the Canadian and the American nations has depended on stories told from the mouth, but also on stories told from books, newspapers, legal statutes, maps, photographs, radio, film, and a variety of other media. On the northwest coast in particular, Canadian and US missionaries, settlers, and lawmakers imposed an imperial, and often a Christian, mapping on the lands they named British Columbia and Alaska with the help of these multimedia stories. Missionaries, few in number but profound in their influence, attacked Indigenous media in an "orgy of destruction" that sought to replace Indigenous creation stories, territorial claims, and kinship relations with Christian ones.[13] Encouraging converts to publicly chop down their totem poles and burn their ceremonial regalia, missionaries sought to impose a new story on the land by exterminating the material forms of storytelling that they so viscerally feared as pagan. While doing so, however, some discovered, perhaps unwillingly, that the Christian story of these lands was not the only one that could be told.

The story of radio mind reveals how invocations of the spirit and its media of transmission were at the heart of the negotiations and contests that made possible the invention of the new Canadian nation. Those who worked at the margins and the center of colonial power, including missionaries, Indian agents, and politicians, talked spirituality when asserting the legitimacy of Canadian sovereignty and when bringing the railway—the spinal cord of colonialism—to Indigenous land. At the same time, Indigenous peoples insisted on their own sovereignty, sometimes even with the help of the same spiritual logics, rituals, and tools of mediation (including the Bible and the printing press) brought to them by missionaries.

Spiritual stories inspired practices of belief that both challenged and consecrated the legitimacy of the Dominion of Canada. Throughout the Americas, colonial sovereignty is still legally premised on a Christian story of the doctrine of discovery, by which a fifteenth-century pope asserted that, with the aim of spreading Christianity, Europeans could autonomously claim Indigenous lands as their own without requiring Indigenous consent. The concept of a Dominion is a subsequent chapter in the story and is a particularly Canadian colonial spiritual invention, drawn from the biblical passage of Psalm 72: “And He shall have dominion from sea unto sea.” A name meant to invent a new political status for Canada as it emerged into its own peculiarly autonomous relationship with the British colonial motherland, “Dominion” at the same time asserted Canadian sovereignty in relation to its American neighbors to the south. This political assertion was also a spiritual claim in the eyes of Du Vernet: “Standing as we do mid-way between the Church in the Motherland and the Church in the United States it should be the constant aim of Canadian Churchmen—born in Canada—to gradually give expression to the Spirit of the Canadian Church in harmony with the Spirit of the Canadian people.”[14] Born in Canada, Du Vernet was born on land that was long contested not only by Canadians, Americans, and the British, but also by the French, the Abenaki, and the Mohawk.

Now that they are older, my children rarely request stories from my mouth. Just before she became a teenager, my youngest daughter would still occasionally ask for them at bedtime, but by then she wanted stories from when I was a child—she wanted to learn more about me and her uncles, or about her grandparents in the “olden days” when they were growing up on farms within the tight-knit Mennonite communities on the Manitoba prairies. I might tell her about how her Opa brought coffee and bread to school for his noon meal, or the time my grandma saved her family when the farmhouse went up in flames. Or I might tell my daughter a story about her Oma and her fourteen brothers and sisters and their long walks to their one-room schoolhouse. I might also tell her about the sod house our Mennonite ancestors lived in when they first came to the prairies from southern Russia in the 1870s, and about how their survival in those early years depended on the help they received from their Métis neighbors. The story would become less restful were I to add that these Métis neighbors were fighting the Dominion government for their right to own land that had been given away to Mennonites.[15]

A bedtime story from the mouth is a gift of relationship—it is an intimate narration that itself creates relationship, reimagines the past, and inspires the future. Stories from my mouth, I realize in retrospect, were significant occasions in my life as a mother, times when my children would stay still long enough for me to imagine for them a world that held just the right balance of danger, challenge, and discovery. These bedtime stories were meant to let my daughters fall asleep secure in the knowledge that they could imagine a future in which animals could talk and peace and justice would prevail, and that they had family who loved them and ancestors worthy of remembering.

At a time when testimony and confession are taking on new significance around the world through government-sponsored processes of apology, truth, and reconciliation for colonial violence and dispossession, we need greater historical awareness of the many-storied past. The 2015 report from Canada's Truth and Reconciliation Commission called the church-run, state-sponsored Indian Residential Schools a systematic attempt at cultural genocide on the part of the Canadian state.[16] Across the country, children were often forcibly brought to these Christian schools, where, among other injustices such as physical and sexual abuse, they were forbidden to speak their languages. Going to bed at night in dormitories lined with rows of cots, they did not hear stories from the mouths of their mothers, fathers, or grandparents, told in Anishinaabemowin, Cree, or Nisg̲a'amk̲; the lucky ones might have heard such stories from their brothers or sisters or other children.

The Truth and Reconciliation Commission shared the stories of the people who offered their testimony long after their days and nights in residential schools. The commissioners then called on Canadians, and the Canadian government, to work together with Indigenous peoples toward reconciliation of this founding violence. Acknowledging and remembering the past, they argued, required steps similar to those taken by some churches, including the Anglican Church of Canada, of repudiating the doctrine of discovery and actively recognizing Indigenous sovereignty and nation-to-nation treaty relationships.[17] Many people have ventured strong critiques of the notion of reconciliation as yet another version of colonial, Christian storytelling. The call of the Truth and Reconciliation Commission to build relationships, repair injustice, and tell stories of the past is a powerful message nonetheless. I offer this book in the spirit of this call, knowing that *The Story of Radio Mind*, despite the cosmic optimism of Frederick Du Vernet, is not necessarily a tale of healing, and that there are always more stories that can be told.

2
A Life on the Border

The past haunts the land, wherever you go. A settler colonial nation is a landscape of sedimented stories, where a group of people, acting in the name of a new nation, has taken over the land of others. Settler colonies, in the words of historian Adele Perry, "were distinguished by their exact method of dispossession, which tended to focus on alienating Aboriginal land instead of appropriating Aboriginal labour."[1] Frederick Du Vernet, like many Canadians in the new Dominion, participated in the collective work of dispossession by making new borders, telling new stories, and naming new towns and nations, with the authority of the British Crown and the Christian god undergirding the effort. These acts of place sought to ground Canada on the land and to consecrate it from above. But even with new names drawn on the land, the past presses insistently on the fault lines of the present. That is, even the most determined amnesia, or the most concrete of buildings, cannot bury the past. Stories of people and their spirits, like subterranean waters, insistently resurface, somewhere, someplace.

Take as an example my neighborhood in downtown Toronto—a place where Frederick Du Vernet once walked. Recently rechristened "Trinity-Bellwoods" by those ubiquitous neighborhood association flags that hang from streetlight posts in many cities, the area is still popularly known as "Little Italy." This is despite the fact that the Italian immigrants who moved here in the 1950s have long been outnumbered by Portuguese families who came to Canada in the 1970s. A nearby street is home to three different Roman Catholic churches all in a single block—one each for Italian, Portuguese, and Spanish speakers. From my porch, I have often watched and listened as parishioners walk together in a procession up the street, holding burning candles, silver reliquaries, and statues of saints, singing, chanting, and imbuing the neighborhood with the power of their god.

Before the Italians and Portuguese moved here, many Jewish immigrants had settled in the area in the 1920s, building synagogues on the tree-lined residential streets, forging a labor movement that crossed lines of religious difference, and raising children who questioned why they learned the "Christian story" at school.[2] And before the Jews, Anglicans and other Protestants had laid claim to the land, erecting red-brick churches to serve the people moving into homes newly built at the turn of the century.

The most significant, but now buried, remnant of the Anglican occupation of the land is the first Trinity College, built in 1851: an ornate neo-Gothic monument to the Church of England's dream of a Christian education that could build a nation. Trinity College has since moved downtown to the University of Toronto campus, but it once lay farther west in a forest of beech, oak, and elm trees. That forest is now Trinity Bellwoods Park, as marked by the streetlight flags.

The park, a popular place for children and young picnickers seeking green space and a place to congregate outdoors, occupies land that was once sacred space for the high church Anglicans among Du Vernet's people. The first Anglican bishop of the Diocese of Toronto, John Strachan—who signed his official name as "John Toronto" in keeping with the protocol by which a bishop literally embodied his diocese—acquired the land for Trinity College as part of his all-encompassing vision for a Christian city. With four of the wards in the city bearing the name of a Christian patron saint of the British Isles, Trinity was located under the watch of St. Patrick, as the 1873 map of Toronto shows (fig. 3). Bishop Strachan had been a major player in the founding of King's College in 1827, the first university in Upper Canada at a time when the Church of England was an established church with privileged status in the colony. The bishop envisioned King's College as a Church of England institution that would prepare young men to serve their new country as doctors, lawyers, professors, and clergy. Livid when the government secularized King's College in 1849, turning it into a university that required no specific confession of faith, Strachan condemned the new University of Toronto as a godless institution. He promptly went to England to seek funding to build a new college that would hew strictly to high church Anglican rituals, theology, and ecclesiastical polity—no Methodist camp meetings or austerely democratic Presbyterians for him.[3]

Strachan found support from such benefactors as the Society for the Propagation of the Gospel in Foreign Parts (SPG), an Anglican organization, supported by the British government, that sent missionaries throughout the Brit-

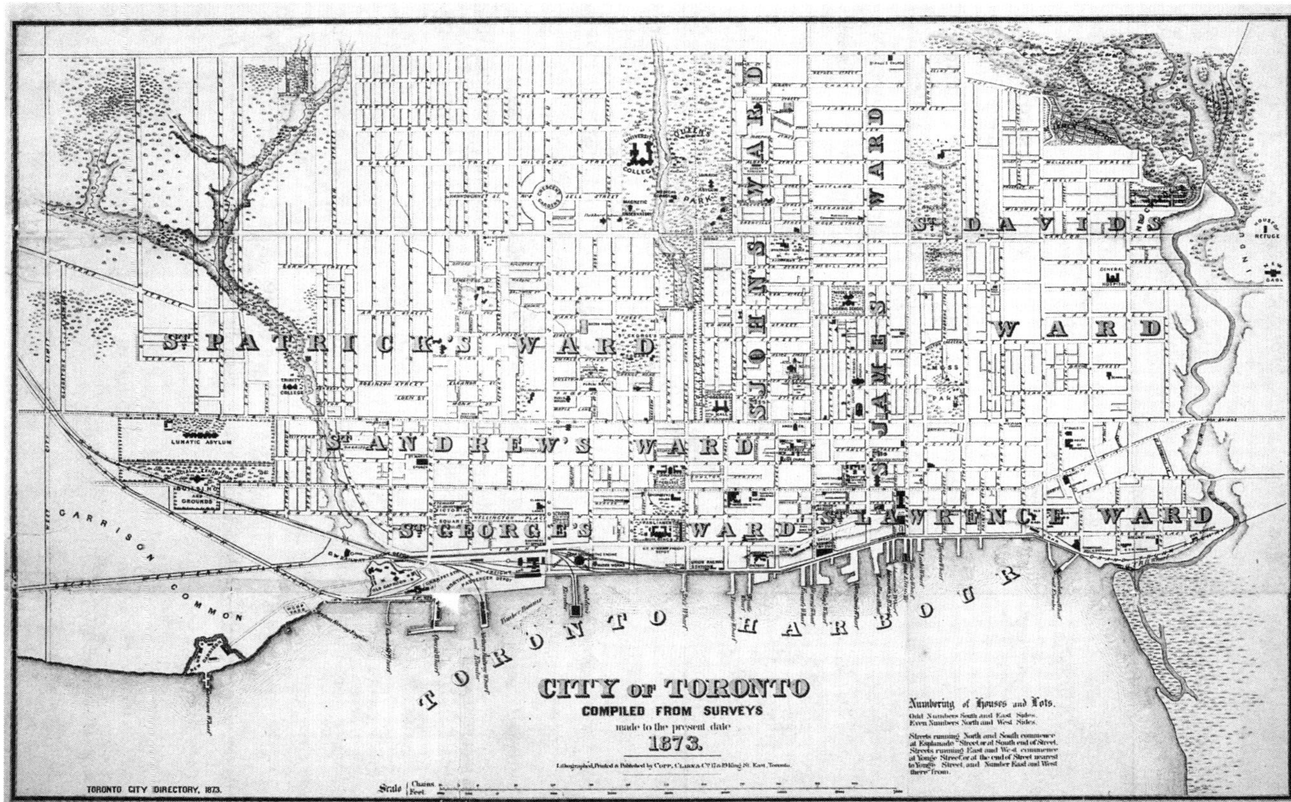

FIGURE 3. *City of Toronto, Compiled from Surveys, Made to the Present Date, 1873* (Clarke and Co.). Photograph courtesy of the Map and Data Library, University of Toronto.

ish Empire in the nineteenth century. The SPG donated to Strachan seven and a half acres of land from the Garrison Reserve, south of present-day Queen Street. The Garrison "reserve" was not land apportioned to Indigenous peoples in a treaty. It was land the Crown—the British monarch—had gifted to the SPG only a few years earlier, in 1845. A savvy speculator, Strachan figured out that he could sell the SPG land for a good profit, on account of the "great mania for railroads" south of Queen Street, and buy a cheaper, larger plot to the north. In 1850, with SPG funds, he purchased twenty acres of "Park Lot 22" from Janet Cameron, the owner of the Gore Vale estate.[4]

When Trinity College was built in 1851, Garrison Creek still cut across the land, wending its way by the college through a ravine, down past the garrisons of Fort York, the site of battles in the War of 1812 where the Americans attacked the British and their Haudenosaunee and Anishinaabe allies, and on to Lake Ontario. Just as most of Trinity College is now buried by earth, trees, and pavement, Garrison Creek, once rich with salmon and traversed by several bridges throughout the city, is now submerged. The creek had become a sewer by the late nineteenth century, and was gradually buried over the years, bridges and all, with the fill dirt from building the streetcar and subway systems of Toronto. The water still moves underground, however, occasionally bubbling up and shifting askew houses that were built on top of its currents.[5]

Before the creek was filled in, becoming tennis courts and baseball fields, and before the building of Trinity College, another story had been laid over the land by John Graves Simcoe, the first lieutenant governor of Upper Canada, who served from 1791 to 1796. Simcoe had commanded the Queen's Rangers, fighting for the British in the American Revolutionary War alongside Frederick Du Vernet's great-grandfather Jacob Ellegood and his great-uncle John Saunders, both British Loyalists. Simcoe envisioned the land that is now my neighborhood as a suitable place for his project of making a brand-new Canadian aristocracy. Inspired by the doggedly straight roads of ancient Roman imperialism and the country estates of the British nobility, Simcoe plotted out the densely forested land in hundred-acre Park Lots along the line of Queen Street. He then bestowed or sold these lots to officers and other would-be gentlemen for them to build their country homes outside the city. This was the origin of Gore Vale, the Cameron estate that was sectioned off to provide the land for Trinity College.[6]

Another new aristocrat, James Givins, lived across the creek from Gore Vale, on Park Lot 23, which he named Pine Grove. An army major in the War of 1812, during which he commanded Indigenous forces fighting against the Americans, Givins later became the chief superintendent of Indian Affairs for Upper Canada. On some occasions, Bishop Strachan and Chief Superintendent Givins worked together for the cause of Anglican missions, telling Ojibwe Methodist missionary Peter Jones that he and his people would be better off "under the superintendence of the Established Church," namely, the Anglicans, who were favored by the Crown with more stable sources of funding. Givins and Strachan were members of a tight-knit band of Anglican men known colloquially as the Family Compact, whose cliquish aristocratic gentility allowed them to concentrate power across a range of colonial ventures, including railroads, banks, real estate, and the Church of England. Across from Givins's property, on the other side of what is now Queen Street, were the Council Grounds of the Mississauga Ojibwe. A place where the Mississauga regularly gathered to camp and hold regional councils, the land also housed the smithy of a Mississauga blacksmith, as well as several cottages and a school, in 1821. By 1845, the government had claimed the land for the Lunatic Asylum, despite the ongoing protests of the Mississauga that the land was theirs.[7]

Before Trinity College, John Strachan's monument to Anglican nation-building, before the Society for the Propagation of the Gospel was granted land as the established church of Upper Canada, and before Simcoe's dream of a new Canadian imperial gentry, the elmy dale and salmon-filled creek was Indigenous land. The Mississaugas fished and canoed the creek, hunted in the woods, and gathered in the open spaces.

These are stories of the land I call home. Trinity Bellwoods is the park where I took my children to play and to swim when they were little, where my husband now walks our dog every morning, and where we play the odd game of croquet or soccer. My mother works as a nurse at what is no longer called the Lunatic Asylum but the Centre for Addiction and Mental Health. Everyone who lives in a city in the Americas can learn a similar history of Indigenous sovereignty and placemaking in their own hometown. For me, it was a particularly unsettling awakening when I finally realized that though I had been researching the life of Frederick Du Vernet as if he were a man who had lived far away in British Columbia, many of the key characters in his story—both people and organizations—had also played a role in colonizing the very land where I live. They turned Indigenous land into property, drawing maps that imposed a grid on the land that spread relentlessly, facilitating my family's ability to buy our plot almost two hundred years later.[8]

The Society for the Propagation of the Gospel in Foreign Parts, a globalized, imperial organization, which paid the salary of Du Vernet's father, a priest in Quebec, and partially supported the missionary labors of Du Vernet himself, once owned the land close to where my house now stands. The SPG owned that land by virtue of one of the most controversial spiritual political claims to territory in the early history of Canada. With the Constitution Act of 1791, every time the British claimed land in Upper Canada—sometimes through negotiating treaties—they set aside a portion of it as "clergy reserves," revenue from which would provide "the Maintenance and Support of a Protestant Clergy."[9] While people such as John Simcoe and John Strachan interpreted "Protestant" to mean "Church of England" (now known as Anglican), many other Protestants considered their own versions of Christianity to be included. In the early nineteenth century, however, the Anglican interpretation was dominant, meaning that the Church of England, many of its parishes largely supported by the SPG, owned a great deal of land.

Du Vernet did not choose to attend the high church Trinity College. Instead, he enrolled as one of the first students in Wycliffe College, the low church, Evangelical Anglican divinity school founded in 1877 in downtown Toronto and relocated in 1891 to the University of Toronto campus. Strong animosity long simmered (and occasionally exploded) between Wycliffe College's and Trinity College's supporters, largely due to their commitments to different collective memories of the Reformation, disagreement regarding the proper relation between church and state, and conflict over proper styles of liturgy. The hardest line of low church, Evangelical Anglicans thought of themselves as inheritors of the Protestant Reformation and saw themselves as a "praying church" and not a "state church." Liturgically, they reviled what they considered to be the popery of those Anglo-Catholic Anglicans who continued to worship with what Evangelicals considered to be superstitious Roman Catholic rituals. Swinging censers of incense and chanting prayers, in the eyes of the Evangelicals, made a mockery of the sacraments in a manner perilously close to what they saw as heathenism.[10]

For their part, the most fervent of the high church Anglo-Catholics disparaged the Evangelicals as austere, ritual-poor enthusiasts with a lack of appreciation for the history of the Christian church. According to the Anglo-Catholics, Evangelicals did not understand the importance of liturgies that spoke to all the senses. In the Anglo-Catholics' view, worshippers needed to be drawn into spiritual union with Jesus Christ through the smell of incense, the sound of a ringing bell, the rhythm of chanting, the sight and feel of richly embroidered vestments, or the taste of the consecrated Eucharist. An Anglo-Catholic priest believed that his sacramental act imbued the Eucharistic bread and wine with the presence of the body and blood of the crucified Lord, while an Evangelical preferred Holy Communion to convey a more spiritual reminder of the sacrificed Jesus. In Toronto, both groups claimed to be the rightful protectors of "the ideals and principles upon which our British civilization has been founded," and both promoted their colleges as the true Church of England seminary in Toronto.[11]

In 1885, the year Du Vernet returned to Wycliffe as a professor of preaching and pastoral theology, *The Calendar of Wycliffe College* asked three "vital questions" about the Bible, salvation, and the vocation of the minister, and provided the correctly Evangelical answers. First, the Bible was the only "authoritative rule of faith," and historical church traditions held no sway in defining orthodox Christianity. Second, sinners were only saved on the merits of their faith, and not by "some sacramental infusion of grace" at the hands of a priest. Third, the job of ministers was twofold: to interpret the Bible and "to testify to Christ." Pious Christians did not require "an order of sacrificing priests" to intervene on their behalf with God.[12] In keeping with a wider anti-Catholicism in nineteenth-century Canadian Protestantism, all these answers were meant to define proper Christianity as the opposite of Catholicism, no matter what the question.

So strong were the liturgical and theological divisions between the Evangelical and Anglo-Catholic camps that once Trinity College decided in 1904 that it had to close up its western Bellwoods campus for financial reasons and affiliate with the University of Toronto, the two Anglican colleges could not find a way to unite. At considerable cost, in 1925 Trinity College built yet another neo-Gothic edifice on Hoskin Avenue right across from the more stolid red-brick building of Wycliffe.

Frederick Du Vernet, however, did find his way across these theological and campus divides. Consecrated on November 30, 1904, as the second Lord Bishop of the Diocese of Caledonia, Du Vernet was recognized by his fellow clergy as a leader in his church. Presided over by William Bennett Bond, the First Primate of All Canada, the consecration took place at Christ Church Cathedral in Montreal. The ritual required three bishops—in those days, all bishops and priests were men—to pray with him and to lay their hands on him, imbuing him with the power of the Holy Ghost and including him within an Anglican genealogy of bishops that the church traced all the way back to Jesus Christ. As Anglican historian Owsley Robert Rowley asserted in 1928: "Any one now elevated to the high office of the Episcopate is the lineal successor of the original Apostles, and receives his authority direct from Christ through that unbroken succession." Du Vernet entered into a long line of male spiritual kinship by undergoing a ritual that collapsed time between the twentieth century and the first. His power as a bishop came from this masculine proximity to Jesus Christ, the "permanent medium of communication between God and man" as the incarnated divine.[13]

After his consecration in the very Evangelical Cathedral of Montreal, Du Vernet was back in Toronto on December 6, 1904, for a visit to the leafy surrounds of Trinity College on Garrison Creek. Perhaps a testament both to his efforts to reconcile low church and high church theological divisions within Anglicanism and to his passion for philosophy, Du Vernet received an honorary doctorate from Trinity College, bestowed on him by the Reverend William Clark, professor of mental and moral philosophy at Trinity. A mere two weeks later, on December 20, having traveled across Canada by railway and steamer boat, Du Vernet alighted on Ts'msyen land. He arrived in the village of Metlakatla, in the northwestern corner of British Columbia, as the newly consecrated bishop of the massive area that the Anglican Church had mapped and renamed as the Diocese of Caledonia.

The SPG, and, by implication, Trinity College and all those who walk in Trinity Bellwoods Park today, was gifted Indigenous land by a British monarch across the ocean. This plot of soil and water dedicated to the pursuit of Christian education was part of a much larger pile of gifts, parceled and sectioned out to churches, settlers, and railways, largely with disregard for the persistent petitions and protests of Indigenous peoples that it was not the Crown's to give away. These petitions and protests have never subsided; they have been re-mediated and re-storied into forms such as the First Story App, which, when downloaded on your cell phone, will tell you the history of Indigenous Toronto—or Tkaronto—as you walk the streets of the city today.[14] These re-mediated petitions insist on continued Indigenous sovereignty, and help show how the gifts of the Crown and the Christian god, and the stories that legitimized these gifts, enacted the spiritual invention of Canada.

Born on the Border

Frederick Herbert Du Vernet was a man oriented to the future, not the past. Quite unlike high church Anglican bishops, such as John Strachan, Du Vernet was an Evangelical Anglican motivated by religious experiment, not religious orthodoxy. Ordained as a priest in Montreal in 1884, Du Vernet was appointed rector to his first parish at St. John's Church in West Toronto, a post he held from 1895 to 1904. In that year, Du Vernet was both promoted and relocated, when he was consecrated as the second bishop of Caledonia in the Pacific northwest (fig. 4). In all these roles, Du Vernet led a life of missionary labors, during which he sought to convert many people to Christianity: railway workers in Toronto, Ojibwe on the Rainy River, and Ts'msyen, Nisga'a, and a variety of settlers on the Pacific coast.

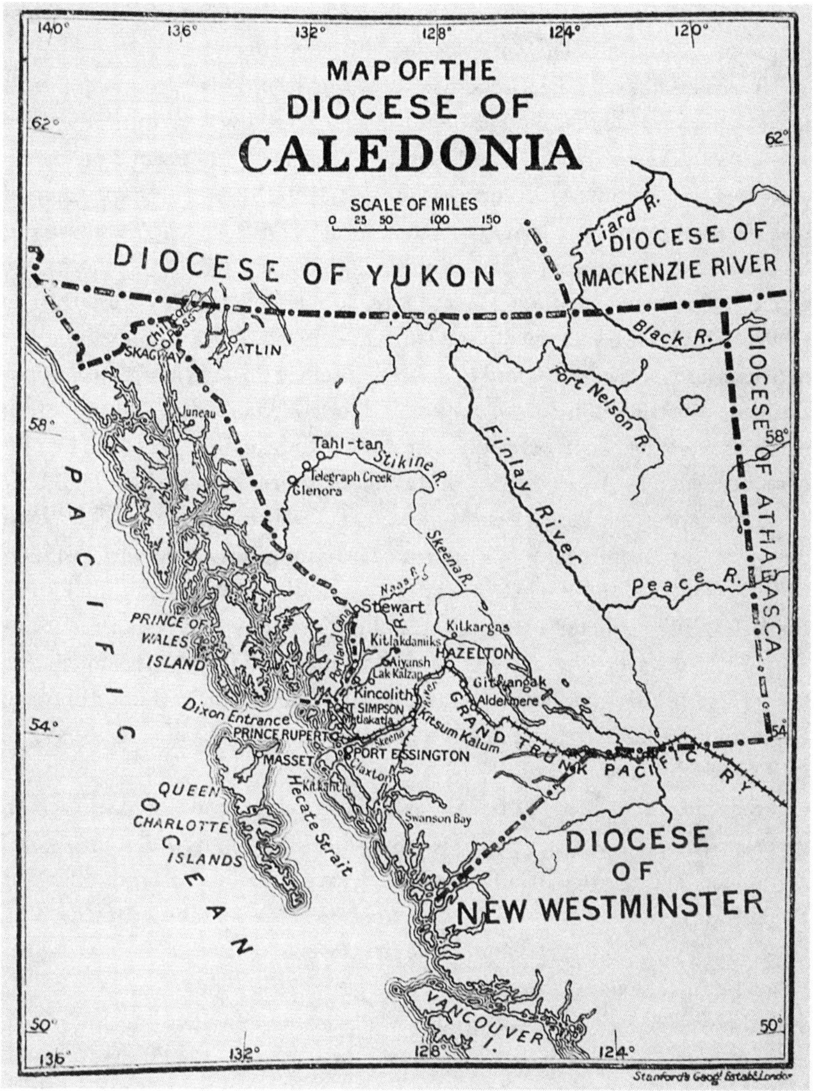

FIGURE 4. *Map of the Diocese of Caledonia.* From *Across the Rockies* (ca. 1912). Photograph courtesy of the Archives of the Provincial Synod of British Columbia and Yukon.

In 1915, he was elected the first metropolitan of the Ecclesiastical Province of British Columbia, which made him the archbishop of Caledonia. He much preferred what he considered to be the more democratic title of "Metropolitan" over "Archbishop," just as he had rejected the title of "Lord" in his everyday interactions as bishop. He also declined to sign his name as "Frederick Caledonia," rejecting the protocol that made a bishop one with the land under his episcopal oversight. He preferred to end his letters with the less amplifying "Frederick Du Vernet, Bishop of Caledonia."[15]

Near the end of his life, Frederick Du Vernet found his "late style," a term used by literary scholar Edward Said to describe how, late in life, writers and artists develop "new idioms" that take their work in new and often revolutionary directions.[16] Du Vernet dedicated himself to a new experimental task unusual for an Anglican archbishop of his day: traversing the border of body and spirit not through prayer or liturgies but through the science of the mind. He pursued a technique he thought would allow people to draw on the power of their God-energized minds to heal each other, to overcome religious divisions and class conflict, and to traverse distance through spiritual communication. He called this power radio mind, or spiritual radio, and thought it was a universally effective fusion of science and the spirit backed up by philosophers such as Henri Bergson and William James, as well as by the Bible.

In retrospect, Du Vernet's late-style vision of radio mind may look idiosyncratic yet also prophetic. In an internet age, two minds *can* almost instantaneously connect, with the help of routers and radio waves. Spirits of all kinds flourish in the mediated realm of telecommunications—that is, communication across distance. But even technological futurism has a past (and a present) rooted in the land, haunted by stories that tell of other visions of how to make nations, how to dwell in one's body, and how to travel across distance in social and spiritual worlds.[17]

Frederick Du Vernet was born on a border, quite literally, and he died on one too. On the road that runs east–west into Hemmingford, Quebec, his birthplace, a long ridge of hills lies about three miles to the south, marking the border between what was then called Lower Canada (now Quebec) and New York State. Today, radio and satellite towers stand as sentries along the ridge, but on Frederick's birthday, January 20, 1860, snowy forests of maple would have been all there was to see. Frederick was the first boy and fourth child born to Frances Ellegood Du Vernet in a span of seven years; over the next decade, Frances gave birth to two more sons, when Frederick was six and nine.

In 1860, Frances was living in the little hamlet of Hemmingford with her husband, Edward, the town's Anglican priest. Edward Du Vernet, ordained in Montreal in 1852, was appointed to Hemmingford's St. Paul's Church in 1855. A poorly built structure, St. Paul's was newly rebuilt as St. Luke's Church in 1860 and consecrated in October of that year, when Frederick was nine months old. In 1868, Edward, Frances, and their five children moved on to another border town, Clarenceville, in the Eastern Townships of Quebec. Clarenceville, like Hemmingford, was in English speaking Loyalist country, between the Richelieu River and the Missisquoi Bay of Lake Champlain, just north of the border with New York and Vermont.

Frances likely felt at home in the Loyalist townships of eastern Quebec, as she had been born in the Loyalist stronghold of Dumfries Parish, New Brunswick, in 1836. On both his mother's and his father's side, Frederick Du Vernet came from families with a long and complicated history of receiving gifts of land and honor from the British Crown. In British North America, being loyal to the Crown—which understood itself to own the land by way of both the Christian doctrine of discovery and the British conquest of the French—had tangible benefits for many. Moving north as people who had fought for or sympathized with the monarchy in the American Revolutionary War, Loyalists sought land, compensation, and legal recognition under the terms of the 1783 Treaty of Paris negotiated between Britain and the new United States of America. Loyalists were a diverse mix of wealthy colonial elites, immigrant farmers and tradespeople, Indigenous nations (who saw themselves as sovereign allies of the British), freed slaves, and slaves forcibly traveling with masters who were both white and Indigenous.[18]

Tens of thousands of Loyalists flooded across the new border all the way from Lake Erie to Cape Breton. For the most part, they rebuilt their lives right along the border's edge, including in the Eastern Townships, despite the concern of then governor-general Frederick Haldimand that settling immigrants from America so close to the new international border would risk spying or treachery. Along with the Loyalists came many Church of England parishes. In the French-speaking, Catholic-dominated province of Quebec, these churches included those built in the newly divided and Anglicized counties of the Eastern Townships, "a sort of buffer zone between the seigneurial lands of the St. Lawrence and the fledgling United States."[19] Farther east, in the Loyalist strongholds of the Maritimes, the territory of the Mi'kmaq and Maliseet, is where Frances's ancestors remade their lives as British subjects living in Canada.

Frances's grandfather, Jacob Ellegood, was a Virginian and slaveholder who lost his land—but not his slaves—in the American Revolution. Ellegood had commanded the Queen's Loyal American Regiment, but in the aftermath of the war, the government of the new nation claimed his Rose Hill Plantation in Princess Anne County, Virginia. In recognition of his loyal service, King George III granted him land on the St. John River in a county named for Queen Anne's son: Prince William County, now part of New Brunswick. Ellegood moved there with his family in 1783, and like other wealthy Loyalists, he brought more than ten slaves with him. He seems to have kept them enslaved. In 1798, "two Black children, the property of Col. Ellegood, named

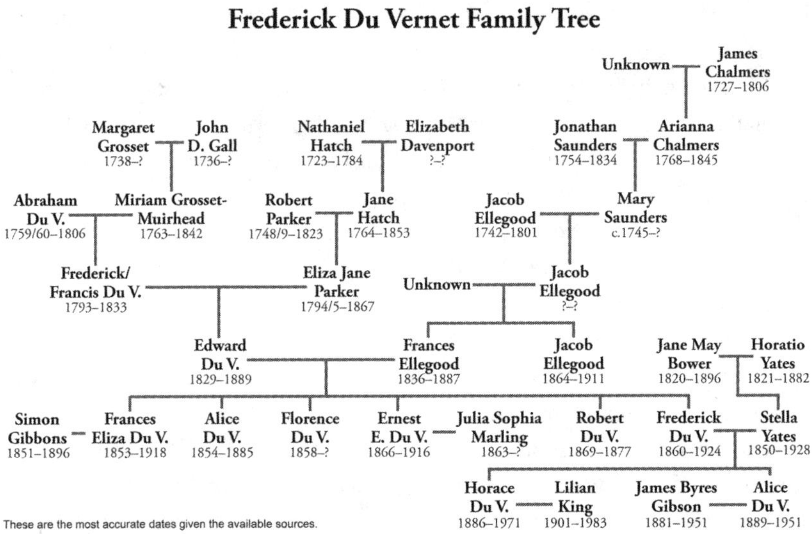

FIGURE 5. Frederick Du Vernet's family tree. Courtesy of Magdalene Klassen and Orvis Starkweather.

Sally and Adam Wise" were baptized in the Church of England in Prince William Parish.[20]

Ellegood's slaveholding continued despite the contrary views of his brother-in-law, Judge John Saunders, with whom he was close. Saunders was a Loyalist officer who had served under Lord Simcoe and shared both Simcoe's and Ellegood's dreams of a landed aristocracy in Canada. When it came to slavery, however, Saunders held the judicial opinion, in 1800, that slavery was not recognized in Nova Scotia. Despite Judge Saunders's viewpoint, slavery was not officially outlawed in the British Empire until 1834. Upon his death in 1801, Jacob Ellegood willed his land and his slaves to his wife, Mary, and four sons, giving to John, his eldest son, Pleasant Wise and her three children, and giving to his granddaughter Rebecca "one negro girl not above 12 years of age to be chosen by her." Ellegood gave his son Jacob, Frances's father, "my negro boy John" and more than ten lots of land.[21] This means that Frederick Du Vernet's grandfather was a slaveholder in 1801. Whether the younger Jacob Ellegood chose to keep or to free his slaves, I have not been able to learn.

The Du Vernet side of Frederick's family came from a different strand of the British imperial story (fig. 5). His father's Huguenot ancestors left Catholic France for Protestant England, only to later move through a wide compass of Protestant imperial networks, thanks to Frederick's great-grandfather Colonel Abraham Du Vernet. Based on a long history of family loyalty to the British Crown, Abraham Du Vernet was the beneficiary of gifts from Queen Charlotte. In 1787, her name was also bestowed, at least for a couple of centuries, on Haida islands along the Pacific coast, renaming them the Queen Charlotte Islands. Abraham had a long career as an officer serving in the Royal Artillery, an imperial army defending British interests. Posted as an engineer in Fort Detroit during the American Revolutionary War, Abraham would have interacted directly with many Indigenous men as they fought alongside the British against the Americans. He likely heard speeches from Indigenous leaders, perhaps even the Mohawk chief Thayendanegea, also known as Joseph Brant, reminding the British of their treaty agreements marked by both wampum and written promises.[22]

While he was serving in the Royal Artillery in Halifax in 1788, Abraham and his wife, Miriam (who would become Lady Miriam when she inherited a Scottish estate in 1817), hosted Queen Charlotte's son Prince William during his royal tour. The prince agreed to be the godfather of Abraham and Miriam's second son. This spiritual kinship was put to good use in 1806 when Abraham, by then living in England, was killed in a cart accident, leaving Miriam a widow with ten children. Prince William granted military commissions and promotions to several of her sons, who then helped build the new Canadian nation. Henry Du Vernet, Frederick's great-uncle, spent twenty years with the Royal Staff Corps constructing the Ottawa River canal works. He led teams of French-Canadian and Irish immigrant men who drilled and blasted the rock out of the Long Sault rapids on the Ottawa River—the site of a historic battle between the Iroquois and the French—to make the Grenville Canal.[23] Henry's brother Frederick also served in the Royal Staff Corps in Halifax, Nova Scotia, and Saint John, New Brunswick.

While in New Brunswick, Frederick Du Vernet (the elder) met Eliza Jane Parker, a woman from another prominent Loyalist family. Like many of the women in the Ellegood and Du Vernet families, the historical record largely considers Eliza Jane Parker notable for the political ambitions of the men in her family: her brothers Robert and Neville Parker both became New Brunswick judges. Eliza and Frederick married in 1816 and set sail for Ceylon, another land claimed and renamed by the British Empire. While in Ceylon (now Sri Lanka), Eliza gave birth to two children; Edward, the younger Frederick's father, was born in 1829 when Eliza was thirty-five. The elder Frederick continued his work building the roads and bridges of the British Empire and became a captain and deputy quartermaster-general in the Ceylon Rifle Regiment. Not only a builder but also an inventor, Frederick was noted by his fellow officers for having devised the screw propeller, an invention for which they claimed he never received proper credit, due to his untimely death. After she returned to New Brunswick with her children, Eliza never saw her inventive husband again; he died of malaria en route from Ceylon to England in 1833.[24]

Edward Du Vernet chose a different imperial path from that of law, the military, or civil engineering when he decided to study for a divinity degree at King's College in Halifax. Soon after, he moved to Quebec, where in 1852 he was ordained as a priest in Montreal. Following his brother-in-law Jacob Ellegood, who had already moved to Quebec in 1849, Edward was first posted in Henryville, then in Hemmingford, and later in Clarenceville. Both Jacob and Edward drew their salaries from the Society for the Propagation of the Gospel in Foreign Parts. Their missions were not to Indigenous peoples, but to the English-speaking residents of Montreal and the rural Loyalist settlers of the Eastern Townships. The Du Vernet engineering and transportation heritage still lured Edward, however, as once in Clarenceville he seems to have caught railway mania. With a group of other shareholders, he incorporated the St. John's and Clarenceville Junction Railway Company in 1870, which was to be a railway running from Clarenceville to St. John's, a distance of about forty miles.[25]

With these complicated imperial crossings in his family's past, Frederick Herbert Du Vernet was a child born into the British Empire and its Church of England, but he was also a child who lived on Indigenous land. As a youth in Clarenceville, he lived next to Missisquoi Bay, a part of Lake Champlain and long a contested watery border. The land of the Algonquin Abenakis, for whom "Missisquoi," or "Mazipskoik," meant "place of the flint," was claimed by the French as their own in the eighteenth century.[26] In 1741, a Sieur Foucault attempted, only half successfully, to settle six families on his seigneury (the French imperial version of a feudal lordship) in the Missisquoi region. After the Treaty of Paris of 1763, in which the French ceded Quebec to the British, British colonial officials bought up the Missisquoi seigneuries, and the government claimed other areas as Crown land and clergy reserves.

The year 1763 was also when King George III declared the Royal Proclamation, acknowledging Indigenous nations' rights to their land "unmolested." Redrawing the boundaries of the British colonies with the Proclamation Line, west of which settlers could not buy or take Indigenous land without the Crown negotiating treaties, the Royal Proclamation is renowned for both igniting the American Revolution and furnishing a legal argument for Indigenous sovereignty that would later be used by the Nisga'a and other nations in their land struggle. Even east of the Proclamation Line, a 1776 map clearly labeled "Indian lands," including those of the "Abenaquis," the "Algonquins," and the "Utawas," in the region of Frederick's childhood. With a second Treaty of Paris in 1783, the British ceded their colonies south of a new border, one that divided Upper and Lower Canada from the United States of America.[27]

By 1868, when eight-year-old Frederick and his family moved to the Abenaki land now named the Eastern Townships, Canada had officially become a Dominion just the previous year. The local Clarenceville Academy was at its peak as a Protestant school, supported by a government grant and meant to prepare young men and women for university. With a curriculum in Greek and Latin, as well as mathematics, English literature, and political economy, the required readings at Clarenceville included Adam Smith and the geologist Charles Lyell, whose scientific approach to the study of earth's history, while still biblical in some respects, inspired the work of his friend Charles Darwin.[28]

Traveling often to Montreal, where his uncle was the rector of St. James the Apostle Church, Frederick lived in the thick of Anglican Quebec. On the morning that Frederick was confirmed at the age of fourteen in Christ Church Cathedral in Montreal—confirmation is the ritual that gives Anglicans the privilege of partaking of the Eucharist—he decided that he was a "Knight of Jesus Christ and had put on 'the whole armour of God.'" Frederick's spiritual awakening, according to a reminiscence by his Caledonia colleague Walter Rushbrook, continued that evening. Listening to a sermon based on the New Testament verse John 6:37, Frederick was further inspired: "After the service he went out into the Cathedral grounds and lifting his face to the starlit heavens there and then consecrated his life to Christ, saying: 'I give myself to Thee Lord Jesus to be used where and how Thou shall choose, and I claim Thy promise "Him that cometh unto Me I will in no wise cast out."'"[29] Whether or not Rushbrook's reminiscence was hagiographic or historical, the unconditional divine love proclaimed in this Bible verse would align well with Frederick's late-style experiments in radio mind.

Frederick Du Vernet's education took an unusual turn when he was a fifteen-year-old student at the Clarenceville Academy. In the fall of 1875, a new teacher came to town: Simon Gibbons, a young Inuit man who, as an orphan in Labrador, had been taken in by Sophia Mountain, a prominent Anglican widow and the orphanage superintendent. Mrs. Mountain eventually became Mrs. Feild when she married her second husband, Edward Feild, bishop of Labrador. Together, the Feilds shepherded Simon into a life as an Anglican priest. How Simon ended up in Clarenceville is unclear, but this Inuit scholar taught the young Frederick Greek and Latin and successfully prepared him for matriculation at King's College in Halifax. That same year, Simon also assisted Frederick's father, Edward, as a parochial lay reader in the Henryville church, a step on Simon's road to ordination as the first Anglican Inuit priest. In 1876, Frederick and Simon traveled east together, enrolling at King's College in Nova Scotia, where Frederick's father had studied. In the spring of 1878, they became family when Simon married Frederick's sister Frances Eliza Du Vernet, known as Fanny.[30]

Little is known about the relationship between Frederick and his teacher, classmate, and brother-in-law, but it is clear that Simon Gibbons was a jovial man who enjoyed his life as a clergyman, traveling throughout eastern Canada, the United States, and Great Britain. While he was priest of a small church by the sea in Lockport, Nova Scotia, Simon and Fanny took in her aging parents: Edward and Frances Du Vernet moved from Quebec back to the Maritimes, where Fanny cared for them. Her mother died in 1887, and her father died in 1889, five years after Frederick had been ordained. Simon was active as a priest—and a Mason—until his death in 1896. As a widow, Fanny tried her hand at missionary work briefly in Japan and eventually settled in Toronto, where she died in 1918. In her will, she left Frederick money for the Diocese of Caledonia, which, in recognition of the time she spent in Japan, he put toward a new building for the Japanese-run mission in Prince Rupert.[31]

Family lore concerning Frederick's youth says nothing about his teacher and brother-in-law, Simon Gibbons. The story of Frederick's teenage years, as told by Sylvia Du Vernet, the wife of Frederick's grandson Ernest, recounts that Frederick ran away from home at fifteen because of his overbearing father. He worked for a time on whaling ships with Cape Breton fishermen, and when he decided to study theology, the story goes, the fishermen offered him a donation to help with his costs of study, which would supplement the scholarship he won from King's College. According to Sylvia, Frederick ended up refusing the scholarship when the terms demanded that he "declare himself a High Church Anglican." The archival record is less dramatic; his time as a student at Nova Scotia's King's College is always duly noted in church biographical records of his life, as is the honorary doctorate the college bestowed on him in 1905.[32] The educational institution that made the most difference in Frederick Du Vernet's life, however, was clearly Wycliffe College, the Evangelical Anglican college founded in 1877, the year Frederick took his first westward journey, to the city of Toronto.

Enrolled in the first class of Wycliffe College, at the age of seventeen, Frederick Du Vernet excelled in his studies, taking home awards for theology, general proficiency, and apologetics. Granted, there was not a lot of competition in the small entering class of 1877 at this brand-new college, but Du Vernet's ongoing participation at Wycliffe as a part-time professor of practical theology, homiletics, and pastoral theology, as well as his role as assistant chaplain between the years of 1885 and 1895, testify to the respect he gained while a student.[33] Having graduated in 1880 with a degree in theology, he moved back to Montreal for two years, where he served as a diocesan missioner. While there, he was ordained as a deacon in 1883 and a priest in 1884.

Returning to Toronto in 1885, Frederick married Stella Yates of Kingston, whom he had met on board a ship sailing to England. Little is known about this shipboard romance, but it was unusual in at least one sense: at their September wedding, Frederick was twenty-five and Stella was thirty-six. The daughter of a prominent Kingston medical doctor, Horatio Yates, and his wife, Jane May Bower, Stella was also from a Loyalist family, but one that retained contact with American relatives. Stella's uncle, American railway baron Arthur Gould Yates, was a witness at her marriage. Just a year later, Stella gave birth to their first child, Horace, in Kingston. Two-and-a-half years later, on March 16, 1888, in Toronto, Stella gave birth to their daughter, Alice.

In their few remaining letters and photographs, Frederick and Stella seem to have enjoyed an amicable marriage in which they worked together in the model of the missionary clergyman and his dedicated, hospitable wife. There are hints that she was herself an advocate for new ways of thinking about bodies and spirits, as Stella openly supported women's suffrage when she served as the president of the women's auxiliary of the diocese, an organization Stella had herself founded.[34] Stella's memorial act, in the wake of Frederick's death in 1924, demonstrates that she understood how important his intellectual and spiritual labors were to him: she donated his library to the Diocese of Caledonia. A brass plate on the wooden bookcase marks the "Archbishop Du Vernet Caledonia Diocesan Library, Bequeathed and endowed, 1925." This library turned out to be a great gift to my research, as on its shelves I found copies of books, such as Henri Bergson's *Mind-Energy* and William James's *The Principles of Psychology*, replete with Du Vernet's careful, and opinionated, marginalia.

As they established their family in Toronto in the 1880s, Frederick and Stella were likely not among the elite of the city in terms of their income, but they would have had ready access to the rich and powerful. In 1895, once Frederick was appointed rector at St. John's Church, they would have lived comfortably in the attached manse. St. John's was poised between two contrasting neighborhoods in west Toronto: High Park, an area with large brick villas housing the wealthy and overlooking a forested three-hundred-acre park, and The Junction, a village that was home to working-class families at what had been the crossing point of several Indigenous trails and now was the intersection of several railways.

Thanks to his own family and career, Du Vernet lived in proximity to both these worlds. His brother Ernest was a prominent lawyer and King's Counsel in Toronto. After a brief time at Clarenceville Academy, Ernest was sent to the most elite boys' school in the country, Upper Canada College, founded in 1829 in Toronto in part through the energetic efforts of Bishop John Strachan. Ernest trained as a lawyer, launching a career that "brought him to a place among the leaders of the legal profession in Canada."[35] He belonged to the most exclusive clubs for the wealthy men of the city: the Albany Club and the Toronto Club. His wife, Julia, was known as an "Old Girl" from Bishop Strachan School, the girls' equivalent to Upper Canada College, and she was regularly noted in the city newspapers for her social appearances.

Ernest and Julia lived not far from Frederick and Stella, but in one of the posh mansions on Indian Road, still today named in a pale echo of the Indigenous trail that once led up from the lake. They later moved to Wychwood, an Arts-and-Crafts-style enclave for the cultural elite of the city occupying land adjacent to one of the oldest Indigenous portage routes in the region, the Davenport Trail. Ernest was an active partner in banking and railway ventures, and gained renown as a lawyer in several high-profile court cases, including the scandalous Massey murder trial.[36] Letters between Frederick and Ernest show that they kept in regular contact about both financial and family matters, and that Frederick gave his brother advice on how to beat out the competition to establish a bank in the newly built town of Prince Rupert.

Frederick Du Vernet's duties as a parish priest, his involvement at Wycliffe College, and his growing commitment to missionary work would have put him in regular contact with the Anglican elite of Toronto, the heirs to the Family Compact. He was a busy man, and these connections would help him in all his roles. From 1895 to 1902, he was secretary-treasurer of the Canadian Church Missionary Association (CCMA), an Evangelical organization founded in 1894 with the goal of sending out properly Evangelical, Canadian missionaries to "do their due part in evangelizing the Heathen and Mohammedan world."[37] Many of these missionaries also went west, to staff missions to Indigenous peoples, which included residential schools. In addition, Du Vernet became something of a missionary-journalist in the 1890s, serving as editor of the *Canadian Church Missionary Gleaner* from 1894 to 1901 and then as editor of a new missionary magazine, *The New Era*, from 1901 to 1904. His editorial role took him on a tour of Canada, including a visit to the Ojibwe of Rainy River, which he transformed into an appeal for funds to support Canadian missions.

These were times of significant change in the missionary work of Canadian Anglicans as they delicately attempted to build their own domestic missionary societies without alienating their church allies and generous donors in England. Du Vernet, with his Loyalist heritage, was at the heart of negotiating this transition. His success in this role, along with his family's prominence in the church, likely contributed to his promotion to bishop in one of the largest dioceses in the country as the diocese shifted from a focus on missions to Indigenous people to ministering to the growing number of settlers.

In his time at the *New Era*, Du Vernet reported regularly on the lives and exploits of missionaries around the world, in Japan, Africa, India, China, Palestine, and South America, as well as at home in Canada. The *New Era* and CCMA offices occupied donated space at the brand-new, state-of-the-art Confederation Life Building at Richmond and Yonge Streets, home to one of Canada's biggest life insurance companies.[38] This was an excellent location for the new missionary organization and its magazine, as they sought to cultivate donors among the growing number of middle- and upper-class Canadians. In the wake of declining support from the British-based organizations, these Canadian donors were fast becoming a financial necessity.

Both the older Society for the Propagation of the Gospel (SPG) and its Evangelical counterpoint, the Church Missionary Society (CMS), had long supported missions in Canada. The SPG understood its mission as directed to both Indigenous peoples and settlers; it was establishing the Church of England by sending out parish priests who would minister to anyone, albeit usually in racially divided churches. The CMS, by contrast, sent its missionaries—both men and women—throughout the British Empire to convert only "heathens," which effectively meant nonwhite people.[39]

Du Vernet also kept his readership up to date on the organizational transitions within Canadian Anglican missions when the CMS-affiliated, low church CCMA merged with the high church SPG supporters into the Missionary Society of the Church of England in Canada (MSCC), under the umbrella of the Canadian church. This union did not resolve the ongoing battles between high church and low church Anglicans, who even debated about how best to convert non-Christians. Acknowledging that some "extremists on both sides will say that their leaders have betrayed them," Du Vernet touted the MSCC as a homegrown missionary organization run by the Canadian Anglican church itself. He argued that as Canadian Anglicans developed increasing autonomy as a national, Canadian church, uniting all the various missionary societies and their finances under the auspices of the Canadian church would mean less confusion regarding the Anglican missionary brand.[40]

A united missionary organization in Canada was increasingly necessary, as British missionary societies were losing interest in supporting work in a country that they no longer considered quite so exotic, as it became more autonomous and began to look less like a colony. Taking a conciliatory approach that would characterize his leadership style throughout his career, Du Vernet urged his readers to give the new united missionary organization a "fair trial." He noted that in negotiating this union, "God's over-ruling hand has been guiding our Church," and he confidently predicted the outcome: "Multitudes in heathen lands will yet praise God for this forward movement."[41] Poised between the church and the city's elite, and in harmony with the colonial goals of the government to assimilate Indigenous peoples and take their land, Du Vernet's confidence was backed by God, capital, and country.

Du Vernet's work with the railway workers of The Junction would have introduced him to a very different way of life in the city. Witness to the poverty and alcoholism in the streets of The Junction, Du Vernet was active in the successful temperance campaign of 1904—a campaign so successful that some parts of the neighborhood remained dry until the year 2000. Du Vernet also developed a housing plan through which railway workers could secure loans to buy their own homes. These firsthand encounters with the great disparity in wealth in a city itself gripped by railway mania may have had some effect on his later cautious embrace of socialist politics.[42]

Du Vernet was sent by the *Canadian Church Missionary Gleaner* on a journalistic "missionary tour" in 1898, and on a train heading to northern Ontario, he found himself sitting next to a "real" socialist, the San Francisco lawyer James Taylor. Du Vernet admiringly called his seatmate "an out and out socialist whose thinking is bringing him nearer to God and mankind. His main principle is—the competitive system is wrong. Cooperation is the true method." Du Vernet took careful notes about Taylor's philosophy for the ideal way of life, including his acrostic spelling out the essentials of life to which all people were entitled:

L.and	he must have a spot on this earth to live
A.ir	[he must have] air to breathe
W.ater	[he must have] water to drink
S.unshine	[he must have] Good sunlight

> Private property tends to rob man of this. Public ownership would secure all these for him. We several times talked about Christian[ity and] this social principle—<u>service</u>.[43]

Du Vernet's work as a bishop, as a social critic, and as a spiritual experimentalist was rooted in these early years on the borders of nations, class conflict, and spiritual politics.

Slow Media

This is one way to tell the story of Frederick Du Vernet's life: relating his genealogy, his family life, his educational formation, his theological dispositions, his career moves. In the rest of the book, I take another approach, one along a less conventional biographical stream. I follow Du Vernet on his westward journey as he interacts with fellow travelers, missionaries, Indigenous people, government officials, and settlers. Du Vernet showed much admiration, for example, for the part-Cree Anglican missionaries Jeremiah and Mary Johnston, who lived in Ojibwe territory on the Rainy River. Once he was Bishop Du Vernet, he worked with the Irish-born James Benjamin McCullagh, a missionary living on Nisga'a land along the Nass River, who was both a valued colleague and a thorn in his side. Odille Morison, a Ts'msyen Anglican from Metlakatla (across the water from Prince Rupert), was an interpreter for anthropologists and government officials, as well as a prominent member of Du Vernet's congregation and friend to Stella and Frederick. Telling the stories of these people as they crossed paths with Frederick Du Vernet helps situate his story.

Over the course of his journeys on Indigenous land, Du Vernet told stories using many media, including print, photographs, and telepathic radio mind experiments. He even told stories from his mouth in sermons and at the Prince Rupert Reading Club. Recounting tales of transformation often imagined as spiritual, such as conversion, as well as those earthly processes often considered secular, such as railway building and real estate speculation, Du Vernet and those around him offer a window onto how Canada was made through stories. Told across traditions of Christian witnessing, legal battles, and Indigenous storytelling, these tales are bound within a spiritual politics that requires untangling. As missionaries, settlers, and Indigenous peoples interacted through stories, they were all shaped by what we in the digital age might now consider relatively slow media: glass plate photography, the printing press, hand-drawn maps, and radio. I tell the story of radio mind through consideration of how these media worked on souls and on the land.

As they were introduced, these media produced and provoked mixed effects. Missionaries journeying in search of souls photographed people and places in service of a story that cast Indigenous peoples as those in need of colonial governance, but they also encountered Indigenous resistance to their cameras. The maps that missionaries helped create through surveying and sometimes negotiating away Indigenous lands were overlaid with anxious and even guilt-ridden stories that they told about Indigenous visions of the land. The printing presses that missionaries introduced to communities far from urban centers produced not only hymns and confessional testimonies but also proclamations of Indigenous sovereignty.

And when a missionary such as Du Vernet encountered radio, a brand-new technology that reimagined the possibilities of human communication across distance, he understood it as a spiritual tool for human unity and personal healing in a way very parallel to the traveling spiritual energies he had long witnessed among Ojibwe, Nisga'a, and Ts'msyen peoples. In retrospect, Du Vernet's optimism for spiritual communication requires some reconciling, in more ways than one. If testimony is a path to reconciliation, as many people now urge, we may want to pause a bit to consider more slowly what baggage comes along with testimony, as both a practice and an idea.

Colonial nations are formed out of pronouncements that are themselves acts of imagination, or practices of belief, trying to will new political powers and relationships into being. The building of the Canadian nation was effected in part through what anthropologist Ronald Niezen has called a process of "spiritual domination," in which Christian convictions about the necessity of converting Indigenous people intertwined with a capitalist imagination of the landscape as ripe for resource extraction. When Du Vernet went west as bishop of Caledonia, the Queen Charlotte Islands—named after a queen who had blessed his ancestors with gifts—were mapped by the Anglican Church as lying within his diocesan responsibility. To rename the land of the Haida after an eighteenth-century fur-trading ship itself named after Queen Charlotte was an act of spiritual invention, requiring imagination, new forms of technological mediation, and stories.[44] Writing the name of a British monarch living thousands of miles away on the new maps of the British Empire, and using it in legal documents, was meant to imbue and reorder the land with the spirit of the German-British Queen.

Spiritual invention bears resemblance to philosopher Charles Taylor's notion of a "social imaginary." For Taylor, our imaginations do not reside only in our own minds. With faint reverberations of radio mind, imagination is also social, giving groups of people a "common understanding that makes possible common practices and a widely shared sense of legitimacy."[45] If, as Taylor argues, social imaginaries are built out of widely shared stories, images, and legends, then it follows that telling new stories can reshape a social imaginary. At the same time, telling new stories—whether about the past or the present—can reshape what a group considers "common" knowledge and practice, and what its members consider to be "shared" terms of social legitimacy.

In the past few decades, the social imaginary of the role of Christianity in the invention of the Canadian nation has profoundly transformed, as Canadian Anglican, Catholic, United, and Presbyterian churches, often pushed by their Indigenous members, have confronted the legacy of their part in the colonization of Indigenous peoples. The Truth and Reconciliation Commission on church-run residential schools for Indigenous children is a potent and imperfect example of this transformation.[46]

Though Du Vernet may have proclaimed that non-Christians—what he called the "multitudes in heathen lands"—would be grateful for the spread of Christian missions, the recent past has not proved him correct. The Queen Charlotte Islands are now Haida Gwaii once again, even on Canadian maps. Mere miles from the watery border with Alaska, and on the self-proclaimed "edge of the world," the Haida Nation, in 2009, negotiated a new protocol with a twenty-first-century queen. The Kunst'aa guu–Kunst'aayah Reconciliation Protocol between the Haida Nation and Queen Elizabeth II (represented by the minister of Aboriginal relations and reconciliation of British Columbia) is a fascinating document of Indigenous sovereign renewal. The protocol agrees to disagree about who is sovereign on Haida Gwaii, in a spirit of what Jeremy Webber has called "agonistic constitutionalism." By this, he means that a constitution—a document that nations live by—is understood to be "a product of a continuing encounter or negotiation."[47] Du Vernet, a man who lived on the borders of many nations and spirits, came to embrace a version of this agonistic openness, after a lifetime of journeys on Indigenous land.

3

Testimonies, Protocols, and Spiritual Stories

Before we follow Frederick Du Vernet's journey westward, we need to consider a longer history of Christian hopes and convictions regarding the ability of stories to enable the practice of believing. Telling the story of a white man who espoused blatant racism and Christian triumphalism, but who also came to question some of the most brutal forms of that racist triumphalism, requires an understanding of the meaning of a story in his context. Augustine in the fourth century, Protestant reformers in the sixteenth, and even the evangelical bloggers in today's social media–infused world—Christians have long imagined testimony and confession as ideal, static-free channels for the spirit. When a wave of missionaries fanned out across the British Empire in the nineteenth century, their storytelling protocols depended on genres of confession and testimony as their most beloved, and deadly, tools in the missionary kit for propagating the gospel. But along the way, on the northwest coast and elsewhere, they encountered and clashed with other storytellers, including Indigenous peoples and anthropologists. In relationships between Protestant missionaries and Indigenous peoples, the words of a testimony were only part of the story. The medium through which people channeled their testimonies, whether a totem pole or a printing press, also mattered.

If a totem pole tells stories with a "spiritual message," is a printing press also a medium of the spirits?[1] Telling stories with tools and technologies such as books, cameras, and radios is not a simple matter of communication. Stories are schemes for ordering a world, offering a cosmology with characters and landmarks to help people find their way. A spiritual story, in the sense I use here, includes many aspects: characters who come from other worlds or have supernatural powers, such as talking animals and miracle workers; a physical setting shaped by an authoritative founding narrative about a people and their land, such as a creation myth; or a plot in which personal or collective transformation is achieved by extraordinary means, such as a divinely initiated flood.

A story—spiritual or otherwise—gains authority and credibility based on who tells it, who listens to it, where it is told, and what medium its teller uses. Indigenous people asserting sovereignty in North America, for example, have fought for the right to use oral narrative as legal, historical evidence in Canadian and US courts, which have long depended on text as the medium for transporting evidence over generations. At the same time, some Indigenous nations and elders place restrictions on the circulation of powerful stories, insisting that tellers and audiences must be authorized through ceremony and protocol to participate in such a story's telling. A story's form of mediation and documentation, its embedding in law, the public audiences to whom it is addressed, and the counterpublics who challenge the story all matter for its power. In North America, an oral narrative passed down by mouth, a story written down as scripture or as history, and a case presented in court as legal precedent enjoy different levels of credibility depending on their context.[2]

According to some scholars, the entire history of the world can be ordered in terms of how humans have mediated stories, truths, and information to each other, collapsing distance with every innovation in communications technology. Dividing history into four "information revolutions" signaled, respectively, by writing, printing, multimedia (including radio), and digital media, Anthony Beavers suggests that with each revolution people gained the ability to circulate writing and images faster, farther, and in greater quantities, making use of an increasingly broad array of the physical senses to communicate information. In Beavers's timeline, the digital revolution marks the arrival of built networks in which human beings and computers together create (and manipulate) information that can be easily stored and readily accessed, but also hidden and forgotten.[3]

These shifts in mediation are perhaps less revolutionary than many have suggested. New media do not completely replace the old, as the continued love of paper books and the revitalization of totem poles reveal. But new information technologies do have real consequences for our hopes and fears about our social relations, for how we understand the mind and its powers, and for the natural environment. In nineteenth- and early twentieth-century missionary encounters around the world, for example, the promise was often that literacy would bring both spiritual revelation and social and economic progress to non-Christian people. The paper on which that literacy depended came from trees. On the Rainy River in the early twentieth century, log booms and the papermaking mills of Fort Frances sent detritus and effluents downstream that killed the fish, polluted the waters, and transformed the lives of the Rainy River Ojibwe. Digital technologies also have their effects: in Nisga'a territory, a molybdenum mine, extracting a rare and costly mineral used in cell phones and other communications technologies, has reshaped the land and poisoned the waters.[4]

Protestants rejoiced over the explosion of communication in the wake of the invention of the printing press; they wanted the Bible placed in the hands of every person. But Christian texts were not the only ones to come off the presses. Accompanying the utopian hopes of Protestants were dystopic fears about what it meant that an increasingly broad group of people could spread their ideas far and wide.[5] Optimistic hopes for communication technologies are never fully realized and are always shadowed by contradictions and fears. Nevertheless, improvements to communication—faster connections, more-pixelated images, smarter smartphones—continue to be widely celebrated.

Communication as Reconciling

The desire and dread embedded in technologies of communication linger as spiritual concerns for both individuals and communities. Communications scholar John Durham Peters has written a history of the very notion of communication that brings these concerns to the surface. Within Western traditions of religion and philosophy, Peters argues, communication has evolved as "the project of reconciling self and other." Driven by a constant hope that to communicate more directly, more immediately, and even wordlessly will make for more-perfect relationships and purer understanding, this ideal of communication as reconciliation is nevertheless plagued by the dilemmas of mediation.[6]

Our instruments of communication—whether words, pictures, phones, laptops, or even brain scans—can never bring us complete clarity in our effort to understand each other. As Peters writes with both scepticism and delight: "The mistake is to think that communications will solve the problems of communication, that better wiring will eliminate the ghosts. Although I am sceptical that the word 'communication' can ever fully shake the ghosts of wordless contact, the term marks out a marvelous zone for inquiry: the natural history of our talkative species."[7] Radio mind, a wireless medium for conveying not ghosts but spiritual energy, takes its place in this longer history of dreams that wordless contact will bring about reconciliation.

Peters's repeated references to the ghosts and spirits of communication—to the lingering hopes of "angelic contact" by which the reality of a spiritual realm could be documented on earth—is echoed in the work of several scholars of religion. Some have argued that religions carry within them particular cosmologies in which some media of communication are considered more convincing or even more natural than others. The binding together of Christianity, Judaism, and Islam as the three "religions of the book" is only the most obvious example of a shared cosmology of mediation. While Christianity has operated with a cosmology in which texts are paramount, other "sensational forms" (to borrow Birgit Meyer's phrase) of communication have also played important roles in Christian piety, including the spoken sermon, the painting, and even the human body, subject to the divine inflowing of the Holy Spirit. Webb Keane has shown the importance of Christianity for the "semiotic ideologies" of colonial modernity, by which he meant the historically specific valuing of certain forms of signs and symbols, including texts, as privileged modes of communication, over against media considered primitive or heathen.[8]

The spectrum of the senses at play in Christian stories of the spirit made it possible for colonial missionaries to find overlaps with the cosmologies of mediation within the cultures they visited, yet at the same time it set up some of the fiercest battles in the missionary context.[9] For example, James B. McCullagh, a missionary who worked under Du Vernet's authority in northwestern British Columbia, dearly loved his printing press and called it an "Iron Pulpit." He saw little of value in the totem poles that told the stories of the Nisga'a, urging them to destroy their poles, or to send or sell them to museums down south or back east. After they abandoned these towering, carved poles of cedar, McCullagh insisted, Nisga'a should tell confessional testimonies rooted in the Bible. Bringing two printing presses to a small settlement on the Nass River, McCullagh was adamant that the Nisga'a should cultivate their most important stories by developing the ability to read a tree that was not carved into a pole but instead milled and bound into a book.

These missionaries were not, of course, entirely successful, and in their wake many forms of testimony remain among Indigenous peoples. Mary Longman, art historian and Indigenous artist, uses the phrase "artistic testimonial" to argue that Indigenous art, both historically and today, has functioned as a politically effective medium that is also spiritually powerful: "In the past 40 years, much contemporary Aboriginal artwork has served two primary purposes: to deconstruct the colonial narrative that has represented Aboriginal people and to rebuild and reclaim the Aboriginal narrative."[10] The testimonial arts that Longman discusses and practices do their work alongside the cultivation of another kind of Indigenous testimony—namely, that facilitated by the Truth and Reconciliation Commission (TRC) of Canada as part of the process of the church and government apologies for the Indian Residential School system of the nineteenth and twentieth centuries.

Truth and reconciliation commissions around the world have made testimony and its public rituals into an ambivalently powerful tool for nationwide introspection and resolution in the wake of violence. More broadly, the world has seen "an unprecedented rise in the production and circulation of and demand for testimony," especially in the aftermath of the Holocaust, in which the testimonies of witnesses and survivors were crucial to its historical reconstruction and criminal prosecution. While some have harshly criticized the Canadian TRC, many Indigenous women and men offering testimonies about their residential school experience have made clear that they valued the opportunity to speak publicly.[11]

Several critics have pointed to the profound irony that the very structure of the TRC is rooted in Christian rituals of confession and Christian theologies of reconciliation. As artist Adrian Stimson of the Siksika First Nation put it: "Instead of the perpetrators having to confess their sins it is Aboriginal peoples who have to confess their pain. We confess our pain and the government assumes the role of the church and gives us an Indulgence, or not, depending on the criteria they have developed. The burden of proof is on us." Stimson has used the testimonial arts to turn this confessional burden on its head in works such as *Buffalo Boy's Confessional: Indulgence*. Testimony, as Stimson's counterconfession clarifies, is not a natural, or neutral, kind of story. Similarly, reconciliation, even in the wake of the TRC naming new principles by which to practice it, has a complicated Christian history. As Jeff Corntassel, Chaw-win-is, and T'lakwadzi point out, "At its core, reconciliation is a Western concept with religious connotations of restoring one's relationship to God." Within Christianity, the death of Jesus has been interpreted as the sacrifice that *reconciled* God and humanity. Even more specifically, reconciliation is a sacrament still practiced in the Anglican Church (mostly among Anglo-Catholics) in which a "penitent" confesses his or her sins to a priest and receives absolution.[12]

Testimony and Confession in Christianity

Thanks to smartphones, satellites, and fiber-optic cables, nearly everyone in North America lives in an age of confessional production in which personal testimony is cultivated, required, and circulated through diverse media, including books, blogs, and social networking sites and apps. And these media all depend on protocols—codes and rules for how to communicate in both social and technical terms. Writing about the control that coding exerts in internet-enabled lives, Alexander Galloway declared: "Today, protocol is our gravity, our oxygen, our pulse." Galloway's critical analysis of protocol infrastructure is helpfully contrasted with the meaning of protocol in Indigenous contexts. Umeek (E. Richard Atleo), writing of Nuu-chah-nulth protocols in the context of southern British Columbia, described protocols as agreements "between consenting parties" derived out of stories.[13] For both Galloway and Umeek, protocol is a necessary structure for living in relationship with others, but it may take very different material forms.

For those who heed its call, confessional production is not easy. Demanding relentless emotional and technological labor, technical savvy, and a way with words and images, producing one's confession in North America is a performance of the self on a stage with well-developed protocols and plenty of judges. Reality shows, blogs, social media, and even old-fashioned memoirs printed in books all work as filters for stories of the self in which people bestow their testimonies on audiences both intimate and unknown, often with a worried backward glance to the real me. As law and literature scholar Peter Brooks has shown, the "modern confessional tradition" in Western culture is a process of self-revelation that can never escape the tension between self-disclosure and self-deception. Or to put it differently, writing about the self means accusing and excusing oneself at the same time; every claim about the self is always shadowed by doubts about mixed motives and the murkiness of memory.[14]

Understanding the significance of spiritual stories—testimonies, confessions, gospels—in specifically Christian imaginations prompts (at least) three questions: First, what kinds of dilemmas does speaking or writing about the self pose for Christian ideals of humility, or what are the ethics of confession? Second, how does mediation—whether by mouth, by pen, or by blog—shape the ethical and social effects of testimonies and confessions? And third, how was the early twentieth-century encounter between Christian and Indigenous forms of storytelling shaped by different cosmologies of mediation, or different underlying understandings and commitments about what counted as the proper kinds of media for ordering and interpreting the world? In other words, what difference did particular media make for expectations about how best to tell stories of how the world works, or how it should work? And how did these spiritual stories establish the legitimacy—albeit contested—of the Canadian nation?

Within Christianity, confession is defined in various ways depending on its context, but let me offer a provisional definition: confession is a form of writing or speaking in which an individual or group acknowledges, often with some guilt in play, his/her/their past actions and dispositions to an audience. Testimony is closely related to confession but has a more confident and less guilt-ridden air; to testify to one's spiritual rebirth (or to scientific results), for example, is on balance more of an act of conviction than an admission of fallenness. The expectation that testimony might lead to "truth and reconciliation" is strongly connected to Christian antecedents of writing and speaking the self, as found in Christian traditions of confession.

With deep roots in practices of narrating oneself to God while allowing others to read along, Christian confession finds its paradigmatic form in Augustine's *Confessions*. Part autobiographical reflection addressed to God and part allegorical exposition of biblical texts, Augustine's *Confessions* continues to provide a template for the Christian practice of writing about the self in order to achieve closer union with God. Augustine's audience, namely God, provided an "authenticity" for his autobiographical reflections about past transgressions and a desired future. As James O'Donnell writes: "'Confession' in Augustine's way of understanding it—a special divinely authorized speech that establishes authentic identity for the speaker—is the true and proper end of mortal life."[15] This divine authorization, however, could not entirely relieve Augustine of the anxiety that accompanied the act of self-revelation.

Never certain that he would be able to stave off temptation in the long haul, Augustine wrote his *Confessions* at once aware of his fallibility and hopeful for the possibility of intimacy with God: "I intend to remind myself of my past foulnesses and carnal corruptions, not because I love them but so that I may love you, my God. It is from love of your love that I make the act of recollection. The recalling of my wicked ways is bitter in my memory, but I do it so that you may be sweet to me, a sweetness touched by no deception, a sweetness serene and content."[16] The anxiety in Augustine's confessional writing stemmed partly from the unacknowledged fact that there were really two audiences for his work: the declared audience of God and the undeclared audience of a public that continues, almost two thousand years later, to read and enjoy his intimate revelations of carnal corruption and divine intervention in both paper and electronic versions.

Confession is a mode of public sharing that is at once intimate and soul baring; its intimacy intensifies its public reverberations. As James O'Donnell argues, "To 'confess' is to find an authentic voice with which to express what is private in a way that can be shared with a wider public."[17] Not simply a dyadic relationship between a sinner and God, the written confession becomes a triangular relationship in which authenticity is determined not only in the eyes of God but also in the more judgmental perspective of the eavesdropping "public." Augustine may have written to God, but his words were, and are, read by fellow human beings.

As the Roman Catholic practice of narrating one's sins to a priest became increasingly regulated within the sacramental ritual of the confessional, confession in Augustine's anxious sense was layered with new meanings. From there, the absorption of confession into the sphere of secular, that is, not church, law was not such a big step, as confession came to be the statement of one's wrongdoing or actions to "the proper authority of the truth of a statement," in the words of the *Oxford English Dictionary*. No longer solely addressed to God, but often with God as a witness, confession in the legal sense was a declaration to someone with the political or legal power to discern its truth.[18]

In the early days of the Reformation, Protestants added to these sacramental-legal meanings of confession by group declarations of faith. Instead of sharing only individually intimate personal stories of their spiritual struggles and failings, they argued over and eventually agreed on corporate "confessions of faith" based on earlier creeds—especially the Nicene Creed and the Apostles' Creed—which were compilations of what came to be authoritative and essential tenets of Christianity. For example, Anglicans prescribed the Thirty-Nine Articles, Presbyterians declared the Westminster Confession of Faith, and Anabaptists adopted the Schleitheim Confession. Christian confession, then, is a way of telling spiritual stories about the self and the community that are meant to be both humble and self-focused in the face of an audience at once divine and human.

Colonial and Secular Confessions

In colonial encounters throughout the early modern world, confession took on yet more dimensions, as Christian missionaries and settlers saw the spreading of the gospel as their duty. In the Americas, one of the most important media that both Catholic and Protestant missionaries sought as evidence of their successful conversion of Indigenous people was the confession in the sense of a testimony of faith. When Indigenous people testified to their newfound faith in Christ, missionaries would write down their words and circulate them back home.

For seventeenth-century Puritan ministers in New England, an Indigenous confession was useful not only as a testimony of the spirit but also as a document for the newly developing "scientific" study of the human soul. Indigenous conversions, as Sarah Rivett has shown, were considered by the settlers to be especially pure transformations, since they thought Indigenous people could have no ulterior motives for self-aggrandizement because of their supposedly primitive state of being. An Indigenous person's testimony of being filled by the "light of Christ" or, even more "purely," a deathbed testimony of an Indigenous child could serve as proof of God's existence, as Rivett argues: "God speaks through the mouth of the dying child, and thus titles [of testimonies] often emphasize the 'verbatim' transcription, 'taken directly from her mouth.'" Part ethnographic text and part empirical data, the Indigenous confession was printed and reprinted in multiple editions for eager audiences who read them for purposes of Christian devotion, entertainment, and the burgeoning science of the soul. In addition to autobiographical, doctrinal, legal, and denominational layers, then, confession was also imbued in colonial America with scientific veracity that made it a sought-after document for the newly developing fields of psychology and anthropology. The confession was a document of the soul and spirit that could be put to use in the service of the most powerful forces in colonial systems of spiritual invention and domination: religion, law, and science.[19]

With roots in earlier Christian forms of autobiography, creed, ritual, and missionary conversion, as well as in scientific and scholarly study, confession has flourished as a genre adaptable to many media and many publics. As Michel Foucault infamously argued in his *History of Sexuality*, confession transformed under the pressures of medicalization and the science of sexology in nineteenth-century Europe, becoming a tool of governing the self. In therapeutic settings, both medical and religious, ongoing revelations of one's personal foibles to a variety of audiences led to a proliferation of increasingly intimate public testimonies. According to Peter Brooks, confession continues to be fueled by a will to share intimate truths: "In a secularized world, the insistence has come to be placed on truth to oneself. And getting at this truth almost necessarily involves a confessional gesture, a claim to lay bare that which is most intimate in order to know oneself, or to make oneself known."[20] As I am arguing, settler colonial America was not, and still is not, a secularized world, if by that we mean a world that does not make use of spiritual stories to exert power and claim land. The compulsion to be true to oneself through public intimacy comes out of a long tradition of Christian confession, which privileges some truths while obscuring others.

Any testimony is partial and dependent on timing, audience, and the impossibility of ever fully accounting for the self. Philosopher Judith Butler accentuates how this partiality is profoundly social—how stories are never just our own: "An account of oneself is always given to another, whether conjured or existing. . . . The very terms by which we give an account, by which we make ourselves intelligible to ourselves and to others, are not of our making. They are social in character, and they establish social norms, a domain of unfreedom and substitutability within which our 'singular' stories are told." In North American Christianity in particular, confession is a gesture of the "singular" individual that is profoundly shaped by a Christian past and a social present.[21]

Long after the Puritan ministers sent Indigenous confessions back to England, testimonies of the spirit were still functioning as the heart of the empirical study of religion, both within religious studies and anthropology. William James, the Harvard psychologist/philosopher of religion, placed testimony at the heart of his wildly popular scientific mediation of the spirit, *Varieties of Religious Experience*, his Gifford Lectures of 1901–1902. Still read today in university religion classes, *Varieties* told a great story by quoting from the autobiographical writings of both famous and unknown subjects. Consider, for example, Maurice Bucke, a Canadian doctor-mystic, disciple of Walt Whitman, and author of the 1901 *Cosmic Consciousness*, who described his own vision thus:

> All at once, without warning of any kind, I found myself wrapped in a flame-colored cloud. For an instant I thought of fire, an immense conflagration somewhere close by in that great city; the next, I knew that the fire was within myself. Directly afterward there came upon me a sense of exultation, of immense joyousness accompanied or immediately followed by an intellectual illumination impossible to describe. Among other things, I did not merely come to believe, but I saw that the universe is not composed of dead matter, but is, on the contrary, a living Presence; I became conscious in myself of eternal life.

Bucke's cosmic consciousness shared Frederick Du Vernet's and William James's optimism for the possibility of a science of the spirit, albeit with a more fiery mystical sensibility.[22]

In some of James's passages, one can still discern how the chapter was first a story from his mouth delivered in an Edinburgh lecture hall. But it was a story from the mouth that was imbued with the authority of science in order to elicit the mystical in its readers. As Courtney Bender has argued, *Varieties* seeks to teach its readers the language of the spiritual, expecting that they will "encounter the residue of others' strongly resonant, singularly authoritative experiences" and will go on to seek their own. A testimony of the spirit is a gift that is meant to provoke a response. For missionaries, telling a story was itself meant to be the doorway to a new set of relationships in which their own testimonies would prompt non-Christians to confess in turn. The practices of believing made out of testimony were meant to transform not only spirits, but also economies, livelihoods, and politics in the Indigenous communities where they were delivered.[23]

Testimony on the Land

The mediation of spiritual stories—the tools and technologies by which testimonies of the spirit are communicated—is a way of placing and naming visions of the spirit in the world. In Protestant cosmologies of mediation, heavily influenced by biblical texts and personal testimony, the speaking subject is a privileged—yet unreliable—witness to the reality of the spirit and a widely expansive cosmos. For many Indigenous peoples, this universal cosmic spirit made little sense in their world in which spiritual stories were firmly rooted in particular places on the land.

Missionaries and Indigenous peoples lived among each other with conflicting, yet sometimes overlapping, understandings of the relationships of stories and spirits. In addition to translating theological ideas and genres, such as God, hell, scripture, and confession, missionaries also used material forms of mediation, such as buildings and clothing, to translate and create the "transcendent." Ruth Phillips shows how seventeenth-century interactions between Indigenous peoples and French and British colonizers "had come to depend on complex translation processes that were rooted in visual *and* verbal expressive cultures. The hybrid forms that resulted drew both on the criteria of material value and on the rhetorical conventions, metaphoric languages, and systems of graphic notation of these two seventeenth-century societies."[24] This hybridity meant that missionaries and their Christian stories were transformed by Indigenous practices of believing. Conflict over the best way to mediate a story—through a ritual confession or a totem pole raised at a feast, for example—raised questions in the minds of both missionaries and Indigenous peoples about how best to cultivate spiritual selves and relations.

Anthropologists and missionaries, in their engagement with Indigenous peoples of the northwest coast, offer two historically parallel perspectives on the significance of mediation. One could argue that both anthropologists and missionaries engaged in the work of confessional production—production that was at once religious, cultural, economic, and political. The work of anthropologist Franz Boas on the northwest coast, for example, was embedded in a profound commitment to written texts as particularly rich objects of cultural and economic exchange.[25] Boas realized that to achieve his ethnographic method, rooted as it was in gathering stories from key informants, he had to convey to the Kwakiutl (now Kwakwaka'wakw) the *value* of the very process of recording a story in a book. To do so, he *translated* the appeal of the book as a form of mediation into Kwakwaka'wakw practice.

Addressing a Kwakwaka'wakw audience, Boas wrote about his collaborator, George Hunt, a Tlingit man adopted by the Kwakwaka'wakw: "My friend, George Hunt, will show you a box in which some of your stories will be kept. It is a book that I have written on what I saw and heard when I was with you two years ago. It is a good book, for in it are your laws and stories. Now they will not be forgotten. Friends, it would be good if my friend, George Hunt, would become the storage box of your laws and of your stories." The translation attempt becomes ambiguous and significant here. First, Boas translates the ethnographic book as the box, and then George Hunt is the box. Both boxes, however, refer directly to the northwest coast practice of crafting bentwood boxes for practical and ritual purposes. Either way, the idea that a box was the proper container for one's most valued possessions became Boas's channel for convincing the Kwakwaka'wakw to give him their stories—along with an agreed on payment in cash.[26]

While many missionaries on the northwest coast also depended on an exchange of stories for cash for their livelihood and their vocation, theirs was usually an exchange quite reverse to that of the anthropologist. The missionary told his or her stories in newsletters, newspapers, and memoirs as a way to generate income from sympathetic audiences in the colonial motherland of England or in Canadian cities.[27] Relying on stories of the degraded heathen, the hopeful convert, or their own bravado and endurance, many missionaries, including Frederick Du Vernet and his colleague James McCullagh, positioned themselves at the center of stories of dramatic redemption.

Protocols and Potlatches

Confessional production is characterized by the incessant urge among Christians to produce and circulate personal testimony through diverse media, including catechisms, newspapers, books, and, now, digital social media. But print culture remains central to the art of Protestant storytelling as both a testimonial and entrepreneurial medium.[28] The plethora of missionary newsletters edited by Frederick Du Vernet and James McCullagh and directed to missionary societies in the United Kingdom and eastern Canada were not simply modes of communication but also commodities that could be bought and sold. The protocols of missionary testimony meant that stories circulated within both ritual and economic exchange.

The missionaries' style of testimony was in sharp contrast to the storytelling rituals among the Indigenous people they were seeking to convert. As Winona Wheeler found in her analysis of the mid-nineteenth-century diaries of Cree Anglican catechist Askenootow (Charles Pratt), he did not turn to a "confessional" mode of self-abasement before God. When he did note what he knew his readers—his missionary bosses—would read as failings, he made use of biblically inflected irony to criticize the paltry support they gave to him and his community. In sharp contrast to the bursts of self-flagellation of either Augustine or James McCullagh, Askenootow noted the limits of writing about the self: "I write least as possible not to deceive God or man, & yet my judgement is with the Lord and my word with my God." Similarly, among many northwest coast Indigenous storytelling traditions, telling a personal story about the self may be considered arrogantly bad form, as many anthropologists have found when trying to elicit life histories from Indigenous elders. Margaret Seguin Anderson and Tammy Anderson Blumhagen, writing of Ts'msyen approaches to oral history, argued that "neither the 'confessional' nor the 'exposé' genres are indigenous to Tsimshian *public* discourse (though they are probably as widely practiced *privately* among the Tsimshian as anywhere else)."[29] For Ts'msyen and other northwest coast nations, the feast (or what anthropologists and colonial officials called the potlatch) works according to protocols of storytelling quite the opposite of a bare-all confession.

The telling of certain kinds of spiritual stories in many Indigenous communities is meant to occur only within face-to-face relations of elders and listeners in which a story must be given explicitly to a listener before it can be passed on. Similar to Anishinaabe storytelling traditions of *aadizookaanag*, or oral tradition, among the Ts'msyen and Nisga'a *adawx* and *adaawak* are a collective heritage passed on from elders to community members who are ready to receive them. Adawx are also transmitted through totem poles, which, when the crests on the poles are interpreted by elders, tell the stories of creation, spiritual beings, and the history of the Ts'msyen or Nisga'a people.[30]

The forms of mediation by which stories of land are conveyed continue to matter. Anishinaabe scholar Leanne Simpson has coined the term "caged knowledge" to warn against allowing traditional Indigenous knowledge to be turned into "data" that helps perpetuate and absolve state-sanctioned colonialism and environmental destruction. Caging knowledge severs it from relations to ancestors and the land: "When knowledge is made into a text, it is translated from Indigenous languages into English, locking its interpretation in a cognitive box delineated by the structure of a language that evolved to communicate the worldview of the colonizers. . . . It is void of the spatial relationships created between Elder and youth. . . . It is separated from the land, from the worlds of the spirits, from its source and its meaning, and from the methodologies for transmission that provide the rigor that ensures its proper communication." In an Indigenous ethics of storytelling, great care must be taken with the means of production—to mediate a story of spiritual power on a mass scale by book or web page to a limitless, timeless audience could court danger, severing a story from contexts of people, time, and place.[31]

That said, many Indigenous people make use of social media to share stories not bound by protocols. Discussing what he calls the "virtual indigenism" cultivated online, Ronald Niezen argues that in the hands of Cree and other Indigenous peoples, the internet has been less a vehicle for self-revelation, and more a channel for collective representation in such a way that websites promote and preserve stories—and languages—as communal resources. Similarly, Idle No More, an Indigenous grassroots movement begun in 2012, became a social media–fueled call to sovereignty across Canadian and American borders and catalyzed an intentionally collective digital movement.[32]

The protocols shaping the mediation of Christian testimony seem to imply that more is better. The mass proliferation of Christian testimonials among a wide range of Protestants—whether today's bloggers or earlier converts and missionaries—appears as the piling up of stories that are focused on asserting both pious virtue and social status, and that often have the added result of accruing wealth through their publication and sale. In other words, Christian confessional production becomes a kind of Protestant potlatch in which there is never too much testifying, never too much intimacy or publicity, and never too much expenditure of the self in the interest of furthering social relations and the kingdom of heaven.[33]

My comparison of Christian confessional production to the potlatch is not accidental. Defined and outlawed by missionaries and governments as a ritual of excessive generosity at the heart of northwest coast Indigenous nations, the potlatch has been a colonial construct with great attraction for many anthropologists and Western theorists, including Franz Boas, Marcel Mauss, and Georges Bataille. A nineteenth-century colonial term for the complex feasting systems of the northwest coast, "potlatch" designated seasonal, ritual feasts that had many purposes, including economic redistribution, the assertion of territorial claims, and social demarcation. During a potlatch, a family or house would give away large amounts of material goods to guests as a "public opportunity to affirm rank and acknowledge wealth."[34] The centerpiece of Marcel Mauss's theory of the gift, the potlatch was also the prime target of missionary and government attempts to convert Nisga'a, Ts'msyen, and other northwest coast Indigenous nations to Christianity and Canadian colonial rule.

Missionaries and government agents in both Canada and the United States suppressed the feasting system, fearing it as a superstitious ritual, but also as an assertion of sovereignty. The Canadian government amended the Indian Act in 1884 in order to ban the potlatch as a supposedly heathen ritual of excessive gift giving in which Indigenous peoples did not understand the true value of material goods. Missionaries thought that the days and nights of feasting and gifting during the potlatch kept Indigenous peoples from being productive participants of capitalism. In the 1916 words of Miss E. J. Soal, CMS Anglican missionary in the Gitxsan territory of Hazelton, British Columbia, the potlatch was a gathering that "as a rule, led to poverty and frequently to murder." Even when banned, feasting persisted as the socially calibrated exchange of goods to mark name and territory, often in parallel with Christmas celebrations. While missionaries and Indian agents sometimes presided over the burning of potlatch regalia, at other times they profited by sending purloined or expropriated artifacts of northwest coast carving, masks, and totem poles to museums or private collections.[35]

At the turn of the twentieth century, Franz Boas and George Hunt used ethnographic analysis of the potlatch to argue against colonial, Christian, and racist constructions of the ceremony by demonstrating how Indigenous people claimed territory and asserted ritual and political authority through the feast system. Their argument was echoed in Marcel Mauss's use of the potlatch as a prime example of his theory of the gift as a system of both economic and ritual exchange that worked through "spiritual mechanisms," including "the one which obliges us to make a return gift for a gift received." Mauss cautioned: "To accept something from somebody is to accept some part of his spiritual essence, of his soul." Spiritual essence was a particularly "dangerous" thing to hold on to, because a gift coming from a person "not only morally, but physically and spiritually . . . exert[s] a magical and religious hold over you."[36] While Mauss was paraphrasing Boas and Hunt in these passages, the tenor of his book suggests that he too adhered to a sense that it was hazardous to hold on to another's spiritual essence for too long, and that his own French society would do well to learn from the potlatch approach to exchange and social relations.

Indigenous writers launched their own critique of the potlatch ban with the help of comparative analysis. Three Nisga'a leaders from the Nass River, Amos Gosnell, William Jeffrey, and Billy Williams, wrote to the *Victoria Daily Colonist* in 1896 to note their own observations about the parallels between Christian and Nisga'a testimonials: "We see in your graveyards the white marble and granite monuments which cost you money in testimony of your grief for the dead. When our people die we erect a large pole, call our people together, distribute our personal property with them in payment for their sympathy and condolence; comfort to us in the sad hours of our affliction. This is what is called a potlatch—the privilege denied us." In framing their protests to government, the Nisga'a often demonstrated this canny analytical ability to draw revealing parallels between the spiritual media of colonial Christianity and their own. They did so before anthropologists and other social theorists discovered that the potlatch is good to think with.[37]

What happens when spiritual essence is given via a story or a confession? Just as a Christian, colonial cosmology viewed the potlatch as a sign of excessive generosity in which Indigenous people misrecognized the true worth of things, so too could an Indigenous ethics of storytelling consider confessional production to be a failure to understand the true worth of stories. In this ethics, spreading one's story of spiritual revelation far and wide to strangers and friends alike misrecognizes the danger of making public what should remain within intimate, and ritually protected, circles. Excessively narrating oneself for the purposes of missionary conversion and missionary fundraising was a spiritual entrepreneurialism that in its drive to convert other peoples' souls and cosmologies of mediation also risked its own.

Early twentieth-century missionaries and anthropologists, the most successful of whom were always good at telling stories from their mouths, both had fraught and commodified relationships with stories, their telling and their gathering. Missionaries and anthropologists did not entirely share the same ideas of what a story was for or how it should travel. In part, this was because anthropologists were usually seasonal visitors who tidied up stories in books once they were back home in the East. Missionaries often remained living among Indigenous people, with all the messy relationships this entailed. In the case of Du Vernet, his testimony of radio mind emerged out of twenty-five years' worth of encounters and relationships with Indigenous people and settlers living in close proximity to him and with the writings of faraway authors. All the while, radio mind was also rooted in his devoted, yet changing, relationship to his god, as he experienced it on the land and waters on which he lived.

In an age of telling stories to the world en masse and often online, the intimacy of narrative both appears and is erased via ever-wider mediations and by ever-more-pervasive technologies. Turning our attention to an earlier time of slow media, we can see that even over a century ago, women and men were worried about how changes in the ways stories were told might shape the possibilities for what it meant to be a human being and a nation. Could stories really bring a new nation into being, erasing the sovereignty embedded in the oral histories of those nations already there? Could stories prompt new practices of believing truly capable of creating new worlds?

Frederick Du Vernet and his fellow missionaries, as well as the Anishinaabeg, Nisga'a, and Ts'msyen they encountered, told stories within and across their cosmologies of mediation—colonial, Christian, and Indigenous. As the land on which they lived became widely, but not universally, imagined as Canada, spiritual stories told through the slow media of photographs, maps, printed texts, and radios helped bind this social imaginary to the land. The Indian Act, residential schools, and broken treaties were tied up in the alliance between church and state that made the story of a Christian Canada seem spiritual, natural, and real. But what is bound can become unbound; what is imagined can be reimagined. As Indigenous people of his time told Du Vernet, and as Indigenous scholars and storytellers today continue to affirm, older stories of the land have abided, as sources of revelation and reclamation, as powerful practices of believing.[38]

4

Picturing the Soul on Manidoo Ziibi

Early on in my encounter with Frederick Du Vernet, an archivist with the Anglican Church of Canada gave me an unexpected gift: a copy of a diary in which Frederick had written down thirteen days of stories from his 1898 trip to the region of the Rainy River and Lake of the Woods, also known in the United States as the Boundary Waters. Compared to his writerly voice as published in church newspapers and letters, the diary brought to life a more intimate portrait of a self-reflective man. A thirty-eight-year-old father with two school-age children, he came to the Rainy River as a missionary-journalist, armed with pen, paper, and a camera. In his efforts to keep a record of what he learned about the Anglican missions on Anishinaabe, or, more specifically, Ojibwe, territory, he ended up preserving stories of Ojibwe women and men who welcomed and chastised him in turn, especially when he sought to photograph them and their world.[1]

On his journey from Toronto to the Rainy River in the summer of 1898, Frederick Du Vernet traveled by train for two days to Rat Portage, a railway town at the northerly tip of Lake of the Woods. He then boarded the steamer *Keenora*, which ferried him south to the Ojibwe reserves of Little Forks, Manitou Rapids, and Long Sault on the banks of the Rainy River. To make the same journey today, visitors would likely find their way to Fort Frances, a town on the Canadian side of the Rainy River, and then drive west along a thoroughfare that still bears the startlingly candid name Colonization Road. That's what government surveyors called the roads that were built to open up "New Ontario" to settlers moving north. Taking a southerly turn off the road about twenty minutes past the town of Emo, visitors will arrive at Long Sault, or what is now once more called by its Anishinaabemowin name, Kay-Nah-Chi-Wah-Nung, the "place of the long rapids."

Here, a visitor will catch sight of the Rainy River again. A wide, snaking flow of water with rapids roiling along the way, the river shifts from a silvery gray to a purplish black depending on the weather. In keeping with its English name, rainstorms come to the river in a flash, bringing winds that threaten to wrench everything and everybody off their moorings. Under sunny skies, the light over the river is clear, almost blinding, and the burial mounds formed thousands of years ago stand out as vivid green reminders of a past before America.

The mounds along the river mark a time when people gathered by its banks to bury their dead, not by digging them into the ground, but by piling their bundled bones into hills of dirt. With time, leaves of mint, hyssop, and milkweed grew into blankets of green, forming mounds at once stable and alive. In his diary, Frederick Du Vernet noted these "prehistoric" mounds and remarked that "the Indians will not allow them to be opened."[2] As they did in 1898, the mounds today signal that this landscape is both ancient and sacred. Now, however, the mounds are the reason for a more recent marker of history: the Kay-Nah-Chi-Wah-Nung Historical Centre, a museum run by the Rainy River First Nations and built into the landscape, combining museum displays, a ceremonial round house, a restaurant, and a guided path through the ancient mounds. First envisioned in the 1970s by the Canadian government as a place to tell the story of the ancient Laurel and Black Duck cultures, it was eventually built in 1998 as a place for the Ojibwe of Rainy River to tell the story of their ancient past and more recent history.

Long before Du Vernet arrived, the river had been a conduit for people of many nations. The Ojibwe called the river Manidoo Ziibi, or "river of the *manidoo*," in recognition of the spirit that dwells in the rapids, where plentiful sturgeon and trout also gather. In the eighteenth century, the Ojibwe gradually pushed the Sioux westward to the prairies, while French and British fur traders, seeking waterways to take them west, negotiated with the Ojibwe for access to the river. In 1783, after the American Revolutionary War, the swift-flowing river, about half a mile wide, was designated part of the international border between Canada and the United States. The Ojibwe, however, continued to live as a nation on both sides of the river. By the 1870s, Canada had promised its newest province, British Columbia, that the government would build a transcontinental railway from coast to coast. To do so, it needed control of a vast swath of Ojibwe territory north of the Great Lakes. The resulting 1873 Treaty 3 sequestered the Rainy River Ojibwe onto seven different reserves along the river and proclaimed the land New Ontario.[3]

Du Vernet's fragmentary diary records eleven July days along the river in 1898; it was what brought me to the Rainy River First Nations on a hot July day in 2012. Bringing the diary back to where it had been written, on the banks of Manidoo Ziibi, I was met with hospitality by Art Hunter of the Kay-Nah-Chi-Wah-Nung Historical Centre. More than one hundred years after Du Vernet's journey, I stood with Art on the banks near the Long Sault rapids, where Du Vernet had plunged into the river to escape the heat and the mosquitos. I was struck by how little the landscape appeared to have changed, yet at the same time, Art and the Kay-Nah-Chi-Wah-Nung Historical Centre made me aware of how it had changed a great deal. The land on the banks of the Long Sault rapids had been "awarded" to the Ojibwe in Treaty 3 in 1873; then confiscated by the federal and provincial governments in 1914, when the seven reserves were amalgamated into one at Manitou Rapids, and the government gave or sold the remaining land to settlers; and finally, partially bought back by the Rainy River First Nations at the end of the twentieth century.

Du Vernet's diary presents an important window onto this tumultuous time on Manidoo Ziibi. With the help of elders and others from the Rainy River First Nations and Kay-Nah-Chi-Wah-Nung, I have been working with students on a "re-mediation" of the diary into a digital exhibit in order to bring its stories, informed by Ojibwe perspectives, to a wider audience. Art Hunter, along with elders Willie Wilson and Dorothy Medicine, told us more of the stories and history of Kay-Nah-Chi-Wah-Nung during our visits to the Rainy River First Nations. We learned that though the mounds still sit gracefully on the land, appearing eternal, they are not. In 1884, one of the mounds was tunneled into by George Bryce, a Presbyterian minister from Winnipeg, who pulled human bones from the carefully packed soil and displayed them during a lecture at the Manitoba Historical Society. His disrespect for the dead extended to the living caretakers of the mounds, as he portrayed the Ojibwe as bloodthirsty "barbarians" who were ignorant of the mounds' significance.[4]

Indian agents, gravel dealers who had bought the land after the forced amalgamation, and pot hunters seeking ancient artifacts had all dug into the mounds, drawn to their antiquity while disdainful of their ongoing spiritual significance in the lives of the Ojibwe. In the 1970s, the mounds were opened once again, this time by a succession of archaeologists working with the help of local Ojibwe people. One of these young men was Art's brother, Al Hunter, who later as chief helped negotiate the land claim that returned the mounds to the care of the Ojibwe.[5]

Over the last two hundred years, Kay-Nah-Chi-Wah-Nung has seen many visitors, and many parties have contended for control over it. Long Sault was an important gathering place for Ojibwe, who found plentiful sturgeon in the rapids and memories of ancestors in the mounds. By the nineteenth century, the river had become a site of great interest not only to the fur traders and treaty commissioners but also to a succession of Catholic, Methodist, Anglican, and, later, Mennonite missionaries. Many Ojibwe of Manidoo Ziibi strongly resisted these waves of missionaries attempting to convert them to Christianity while at the same time accommodating particular Christian missionaries up to a point.[6]

In both 1849 and 1854, the Ojibwe Grand Council refused to allow Methodists to establish missions, but gradually allowed the building of schools and even some churches. Then, in 1873, the council, led in part by Mawedopenais, a chief of Kay-Nah-Chi-Wah-Nung, negotiated a treaty with representatives of Queen Victoria of Great Britain. The way the Crown's representatives told the story, in English, the Ojibwe had agreed "to cede, release, surrender and yield up to the Government of the Dominion of Canada for Her Majesty the Queen and Her successors forever, all their rights, titles and privileges whatsoever, to the lands included within the following limits . . ." In return, they were to receive reserve lands, farming equipment, hunting and fishing rights, and financial compensation. The Grand Council of Treaty #3, however, asserts that the government of Canada's version does not tell "the full story" of the treaty: government accounts misrepresent the "spirit and intent" of the treaty and ignore the assertions of leaders such as Mawedopenais, who insisted that "the Great Spirit planted us here" in order for the Ojibwe to govern themselves and their territory. In the wake of Treaty 3, Long Sault became one of the largest reserves on the Rainy River, forming a block of almost eleven thousand acres (fig. 6).[7]

By the 1870s, Anglican missionaries had driven off other Christian competitors, but they remained only mildly successful.[8] They established schools on several reserves along the river, but churches were few. In Long Sault in particular, it was not until 1896, with the arrival of the Swampy Cree Anglican missionary Jeremiah Johnston, that the first church was built. By the time Jeremiah and his wife, Mary, arrived at Long Sault, the Ojibwe had experienced twenty years of the government of Canada's ongoing project of Indigenous assimilation.

In 1876, the government of Canada had enacted the Indian Act, a sweeping set of laws that tried to classify and regulate the lives of Indigenous peoples in minute detail, making them wards of the state under the authority of Indian agents who wrote yearly reports detailing reserve life. In 1880, the government of Canada made one of many amendments to the Indian Act, prohibiting most of the people that it classified as Indians, including Ojibwe of the Rainy River, from selling their agricultural produce off the reserves without

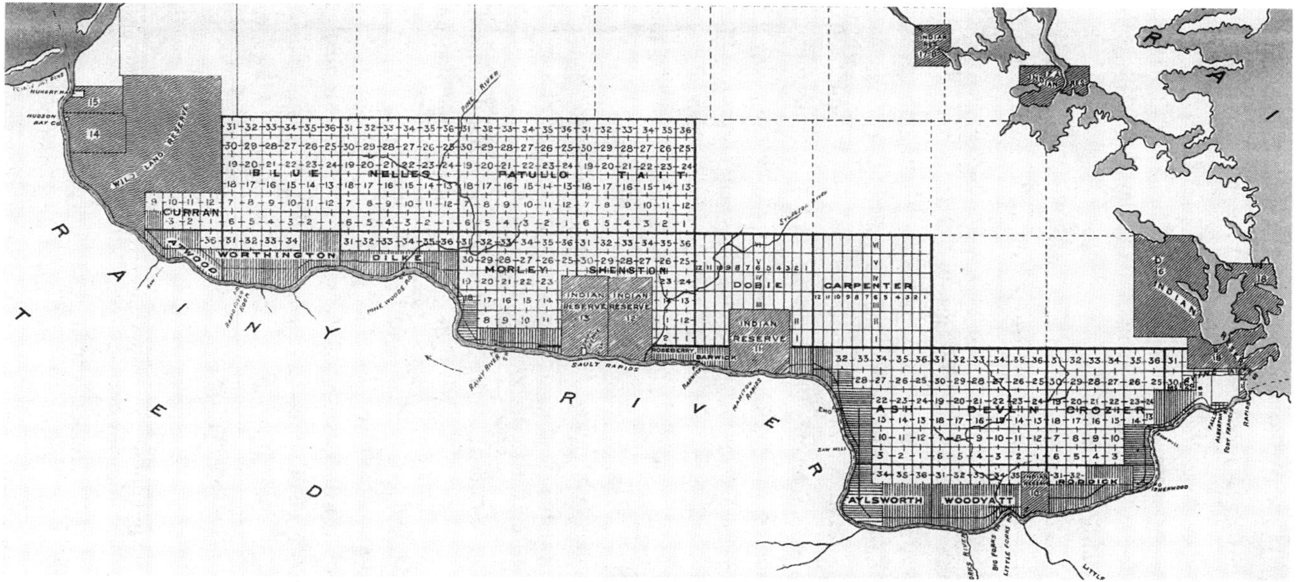

FIGURE 6. Detail of a map of the Rainy River District, with Long Sault at "Indian Reserves 12 and 13." From Frank Yeigh, *The Rainy River District, Province of Ontario, Canada: An Illustrated Description of Its Soil, Climate, Products, Area, Agricultural Capabilities and Timber and Mineral Resources, Together with the Laws and Information Pertaining to Free Grants and Homesteads*, 3rd ed. (Toronto: Ontario Department of Crown Lands, 1894). Photograph courtesy of Thomas Fisher Rare Book Library, University of Toronto.

the permission of an Indian agent. Harvesting vegetable gardens without the ability to sell the harvest led to piles of rotting produce. Under the restrictions of the Indian Act, there was little motivation for the Ojibwe to do what the government supposedly wanted—namely, for them to become agriculturalists and give up hunting, fishing, or wild rice gathering. Repeated small pox epidemics and the environmental destruction of the forests and the waters brought on by the logging industry combined to devastate Ojibwe families and communities along the river.[9]

In 1895, the Dominion government again revised the Indian Act to outlaw anyone encouraging or participating in an "Indian festival, dance or other ceremony of which the giving away or paying or giving back of money, goods or articles of any sort forms a part." Casting its net across the continent, this amendment applied to both northwest coast feasting practices and the Midewiwin, or Grand Medicine Society, of the Anishinaabeg. When Jeremiah Johnston arrived at Manidoo Ziibi in 1896, the "pagans" he sought to convert could end up serving jail terms of between two and six months for practicing their own ceremonies. After 1892, fishing and wild rice gathering also were endangered, when the Dominion government gave up on protecting Ojibwe fishing rights, and American and Canadian fishermen swarmed to the river to catch sturgeon, filled with lucrative caviar, drastically depleting the stocks through overfishing. In 1898, the government of Ontario passed a law requiring Canadian lumber to be milled at Canadian pulp and paper mills, increasing the volume of paper production and thus sending even more pollution westward down the river.[10]

The obstruction of Ojibwe agriculture ran contrary to the support promised in Treaty 3, and the government used the results of this obstruction to argue that since Ojibwe were supposedly not sufficiently productive farmers, their land could be commandeered and given to white settlers. In 1914–1915, the combined forces of the Ontario and Canadian governments amalgamated all seven reserves—each of which had its own family and local histories—into one reserve at Manitou Rapids, east of Long Sault.[11] Colonial laws, resource extraction, and the increasing presence of white settlers on both the Canadian and US sides of the Rainy River placed intense pressure on the lives and land of the Ojibwe.

The Anglican missionaries are now long gone, but Kay-Nah-Chi-Wah-Nung remains a place where both the land and the people seek to remember the past. The Rainy River First Nations marked the centennial of the forced amalgamation in 2015, and the circular pavilion on their powwow grounds bears the names of the seven former reserves. The community still remembers, and lives with, with the traumatic effects of the forced move. This respect for memory, in all its beauty and ugliness, made Kay-Nah-Chi-Wah-Nung a powerful place to bring a diary written by an Anglican missionary who came to Manidoo Ziibi carrying a camera and a spirit of conversion with him, but who ended up himself feeling changed, if not entirely converted, by his encounters with Ojibwe people and practices.[12]

Photographic Events

Taking his first journey west as a missionary-journalist, Frederick Du Vernet set out to document the state of Anglican "Indian missions" in western Canada for the *Canadian Church Missionary Gleaner*, a newsletter published for Anglican audiences in Canada and Great Britain. Upon leaving Rat Portage, the steamer *Keenora*, with Du Vernet aboard, traveled through a region of lakes, islands, and rivers marking off what had only recently become the borders of Manitoba, Ontario, and Minnesota (fig. 7). Entranced as he was by the landscape and the people, Du Vernet was also dismayed by what he considered to be heathen practices.[13]

Despite years of trying to convert the Ojibwe, Catholic and Anglican missionaries in the area had little success to show for their efforts. Both the reports of the government Indian agents from that time and Du Vernet's own account admit as much: In the 1898 *Annual Report of the Department of Indian Affairs*, the Long Sault and Manitou Rapids Bands were said to total 124 people, with the "great majority [being] pagans."[14] What emerges from Du Vernet's diary—sometimes through zealously Christian prose and sometimes via a protoethnographic style of writing—is a picture of an Indigenous culture with strong spiritual traditions of its own, ably protected by men and women of the Treaty 3 reserves he visited.

An avid photographer and frank diarist, Du Vernet made sure to keep his camera close to his side throughout the trip to Manidoo Ziibi. His diary of the tour served as the basis for articles he wrote as the editor of the *Gleaner*. Only one of the published articles from the Manidoo Ziibi portion of his trip has survived, the diary is truncated, and none of the photographs remain. These gaps aside, the diary contains many fascinating accounts of the significance of what scholars call the "photographic event," meaning photographers' negotiations with their subjects and the technical labor required to take a photograph.[15] Du Vernet's written stories of the resistance to and requests for photographs that he encountered among the Ojibwe are a revealing lens on how the event of taking photographs marked his longing to capture spiritual stories and presences. At the same time, his stories record, however fleetingly,

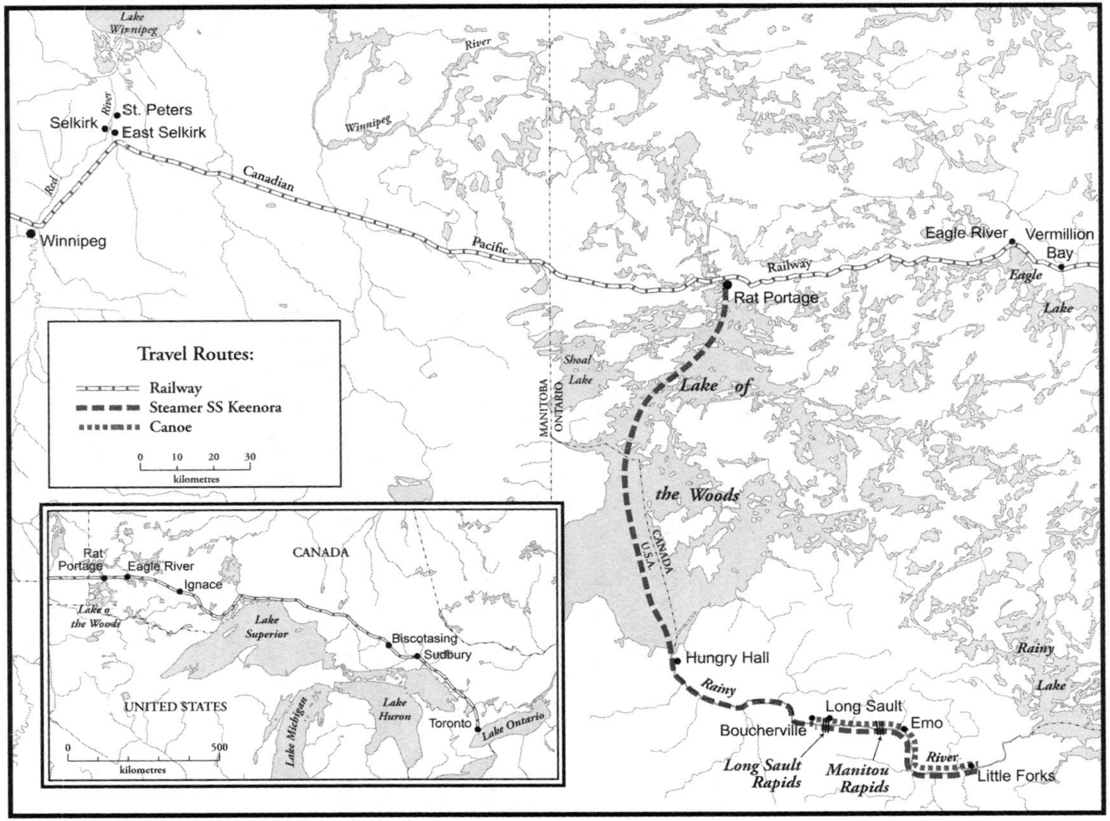

FIGURE 7. Map of Du Vernet's journey to the Rainy River in 1898. Courtesy of Douglas Fast.

a corresponding Ojibwe ambivalence about what such kinds of capture might entail.

For missionaries, the photographic event could build or hinder new relationships with the people whose photos they wanted to take. When framed out of its local context, a photograph could serve as a witness to missionary success in order to encourage generous donations, especially when printed in missionary newsletters or illuminated in the lantern slideshows that missionaries produced as a mix of evangelism and entertainment. In more private moments, a missionary could look at a photograph after the fact, prompting any number of reactions, reminiscences, and feelings of solidarity. Photographs could tell stories, provoke memories, imprint on the soul, and testify to the workings of the spirit. Protestants used photography to enable their "spiritual sight," or their ability to see how the spirit was at work in the everyday world. Placing the missionary's sense of spiritual sight within the same frame as what Gerald Vizenor has called the "imagic presence" of the Ojibwe, it becomes evident that all parties to the colonial encounter understood visual imagery to have a power beyond that of the merely documentary.[16]

Jeremiah and Mary Johnston, Du Vernet's hosts on Manidoo Ziibi, both could speak Anishinaabemowin, or what they then likely called Ojibwe. Their approach was attuned to the Ojibwe emphasis on hospitality, consensus, and respect. Refusing to force himself on people, and hesitant to sing or pray in their homes unless invited to do so, Jeremiah had a slightly better success rate with bringing Christianity to the Ojibwe than earlier missionaries. He managed to clear some land and build a house, as well as erect a church and a small graveyard. Besides Du Vernet's diary, there are few historical sources to tell us about the Johnstons' mission at the Long Sault rapids during a critical time in the lives of the Manidoo Ziibi Ojibwe, some of whom were Christian, but most of whom were not.

Frederick was clearly captivated by Jeremiah and Mary and was very impressed with their commitment to their mission. He noted with some awe Jeremiah's past military service in the Anglo-Sudan War as one of several hundred Indigenous and Métis "voyageurs" sent to navigate the Nile during the 1884 British campaign to rescue General Gordon from the siege of Khartoum. He took care to note that Jeremiah "deepened" his faith while on the Nile, giving his Bible away to a "native" and meditating in the desert. According to Du Vernet, Jeremiah was raised by his Cree Christian mother and had "grown up a Xian [Christian]." Jeremiah's English father seems not to have been part of his upbringing, and his mother saw to it that her son was formally educated. He eventually sought out theological and missionary training at the Anglican St. John's College in Winnipeg.[17] He was the ideal "Christian Indian" for missionary work, in the eyes of the Anglican Church: educated, capable of conversing in Anishinaabemowin, and with more experience traveling the British Empire than many Canadian missionaries.

Mary Johnston told Frederick many stories, which he carefully wrote in his diary. In addition to stories of Mary's seafaring bravery, when she rescued both her children and fully grown men from stormy waters, Frederick also recorded stories that Mary told him about "Christian Indians" from the northern Manitoba mission of Jack Head. One story related Mary's disappointment when a young woman named Kitty (or Kittie) continued to participate in the Ojibwe ritual of the "medicine tent" even after her baptism. Facing serious illness, Kitty had been "persuaded by her husband to renounce Xy + go thro: the medicine tent. Mrs Johnston heard this and was very much disappointed as 'Kitty' seemed a good Xian girl." Mary recalled to Frederick how she alone had comforted Kitty during her dying hours with Christian hymns and prayer, only to be shocked at the preparations Kitty's father had made for her burial:

> When [Mrs. J.] got [to the grave] she found that though the body was not cold she was painted and fastened up in a blanket in a sitting posture for heathen burial. Mrs. J. turned to Kittie's father [and] said "What does this mean—Kittie was one of our Xian girls I cannot have her buried like a heathen." The old man said, "do as you like." So she went home + got some clothes and asked some Indians to make a coffin + they came + washed the Indian girl + laid her out. [Mrs. J. was] Watching by her the rest of the night with only the old Indian in the house for none of the rest would come near. The next day she had them gather together. They sang a hymn + had a prayer in the house + at the grave she asked a Xian Indian to offer up prayer.[18]

The medicine tent that Mary Johnston condemned was a space in which men and women trained as ritual experts could address the spirits, cure family and community members, and even communicate mind-to-mind across great distances. Declared to be heathen practice by Christian missionaries and censured by government Indian agents, the medicine tent nevertheless continued as a primary mode of healing for a people barraged by diseases and hunger brought on by colonial rule.[19]

Mary Johnston's story of a woman who combined Ojibwe rituals with those of Christianity was the kind of detailed story that Du Vernet told repeatedly in his diary. In these stories, photography often emerges as a character in its own right, an act and technology that mediated not only images but also relationships among Du Vernet, the Johnstons, and Ojibwe men, women, and children. In the eleven days on the river recorded in his diary, Du Vernet describes taking nine photographs, though he likely took more. The photographic events he thought worthy of description included photos taken at the request of his fellow Christians, who wanted their family members preserved on film. He also described more awkward and even hostile interactions in which non-Christian Ojibwe refused to take part in his picture taking. In all his photographs, including those meant to document church buildings and schools, he considered it important to include local people in the frame, but his compositions did not always work out as planned, for technical and interpersonal—or perhaps spiritual—reasons.

The Soul of Photography

Can a photograph steal a soul, or even bring back the dead? In the early days of photography, this was a question that haunted many people as they contemplated the uncanny likenesses that photography captured on paper. In nineteenth-century Europe and North America, spirit photographers claimed to catch the spirits of dead loved ones on film, processing their ghostly images back into presence. Cameras and their effects traveled widely around the world in the hands of colonial anthropologists, missionaries, tourists, and entrepreneurs looking for a captivating image; they were met with both hostility and incredulity.[20]

As people from different sensory and spiritual cultures met each other with a camera in between them, the photographic events that ensued offer a glimpse of the unnerving closeness of face-to-face colonial encounters. Ethnographic, literary, and historical accounts of the cultural encounters provoked by these photographic events have often made mention of the idea that "natives" believed that a photograph could steal the soul of its subject. The soul-stealing photograph, however, is by no means an innocent idea. Both missionaries and the people they sought to evangelize understood photographs to have powerful spiritual effects, albeit for different reasons.

Many scholars have argued that the soul-stealing photograph was a stereotype that colonizers imposed on what they thought were naïvely superstitious natives. Alternatively, other scholars have suggested that for an Indigenous person to think that a camera and its owner could function as a kind of "vampire" with predatory motives was a valid, and sometimes tactical, belief that made sense in colonial contexts. Heike Behrend uses the term "photo magic" to describe the efforts of European missionaries in colonial East Africa.

Behrend shows that missionaries quite explicitly used photography both to spread the gospel and to make what they hoped would be a dazzling display of the superiority of their own supernatural power. These nineteenth-century German missionaries were sure that by fixing onto paper the faces of those they hoped to convert, they could prove the power of their god. They even borrowed from other supernatural practices of photography back home to argue for the spiritual efficacy of their imagery. For example, they cited the Spiritualist practice of spirit photography, in which photographers claimed to have captured on film the spirits channeled by mediums during séances. In other words, Heike Behrend writes, these missionaries "converted technology into magic."[21] Even today one could argue that in the age of social media, photographs have a treacherous ability to destroy if not a soul, then at least a reputation.

Along Manidoo Ziibi, the camera was one more technology in a long tradition of image making. Reflecting on technologies of storytelling, Ojibwe writer and poet Louise Erdrich has argued that the trope of the soul-stealing photograph makes no sense in the watery regions of "Ojibwe country." Erdrich describes how, in Anishnaabemowin, the root word *mazina* is at the heart of a constellation of concepts dealing with images, books, pictographs, and more: "*Mazinaakizo*. To be photographed. (Nothing about stealing souls in the word mazinaakizo. Photographers did not take Ojibwe souls, it wasn't that easy. Soul theft required the systematic hard work of inventive humiliations and abuse by the government and by Catholic nuns and priests.)"[22] Erdrich demystifies the photograph's effects on the soul in order to draw attention to emotional and physical brutality mediated not by cameras but by residential schools in both the United States and Canada.

Manidoo Ziibi and its surrounding region had a varied history of visual documentation long before Du Vernet's 1898 visit. For centuries, the Ojibwe had painted on rock to tell stories of spirits in specific places. They also drew images on bark scrolls to tell their stories of creation, of human-divine interaction, and of ritual systems such as the Midewiwin society. White settlers also turned to visual imagery in their nineteenth-century encounters with the Ojibwe. The Canadian painter Frederick Verner, who built his artistic career on romantic paintings of the Ojibwe, first visited Ojibwe territory in the company of the lieutenant governor of Manitoba, as he went to negotiate Treaty 3 in 1873. As art historian Maureen Ryan has shown, Verner's 1873 paintings of the Rainy River and other sites were part of a broader visual culture of "imaginative appropriation" that assisted the Canadian seizure of Indigenous land, partly through painting scenes that enabled the persistent colonial rhetoric that "Indians" were a "dying race" (plate 1). Ryan argues that the subdued hues of *On Rainy River at Long Sault* depicted a "traditional" Ojibwe settlement, which appeared to urban, southern eyes as temporary in construction, occupied by people in need of "humanitarian" aid. Late nineteenth-century studio photographs of Ojibwe families in elegant, often beaded, clothing tell another story. Most Ojibwe on the Rainy River would have seen photographic images in newspapers and postcards, and many would have posed for photographs in towns in Minnesota or Ontario or for visiting photographers.[23]

Whether or not Du Vernet thought that cameras could steal the soul, taking photographs led him to contemplate the very notion of the "soul," or the "spirit." As a journalist who wanted to tell stories of missionary work on the Rainy River to Christian audiences throughout Canada, Du Vernet considered photography to be such an important medium of testimony that it was worth the trouble to haul around on his journey the bulky equipment of a dry plate camera. His efforts, often focused on conveying the spiritual lives of others, are mirrored by the work of many other missionary photographers at the turn of the twentieth century.[24]

Twelve years after Du Vernet visited Manidoo Ziibi, one of the more celebrated documentarians of the Ojibwe, American ethnographer Frances Densmore, was the photographer of the *Ojibwa Wigwam at Manitou Rapids* (fig. 8). Like Du Vernet, Densmore was an Anglican—or in the United States, an Episcopalian—who also recorded late nineteenth-century "missionary journeys" to the Ojibwe with the camera, the pen, and the voice-recording technology of wax cylinders.[25] Du Vernet's desire to visually record his encoun-

FIGURE 8. Frances Densmore, *Frame of an Ojibway Wigwam at Manitou Rapids Reserve in Ontario, Canada* (1920). Photograph courtesy of Minnesota Historical Society (13166).

ters with the Ojibwe, then, was part of a much wider practice of committing Ojibwe people and landscapes to a visual record with complicated political and spiritual effects.

The Promise of Presence

The photograph has been the focus of a great deal of theorizing for its capacity to both depict reality and distort it. Photography's uses as historical evidence and nostalgic evocation make the photograph a material witness that is at once trustworthy and unreliable, emotionally charged and emotionally deadening. Roland Barthes, in perhaps one of the most famous meditations on the photograph, was acutely aware of the multivalent power of photography to provoke by its shock value—or what he called the *punctum*, the wound—and to pacify by its ubiquity. Since their invention, photographs have grown increasingly commonplace, and in their commonality they often serve not as illuminations of the unexpected but as veils of the banal. Nevertheless, Barthes continued to believe in the "magic" of some photographs not only for their "evidential force" but also for their potential to carry the soul. He showed this most evocatively in his discussion of the winter garden photograph of his much-beloved mother, taken when she was a girl.[26]

For Barthes, this photo (which he does not display to his readers) is the only one that conveys the "air" of his mother to him: "in which I discover her: a sudden awakening, outside of 'likeness,' a *satori* in which words fail." The air of the photo, "given as an act of grace," restores, even re-ensouls, Barthes's dead mother to him in his grief: "In this veracious photograph, the being I love, whom I have loved, is not separated from itself: at last it coincides. And mysteriously, this coincidence is a kind of metamorphosis. All the photographs of my mother which I was looking through were a little like so many masks; at the last, suddenly the mask vanished: there remained a soul, ageless but not timeless, since this air was the person I used to see, consubstantial with her face, each day of her long life."[27]

For Barthes, the photographic air that can effect this metamorphosis, this ensoulment, is refracted through grace, a concept from his own Protestant heritage. He also alludes to satori, a concept Barthes understood as being from Japanese Zen, but which also has its own history of Protestant inflection from William James and D. T. Suzuki. If we take him at his word then, for Barthes, the viewing of certain photographs offers a "certificate of presence" that is not only an insistence that the photographed object existed, but also, potentially, a path to copresence that allows a "metaphysical" contact with another soul.[28]

Fifty years earlier, in a qualitatively different photographic age, but one in which photographs were still relatively ubiquitous and politically powerful, Walter Benjamin offered his own reflection on the "magic" of photographs: "The most precise technology can give its products a magical value, such as a painted picture can never again have for us. No matter how artful the photographer, no matter how carefully posed his subject, the beholder feels an irresistible urge to search such a picture for the tiny spark of contingency, of the Here and Now, with which reality has so to speak seared the subject, to find the inconspicuous spot where in the immediacy of that long-forgotten moment the future subsists so eloquently that we, looking back, may rediscover it." Similar to his conviction that handwriting could reveal the unconscious, Benjamin understood photography to have the capacity to reveal the obscured, thus making possible the "rediscovery" of what the future looked like in the past. For Benjamin, this contact with immediacy came at a price, however, in that photography was also a tool of fascist surveillance and capitalist creation of desire.[29]

Benjamin showed that a photograph is a form of mediation that we attend to with caution, acknowledging its power as both magical and tyrannical. This was especially true for missionary photography. What Benjamin and Barthes demonstrate is that even within the canons of Western critical theory, the photograph has carried with it spiritual effects. As a carrier of the soul of the dead and a channel for the visceral "immediacy" of the past, the photograph is far from one-dimensional. With access as well to the photographic events that lie behind the image on paper—or onscreen—these spiritual effects come into even sharper relief.

Photography—both as technology of representation and as testament to human relationships—conveyed the complex ambivalence of Protestant testimonies in a way that is particularly charged when thinking about the past in a settler colonial context. How can we know today what kind of testimony a photograph was meant to witness? What kinds of stories did early twentieth-century Protestants hope that photographs might tell? In addition to the testimony of the eyewitness account and the propaganda of missionary evangelism is another more-difficult-to-pin-down quality of presence, in which the photograph operates in a realm of piety or spiritual encounter. David Morgan has argued that early twentieth-century Protestants lived with a visual piety in which they hoped that photographs might "reanimate a world bereft of spiritual presence."[30] Their yearning for a vision-rich spirituality, however, depended on the same technologies that would facilitate their attempts to outlaw and obliterate the visions of Indigenous peoples.

Protestant Photo Magic

Bringing together Du Vernet's diary with the materiality of photographic testimony—its evidential force, its visual piety, and its capacity to cultivate and destroy relationships with others, dead or alive, human or spirit—illuminates the photo magic of Frederick Du Vernet. As he encountered the Ojibwe with their own traditions of spiritual sight in which religious visions and their visual depiction were a primary mode of teaching, Du Vernet's photographic zeal had its roots in a Christian pedagogy and aesthetics of visuality. Seeing the land with the eye of the photographer brought him to record it with poetic appreciation. Aboard the SS *Keenora* close to Hungry Hall, one of the seven Rainy River reserves, he noted that "one spot especially[,] where the light green crop of grain with a little cottage was perfectly reflected in the still water[,] lives in my memory."[31] His word pictures, documenting what could well have been a crop of grain raised by Ojibwe farmers, narrate the transformation of the land.

When he needed to send his heavier bags ashore at the Long Sault rapids so that he could travel light when returning by canoe from Little Forks with Jeremiah Johnston and Charlie, their "Indian" guide, Du Vernet made sure to keep his camera with him. He would not have been able to use the bulky camera as he "twisted and turned" seeking comfort in the canoe, but by his description of his "first experience" of running the rapids, he did not care: "When we got to the head of the rapids we all sat down lower in the canoe I put my paddle in then came the first 'Chute'. [A] log ahead made Mr. Johnston change his course a little + a mass of spray broke over the Canoe. On we went running the three 'Chutes'[.] It was very thrilling."[32] These moments of vivid description in his diary have an intimacy and liveliness that a photograph would not have captured.

On several occasions, Du Vernet carefully recorded the gestures and words of resistance that Ojibwe elders offered to his missionary tour, especially when he wanted to take their pictures. He also noted those who sought out his camera. Many of the pictures taken by Frederick Du Vernet were of his hosts, the Johnston family. In his diary, Du Vernet recounts how both Jeremiah and Mary requested that he take photographs for them for different purposes:

> Back of the Church is the graveyard, with two or three marble stones + a wooden cross[.] [A]s the Indians take great care of their graves it is right that the Christians sh[oul]d do the same. I took a photo of the Church from near the flag staff + one of the graves as Mr. J wanted to send a picture home to England to the relatives of a former Catechist to whose memory the white marble cross has been erected. In front of the Church I had Mr Johnston Mrs Johnston Florence 13. Beatrice 11. Isabel 9. + Samuel the baby boy (16 months). Mrs J. is very anxious to have a picture of her boy as he is delicate[.] [S]he has lost six children.[33]

Jeremiah Johnston wanted a photo of the Christian grave marker commemorating his deceased coworker, Joseph Edwin Wain, to send to Wain's relatives in England, while Mary Johnston, amid her anxious uncertainty about her child's health, and in the knowledge of her six dead children, sought a photo of the living, hoping to fix an image of her family.

Du Vernet's camera could capture an image of the gravestone that testified to the memory of the catechist who had claimed the land—and planted the flag—for both Christ and Queen. It could also document a sickly child for his worried mother. Du Vernet happily obliged, composing what he hoped would be fine images, using his knowledge of light conditions and photographic techniques.

Touring Long Sault with Jeremiah Johnston, Du Vernet often noticed the placement of graves, both traditional Ojibwe and Christian. He noted in his diary that the grave of the "old chief" (likely Chief Mawedopenais) was by the riverbank, and was particularly fascinated by a very well-tended set of Ojibwe grave houses. He declared his hope that he could take a photograph of the graves at some point, and then went on to describe them with great specificity, echoing the details of Mary's story of Kitty's death:

> The three graves are covered over with a pointed roof. [A] flag staff with a white flag at top another half way up stands at the foot of each grave[.] [T]he bodies are put into the grave in a sitting posture then branches put across + about a foot of earth placed over this. + a little house built over this[:] it is side ends + a roof in the one and there is always a little door + a shelf below this[.] [A] spirit is supposed to come in + out of this door + get what is placed there + on the [boughs?] round the grave.[34]

Even in the midst of his missionary zeal, Du Vernet stopped to reflect with appreciation on how the Ojibwe cared for their dead, considering their upkeep of graves to be a good example for Christians. Seeing these graves through the eyes of a photographer may have helped Du Vernet step out of his role as evangelical proselytizer and into a space in which he could pause to seek some level of understanding of the culture he was encountering.

With his camera trained on the people and graveyards of Manidoo Ziibi, how might Frederick Du Vernet have understood the spiritual effects of a photograph on a soul? The *Oxford English Dictionary*, a reference work steeped in an Anglo-Protestant etymology, defines the soul as the animated "principle of life" within a human being.[35] For many nineteenth-century Protestants, the soul was firmly lodged in the individual human being, but was ideally in fluid communication with God—in fact the soul, if properly attended to, was directly animated by God and the Holy Spirit. One needed to tend carefully one's soul, using a range of sensory techniques: reading the Bible to listen for its lessons; praying regularly in formal, communal liturgies, with family at home, or alone at one's bedside or in the beauty of nature; and attending weekly church services that would include hymn singing, the Eucharist, and other seasonal rituals. For clergy, an extra task of tending one's soul included dedicating oneself to the care of the souls of others within one's parish or charge.

Just as various Christians have diverse understandings of theology, including about what the soul is and how it should be tended, so too are there "many ways of being Ojibwe in the past and in the present." That said, many Ojibwe also believed in a "soul-spirit" directly animated by a creator, gichi-Manidoo, who brought the world into being. As Ojibwe scholar Basil Johnston phrased it: "Following the example of Kitchi-Manitou, every person is to seek a dream or vision within the expanse of his or her soul-spirit being and, having attained it, bring it into fulfillment and reality." A network of many *manidoog* ("spirits," s. *manidoo*) also aid in this difficult process of spiritual discernment as spiritual guides who inspire storytellers to recount visions and prophecies and to interpret the symbolism of the images on rocks and birch-bark scrolls. Listening to manidoog speaking through lightning's electricity or the force of the wind would ideally lead also to listening to the stories of the elders and heeding their messages, appropriately caring for the spirits of the dead and their grave houses or burial mounds, and participating in communal rituals as the seasons required.[36]

In his study of Ojibwe elders, scholar of religion Michael McNally points to two kinds of soul-spirit lodged within each person. The *jiibay* is a soul seated in the mind that can wander from the body in sleep or trance and that "lingers for a time" after physical death, akin to a ghostlike spirit. The *ojichaag*, the second soul, is more firmly housed in the heart, as the source of animation of the human person, somewhat parallel to the conventional descriptions of the Christian soul. McNally explains that, ideally, the soul matures over the life cycle, such that when an Ojibwe man or woman becomes a *gichi Anishinaabe,* they are an honored elder who is most fully human as well as most powerfully able to aid the flow of spiritual relations within the community of humans, animals, nature, and the manidoog.[37]

These interrelated Ojibwe understandings of soul and spirit—jiibay, ojichaag, manidoo—both overlap and differ from those the missionaries brought with them. English and Ojibwe translators of the Anglican Book of Common Prayer, including the Ojibwe Anglican priest John Sanders whom Du Vernet met en route to Rat Portage, sought words in Anishinaabemowin that could convey Christian meanings—for example, by using variations of gichi-Manidoo for the Christian god and of gichi-ojichaag for "Holy Spirit." As Basil Johnston argues, however, the concept of manidoo was broader than the Christian notion of spirit, encompassing aspects of the world that Christian spirits did not usually include: "Depending on the context, they [Ojibwe] knew that in addition to spirit, the term also meant property, essence, transcendental, mystical, muse, patron, and the divine."[38] Translating the soul-spirit in encounters between missionaries and Ojibwe required rethinking Christianity in a new language. As the revisions to the Indian Act outlawing Indigenous ceremony demonstrated, however, missionaries undertook their attempts to understand or translate Ojibwe souls and spirits backed up by a law that stacked the terms of translation in their favor, by criminalizing Ojibwe practices of the soul-spirit.

Du Vernet used the word "spirit" only twice in his diary. The first time was in describing Ojibwe grave house rituals (fig. 9). Though he likely did not know the word "jiibay," his reference would correspond to this spirit that lingered at the grave. His second reference occurred when describing a "medicine tent" ritual for protecting a family from what he called an "evil spirit." He used the word "soul" only once in his diary, as a term designating a person, when he recounted a story of morning prayers said around the breakfast table at the Little Forks Reserve. While he knelt with his fellow missionaries as they prayed in Ojibwe, some visiting non-Christian Ojibwe sat in their chairs quietly remarking to each other about the scene. Du Vernet recalled: "It was an opportunity[.] I prayed earnestly for the souls in heathen darkness[;] the man sat with half closed eyes." Whether the man with half-closed eyes was praying or sleepy, Du Vernet does not reveal, but he did take care to note that just before these prayers, "an older Indian Woman (who had opposed the mission [by] pulling up the stakes when the land was marked off) opened the door + seeing us at breakfast slammed it again."[39] This elder's door slam echoed her earlier physical assertion of sovereignty, pulling up the stakes that the missionary Mr. Bagshaw had pounded into the earth.

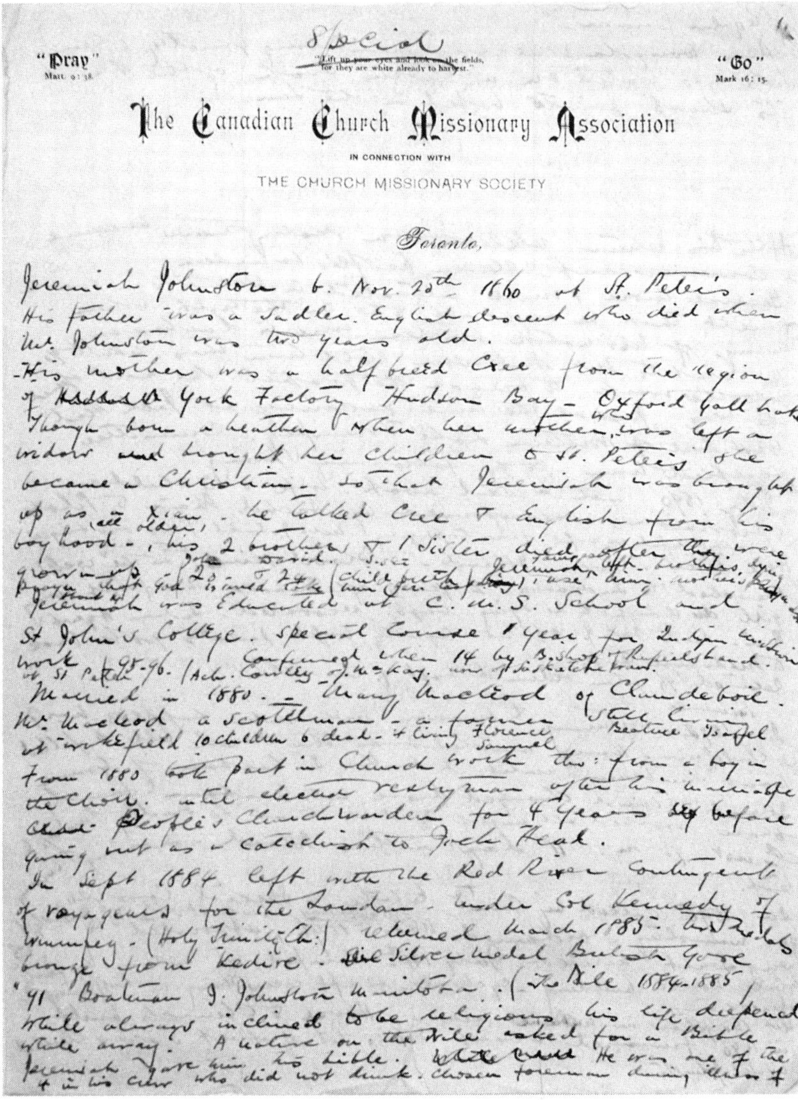
Special

"Lift up your eyes and look on the fields, for they are white already to harvest."

"Pray" Matt. 9:38

"Go" Mark 16:15

The Canadian Church Missionary Association

IN CONNECTION WITH

THE CHURCH MISSIONARY SOCIETY

Toronto,

Jeremiah Johnston b. Nov. 20th 1860 at St. Peter's.
His father was a Sadler. English descent who died when
Mr. Johnston was two years old.
His mother was a halfbreed Cree from the region
of York Factory Hudson Bay – Oxford Hall lake
Though born a heathen when her mother was left a
widow and brought her children to St. Peter's she
became a Christian – so that Jeremiah was brought up
up as a Xian [illegible] – he talked Cree & English from his
boyhood – his 2 brothers & 1 sister died after they were
grown up [illegible]
Jeremiah was Educated at C.M.S. School and
St John's College. special Course 1 year for Indian [illegible]
work [illegible] 95–96. (Arch. Cowley [illegible]) Confirmed when 14 by Bishop [illegible]
Married in 1880 – Mary Macleod of Clandeboye.
Mr Macleod a Scotchman – a farmer still living
at Wakefield 10 children 6 dead – 4 living Florence Beatrice Isabel Samuel
From 1880 took part in Church work thro: from a boy in
the Choir, until elected vestryman after his marriage
People's Churchwarden for 4 years before
going out as a Catechist to Jack Head.
In Sept 1884 left with the Red River Contingent
of voyageurs for the Soudan under Col Kennedy of
Winnipeg – (Holy Trinity Ch.) returned March 1885. [illegible]
bronze from Kedive – Silver Medal British Gov.
'91 Boatman J. Johnston Manitoba. (The Nile 1884–1885)
While always inclined to be religious his life deepened
while away. A native on the Nile asked for a Bible
Jeremiah gave him his Bible. [illegible] He was one of the
[illegible] in his crew who did not drink. chosen foreman during [illegible]

FIGURE 9. Page from Frederick Du Vernet's "Diary of a Missionary Tour" (1898). Photograph courtesy of The General Synod Archives, Anglican Church of Canada (M81-41).

When Du Vernet found his chance to photograph both the church and the Ojibwe graves at Long Sault, he again met with resistance from another woman elder: "After dinner I felt that as the air was so clear + the beautiful fleecy clouds were rolling across the sky I must take the last two pictures that I had available so about 2:30 p.m. took one of the Church from the middle of the garden. Mr. J. Mr. S. standing near the Church." Encountering full cooperation from Jeremiah Johnston and William Swalwell, the two missionaries in front of the church, Du Vernet found a very different reception when he tried to take a photograph of an Ojibwe elder in front of the graves:

> I went with Mr. J. to take a picture of the three graves [of] "grandfather"'s Grandchildren. We saw old "grand"mother who is so opposed to Xy outside her house. When we asked her if she w[oul]d come and sit by the graves on the chair there she refused remarking in reply to our promise to send her a picture if we did. "If I thought I could get something to eat out of the picture every time I looked at it I might come" I had Mr. J. sit in the chair instead. The women all disappeared into the houses.[40]

The grandmother's refusal to be photographed at her grandchildren's graves could have sprung from a number of motives, including her strong opposition to Christianity, and thus to this missionary visitor from the south. She may also have suspected that the photograph would provide Du Vernet with more nourishment than it would her. At a profoundly emotional level, she may have been refusing to be a photographic decoration at the side of the graves of her grandchildren, who had all died far too young.

Much of the elder's resistance may also have come from the spiritual significance of Ojibwe graves. Recall that the Ojibwe grave was a house for the jiibay, or the spirit of the dead that lingered there. To properly respect the jiibay, the grave houses demanded care, and the names of the dead were not to be uttered. A grandmother or grandfather, as a particularly mature soul with the power to communicate with the spirits, had a special responsibility to care for the grave houses.[41] Posing for a photograph taken by a stranger in front of her grandchildren's graves would be a gesture of disrespect.

Ojibwe elders with strong opposition to Christianity appear often in Du Vernet's account, always stepping out of the frame before he can capture them on film. Writing of Manitou Rapids, a reserve well known for its consistent refusal to allow missionaries to establish churches, Du Vernet recounted missionary Jeremiah Johnston's thwarted attempts to convince "the chief medicine man" Great Hawk to allow him to conduct Christian services in the community. After initially refusing, Great Hawk relented, allowing Johnston to speak to a crowd in the schoolhouse, but only briefly: "Very soon the old Chief stopped him 'That will do. You can talk about the School but you must not talk about your God.' and turning to the people he ordered them all out 'Go out. Go out' he said + opening the door he drove them all out." Meeting Great Hawk himself at the Manitou Rapids schoolhouse on the afternoon of July 15, 1898, Du Vernet hoped for a photograph of the Ojibwe leader:

> The old Chief in reply to my remark that I hoped they were pleased with the progress which the children were making in the School said they were not[.] [T]hey thought that their children ought to get on faster[.] [T]hey fail to see that unless they will send them regularly they cannot expect much improvement. The parents say before the children, "We can't get them to go if they do not want to go." After this pow-wow in the School house I went out to get my camera, gave George [Great Hawk's grandson] a pin. It was a dull day. I forgot to open the diaphram of the camera as I should but the mosquitoes were thick! The old Chief stood with his back towards me at first + was walking away, but Mr. J. coaxed him to come + he stood for a moment then moved.[42]

Du Vernet would have required his photographic subjects to remain still for several seconds or even a minute in order to allow the image to be properly recorded on the glass plates of his camera.[43] If this image had survived the years, Great Hawk would likely have been blurry, or not there at all.

Great Hawk's resistance to the photographic event highlights how photography demanded time and stillness during which the gaze and machine of the photographer tried to control the subject's body. Great Hawk's refusal to stay still, like his refusal to let preaching take place in the schoolhouse, indicated his awareness of the high cost of being subject to both the gospel and the camera.

Back at Long Sault, Du Vernet demonstrated again how not only spiritual but also technical troubles thwarted his photographic pursuits: "As Mrs. Johnston was so anxious to have Sammie's picture, about 10 o'clock I had him sitting in his chair below the house so that part of the river might form a background but also for the first time I exposed on a plate already used + so have no doubt spoilt the group taken in front of the Church on Monday morning. I tried another and yet another. I feel the last one was a failure as I did not hear the return click of the shutter. Never mind it pleased them."[44]

The Ojibwe grandmother had refused Du Vernet's offer of a photograph as an insufficiently material gift—as she noted ironically, a picture was not food and meant nothing to her. Great Hawk neither wanted to hear the biblical stories of the missionary gospel nor did he want his image carried back to Du Vernet's home as part of a missionary story. By contrast, Mary Johnston anxiously sought a picture of her son Samuel as a record of his presence in a future she worried he might not live to see. Du Vernet's repeated attempts to grant her wish, and his rather flippant reply to himself upon realizing that the photograph was likely ruined—"never mind it pleased them"—suggests that while he understood Mary's desire, in the end he agreed with the Ojibwe grandmother. Photographs were really not that important after all; it was the photographic event—whether resisted or accommodated—that counted.

Du Vernet was not seeking to mediate a pure Ojibwe culture with his diary and his camera. He was well aware of the negative effects of the railway and drunken white settlers on Ojibwe communities. His goal was to photograph Ojibwe lands and people as "religious," whether traditionally Ojibwe or more recently Christian. Taking photographs punctuated all his visits to churches and schools—he hoped his photos would serve as evidence of the success (however limited) of the Anglican missionary endeavor among the Ojibwe, as well as serve more interpersonal goals of commemoration and presence for his co-laborers. The pacing of dry plate photography, however, meant that ritual movements and intense physical activity were not subjects of Du Vernet's camera. When Du Vernet was an active participant in what he detailed—whether a state-sanctioned Eucharist, a government-outlawed medicine tent healing ceremony, or his first time rushing down rapids in a canoe—his camera was not in action.

For example, writing of the church service on what he declared to be his "first Sunday in a mission to the heathen!" Du Vernet elaborately described the Communion ritual and each of its participants with words, but not photographs: "In front of the pew where these were sitting was an Indian lad about 12, a Xian. Back of Mr Wood was an old Indian Thomas Bunyan, a Christian (one of) whose sons is buried in the Churchyard. the other was with him in Church though ill. Another still older Indian who came in late calls himself Mr. Johnston, grandfather. he is interested but is still a heathen. His wife being strongly opposed to Xy."[45] Mr. Johnston's wife was likely the grandmother who refused to be captured by Du Vernet's camera; her husband, however, was willing to listen to him in church.

Many of the people whom Du Vernet called Christian Indians were, in his description, poised on a tentative line "facing both ways" between traditional Ojibwe practices and Christianity. Du Vernet seemed aware of their dual interests and commitments in his attempt to translate the spiritual power of Communion by way of the English words of treaty and covenant: "I administered the bread + Mr. J. the wine. (treaty covenant) There were 8 Cmts. [communicants] besides the 2 Clergymen. 4 white people four Indians. Mrs Crow. her 2 daughters + Mr McLeod. A solemn feast. very quiet."[46] In keeping with Anglican ritual practice, those who partook of Communion had first been baptized and confirmed, so they had stepped further over the line toward Christianity.

The only extant article based on Du Vernet's diary also referred to the idea of a treaty covenant: "Knowing that all the Indians were familiar with the thought of a treaty, I endeavored to fix in their minds the idea of a Covenant Feast." Expressing "great joy . . . to have the privilege of preaching to the Indians, even though it was through an interpreter," as well as sharing his anxieties about those who remained outside of his church, Du Vernet's published account of the church service is remarkably similar to the diary. His translational gambit of "treaty covenant" suggests that he understood the bread and the wine of Communion to be akin to the treaties signed between the Queen and the Ojibwe; a promise to the Queen was also a promise to Christ. The idea that white Christians and Ojibwe Christians enacted a liturgical echo of the treaty in consuming the bread and the wine, the body and blood, could have fit well with Anishinaabe convictions that treaties were sacred promises, watched over by the Creator, requiring ritual care.[47] Which Anishinaabemowin words Jeremiah Johnston used to convey the idea of a treaty covenant, and how far Du Vernet would have gone with his comparison would be worth knowing: Did the Ojibwe take in the body and blood of the divinely sanctioned Queen in signing their treaties; did the Queen and her representatives ritually consume the Ojibwe's manidoog?

In his written attempts at translating Ojibwe rituals, Du Vernet is both respectful of and repelled by Ojibwe practices of the medicine tent and grave houses. His description of one encounter while walking through Long Sault with Jeremiah Johnston reads in part as a missionary condemnation of the heathen and in part as detailed ethnographic field notes, similar to his minute recounting of church services:

> Hearing a sound of incantation we went into a house. It was being used as a medicine tent. [A] man + his wife who had lost their son two weeks ago were propitiating the evil spirit that the rest of their family might be left alone. These two were sitting in one corner on the matting which went round the house on cedar twigs[.] [N]ear the end in the middle was an altar like pile of clothing bead work and surrounded by two tin dishes these were a sacrifice to pacify the deity. The sacrifice being afterwards divided among the medicine men. The medicine men (3 of them sat in a row) one was swaying forward repeating a meaningless refrain. incantation. [T]he other two, Chief Cut-leg and another with a pipe in his mouth, would interject "A-yah." In front of the man repeating the word of incantation was a tin rattle partly filled with shot [and] a pan of broth. In the middle of the floor near the door were two kettles of broth. made out of a dog which had been killed. called "the Dog feast[.]" [B]eside this was the tom-tom

> a wooden cask with a tight leather head. Chief Cut-leg got his crutches and hobbled out muttering something which Mr. J. took to mean that our presence was not desired there but we stayed on for a little while. It was most interesting but very sad. [T]his propitiation offered in ignorance to a higher power. Even tho: it was all such a fraud, the medicine men getting the spoils I stood with uncovered head with a feeling of reverence as it was a degraded + ignorant cognition of a Superior Being in whose hands lay their destiny.[48]

Entering a medicine ceremony for two grieving parents uninvited, the missionaries violated protocol and knew it. Impressed by the power of the ceremony despite himself—"most interesting but very sad," "a feeling of reverence" in the face of a "fraud"—Du Vernet recorded and experienced the ceremony lodged within his own commitments to a Christian "Superior Being."[49]

Despite Du Vernet's missionary fervor, something of the power of Ojibwe practices of believing broke through his zeal. Noting Chief Cut-leg's muttering exit, the grandmother's caustic refusal to be photographed, and Great Hawk's opposition to Christian preaching, Du Vernet's habits of recording show that he knew, on some level, that what he called ignorance was, in truth, resistance. Fascinated and moved to reverence by the graves and by the incantations of Ojibwe spiritual leaders taking care of the spirits, Du Vernet sought to record his encounters using photographic images and the written word. In the end, his diary leaves us with a portrait of how the act of taking a photograph was embedded in social relationships in which the missionaries and the Ojibwe cultivated and contested the workings of the spirit. Taking a photograph could be an act of colonial aggression yet also a gesture toward a future of relationship.

Capturing images of new people, places, and rituals that provoked in him both "feelings of reverence" and condemnations of "heathenism," Du Vernet was well aware that his photographs would record his face-to-face interactions across changing and contested terrains of colonial power. At some moments, his reaction was that of the Christian missionary eager to eradicate Ojibwe practices in the name of Christian unity. At other moments, he took Ojibwe approaches to ritual and community as exemplary for Christians, as in the case of their care of graves. And at yet other moments, he noted with remarkable awareness when Ojibwe elders openly, and with much wit and strong argument, shared with him their disgust for his goals.[50] Whether his photographs would have portrayed the Ojibwe as a "dying race" we cannot know, but taken as a whole, his diary does not do so.

Photographic Testimony

Du Vernet wanted his photographs to tell a story of Jeremiah and Mary Johnston's successes, and to document Christian presence on Ojibwe land. His later experiments with technological mediation—especially under the guise of what he called radio mind—also took shape amid his work as a missionary among Indigenous peoples once he had moved to British Columbia. In the presence of the supposedly heathen soul, the communication technologies of photography and radio played a large role in Du Vernet's spiritual imagination. The photographic event was a means by which he sought to develop relationships with his Christian colleagues and to document a kind of spirituality that was foreign yet intriguing to him. At the same time, Du Vernet's attempts to take photographs exacerbated the resistance Ojibwe elders showed to his missionary project.

In light of Du Vernet's experiences, Louise Erdrich's contention that Ojibwe cosmology is not one in which photographs were thought to steal souls rings true. Instead, the Ojibwe elders who resisted Du Vernet's camera may well have thought that his photographs were another attempt to steal their land and literally re-vision it as "Canada." Imagining Canada required the media of communications technologies—including the visual documents of photographs, mining surveys, paintings, and maps plotting out colonization roads.[51] At the same time, however, photography is too ambivalent a medium to be given only one meaning—photography itself allows for a multivocal storytelling on the part of both the photographer and the photographed, as well as for those who look at the photos long after their taking.

Photographs do the work of turning human beings into singular individuals. Framed in a limited space that can never fully display the networks of human relationships that make us who we are, photographs freeze their subjects into place, without telling the viewer much, if anything, about their relationships or inner life. Roland Barthes had to go through piles of photographs until he could find the one that conveyed his mother's soul to him—he had to work hard to produce the desired connection among memory, feeling, and image. The Ojibwe elders who turned their backs on Du Vernet were also turning their backs on his religion, which sought to make each of them an individual soul who would not only give themselves to Jesus Christ but also become settled workers in the newly imagined nation of Canada. The old woman who pulled up the stakes for the church could have been saying: "You cannot turn our land into real estate." The grandmother who refused to allow Du Vernet to photograph her at the grave could have been saying: "You cannot frame me as a sign of a future never to come by posing me next to the graves of my grandchildren."[52]

The development and spread of photography in the nineteenth century occurred at the same time as the most intensive development and spread of missionary Christianity. Can we then go further to say that photography itself was a carrier of the very concept of the "soul" in a Christian guise? And in turn, that colonial photographers were not trying to steal souls, but were instead trying to make souls in their own image? Photography, a process of being made to stop, to be looked at, and then to potentially look at oneself after the fact, embodied a kind of psychagogy—a training of the singular soul and the psychic processes that formed it.[53] Whether in the case of the Ojibwe grandmother who refused Du Vernet the right to take her picture, or in that of Mary Johnston, the mother who requested that he take a photo of her fragile son, the camera was a particular kind of tool for creating relationships between people, between the present, past, and future, and even between people and their visions of the spirit or spirits.

Pictures of the dead, whether in family albums or spirit photographs, made for new possibilities within Christian theologies of bodily resurrection, in which the soul, that part of the human that survives death, was in some ways mediated to the living via the photograph. While a photo of a spirit hovering over a Spiritualist medium may not have been widely convincing, a photograph of a face—beloved or renowned—comes closer, with all the promises of future presence that Christian theologies of immortality imply.

These promises of presence, however, are not limited to Christian cosmologies of mediation. Photographs contain within them multiple possibilities of interpretation and memory and can be used to tell many different stories. They can even be put to the use of "photographic sovereignty" to reclaim Indigenous land.[54] The photographs of ethnographer Frances Densmore have moved through such a transformation. Her beautiful black-and-white images of wigwams at Manitou Rapids now hang on the walls of the Kay-Nah-Chi-Wah-Nung Historical Centre, framed within a narrative of Ojibwe sovereignty.

Photographic Postscript

When I first turned to writing this chapter, I could only count on my imagination to bring the Johnston family to life. I could envision little sickly Sammie, the Johnston toddler, sitting in his chair by the river, posing for the white man from Toronto. Not having Du Vernet's photographs to hand was in some

FIGURE 10. The Johnston family (ca. 1905). Photograph courtesy of the Minnesota Historical Society (100140).

FIGURE 11. Jeremiah Johnston and Arthur Richardson, wearing their military medals, Long Sault (ca. 1905). Photograph courtesy of the Minnesota Historical Society (100139).

FIGURE 12. The Johnston family, White Earth, Minnesota (ca. 1910). Photograph courtesy of the Minnesota Historical Society (57537).

ways a benefit to me, as in their absence his descriptions of the photographic event stood out to me all the more starkly. Nevertheless, I was exhilarated to discover that later photographers had improved on Du Vernet's photographic failures. A set of photos in the collection of the Minnesota Historical Society includes the family of Jeremiah and Mary Johnston in various poses. The earliest may be a family photograph posed in a photo studio, perhaps in Fort Frances. Judging from Samuel's age, and the existence of his three younger brothers, I would date the photograph at about 1905 (fig. 10). Sammie clearly made it through his sickly toddlerhood thanks largely, I imagine, to the fortitude and care of his mother, Mary.

Another photograph taken at Long Sault itself, sometime between 1902 and 1907, features Jeremiah Johnston with Arthur Herbert Lindsay Richardson, a North-West Mounted Police officer recently returned from the second South African War (1899–1902) (fig. 11). Both men sit outside, relaxed in kitchen chairs, sporting their military medals for valor. Richardson is wearing the Victoria Cross, which he received in 1900 in South Africa. Johnston is wearing the Khedive's Star and the Silver Medal for Sea Gallantry for his service with the Gordon Expedition in British-occupied Sudan in 1884–1885, medals Du Vernet was careful to record in his diary. These medals were likely

FIGURE 13. Bella Johnston as an "Indian Maiden" (ca. 1905). Photograph courtesy of the Minnesota Historical Society (57534).

not the only ones on the reserve, as Ojibwe homes could have also housed treaty medals, given by the government in recognition of Treaty 3 and kept as material markers of treaty promises. As Cree and English, missionary and seaman, and host for the Mountie on the reserve, Jeremiah Johnston was situated at many intersecting stories and identities, especially when viewed with the help of Du Vernet's diary.

Other photos of the Johnstons, once they moved to White Earth Reservation in Minnesota, display their growing family and expanding circumstances—for example, as they posed outside the Episcopal rectory of St. Columba's (fig. 12). Several photos of their daughter Bella have also survived, including a group in which she is dressed as an "Indian maiden"

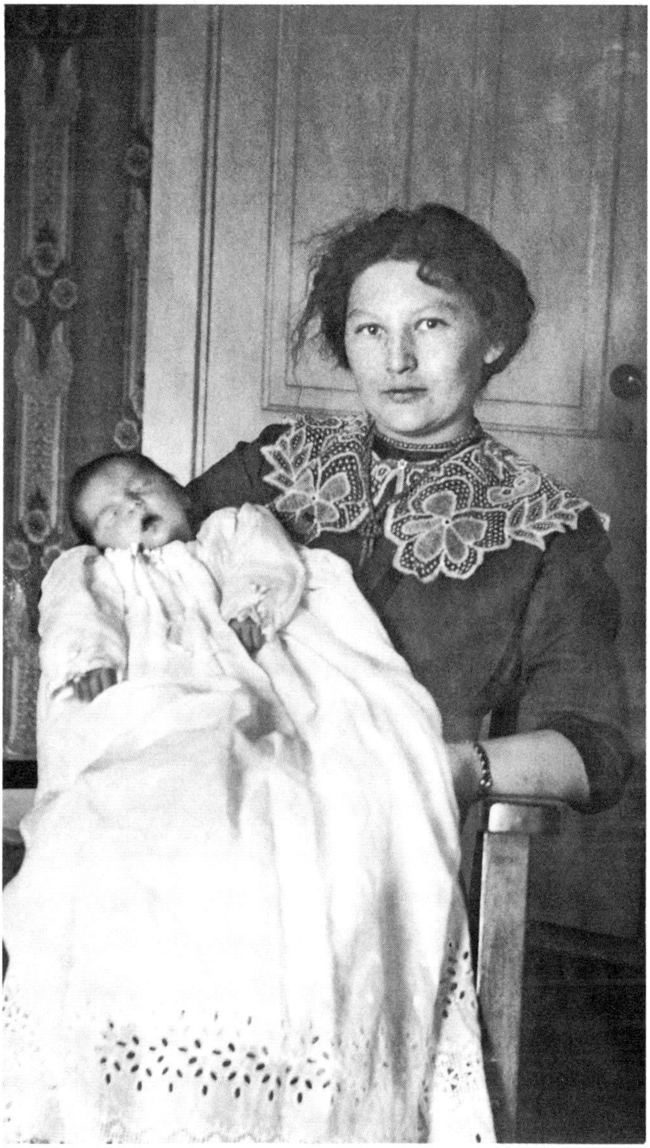

FIGURE 14. Bella Johnston Dailey and her daughter Letitia B. Dailey (1912). Photograph courtesy of the Minnesota Historical Society (GT3.13 r64).

(fig. 13). Another surviving photo of Bella, one that her mother would most certainly have loved, shows Bella Johnston Dailey as a new mother, with her chubby baby Letitia (fig. 14).

Du Vernet was not alone in wanting to photograph the people and places he encountered on his missionary tour of Manidoo Ziibi. Like Du Vernet,

Frances Densmore was also fascinated by Ojibwe graves and took several photos of them in different locations, just a few years after Du Vernet's visit. Unlike the images of Jeremiah Johnston and his family, the photos of these grave houses cannot be viewed as snapshots on the Minnesota Historical Society website, since Ojibwe communities have successfully counseled the historical society that these images are too sacred to display so publicly. To do so would disrespect Ojibwe protocols for the tending of graves and the uses of photographs.

The old Ojibwe grandmother who turned her back on Du Vernet was not able to stop him from photographing the graves of her grandchildren, nor were other Ojibwe able to restrain Frances Densmore from photographing their houses for the dead and their jiibay. By today, however, Ojibwe communities have convinced others that these images of the spirit require very careful handling. The photographic event, far from being a thing of the past, remains alive and relevant today, and is still doing complicated work on spirits and souls, and the stories that we tell about them.

5
Map Is Territory

Frederick Du Vernet first set foot on Ts'msyen land on December 20, 1904, at Metlakatla, the Sm'algyax word for "saltwater pass." A city dweller without the "hip gum boots" necessary for sloshing his way to land, the bishop was "packed" to shore on the back of a Ts'msyen sailor.[1] Freshly consecrated as the second bishop of Caledonia, Du Vernet had been promoted from parish priest and missionary journal editor to chief priest of all the Church of England churches and missions in a two-hundred-thousand-square-mile area of coastal waterways, forested mountains, and sleeping volcanoes. The Diocese of Caledonia was a spiritual invention produced back east through a quixotic church-led mapping project that hoped to make diverse Indigenous territories into Christian and Canadian land. Arriving at Metlakatla, his first episcopal seat, Du Vernet entered a rain-soaked fusion of land, sea, and forest that was very remote from the centers of Canadian imperial power, as colonial and missionary maps told the story (fig. 15).

Frederick came from a long line of men who drew maps in order to claim Indigenous land. His great-grandfather Abraham Du Vernet was an officer of Britain's Royal Regiment Artillery, a military unit of engineers and "men of science" who surveyed the land and rivers of British North America to turn them into roads and canals. Abraham saw active duty as a lieutenant in the Royal Artillery during the American Revolutionary War, and traveled throughout the Great Lakes region, together with his fellow officer and relative Henry Du Vernet. Henry also had a surveyor's eye, drawing a remarkable map of the Miami River (in what is now Ohio) in 1778, when it was the site of battles between the Americans and the British, who were joined by their allies from the Miami Nation. Henry's map told a story of the Miami and the Cana-

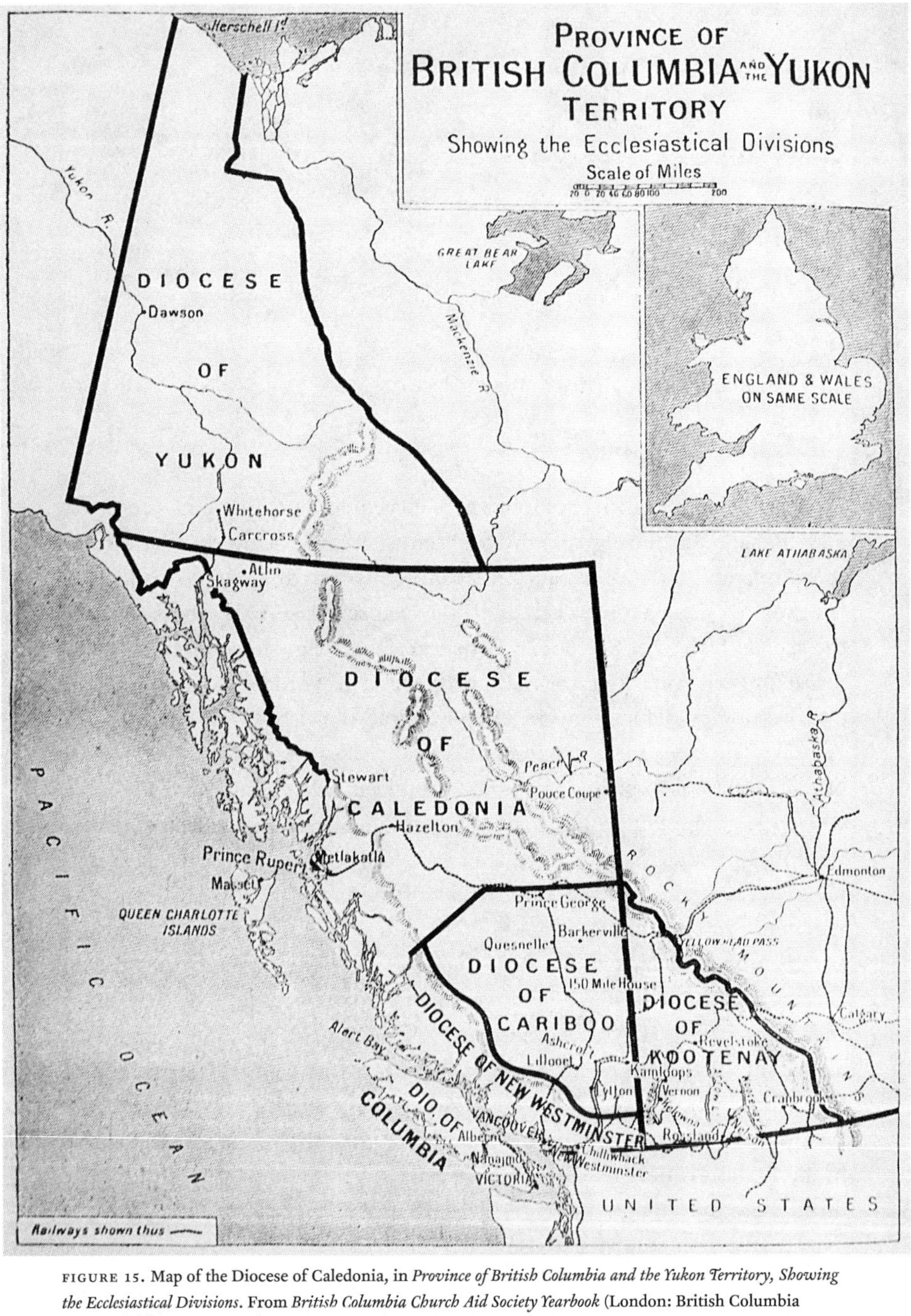

FIGURE 15. Map of the Diocese of Caledonia, in *Province of British Columbia and the Yukon Territory, Showing the Ecclesiastical Divisions*. From *British Columbia Church Aid Society Yearbook* (London: British Columbia Church Aid Society, 1911). Photograph courtesy of the Archives of the Provincial Synod of British Columbia and Yukon.

dians living alongside the river. Unimpressed by the French, he commented approvingly on the "clean interiors" of the cabins of the "Maumee" (fig. 16).[2]

Abraham's son Henry, Frederick's great-uncle, also became a surveyor and engineer who drew maps and painted pictures that imagined Canada into existence. As part of a bid to stave off American aggression, the younger Henry traveled from England in 1819 to remap the land and waters around the Ottawa and St. Lawrence Rivers, turning them into the canal system of early Canada. Henry's 1831 map of the rivers around the island of Montreal plotted out a plan to tame the Ste. Anne Rapids, but it told no stories of the people living nearby—not the Algonquin, the Mohawk, or the settlers. His map was a tool for discerning whether to build new canals or blow up rocks in order to allow ships and their cargoes to more easily navigate their way back and forth to new settlements growing along the rivers. The Sainte-Anne-de-Bellevue Canal was opened as a "navigable waterway" in 1843. By the 1970s, the canal was no longer a hub of commercial traffic, and it gradually became a "National Historic Site," deserving of "commemorative integrity" in recognition of its role in opening the land and rivers to colonial settlement.[3]

Abraham and his son Henry drew maps when working as military officers and engineers who served the Crown. Frederick Du Vernet followed in his ancestors' footsteps not as a draftsman and a soldier but as a storyteller and a missionary. Frederick used the maps of others as pragmatic tools to settle disputes over property with his colleagues, with rival Christian missions, with white settlers, and with Indigenous peoples. He understood his missionary responsibility as claiming ground before other churches could do so: "In a new country the first Church to occupy the ground wields an immense advantage. The foundation period. Should we show less faith in the West than [does] the Commercial world."[4] Encouraging his church to take an interest in the Pacific northwest with the same avidity as the fur-trading and railway companies that had sought out territory in the region, Du Vernet pointed to the spiritual riches of the "new" country.

Du Vernet used maps to tell stories that were "replacement narratives," the phrase Jean O'Brien has given to a "genre of local history writing that became crucial in defining Indians out of existence." As O'Brien notes in the context of New England, Protestant missionaries and ministers swelled the ranks of local history writers who detailed the "firsts" of the settlers and the "lasts" of the "Indians", as they purportedly died out. These ministers and missionaries bestowed names from biblical stories—and sometimes their own names too—on the land, in what became a "cartographic erasure" of Indigenous stories rooted in place. Even Du Vernet's name found its way onto early

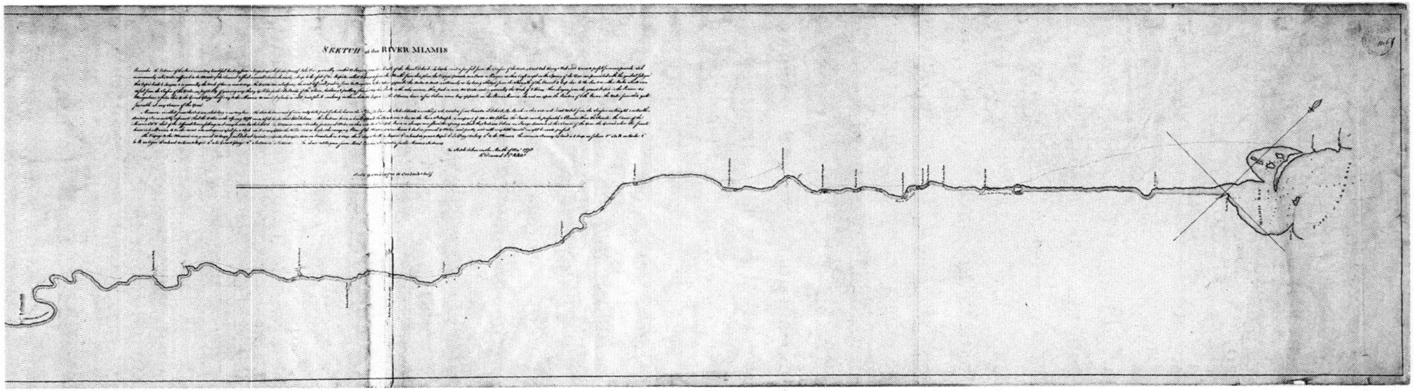

FIGURE 16. Henry Du Vernet, *Sketch of the River Miamis* (1778). Photograph courtesy of the Library and Archives Canada.

twentieth-century maps, in a largely failed bid to replace Ts'msyen stories of the land.[5]

Replacement narratives never quite erased earlier stories. Du Vernet's most creative storytelling with maps was haunted by his anxiety about the stories and people he knew from the Indigenous world he was seeking to rename. He knew that turning Kaien Island into Prince Rupert laid new stories, new royalty, and new goddesses and spirits onto land and water that had already been named by Ts'msyen, Nisga'a, and other Indigenous peoples; the careful notes he kept of their names for the world displayed as much. To paraphrase the writer Hugh Brody, the "maps and dreams" of settlers, missionaries, and colonial officials were superimposed on those of Indigenous peoples, often with very violent effects, but never with complete displacement.[6]

The maps that built the "New World" nations were what some geographers call "performative" maps, embedded with histories, visions, and colonial spirits. Maps are also elements in missionary retellings of Indigenous land, by which the land is embedded with Christian myths and rituals. Colonial mapping was not a one-way process of imposing an external vision on the land, but a hybrid process combining Indigenous territorial knowledge with the techniques and motives of colonial surveyors, as Kapil Raj has shown in the context of colonial India.[7] Similarly, the maps I consider here performed Christian reimaginations of Indigenous space, but depended on sustained and conflicted relationships between missionaries and Ts'msyen and Nisga'a people to do so.

Arrival

Standing on the northwest edge of the continent, Frederick had arrived at his new home without his family. His wife, Stella, was more than three thousand miles away, staying behind in Toronto to take care of Alice and Horace, their two teenaged children, while Frederick settled into his new role. Frederick was grateful for and a bit overwhelmed by the piles of Toronto newspapers that Alice sent to keep him up to date. Both Stella and Frederick were worried about Horace, who was struggling to find his way and to graduate from high school. Whether or not his family in Toronto was far away from Frederick's thoughts, they were thousands of miles and a long voyage away from him in the flesh.[8]

Du Vernet's new post was the internationally renowned village of Metlakatla, a community founded in 1862 by William Duncan, a controversial

FIGURE 17. Eastern portion of Metlakatla, showing the cannery buildings on the left (ca. 1895). Photograph courtesy of the Royal British Columbia Museum and Archives (C-08105).

lay missionary with the Anglican Church Missionary Society, together with Ts'msyen men and women who had joined his Christian experiment. Metlakatla was the first successful mission village in the diocese, but by 1904 it was a community with a history of scandal and struggle. More than half of the original Metlakatla community, along with the missionary William Duncan, had left for Alaska in 1887 because of an ongoing dispute with William Ridley, the first bishop set to watch over Caledonia. The church had burned to the ground in 1901.[9]

Duncan's vision for Metlakatla had been utopian and strict. He sought to establish a Ts'msyen settlement outside of the "corrupting" influence of the Hudson's Bay Company trading post of Fort Simpson. Together with about fifty Ts'msyen, he founded Metlakatla as an orderly row of clapboard houses where the inhabitants could be self-sufficient and industrious. Duncan demanded that they adopt family arrangements, occupations, and virtues that matched a Christian ideal of working-class lifestyles reminiscent of his motherland. With a church, a school, a girls' mission house, a store, a fish cannery, and even its own jail, Metlakatla was designed to serve all the needs of settled, town life, as postcards of the settlement conveyed (fig. 17).[10]

Duncan's utopian Christian community was lauded to the world as a success by such notable entrepreneurs as Henry Wellcome, who, thanks to his friendship with Duncan, amassed a large collection of northwest coast masks, boxes, and ritual artifacts, now housed in the British Museum. In reality, however, Metlakatla was riven by conflicts over Ts'msyen land rights, Anglican sacramental politics, and persistent questions over sexual improprieties and gender roles. Rumors that Duncan—a bachelor—had fathered a child with one of the young women in his mission house troubled his superiors and community members alike.[11]

His Anglican chiefs also considered him to be overly controlling in ritually scandalous ways, in that he denied Metlakatlans the chance to partake of the Eucharist. Duncan feared that Ts'msyen Christians would not be able to tell the difference between what he considered to be their former "cannibalistic" practices and the Christian rite in which the faithful ingest the body and blood of Christ. His benefactor Wellcome praised Duncan's "simple" approach with florid language, insisting that the Ts'msyen "who had tasted human flesh in their days of heathenism, benighted as they then were, would have recoiled with horror, at the bare thought of consuming, even by emblem a part of one of their gods!" From the Ts'msyen perspective, however, the heart of the issue was two acres of land.[12]

In 1864, James Douglas, the governor of British Columbia, had created a reserve of two acres at Metlakatla for the use of the Anglican Church Missionary Society, which was quickly occupied by Duncan and the Ts'msyen. In 1879, William Ridley, the first bishop of Caledonia, arrived from England after a career as a missionary to India to watch over the controversial mission and its increasingly renegade missionary. The new Diocese of Caledonia, established with Ridley's episcopate, encompassed much of what is now called northwestern British Columbia.

William Duncan actively resisted the supervision of his new bishop. Duncan was not an ordained priest: he had no sacramentally bestowed powers that gave him status in a Christian colonial world. Duncan's power came from four main sources: his stubborn evangelical certainty that Jesus Christ died to redeem sinners; his own escape, along with those Ts'msyen who joined him in Metlakatla, from a devastating smallpox epidemic in a neighboring village; his seemingly endless entrepreneurial energy, which included his control of the village store; and his well-chosen friends among the Ts'msyen elite. By contrast, Ridley was a man fully consecrated with the powerful title of a bishop: the Christian version of a chiefly name that gave him the ritual authority to baptize people, ordain priests, administer the Eucharist, and hold territory—or real estate—under the collective authority of the church.[13]

After dismissing Duncan from the Church Missionary Society for his stubborn refusal to follow church orders, Ridley insisted that the two acres on Metlakatla belonged to the church. Duncan and most of the Ts'msyen insisted that the land belonged to the Ts'msyen, and the CMS had only held it in trust. After a protracted and hostile battle, the majority of Metlakatlans and Duncan, with the help of Henry Wellcome, appealed to the United States government for land across the border in Alaska—Tlingit territory. Here, they established the settlement of New Metlakatla in 1887. Back in Canada, in 1888 one of many waves of land commissions in British Columbia established—without a treaty—a larger Metlakatla reserve, an area on the mainland and surrounding islands, including much of Kaien Island.

When Frederick Du Vernet arrived at Metlakatla in 1904, he entered a fractious environment where mapping the land was a continual source of political strife and scandal. The authority of both ritual and property were not at all settled questions. The legal status of church lands within the Anglican diocese, as well as the legal status of British Columbia as a province, was still at issue between the Ts'msyen and the settlers. The Ts'msyen, along with all the other Indigenous nations in the Pacific northwest, had repeatedly insisted that they had not given up title to their land: they had signed no treaties and had never agreed even to the concept of a "reserve."[14] The land belonged to them not through deeds of property and surveyed maps, but through their own ancient adawx and feasts that claimed territory through stories and ritually bestowed clan names.

Even James McCullagh, a CMS missionary who lived among the Nisga'a just up the Nass River from Metlakatla, knew that the colonial maps and surveys oriented by the Indian Act had not erased Ts'msyen and Nisga'a ways of naming and holding land. Just as the Indian Act had outlawed the medicine tent among the Ojibwe, so too had it deemed the potlatch illegal in 1885. Nevertheless, the feasting system persisted all along the coast, sometimes becoming a source of tension between Indigenous Christians and Indigenous non-Christians. In an 1899 address entitled "The Indian Potlatch," which he gave to the annual meeting of the Church Missionary Society in Metlakatla, McCullagh provided a detailed ethnographic account of the Nisga'a feasting system worthy of any anthropologist of his day. The potlatch, or the feasting system, conferred clan names on men and women thought to be worthy of the power, and crests and totem poles told the stories of their territory, their ancestors, and their interactions with the world of spanaxnox, animals, and other spirits.[15]

Clarifying that "potlatch" was a term invented by the "white man" that conflated a variety of different feast systems, McCullagh argued that the potlatch was not primarily a religious event but a political act: "the systematized form of tribal government based upon the united suffrages of the clans."[16] The potlatch, McCullagh claimed, was the Nisga'a form of an election that distributed both territory and goods. Having recognized the political significance of the feasting system, he proceeded to offer suggestions for how to destroy it.

Banning the potlatch was an ineffective legal approach, McCullagh argued. Instead, he pleaded for a law that would protect the "Christian Indians" who had tried to step out of the potlatch system of social and economic debts. It was the potlatch system, he said, that kept drawing his Christian converts back to traditional Nisga'a practices. The government should draw up a new law, he advised, ensuring that "a chief wishing to become Christian and civilized should have his rights assured to him by law—the Potlatch should not be allowed to deprive him of his rights."[17] Delivering his message to his fellow missionaries at their meeting in Metlakatla, he would have underlined what they already knew: Indigenous land was held collectively by virtue of the authority of spirits, stories, and laws that were neither Christian nor colonial.

Throughout the many land commissions that regularly revisited their territories, and until today, Indigenous peoples on the northwest coast have been remarkably consistent in their resolve that the land belongs to them, regardless of what surveyors and their maps have had to say. With the same resolve shown by "an older Indian Woman" whom Du Vernet met on Manidoo Ziibi, Ts'msyen and Nisga'a women and men repeatedly pulled up the stakes of surveyors and challenged the arrival of settlers. They insisted on the continuing power of their own stories of how people belonged to land and land belonged to people.[18]

Cosmologies of Land

Benedict Anderson's insight that maps were indispensable tools for colonial seizure of land and Jonathan Z. Smith's 1978 book *Map Is Not Territory* together provide an important lens for thinking about what I call cosmologies of land: religiously authorized visions of what land is for, who owns it, how it is mapped, and where sites of spiritual power are located. Smith argued that scholars of religion must forgo the concept of "sacred space" as a timeless, apolitical claim. Instead, Smith suggested a "locative" understanding of religion that accounted for history and the ideological power of "imperial leaders." Always sharply critical of "metaphysical hierarchies" and scholarly universalizing (but not of scholarly comparison), Smith has been particularly suspicious of uses of the words "religion" and "sacred" in ways that deny the histories of colonial power and knowledge production. For Smith, "in the locative map of the world, we are encountering a self-serving ideology which ought not to be generalized into the universal pattern of religious experience and expression." Asking his reader to note the power embedded in mapping, Smith made a fascinating distinction: a locative approach to mapping was one in which "homeplace" mattered, and in which this place was even a "central religious category."[19]

Juxtaposing this locative, imperial religion based on homeplace with a diasporic religion of travelers far from home, Smith contended that diasporic religion inverted the ideological significance of land, homeplace, and religious authority. In diasporic religions, "rather than being born into a divinely established and protected land whose glories one celebrated, one was initiated (reborn) into a divine protector who was tied to no land."[20] This landless divine protector drew power from transcendence apart from specific places on earth: he was a new kind of imperial leader who could be everywhere, and nowhere, all at once.

Smith insisted that scholars of religion had to abandon their stereotypes of "primitives . . . without history" passed down along generations of theorists of religion. He also decried a universal theory of religion that stood outside history or earthly matters and posited all power in a transcendent sacred. Instead, to study religion was to analyze how politics, power, and the colonial and trading interventions of "the white man" profoundly shaped the myths and rituals of "natives." Calling for a rigorous reflexivity rooted in careful attention to sources, Smith cautioned scholars of religion to think twice about what scholarly perspectives, or "maps," make visible, what they obscure, and why scholars still need them. He wrote: "We need to reflect on and play with the necessary incongruity of our maps before we set out on a voyage of discovery to chart the worlds of other men. For the dictum of Alfred Korzybski is inescapable: 'Map is not territory'—but maps are all we possess."[21] But when thinking about Christian colonialism, is this really the case?

Map Is Not Territory has been very convincing to scholars of religion—it is even cited in an almost songlike manner; everyone knows the meaning of the refrain. But taking seriously Smith's call to understand the ideological power of locative cosmologies requires doing the same for what he calls the diasporic "transcendent" cosmologies. A god who could travel anywhere, who did not live at the mouths of rivers or at the base of a cliff—a diasporic transcendent deity who requires no rooting in a particular place—starts to look a lot like the white man's Christian god in his colonial encounters with Indigenous peoples.

As Aileen Moreton-Robinson has written in *The White Possessive*, postcolonial theories that privilege migratory, diasporic subjects who wander the world cannot account for the significance of how specific lands, or homeplaces, matter to specific peoples. Maps are not solely metaphorical tools that enable a people to chart—however mistakenly—the worlds of other people. Colonial cartography was also a medium through which white men told and made real a story of colonial possession. Realizing this changes the refrain: map *is* territory. The *Oxford English Dictionary* defines "territory" as "the extent of the land belonging to or under the jurisdiction of a ruler, state, or group of people." With this definition in mind, it becomes clear that maps are crucial in the work of turning land into territory.[22]

A vigorous discussion of critical cartography in Indigenous studies shows the territorial power of mapping by storytelling. The concept of nominative cartography, in particular, describes the ways that maps act as tools of naming that both erase and create stories. Mohawk anthropologist Audra Simpson uses another revealing phrase, introducing the idea of cartography as "theaters of apprehension." Gesturing to the many meanings of apprehension here—namely, to see or understand something as well as to fear it and grab it—Simpson marks cartography as a key tool in the story and infrastructure of colonial dispossession.[23]

The Spinal Cord of Colonialism

As the second bishop of the Diocese of Caledonia, Du Vernet was to serve as both peacemaker and chief missionary not only in Metlakatla but also in missions spread throughout a vast area that included the traditional territories of the Haida, Ts'msyen, Nisga'a, Gitxsan, Tahltan, and Haisla nations. Du Vernet arrived at a crucial time in the lives of these nations: the moment when the railway was making its way to the coast, bringing not only an onslaught of settlers but also new battles over land. All along the route of the Grand Trunk Pacific Railway, Indigenous nations struggled against a foe with deeper pockets than the churches. The railway company surveyed the land in search of the straightest line and the most navigable terrain for its engines. Considering Indigenous reserves and cemeteries no barrier, the GTP convinced the colonial government to move the living and the dead to reach its goal.[24]

The railway required Du Vernet to face in a new imperial direction—toward the expansion of what was called "white work" in anticipation of the settlers who would flock to what the GTP maps advertised as "2,000,000 Acres of Agricultural Land" along the northern rail lines of British Columbia (plate 2). Once the rail terminus was built, Du Vernet began to understand his work not only as supporting the "Christian Indians" of Metlakatla and surrounding communities but also as contributing to the building of an imperial city on the edge of the empire.

Du Vernet must have cultivated respect for his work among his colleagues both back east and on the coast. He eventually became the metropolitan—leading bishop—of the newly amalgamated Ecclesiastical Province of British Columbia in 1915, in the first years of a world war that would empty his territory of many of its men, including the missionaries and clergy whom he had worked hard to call to a vocation in the northwest. The missions of the Diocese of Caledonia were concentrated in the treaty-less Indigenous territories of the northwest coast, but the diocesan boundary technically stretched to the edge of northeastern British Columbia, which included the Athapaskan lands of Treaty 8, the only treaty that reached into British Columbia's borders.[25] But it was only in 1915 that Du Vernet turned significant attention to this northeastern region. Upon becoming archbishop of Caledonia and metropolitan of all British Columbia, the scope of Du Vernet's territorial responsibilities grew to an enormity impossible to fully fathom, let alone personally oversee. It is perhaps no wonder then, that in the face of such vastness, he eventually sought to overcome distance through the application of telepathy, or what he saw as the science of spiritual radio.

From the beginning of his travels through the foggy lands and waters of the northwest coast, Du Vernet knew that even though he traveled in what was called the Dominion of Canada, he was on Indigenous land. His notebooks and letters are filled with detailed descriptions of the people and lifeways of the Nisga'a, Ts'msyen, Haida, Tahltan, and Gitxsan nations on the Skeena and Nass Rivers and along the Pacific coast. On one page of a notebook crammed with short histories of the Indigenous missions in the diocese, he noted how the terms of union of British Columbia with the Dominion of Canada in 1874 resulted in the transferring of "Indian Reserves" to the Dominion government, and that an initial reckoning of eighty acres per Indigenous family became twenty. He added that in 1876 (the same year that the Indian Act first came into effect) the two levels of government agreed that "any land taken off a reserve shall revert to the Province."[26] By the time he wrote this, he had probably already learned that this last point was considerably more complicated.

His notebooks are also filled with "firsts"—his first service given in a church, the first church built in an Indigenous village, and the first baptisms he performed. He recorded the names of children and adults whom he baptized at each service, gave lists of lay readers he had licensed, and noted the numbers of Haida, Ts'msyen, Nisga'a, and Tahltan children attending day schools in their home communities. Late in his life, in the wake of his radio mind experiments and while he was confined to bed rest on account of a weakened heart, he crafted his own chart of how many confirmations he had bestowed on the people of his diocese. Between 1905 and 1924, he confirmed 534 men and 586 women at more than 43 churches stretching from Massett on Haida Gwaii to the new white settlements of the Peace River Valley, on the northeastern boundary of British Columbia. As archbishop, he also made a few trips south to Vancouver, to confirm the faithful at Christ Church Cathedral. According to his lists, on his many journeys he confirmed Haida, Nisga'a, Ts'msyen, Tahltan, Gitxsan, white, Chinese, and Japanese people in the ritual that enables baptized Anglicans to receive the Eucharist.[27]

Traveling was a constant theme in his notebooks and letters from the beginning of his work. With no road access to Prince Rupert for the entire time that he lived there, Du Vernet depended on steamers, fishing boats, canoes, the railway, and his feet for "moving amid the mountains." In February 1905, writing a letter to Stella while on board the steamer *Tees*, en route to the Ts'msyen village of Kitkatla, Du Vernet urged his wife: "Do not worry over me or over the Commission about land etc. only keep quietly working for me + the diocese."[28] Stella may have been worrying over a growing media scandal about the British Columbia government granting special—and illegal—favors to the Grand Trunk Pacific Railway in its 1904 purchase of land on Kaien Island. The same day that he wrote to Stella, Frederick also wrote a draft for an article about his missionary exploits, which may well have caused his wife to worry had it been addressed to her:

> Bishop Du Vernet has lately accomplished what few white men ever attempt[:] a trip up and down the Naas River in winter travelling in an open boat to where the ice was strong enough to hold and then trotting behind the dogsled with an occasional rest upon the sleigh when the trail was good. On his return trip it was too stormy to take a boat from tidewater down to the river's mouth, so accompanied by two Indians he made his way along the rocks and broken ice on the water's edge climbing up and down steep cliffs where they jutted out into deep water.[29]

Just as he felt the thrill of running the rapids on Manidoo Ziibi thanks to his Ojibwe guide Charlie, so too did Du Vernet enjoy the excitement of dogsledding and rock-climbing with the help of his "Indian" guides. Writing about himself in the third person, accompanied this time by unnamed Indigenous men, he was the hero of the story, standing at center stage (fig. 18).

Like Manidoo Ziibi, the Nass River had long been a thoroughfare for fur

FIGURE 18. Bishop Frederick Du Vernet, early Prince Rupert (ca. 1908). Photograph courtesy of the Prince Rupert City and Regional Archives (P2004-056-6448).

traders, Hudson's Bay Company employees, miners, and missionaries, so it is unlikely that Du Vernet was quite so unusual a white man as he claimed. In fact, one of the goals of his trip was to visit the Nisga'a village of Lakkalzap, a mission fought over by Methodist and Anglican clerics—white men—for many years.

The Nisga'a of Lakkalzap greeted the new bishop with a lavish welcome: the firing of a gun salute, fireworks, music from a brass band, and an address by the chief of the council. In an optimistic tone, Du Vernet noted, "This is the place where under peculiar circumstances the people of their own free will and as a united body renounced their allegiance to the Methodist Church and came over to the Church of England." Recounting that the Nisga'a were overjoyed by the new unity of "Christian Indians" all along the Nass, Du Vernet also noted that the Lakkalzap Nisga'a had taken strong measures to attract the Anglican clergy: "For more than three years past the Church of England missionaries refused to listen to the petitions and deputations of the Lakkalzap people to be taken over but when the ultimatum came and they announced their decision to return to heathenism if not received into the Anglican Church only one course was open in the interest of Christianity on the Naas." As Du Vernet would learn, the Nisga'a often set the terms of their engagement with the church. They were especially determined to have white men ordained by the church as their Christian guides, while they kept their own Nisga'a political and spiritual leaders.[30]

The insistence of the Lakkalzap Nisga'a that the Anglican Church take them on (rather than take them over) required the Methodist and Anglican churches to come to an agreement that involved the exchange of money and land title, and what amounted to a noncompetition clause. The Methodists and the Anglicans had long challenged each other's maps of their missionary territory in northwestern British Columbia. In this, the Methodists shared the perspective of the Nisga'a: the map of the Diocese of Caledonia was an Anglican fiction. The bishop brokered a deal with Robert Whittington, superintendent of Methodist Indigenous missions. Du Vernet convinced Whittington to accept payment for some church buildings on Lakkalzap land in exchange for the Methodists leaving all the missionary activity on the Nass River to the Anglicans.[31]

Both missionaries realized, however, that they could not conclude their own deal without the participation of the Nisga'a. In his letter to Whittington in February 1906, Du Vernet commented in particular on the cleverness of the Nisga'a distinctions of ownership:

> With great acumen, the people of Lakkalzap draw a distinction between what was bought with Methodist Missionary money, and what was bought with their own money, for their own use and the use of the village. They acknowledge that the Methodist Missionary Society put $2000 into the Church Building and although they subscribed also, they lay no claim to this, but are prepared to build a new church. The Council has given you due notice, that on account of the new survey the Methodist Church must be moved within 6 months. They draw a further distinction between what was put into the Church at the time it was opened, and what they have since bought with their own money for their own use. For this reason they are willing to put back the benches and the lamps, but the bell, the organ and the stoves are, they claim, their own property bought with their own money for the use of the people of Lakkalzap, e.g. the bell serves for various municipal purposes.[32]

The new survey of land Du Vernet mentioned revealed that the Methodist church was on Nisga'a reserve land, a territorial incursion that Indigenous groups often resisted; they allowed churches to be built, but the land remained theirs. A mere building, the Methodist church had to move, leaving behind the land belonging to the Nisga'a as well as the things that were theirs, because they had paid for them with their own money. The earlier renaming of Lakkalzap as Greenville after a previous Methodist missionary was similarly transient; though it is still sometimes referred to informally as Greenville, the official name of the village is now Laxgalts'ap.

Du Vernet's lawyer was not convinced that the Methodists would keep their word to leave the Nass Valley to the Anglicans, but the bishop went ahead with his deal anyway, paying the Methodists for the church building. Perhaps recalling the earlier disputes between the Ts'msyen and the Church Missionary Society over the very same question of whether the church owned the land in Metlakatla, Du Vernet was clear in his summary of the situation that neither the Methodists nor the Anglicans held title to the land: "To sum up the whole matter: The authorities of the Church of England are prepared to negotiate with the authorities of the Methodist Church for the purchase of property bought with the money of the Methodist Missionary Society, but in regard to all property bought by the people's own money for their own use on their own reserve, the authorities of the Methodist Church must settle any dispute as to ownership before the Indian Agent. Where there is no legal title there can be no proper conveyance and therefore no sale."[33] Underneath Du Vernet's assertion about title lay a deeper conflict over the ownership of the land, which had long been contentious and unresolved.

For the Nisga'a and other Indigenous nations, title was a concept that they used cautiously but doggedly, insisting that their land included much more than reserves that had been allotted to them over the course of their colonial interactions with Canada. Engaging with the language of title did not mean they relinquished their own language for holding territory. As historian Nicholas May writes: "The imposition of reserves and subsequent grabbing of their lands without any negotiation had deeply offended a touchstone of Nisga'a culture, namely its concern for the proper holding and transfer of house titles and the lands, the *ango'oskw*, connected to them. In demanding a treaty Nisga'a proposed in a language the K'amksiiwaa [settlers] could comprehend their longstanding practice of making public and transparent all claims regarding the establishment or transfer of property, which they practiced in their *yukw* (settlement feast)."[34] In addition to the yukw, the spanaxnox, the adawx, and totem poles also materially testified to Indigenous collective ownership.

The Kaien Island Land Grab

If two acres of land could provoke the exodus of the Ts'msyen and Duncan from Metlakatla in 1887, the 13,567 acres of what Ts'msyen today call the

"Kaien Island land grab" of 1906 incited controversy and land claims that are still ongoing. For railway companies to lay down their tracks, they had to first gobble up land across the North American continent; sometimes they received this land as gifts—or grants—from governments; other times they bought it at radically reduced prices. When the territory they sought was explicitly Indigenous reserve land, as in the case of a large part of Kaien Island, the railway companies faced more-complicated negotiations. The Grand Trunk Pacific Railway secured its coastal land by soliciting gifts from the British Columbia government and negotiating with the Ts'msyen. Frederick Du Vernet assisted the railway in its efforts.[35]

In early 1906, George Morrow, the Indian agent at Metlakatla, and Frederick Du Vernet, the Metlakatlans' bishop, counseled them as they negotiated with the GTP over the purchase of almost fourteen thousand acres of land designated as an Indian reserve on Kaien Island, Digby Island, and the mainland. Though records of this deal are scant, apparently the Ts'msyen started the negotiations at $10.00 per acre and the railway company at $5.00; they settled on $7.50. Remembered today by legal scholars for its implications in terms of whether land "surrendered" by Indigenous nations reverted to federal or provincial jurisdictions, the Kaien Island purchase is the subject of an ongoing land claim by the Metlakatla First Nation.[36]

Confident that it had purchased the land, the GTP commenced mapping a new city across the water from Metlakatla in the spring of 1906. As George Morrow reported to the superintendent of Indian Affairs in Ottawa: "Metlakatla to-day is used as the headquarters of the Grand Trunk Pacific railway while their engineers are engaged in laying off a townsite, and making a survey of a harbour for the Pacific coast terminus of this company within two miles of the old historic spot" of the mission village. Morrow retrospectively mused that "this terminus must consist more or less of Indian lands belonging to these people. The opening up of this reserve enhances the value of all of it, and brings employment and business to the very door of these people." He also noted however, that the Ts'msyen did not share his vision of enhancement: "I may add that I was keenly disappointed quite recently when a few of them engaged with the engineers gave up work, with hardly a moment's notice, stating that they were not satisfied with the wages paid; but my belief is that the reason they gave up the work was on account of the new experience of having a master over them from 7 a.m. till 6 p.m. However, they will gradually fall into line, and when they do so will prove good faithful labourers."[37] What Morrow's paternalism did not acknowledge was that Ts'msyen dissatisfaction with their wages was likely exacerbated by their ongoing concerns about the terms of the Kaien Island sale.

Whether or not the men of the Dominion Hydrographic Survey understood the significance of the "old historic spot" where they worked, they turned their encounters with the land and sea into maps that were both "topological and cosmological representations." They brought their cartographic and hydrographic tools to the task, using levels called spirit vials to grade the land and plumb lines to sound the depths of the harbors. They also received spiritual sustenance from the bishop. As the *Victoria Daily Colonist* told its readers, the survey crew tasked with finding the best spot for the railway terminus "warmly welcomed" Du Vernet to their camp on Kaien Island, where he administered the Eucharist to them. The *Colonist* called this "the first religious service ever held on Kaien Island."[38]

This "firsting," to use Jean O'Brien's term, was subtle in its erasure of Indigenous presence compared to the claim of the *Church Missionary Gleaner* when describing the same event: "On Easter Day, 1906, the present site of Prince Rupert was primeval forest, and Kaien Island was uninhabited. On May 20, 1906, Bishop DuVernet held the first religious service on the island, and on June 17 the first religious service at Prince Rupert, the latter being held in the dining-room tent of the Grand Trunk Pacific survey camp."[39] This firsting text may well have been written by Du Vernet himself and sent to his *Gleaner* colleagues.

The Ts'msyen had lived in villages, gathered shellfish, tended gardens, and buried their dead on Kaien Island for centuries. The surveyors, railway workers, and missionaries all knew this; at times they had literally dug up the bones. To these men, however, Ts'msyen practices did not look like "religious services" when Christian rituals were the measure. The 1895 revision to the Indian Act said as much, outlawing Indigenous "ceremonies" such as the potlatch—deeming them not religious—in part because they involved "the giving away or paying or giving back of money, goods or articles."[40] A Eucharistic service in which the priest consecrated the bread and wine into the "real presence" of Jesus Christ, and then gave them to the communicants in exchange for their faith, and likely monetary offerings, too, was not outlawed. The diasporic, traveling Christian god had a spiritual jurisdiction that was recognized by earthly colonial law.

In addition to the missionaries' descriptions of Indigenous ritual practices, anthropologists such as Franz Boas, Edward Sapir, and, later, Marius Barbeau wrote their own accounts of visiting the region. An archaeologist employed by the American Museum of Natural History, Harlan I. Smith visited the Metlakatla area in 1909, cataloging many ancient shell middens and noting repeatedly that "Indian houses and gardens" were built atop these heaps of shells. Smith noted many petroglyphs grooved into the rocks along the Nass

River and around Metlakatla, as well as graves. A railway agent contributed to his research, as Smith noted in his *American Anthropologist* article: "On the northern side of Skeena river, on the right-of-way of the Grand Trunk Pacific Railroad, near grade mile-post either 85 or 87 are graves, according to Mr. H. Blake, a railroad employe [*sic*] residing in Prince Rupert, British Columbia."[41] In search of antiquity, Smith could not ignore that Ts'msyen people—both alive and dead—still inhabited the places now called Digby Island and Prince Rupert.

Pure Speculation

By 1907, a GTP map depicted the yet-to-be-built railway wrapping around the western perimeter of Kaien Island. The map also christened the land Prince Rupert, a name chosen by way of a national contest, in honor of the reputedly roguish first governor of the Hudson's Bay Company, a cousin to King Charles II (plate 3). Prince Rupert, who lived in the seventeenth century, had never traveled to Canada, but for over two hundred years Rupert's Land, a vast swath of Cree, Ojibwe, and Inuit territories west of Hudson's Bay, carried his name. Applying the prince's name once again to Kaien Island, even before the city had been officially founded, sought to replace the long history of Indigenous presence on the island by renaming it.[42]

The surveyors camped on Kaien Island because its deep harbors were well suited to a northern rail terminus where lumber, minerals, and goods could be loaded onto ships and freighters heading east to China and south to the Americas. Du Vernet's ministrations to the survey camp, and his earlier negotiations in the land deal, laid the ground for his friendships with GTP officials, including James H. Bacon, the chief harbor engineer, and Mr. Dodge, the head of the survey crew. He even posed for photographs with some of these men, standing at the railway worksite sporting his clerical collar and a jaunty sailor's cap (fig. 19). By the end of 1906, the GTP had a survey in hand and was preparing to sell off prospective town lots at a great profit.

The railway's purchase of Kaien Island—at bargain rates—became a political scandal not because of concerns about the dispossession of the Ts'msyen, but because politicians and citizens down south worried that the railway had, once again, fleeced the government. In March 1906, the Kaien Island Investigation was held in the provincial capital of Victoria, during which mapmakers were questioned in great detail about the lines they drew around and about Kaien Island.[43] But the Grand Trunk Pacific Railway's purchase of Ts'msyen land held fast.

FIGURE 19. Mr. Bacon, Bishop Du Vernet, and Mr. Atwater (1910). Photograph courtesy of the Library and Archives Canada (Charles Hays Fonds).

In a September 1906 letter to his brother Ernest, a Toronto lawyer who was a partner in a new bank, Frederick narrated in great detail the process of surveying Prince Rupert and the intricacies of buying its newly made lots from the GTP. Having heard from Stella that his brother might be interested in establishing a bank in Prince Rupert, Frederick gave Ernest some cautious advice: "There is absolutely no land worth anything for sale within several miles of the townsite of Prince Rupert—rocks and mountains." The land *within* the townsite, however, was hot property: "I hear that men with millions of dollars are waiting to buy up everything they can. I fear this will retard progress."[44] Fantasy maps crafted by the railroad helped drive this land speculation.

With the close of the Kaien Island Investigation in Victoria, marketers for the Grand Trunk Pacific Railway, led by their chief booster, company president Charles Hays, quickly told a new story about the land. With maps, brochures, and advertisements, they eagerly narrated how Prince Rupert would become a city to rival southern counterparts like Vancouver, Victoria, and even San Francisco. Railway barons and politicians alike had heralded Prince Rupert as either the "Gateway to the North" or the "Gateway to the Orient." Alongside stories of cargo ships and freight trains were aesthetic dreams for the new city. Charles Hays hired the Boston architectural firm of Brett & Hall to design the plans for the imagined city. Architect George Hall, mentored by Frederick Olmsted of Central Park fame, designed a township with curving streets lassoed by the railroad (fig. 20). Another architect famous in his day, Frances Rattenbury, drew up plans for a grand hotel that would rival the legendary Empress Hotel in the provincial capital of Victoria.[45]

Worried that the Toronto and Seattle newspapers were encouraging "pure speculation" by "booming" the town lots along the railway, Frederick was nonetheless willing to engage in some modest speculation himself, with the help of his GTP friends: "Mr. Russell has applied for me and the application is endorsed by Mr. Bacon, the Chief Engineer and Mr. Pillsbury the Head Engineer on the spot. I am thinking of putting up a readymade house with 3 rooms ($200 + o.g. at Vancouver) the foundation is extra. But such a building can be easily moved later. Such a building would suit for a temporary bank." Not quite offering to take a risk with his brother on the enterprise, Frederick returned to a note of caution: "You understand that as the G.T.P. own all the land and none is on the market permission to erect a building where the Engineer says + subject to removal at his order must be obtained. Don't be misled into buying land out here without knowing what you are doing." Very grateful to Ernest for taking care of Horace, his struggling son who was still in Toronto, Frederick always signed off his letters as "your affectionate brother."[46]

Du Vernet grumbled repeatedly that the powerful Senator Cox, a Toronto-based financial magnate with a vast network of banking and insurance companies and a strong commitment to the Methodist Church, would likely get all the business in Prince Rupert, since his Bank of Commerce arrived first on the ground. Nevertheless, Frederick counseled his brother that he could get rich by being quick, giving him some inside information about the $100,000 payment the Ts'msyen were to soon receive for selling part of

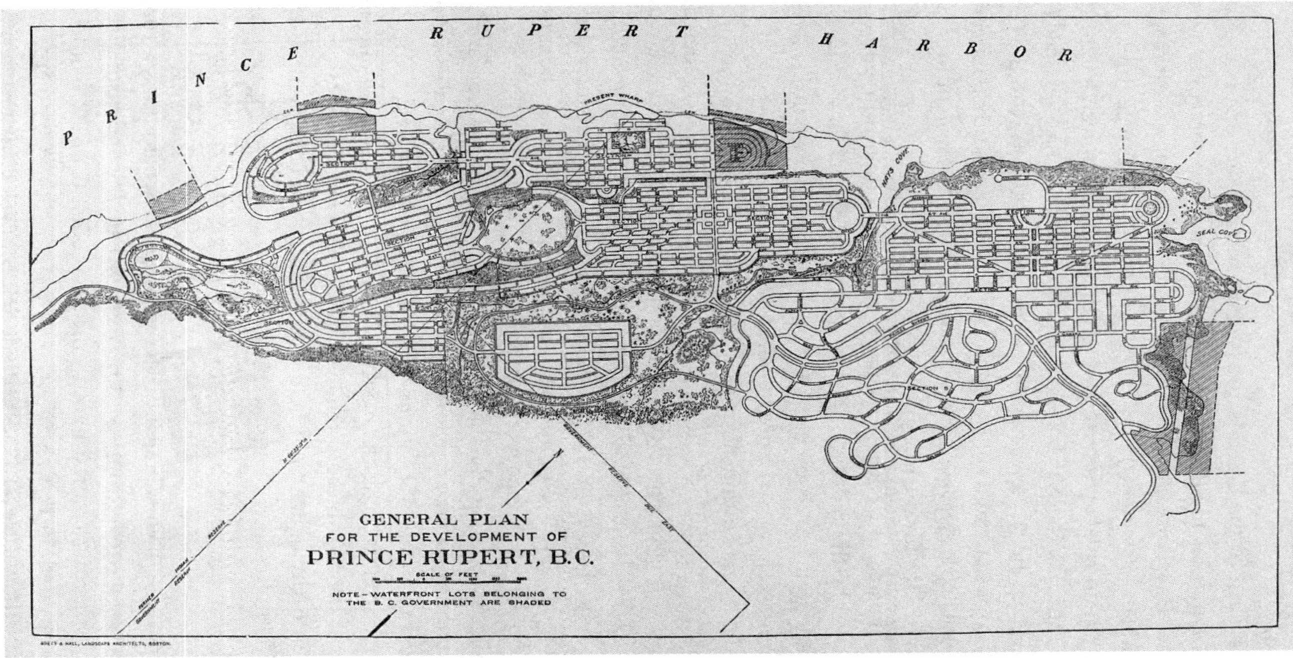

FIGURE 20. *General Plan for the Development of Prince Rupert, B.C.* From *Prince Rupert, British Columbia: The Pacific Coast Terminus of the Grand Trunk Pacific Railway* (Montreal: Grand Trunk Pacific Railway Company, 1911). Photograph courtesy of the Thomas Fisher Rare Book Library, University of Toronto.

their reserve to the railway: "The Indian Agent + I are going to encourage the native people to put their money in a bank. If your bank were first on the spot it would no doubt get much of what is going except that the Post Office does its banking with the Bank of Commerce."[47] Having already counseled the Ts'msyen in their negotiations with the GTP, Du Vernet was ready to go one step further and recommend that they become not only churched but also banked.

Acting as a go-between for the Ts'msyen and the government, Du Vernet ferried their cash to Metlakatla: "Last Monday Bishop Du Vernet, acting for Indian Agent Morrow, came over here from Prince Rupert and paid the people the balance of the money due for land surrendered to the King, August 17th, 1906. A small amount had been held back from each at the time of the former payment to allow for certain disputed claims. These cases, six or seven in number, were decided at Ottawa, and those allowed have now been paid in full. There were also about a dozen garden claims which were likewise finally disposed of, the price paid being from $100 to $200 for each garden."[48] Du Vernet's fears of rampant speculation and concern for the saving habits of the Ts'msyen sat uncomfortably with his urge to claim his own town lot and to help his brother benefit from the money that would change hands with the selling of Ts'msyen land. Du Vernet's ambivalent advice to his brother—think twice before you buy—suggests that he was not entirely convinced of the wisdom of his brother coming to town. It seems that in the end, Ernest did not invest in Prince Rupert.

Frederick was not alone as a settler with doubts, however subtle, about practices of buying and selling Indigenous land in a province that had never truly settled questions of Indigenous title. As legal historian Hamar Foster has written, "The idea of Indian title was an uneasy compromise between two competing but unevenly balanced thoughts: that Aboriginal people ought to enjoy some rights to their traditional lands, and that industrial, capitalist civilization would improve everything it touched, especially the bank balances of those who were in its vanguard." Missionaries such as Du Vernet were often in the middle of this uneasy compromise: defending Indigenous rights to (some) land while also assuming that increased white settlement and the "improvements" of capitalism were inevitable, and benefiting from them along the way.[49] Du Vernet's careful attention to the real estate dealings of the Anglican church and his own personal land purchases show that he thought that for the Dominion government to map the land and to give or sell it to the church, the railway, the banks, and the settlers was a story of progress.

The Last Big Blast

The "Last Big Blast" on January 21, 1914, would have shaken the earth and pounded ears for miles around, as rocks, mud, and scrub flew into the air in one last burst of dynamite. The rock had to fly to make way for the realization of the vision: the city, the railroad, and the new citizens that would create Prince Rupert. The local paper reported often on the blasts, forewarning residents of the scheduled explosions, but even so there were fatalities—people, often children, who didn't quite get out of the way in time. Photographers waited nearby to catch the magnificence of the destruction of what they took to be inanimate matter, not recognizing the "sentient and knowing" beings that a Ts'msyen viewer might have sensed in the rocks.[50] The blasts were a sight to see, a moment of history to record over and over again, to tell the story of making of a city out of the earth. Prince Rupert's most active photographic entrepreneurs, the McRae Brothers, took many pictures of the blasts, both "first" and "last" (figs. 21–23).

The dreams of Prince Rupert's glory were never fully realized, remaining visible largely on maps. City booster Charles Hays died in the sinking of the

FIGURE 21. *Before the Blast, Apr. 24th, '13*, Prince Rupert, BC. Photography by the McRae Brothers. Photograph courtesy of the Royal British Columbia Museum and Archives (A-00455).

FIGURE 22. *Moving Mountains at Prince Rupert B.C. in Apr. 24th, '13*. Photography by the McRae Brothers. Photograph courtesy of the Royal British Columbia Museum and Archives (A-00456).

FIGURE 23. *The Last Big Blast, Prince Rupert B.C., 21 Jan. 1914*. Photography by the McRae Brothers. Photograph courtesy of the Royal British Columbia Museum and Archives (A-00457).

Titanic in 1912 and with him went a good deal of the optimism and funding for the city; he remains immortalized as the city founder in a bronze statue and plaque near the city hall. Two years after his death, the railway was joined, as Du Vernet noted with some drama: "April 7th 1914 two ends of steel of G.T.P. met a mile east of fort Fraser. April 9th train through to P.R. Regular trains from East began running Sept. 3 (?), 1914." Despite all its sweetened land deals and profiteering, the Grand Trunk Pacific Railway went bankrupt and was nationalized by the Canadian government in 1919. That same year, the cozy relations between the railway and the missionaries went sour, when the railway abolished clergy passes. Du Vernet lamented to supporters in Britain: "This is a hard blow on me for I travel many thousands of miles on the G.T.P., the C.N.R., the White Pass Railway, and the Edmonton, Dunvegan and British Columbia Railway."[51] He hoped he could negotiate at least half-fare privileges for his clergy.

Reminiscing late in life on "pioneer days," Du Vernet reflected in his notebook on how much the physical landscape of Prince Rupert had changed with the coming of the railway. Recalling pleasant Sunday afternoons with Stella in the early days, he wrote: "Our Church Hall stood at the bend of the St. nothing [was] beyond this but a spruce clad hill. Sunday aft. Mrs. DuV. & I [hiked there]. Where is this hill today. 2nd Ave & 5th St go through it. A good illustration of how faith can remove mountains, for if there had not been unbounded faith in the future of this city such a work would never have been accomplished. I was always an optimist."[52] Optimist or not, faith did not remove mountains all by itself. Dynamite was necessary to get the job done. A 1908 photograph of the hillside of Prince Rupert was likely meant to be an optimistic portrait of progress, featuring wooden shacks, the new hotel, and the church hall peeking out beside it. But faith in progress also left the land scarred and naked, trees stumps clinging to the earth, their trunks milled into lumber (fig. 24).

The dynamite would never have been laid on the ground without a vision at once Christian, capitalist, and colonial: faith *was* required to move the mountains. Such violent destruction could only occur when authorized by spiritual imaginations that remapped the land as property that held resources waiting to be extracted. On the northwest coast in the early years of the twentieth century, the spiritual vision of the Canadian nation was most plainly established by the blasting and remapping of Indigenous ones.

Missionary Real Estate

Having experienced the intensity of negotiating the Kaien Island land deal just a year into his duties, and knowing the history of the missionaries'

FIGURE 24. Prince Rupert with the Anglican church hall in view on the "spruce clad hill" after the trees were cut down (August 13, 1908). Photograph courtesy of the Prince Rupert City and Regional Archives.

struggles over land in Metlakatla, Du Vernet understood well the politics of Indigenous land. Under the Indian Act, Indigenous people could not preempt land or vote—two defining features of what might be called secular citizenship. They could only own land collectively, in the form of "reserves," but even that ownership could be threatened if the population of the reserve dwindled—or if a railway company applied pressure.[53] With different emphases, both the Nisga'a and the missionaries contested this law, arguing that the right to own land would allow Indigenous people to become full-fledged citizens. The Nisga'a and other coastal nations, however, insisted that their collective land claims must first be settled before they would seek to own real estate as individuals. More widely, Indigenous nations repeatedly insisted that churches built on Indigenous land were just that—buildings given space on land that remained their own territory.

Du Vernet's notebooks are filled with references to real estate—the buying, selling, and deeding of land that had been mapped out by chains or lots. In 1909, as the president of the Prince Rupert Ministerial Association, which also included a Roman Catholic, a Methodist, and a Presbyterian, he was delegated to write to Premier Richard McBride to request that the province sell city lots to the churches at reduced rates: "We respectfully point out that as the rush for lots will most likely be unprecedented and powerful syndicates will crowd others out it could be a most becoming act on the part of the Provincial Government to ensure that Church corporations animated by unselfish motives should be given an opportunity to secure favourable sites." The Ministerial Association, while notably ecumenical, had shut out the Salvation

Army from its club, so the Army adjutant had to write his own letter a few months later. None of the letters worked, however, and the premier turned them all down, in the politest of terms.[54]

For Du Vernet, the lot number of a church was as important as the saint's name bestowed on it. When noting the history of the Anglican churches in his diocese, he regularly began his description with the lot number immediately after the church's name. He painstakingly transcribed the words of dead people's wills and living people's conveyances, that is, the transfer of property between two people through a written deed. Du Vernet also recorded the details of many Certificates of Indefeasible Title and Certificates of Allocation, the latter being a tool by which Indigenous councils allowed the Anglicans to build churches on their land without selling the land. He made lists of lot numbers in all the missions and settlements in the diocese, and drew pencil sketches of church property abutting Indigenous reserves and bordering the lots of the Hudson's Bay Company along the Peace River.

He also told survey stories like this one in Telegraph Creek, Tahltan territory: "Mission building stands on land not included in reserve when it was surveyed Crown land. For the use of the Missionary Society so long as it is used for missionary purposes. The agreement with Crown Land department. Building erected by Mr. Stephenson (carpenter). $1000. Fence extra." The Crown regularly granted Christian churches the right to use of land, even before the Dominion of Canada existed. A note added at the top of this narrative amended the story with a common ending for churches in the area: "Building burned down."[55]

Du Vernet also recorded dozens of transactions by which he held land as a corporation sole. This is the legal term for holding property by virtue of a ritually bestowed name. As bishop of Caledonia, Frederick Du Vernet owned acres and acres of land in his ecclesiastical role, but this was not land that he could register under his own personal name. Ritually invested with the name of bishop, which allowed him to hold collective property for the church, Du Vernet was imbued with authority parallel to that of a clan leader among the Nisga'a or Ts'msyen: he held collective land for the good of the community that would not pass on to his heirs and would not remain his were he to retire from his episcopate.

In an illuminating exchange of letters with a law firm in the provincial capital of Victoria, Du Vernet argued repeatedly for the special privilege of the church to own land as a corporate, or collective, body, as represented by the bishop as a corporation sole. As a legal concept, the corporation sole had long been "a curious freak of English law" that ensured continuity of church property by designating an ecclesiastically sanctioned individual as holding the fee simple, or title, to a piece of church land not as a person but as a legal entity. Most commonly, for example, a bishop would own church property as a cleric who was a man, but who was also the "secular, legal embodiment of the church." As Perry Dane has argued, the corporation sole was an individual who was a collective representation, poised at the juncture of secular and church power as an "extraordinary, irregular, custom-tailored effort at translating religious principles into secular terms."[56] The Canadian state could recognize the right of the chief priest of the Anglican Diocese of Caledonia to buy and sell land as a collective representation, but refused to acknowledge the right of clan leaders of the Nisga'a or Ts'msyen to transfer their land through similar processes. Ritual familiarity bred political privilege.

Du Vernet developed something of an obsession with sorting out the extent of land throughout the diocese that the bishop owned as a corporation sole. This was perhaps due to an early dispute with the previous bishop of Caledonia, William Ridley (the same one who, ironically, had fought with the Metlakatlans over the Church Missionary Society's collective ownership of "Mission Point"). The retired bishop had tried to sell privately some land in Port Simpson that was registered as owned by the bishop of Caledonia as a corporation sole. Even though the buyer had deposited her money, Du Vernet would not be swayed, writing to her lawyer: "It seems to me so highly improbable that Bishop Ridley in the days of his full mental vigor should have allowed his private property to be registered in the name of 'The Lord Bishop of Caledonia' knowing as he did that such was a 'corporation sole' that in the interests of the Church I must ask for further proof before I hand over Church property."[57] There was no possible way, Du Vernet argued, that the previous bishop could have mistaken church land with his own.

With the proof from the retired bishop who had moved back to England not forthcoming, Du Vernet refused outright to hand over the property, declaring in a 1910 letter that he could not enact a "violation of my trust as a 'corporation sole.'" Tempering his refusal with notes of sympathy for Ridley in his "declining years," Du Vernet stood fast to his ritual obligations: "Personally I am willing to do all in my power for him but 'a trust' in an official capacity is a sacred thing." Du Vernet sought to imbue his own legal responsibilities with sacrality, but he did not turn to parallels with the sacred trusts by which Ts'msyen and Nisga'a clans had held the land since "time immemorial."[58]

Du Vernet's commitment to the sacred authorization of collective ownership of church territory was mirrored in his commitment to the Anglican ritual of "consecrating" a church. In addition to taking great care to catalog church property by the cartographic systems of survey grids and legal map-

FIGURE 25. Kincolith church (ca. 1905). Photograph courtesy of the Northern British Columbia Archives (Archdeacon W. H. Collison Fonds, accession no. 2009.7.1.124).

ping concepts such as "Crown land," "reserve," "certificates of allocation," and "corporation sole," Du Vernet repeatedly noted his first visits to churches and his ritual labor of consecrating these buildings as Christian space. He recorded the proper ritual refrain in his notebook, using a framed document hanging in the vestry of the Nisga'a church at Kincolith as an example: "Certificate of consecration: This church named Christ Church of Kincolith situated at the mouth of the Naas river is now consecrated this 30th day of September in the year of our Lord Nineteen hundred, according to the usual rites of the Church of England and is thereby dedicated forever to the Worship of God, the Father, Son, and Holy Ghost (signature of the Bishop)."[59] This ritual of consecration that blessed a church built at the mouth of the river placed a new trinity of spirits on top of those sbi-nax̱nok̲ already there (fig. 25).

Discarding the Map

Du Vernet also bought land as a man, not a bishop, holding plots on both the Skeena and the Nass Rivers (fig. 26). He recommended to other settlers

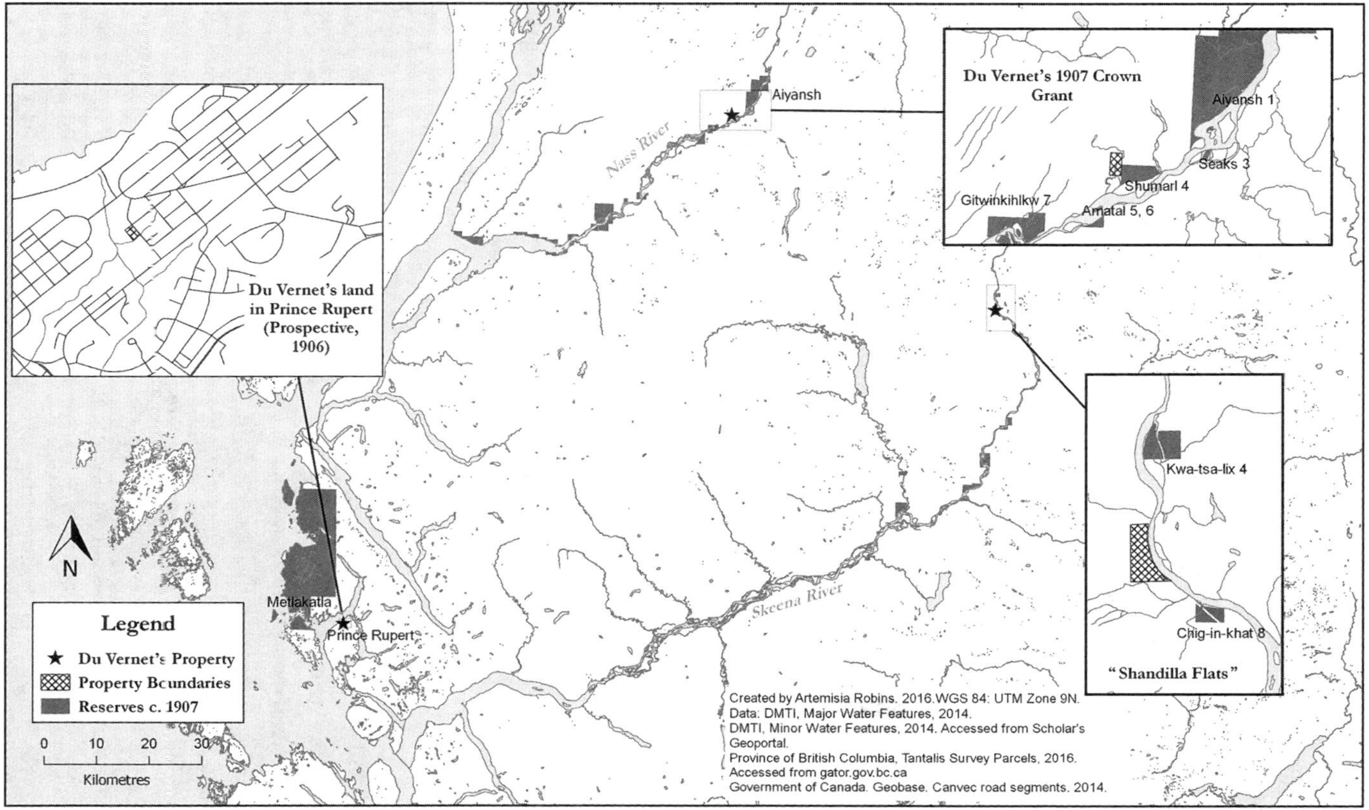

FIGURE 26. Map of Du Vernet's properties in northwestern British Columbia at the time of his death in 1924. Courtesy of Artemisia Robins.

that they do the same. By the early twentieth century, the missionaries were encouraging settlers from eastern Canada, Great Britain, and Europe to move to the Nass Valley, hoping that the newly imagined city of Prince Rupert with its proposed railway terminus would prove attractive to farmers from more densely populated regions. The Nisga'a, for their part, openly opposed white people settling their lands. In 1907, when Joshua Priestley, the first settler, showed up to claim land next to the Nisga'a reserve, his arrival and his claim of ownership was quickly disputed by the Nisga'a in letters and in face-to-face meetings. Priestley claimed that Bishop Du Vernet and the missionary James McCullagh had directly entreated him to come to the Nass Valley, and he was angry to find the Nisga'a not as welcoming.[60]

An ongoing conflict between Joshua Priestley and Nisga'a leaders reveals the Nisga'a's strong refusal of colonial maps. Head chief Alfred Skadeen, along with "all the rest of the chiefs," wrote collectively to Joshua Priestley in February 1907, insisting that Priestley had preempted a plot of land that was Nisga'a territory, and that he must return to the "Bishop's land" downriver: "We will take one canoe and load it, both you and your goods and we will send you down. We will cut down any kinds of timber or any trees we want and you will not speak for it because that timber land belongs to us. Hoping to be answered soon." Priestley wrote with anger and panic to Superintendent Frederick Hussey of the provincial police in Victoria, claiming that the Nisga'a had threatened him with violence.[61]

In the spring of 1908, provincial constable Alfred Carter came with Commissioner O'Connell to the Nass Valley to hold a meeting with the Nisga'a and Priestley in the schoolhouse at Aiyansh. Carter despaired of Priestley's approach, calling him "a man devoid of tact, and one that does not understand the ways of the Indians, or the conditions of the country, and to all appearances, in my opinion, never will."[62] With the missionary James McCullagh serving as translator, the Nisga'a chiefs, one by one, stated their concerns with Priestley's preemption, repeatedly asserting that he should return to Bishop Du Vernet's land.

Chief James Ksidiyawug testified: "We heard last spring that this Whiteman was coming to live upon the Bishop's land. He came and put his freight out there, and came up as it were for a short time to Aiyansh. Behold, he goes and stakes la [*sic*] land opposite, and even sets his stake upon a part of our reserve." Chief Ksidiyawug described how Priestley refused to listen to the Nisga'a, so "we told him to get out altogether and go to the Bishop's land for which he had originally come here. It is evident to us that that man is in the wrong, because he tries to take advantage of us and so creates bad feeling and excitement among us. Therefore the people request that he go down to the Bishop's land for which he came and which is already surveyed."[63] The bishop's land was a grant of Crown land that Du Vernet had claimed but had not "improved." He may have wanted to have a settler to farm and then purchase the land from him, but he still owned the land upon his death.

A younger member among the chiefs, Andrew Mercer, put the matter of maps most sharply:

> I have been asked by the chiefs and people to explain as fully as possible to the Commission the reason of our objection to Mr. Priestley's taking up land here. The principal reason of our objection is that We ourselves are not yet satisfied with what has been reserved for us. . . . We felt very much aggrieved last winter and troubled among ourselves about this land question, for it is FOUR YEARS now since we have seen an Indian Agent in this district. Consequently we have discarded the map of the reserves drawn up by the Indian Department. We want more land, and we do not see that there is much room around us for settlers in view of what we require for ourselves.[64]

Discarding the map, Andrew Mercer and the chiefs refused the narrative that described their land as belonging to the Crown.

With Indian agent George Morrow rarely venturing up the Nass River, Chief Timothy Derrick was pointed in his criticism of both the agent and the Indian reserve as a "way of deceit:"

> We also see from reserves outside of us that they are not really the property of the Indians: the White man buys a part of one reserve and the government takes the money. Therefore it is much better for us from henceforth to have no Indian Agent and no Indian Act. It is much better for us to have just a good Magistrate who would lead us and guide us with regard to the law. Further, I have observed that an Indian reserve is not secure. . . . We have come to the conclusion therefore that it is much better for us to try to hold of ourselves the inheritance which God gave our fathers at the beginning. I thank the chiefs who have come to see us. I see that we worship God in common and am glad. That is all I have to say.

Timothy Derrick rejected the Indian Act by way of a common god. His argument, however, left Mr. O'Connell somewhat confused about which reserve he meant "as having been bought by the Whiteman and the money retained by the government." Derrick succinctly replied: "I mean the Metlakatla reserve."[65]

Andrew Mercer and Timothy Derrick discarded reserve maps and rejected the Indian Act, but they did not entirely reject the authority of Canadian law. Andrew Mercer's mix of candor and accommodation in this testimony was in keeping with many of his other letters and speeches. In a letter on behalf of the Indian Land Committee to the *Prince Rupert Evening Empire* in 1912, which Du Vernet most likely read, Mercer expertly critiqued how colonial authority rested on both maps and the Bible:

> If the surveyor and those that have staked pieces of land up in the Naas valley wish to come again, let them go to Ottawa first and make the government settle our land. And if our land is settled, then let the surveyor and those that have their stake come again, for we do not want to stop them. But we want a full settlement. Also we want to right of what is lawful. Same thing as you want to do right, as you all perceive it from the Holy Bible. Whenever the J.P. or a judge were in court they used Bible for to do right. We also see and read in it, in the Holy Bible, that "Cursed is he that removeth his neighbor's land mark," and that you break one of the Ten Commandments, "Thou shall not covet," for you have knock us down and take our possession.[66]

Mercer was a persistent critic who repeatedly articulated how colonial maps were rooted in Christian stories and spirits. He called on Canadians to be accountable to the laws and commandments embedded in their stories.

Stealing the Light

By the end of his life, Du Vernet became retrospective about his role in the making of the city of Prince Rupert and came to tell stories of maps and money. Lingering questions about his role in the railway's purchase of Indigenous land bubbled up in these stories. In an undated reminiscence likely written near the end of his life, he recalled his interactions with the feisty newspaper editor John Houston. Founder of the *Empire*, Prince Rupert's "first" newspaper, in 1907, Houston was notorious for his harsh critiques of railway companies. He quickly became a target of James Bacon, the GTP harbor engineer, who locked up Houston's printing press in a warehouse, saying that Houston did not have the right to publish on GTP property—which included all Kaien Island. Houston was not so easily silenced and arranged for his paper to be printed in Victoria, until the GTP relented and allowed him to set up shop again.[67]

One of Houston's editorials questioned the role of the missionaries in the sale of Ts'msyen land, and Du Vernet was not pleased. Though respectful of

Houston's "righteousness," Du Vernet recalled his own righteous urge to preserve his honor, even on Sunday, a day of rest:

> One Sunday morning [I] picked up [the] Empire [and read] an editorial in which the writer was trying to get a good crack at Mr. Morrow the Indian Agent + in speaking of the Metlakatla land deal he referred to both the temporal + spiritual advisers of the Indians in no complimentary terms as though both had received bribes from the G.T.P. . . . As my conscience was quite clear, I felt even though it was Sunday aft[ernoon] I must [spend] the hour in his den. . . . [I asked] "Mr. H what do you mean by this editorial?" [He replied] "Don't mean you anyway." But I was not to be put off. . . . I said to John H. "You are a preacher of hard righteousness just like myself. You hit what you believe to be wrong and I admire this. But you have made a mistake this time in hitting the missionaries."[68]

Du Vernet did not ask John Houston to publish a retraction, so he was all the more pleased to note that the editor clarified in the next week's paper that he was not casting aspersions on the missionaries.

A second story suggests that Du Vernet's conscience might not have been entirely clear. At an open meeting of the Prince Rupert Reading Club, on May 12, 1924, just three months after he had publicly demonstrated the power of radio mind to an eager youthful audience at the offices of the Prince Rupert newspaper, he read a story of his own composition. Starting out with the recognition that Prince Rupert was built on what had once been the hunting grounds of the "Tsimshean Indians," Du Vernet went on to recount a legend from "the beginning of time" when the land was in perpetual darkness.[69]

Weeget, the hero of this land, decided to disguise himself as a frond of hemlock so that he could float up to Heaven to discover the secret of how to bring light to the world. The Daughter of Heaven accidentally ingested the hemlock frond, allowing the "spirit of Weeget" to grow inside her, and eventually she gave birth to a little boy who himself had the "spirit of Weeget" inside him. The little boy, with the spirit of Weeget urging him on, became fascinated by a "golden ball of light" belonging to the King of Heaven. Every day he rolled the ball closer and closer to the edge of Heaven, until one day the ball plunged to the Earth, to bring light to the Ts'msyen. They named the spot where the ball fell Weeget's Point. And here I will let Du Vernet's telling take over:

> Any Tsimshean will tell you the exact spot where this Ball of Light first touched the earth. The place is not far distant on Digby Island, half way between Prince

> Rupert and Metlakatla, near the southern end of what is known as Venn's Passage. The name, Weeget's Point is not to be found on any map to-day, another name has taken it's [*sic*] place.
>
> Nearly all the land on which the city of Prince Rupert now stands and also the whole of Digby Island and part of the mainland to the north was Indian Reserve, prior to 1905. After the Grand Trunk Pacific Railway determined that Tuck's Inlet was the best harbour available on the northern Pacific coast, it became necessary for them to secure land upon which to build their terminus. . . . Before the Government could lift the reserve the Tsimsheans at Metlakatla had to be consulted. Negotiations took place with the result that the Indians agreed to sell part of their Reserve for a large sum of money [a little more than $100,000]. . . . It was decided by the natives that the dividing line, between the land which should be kept and the land which should be sold, should run down the centre of the famous Weeget's Point. The final agreement was signed in the presence of four men. Two appearing for each side. The Tsimsheans were represented by their Indian-Agent, Mr. George Morrow and the Bishop of Caledonia.
>
> In the re-naming of the places by the Dominion Hydrographic Survey Weeget's Point was called Du Vernet Point, in honour of the Bishop who had acted on behalf of the Indians during the lengthy negotiations already described.
>
> With the change of the name of this point and the passing away of the older Tsimshean Indians, few of the white people are likely to hear from the natives this local legend of the great Weeget and how Light first came to this northern country. I have told you this story as it has been handed down among the Tsimsheans from generation to generation. It is not difficult for us to see in this Indian legend some faint resemblance to the grand old story, enshrined in the Bible, of the coming of Christ to be the Light of the World.[70]

One of the longest stories that Du Vernet recorded, "The Golden Ball of Light" was a replacement narrative that stuck his name on one of the most spiritually powerful sites on the coast: the territory marked by the meeting of heaven and earth.

Who told him this story? Where and when did he come by it? The story of Weeget, or for the Nisga'a, of Wiigat-Txeemsim, is one that can be widely shared; its telling is not bound by protocols of "private property." My guess is that he heard the story from Odille Morison, a Ts'msyen woman from Metlakatla, who, with her English-born husband, Charles, had long been a prominent Anglican member of the diocese. Morison had herself recorded Ts'msyen stories for a white audience, both by sending stories to the anthropologist Franz Boas for his own ethnographic collection and by publishing her own accounts of Ts'msyen "proverbs" in the *Journal of American Folklore* in 1889.[71]

Morison was a complex woman at the intersection of several nodes of colonial and Indigenous power. The daughter of an important Ts'msyen midwife and healer and a French-Canadian Hudson's Bay Company employee, Odille married Charles Morison, also a Hudson's Bay Company employee. Odille was what Maureen Atkinson has called a "community correspondent" and "cultural intermediary" who worked hard to balance several roles: motherhood, community leader, biblical translator, ethnographic collector, and translator for colonial government officials and missionaries alike.[72]

A set of photographs pairing Odille with Stella and Charles with Frederick suggests that the two couples shared a familiarity with each other. Taken on a porch at Kitkatla, a Ts'msyen village, Odille sits with her arms folded and with Stella standing behind her, both women dressed elegantly, looking pleasantly at the camera (fig. 27). Frederick and Charles pose similarly, with the archbishop giving the honor of the chair to Mr. Morison, a man he had licensed as a lay reader in the church (fig. 28). In his own reminiscences, Charles wrote of Du Vernet with fondness: "He is the very best of company socially and enjoys a joke; he never spares himself and is a tremendous worker. The more you get to know him the more you get to love him."[73] The Morisons and the Du Vernets had the time to tell each other both jokes and stories.

If Odille Morison did tell the story to Du Vernet, she cannot be held responsible for his errors in the retelling. It is not clear why Du Vernet thought that younger Ts'msyen would not share the story with white people—because they did not want to, because they no longer remembered it, or because they thought the white people would not listen? Du Vernet's recounting of the legend of the Golden Ball of Light was not a version that was faithful to the story that Ts'msyen elders handed down across the generations. His double parallel—between Weeget who brings light and Du Vernet who brings the railway and between the light of the Golden Ball and that of Christ—is not in the generational tale that has survived today.

Now, few people in the region, whether Ts'msyen or not, could tell you where to find Du Vernet Point, save for the skippers of boats who regularly read nautical maps. Aside from the official hydrographic map, the only other map on which I have found Du Vernet Point marked is a 2013 environmental assessment report commissioned by the company applying to establish a Liquefied Natural Gas terminal at Prince Rupert, the latest resource extraction hope for the region's struggling economy. I talked with one skipper who was not sure of the location of Du Vernet Point, but suggested that I might be

FIGURE 27. Stella Du Vernet and Odille Morison (ca. 1920). Photograph courtesy of the Diocese of Caledonia Archives.

looking for the "Man-who-fell-from-Heaven" petroglyph, in Metlakatla. This petroglyph, however, tells a different story of a creature crossing the border between heaven and earth.[74]

Du Vernet's "local legend" was a complicated replacement narrative; he sought to legitimate his controversial role in the birth of the railway and the city at the same time that he tried to naturalize Canadian sovereignty through reconciling Ts'msyen, biblical, and hydrographic narratives. The typewritten manuscript bears two titles, both in Du Vernet's handwriting: the first, "Let there be Light," he crossed out, adding just below it, "The Golden Ball of Light" (fig. 29). Though his revised title nods to Weeget's story more than

FIGURE 28. Frederick Du Vernet and Charles Morison (ca. 1920). Photograph courtesy of the Diocese of Caledonia Archives.

to that of Jesus, his conclusion has a different effect. Laying the Christian story of the "Light of the World" over the story of the "Golden Ball of Light," Du Vernet's pencil quite literally traced Weeget into Jesus.

Du Vernet was also wrong in another sense. His version of the legend of the Golden Ball of Light, including his retelling of his role in the land negotiation and renaming, is not a version of the story that is faithful to the one the Ts'msyen have handed down across the generations. Ts'msyen and other northwest coast nations continue to actively tell each other and "white people" the story of when Weeget—also called Raven—stole the light. In museums, ethnographies, art, and dissertations, Indigenous artists and sto-

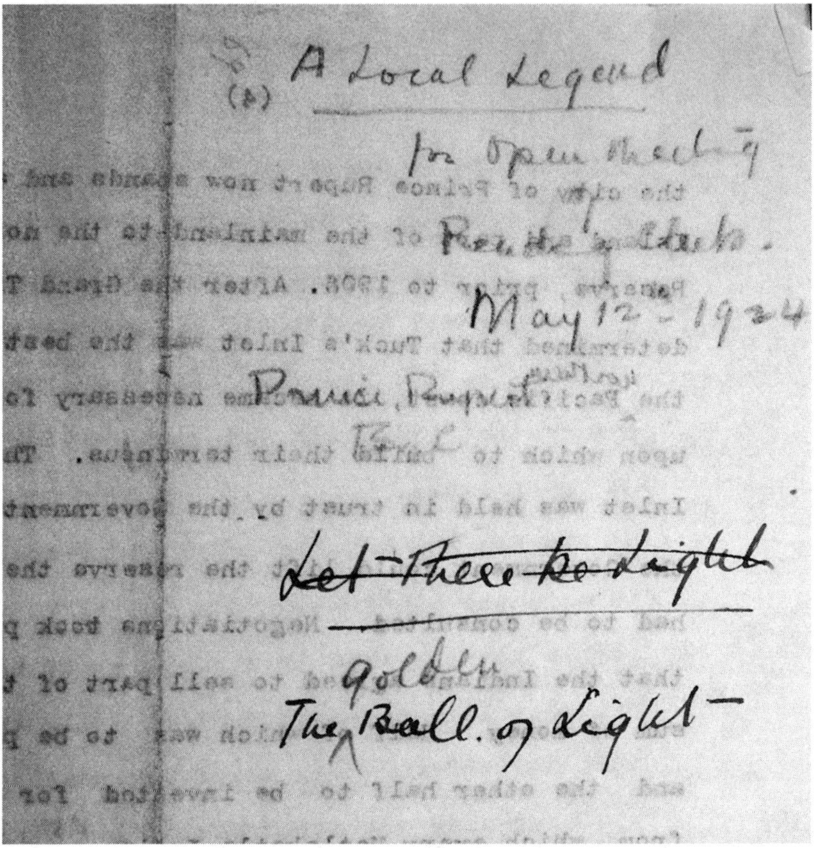

FIGURE 29. Du Vernet's "The Golden Ball of Light" manuscript (1924). Photograph courtesy of the Diocese of Caledonia Archives.

rytellers recount the story of Weeget/Raven and stories of the ancient origin of Prince Rupert as a way to establish both their sovereignty and their cosmology.[75]

In the 1950s, Ts'msyen ethnographer William Beynon told the story of Raven stealing the light in several anthropological publications. In 1959, the Kitwancool of the Nass River watershed recounted how one of their totem poles records the story of their ancestors' departure a thousand years ago from Ke-an, a village on the land where Prince Rupert now stands. Tlingit artist Preston Singletary's glass sculpture *Raven Steals the Sun* vividly tells the story at the *Our Universes* exhibit within the National Museum of the American Indian in Washington, DC. *Raven Brings the Light,* a children's book published in 2013, stunningly illustrated by Roy Henry Vickers, a man born in Laxgalts'ap, carries the story to a new generation of readers.[76]

Most remarkably, Patricia Vickers, in her PhD dissertation about the power of political and spiritual transformation generated by Ts'msyen ayaawx, tells many versions of the story of Txeemsim (or Weeget) in a manner that resonates profoundly with radio mind. Explaining that stories of Txeemsim bringing the light are stories of betrayal, creation, and the relief of suffering that belong to everyone and thus can be shared, Vickers also noted which elders gave her permission to tell the Txeemsim ayaawx. Calling on churches to pursue reconciliation through recognition of their wrongdoing and respectful engagement with Indigenous ancestral traditions, Vickers drew strong parallels between Christian and Ts'msyen views of the mind: "Harnessing the mind requires spiritual discipline through ritual practice." With words that could have come from *Spiritual Radio,* she continued: "Our thoughts and intentions are like a rock tossed into the water creating ripples on the surface of the water that extend outward impacting other living beings. To have intentions and thoughts that extend toward spiritual balance and peace can create transformation." For Vickers, however, thoughts must be bound with ceremony that "strengthens the heart" and refuses "the internalization of colonial delusions."[77]

Similarly attuned to the spiritual power of the mind, novelist Eden Robinson tells a new story of Wee'git in *Son of a Trickster*, her novel about a 'Namgis/Heiltsuk teenager finding his way in a family shaped by enduring spiritual lineages, the aftereffects of the violence of colonial dispossession and residential schools, and the precarious resource economies of northwestern British Columbia. As Jared faces animal spirits both curious and predatory, he slowly comes to grips with the knowledge that he is the son of Wee'git and a spiritually powerful mother, and he seeks to tame his own unbidden power to step out of his body and to communicate mind-to-mind. In order to survive, he must learn to accept what Robinson calls the "simultaneousity" of magic: "Think of magic as a tree. The root of supernatural ability is simply the realization that all time exists simultaneously."[78] These old and new tales of tricksters, cosmologies, and sovereignty demonstrate that stories circulate in cycles of memory, in which plots and heroes can be remapped, and spirits can rise and fall and rise again.

In rewriting the story of Weeget at the same time that he was venturing into the realm of radio mind, Du Vernet acknowledged the power of Ts'msyen maps and stories. His acknowledgment offers a twist on Nicholas May's assertion that the Anglican missionaries could not see the light as the Nisga'a did: "It is a testament to the utter opacity of Nisga'a symbols and metaphors to these missionaries that a religious culture that conceptualized the cosmos in terms of light and its many refractions should appear over and over in their writings under the phrase 'heathen darkness.'" May notes that many of the CMS missionaries, with their "low church" Evangelical anti-ritualism, "cast a suspicious eye on the symbols, rituals and metaphorical play employed by some within their own Church of England. The trickster Raven stood no chance with them, no matter how illuminating the light he carried in his beak."[79] Du Vernet's story, even with his failed renaming of the land and his futile attempt at a Christian ending, suggests that the trickster Raven did work his magic in the end.

Du Vernet thought Prince Rupert was his land, and he made Weeget his story. He traced the "faint resemblance" between Weeget and Christ, and then narrated how his very own name would obscure any memory of the trickster provoked by the land. Du Vernet participated in a practice of believing that spiritually imagined the reality of Canada with the help of the Dominion Hydrographic Survey, at the same time that he left behind a Ts'msyen story that would undercut and disrupt this very dominion. His was an ambivalent practice of believing that he enacted often in his life as a missionary. Though it is impossible to know definitively, perhaps Du Vernet told this story in part to confess to, and exonerate himself of, responsibility for negotiating the Kaien Island land grab. Writing down the story of Weeget so that he could tell it aloud to the people of his city, Du Vernet left behind a record that sheds light on his own ambivalent colonial spirit.

Maps were a mode of storytelling for the bishop and his fellow missionaries, as they worked to make their churches the centers of new colonial communities. The Nisga'a and the Ts'msyen, however, had their own "maps of sovereignty," a phrase that Perry Dane has used to depict the "multiple legal realities" that embed not only US and Canadian but also Indigenous jurisdictions in the land.[80] Putting the plurality of spirits back into the maps and the stories that literally made Canada demonstrates how maps mediated cosmological and capitalist visions of the land all at once. Reading these maps alongside the stories of missionaries, Ts'msyen, and Nisga'a suggests that the colonial spirit was one that rested its contested authority on Christian topologies that never successfully renamed those that were there first.

6
Printing Presses in the Promised Land

The lines of a map orient the mind by playing with scale, granting a bird's-eye view of the world, making faraway places into destinations. A printing press plays with letters and spaces, transforming trays of metal type into words that pull a reader into the mind of a writer. A slower medium than radio or the internet, print nevertheless has a powerful ability to transfer the thoughts and visions of one person to another. As objects that travel, maps and texts can find themselves in the hands of readers anywhere, calling on them to imagine new worlds. Telling a before-and-after story of a printing press that melted in a fiery blaze, this chapter follows Frederick Du Vernet in his relationship with one of his longest-serving missionary colleagues, the Irishman James Benjamin McCullagh, as they grappled with the promises and unexpected properties of print.

For its power to make stories mobile and proliferating, the printing press was a beloved tool of Protestant missionaries. As James McCullagh put it in a 1914 issue of the *North British Columbia News*: "I want you to give me an iron pulpit, one in which I can stand and speak, and preach and teach, and be heard over the whole valley, and even here in England. This iron pulpit is a printing press!"[1] A paper printed in England by Church Missionary Society (CMS) supporters and filled with stories by the missionaries of the Diocese of Caledonia, the *North British Columbia News* was the latest in a string of newsletters and papers that McCullagh had founded from his mission at Aiyansh on the Nass River. Some were printed locally by his mission printing press and others were printed in England, yet all these publications prominently featured news of McCullagh in his ongoing attempts to convert the Nisga'a of the Nass Valley. Unable to fully control McCullagh's voluminous and often vainglorious print production, Bishop Du Vernet sometimes found himself at odds with the missionary and his fondness for the printing press, but he could not do without either of them.

Frederick Du Vernet had little of the brashness of his Irish colleague, but after his many years as an editor of the *Canadian Church Missionary Gleaner*, he also recognized the power of print. He knew that a daily discipline of writing stories that traveled around the world on paper was what kept the "missionary writing machine" chugging along. As bishop, Du Vernet spent much of his time traveling to the villages and towns of his diocese as the "chief pastor" to his missionaries and lay people, writing about his visits after the fact. Recounting in December 1906 a more than four-week visit across the Hecate Strait to the Haida mission at Massett, he described his approach: "I find it a good plan to stay long enough in a mission to thoroughly enter into the life of the people so as to be able to understand the conditions which prevail."[2] He visited every family in the village, going door to door with the resident missionary, William E. Collison. The son of longtime CMS missionary William Henry Collison, W. E. Collison had grown up on the northwest coast, spoke fluent Sm'algyax, and was learning the Haida language.

Du Vernet depended on the young man to translate for him, since he could not speak the Haida language himself. With his photographic eye and his language inability, he no doubt appreciated Collison's approach to telling the gospel story with not only words but also pictures: "At the Thursday evening prayer-meeting a Scripture picture is thrown upon the street by a fine lantern and one of the natives taught by Mr. Collison gives an address upon the subject. The average attendance is about 90 and the people seem to thoroughly enjoy the meeting."[3] Collison likely displayed not only scriptural stories but also photographs of Indigenous Christians. Lantern slides housed in the Diocese of Caledonia archives include an ecce homo image, produced in England, depicting a very white Jesus crowned with thorns, blood dripping from his forehead (fig. 30). They also include locally produced images of missionaries and Indigenous people, including a wedding couple posing outside of a church and the Indian Land Committee assembled at Aiyansh (plates 4–5). Collison and his Haida coworkers made clever use of the medium of light to tell a story. McCullagh, however, was fully committed to paper, so much so that he brought not one but two printing presses to the Nass Valley.

Despite McCullagh's and Du Vernet's optimistic writings in missionary newsletters, the growing Nisga'a "unrest" on the Nass River, channeled through letters, oral stories, and printed protests, pressed on the minds of both men. Two men living far from the lands of their birth, the missionaries' answers to the Indian Land Question were not always consistent or coherent. In their uncertainty, they depended on media that could tell stories close up

FIGURE 30. An ecce homo lantern slide (ca. 1910s?). Photograph courtesy of the Diocese of Caledonia Archives.

and broadcast them afar in order to make spiritual political claims that they hoped would turn their new promised land into Christian territory. That they could look on the rivers, mountains, and lava beds of the Nisga'a "valley of eternal bloom" as lands promised to them was a conviction born out of a Christian story of evangelization combined with an evolutionary story of white supremacy.[4]

Emboldened by the white possessive, the missionaries understood that being white men gave them a peculiar ability to *hold* property as legal subjects of the British Empire and to *take* the land of Indigenous peoples, by way of printed deeds that asserted their ownership. Theirs was an anxious possession, however, thanks to their awareness of what the Nisga'a had clearly spelled out for them in person and in print: "We never will admit that our ancest[o]rs possessed no right or title to these lands simply because there was no White man on hand to give them a title."[5] Papers that mapped possession were not enough to truly claim Nisga'a land, and the missionaries knew this.

Indigenous Print

Long heralded as one of the secrets to success of Martin Luther and other Protestant reformers, the printing press made a new scale of mass communication possible in the sixteenth century. Printers published everything from vernacular biblical translations to sermons to pamphlets decrying the power of the pope or the wealthy, landed elite. The printing press mobilized spiritual political movements across Europe. At the same time, some scholars have argued, the printing press created a spirit of "epistemic Protestantism" in which solitary, silent practices of reading helped make individualism both a symbolic virtue and a moral practice. As literacy increased among Christians, reading and writing became fundamental ways to know the self and to change the self. Some missionaries considered biblical tracts to have the power to heal would-be converts, even if they could not read.[6]

Protestants were especially diligent in making the most of the printed word and image as a vehicle for producing and circulating testimonies of Christians, both Indigenous and settler. They used global networks of print and distribution to build imperial "imagined communities" that framed North America as a site for conversion and settlement. Missionary networks of print culture intersected with colonial networks of power; they were didactic media overflowing with instructions for feeling colonial and Christian. They also firsted the settlers and lasted the "Indians" out of the story.[7]

For a missionary to set up a printing press on Indigenous land, however, cooperation was usually required. Just as with language translation, there was no way for missionaries to work with the heavy machinery of a press or to print in the languages of Indigenous peoples without their help. Print "became Indigenous" to the Americas through the labor of Indigenous peoples, as the Aiyansh printers, including Paul Mercer and Charles Morven, exemplified. McCullagh acknowledged the Nisga'a men who worked with him, but considered himself the printer in charge. A 1900 issue of the Aiyansh-produced *Caledonia Interchange* spelled out McCullagh's conviction that the spiritual must be "materialized" and the material must be "spiritualized" in the work of the missionary. He argued that missionaries were "spiritual agents engaged in a spiritual work which can only be accomplished by spiritual means," but they also needed to embrace the "monotonous routine of work" that characterized the missionary's day as a teacher, medic, and printer.[8]

McCullagh was not alone in materializing his missionary printing dreams. Just to the east in Athapaskan and Cree language territory, Catholic missionary Father Émile Grouard worked on printing in Cree syllabics and English at almost the same time that McCullagh was printing Nisga'a texts in Latin characters on the Nass River. Across the world in New Zealand, Anglican missionaries also turned to print with a colonial spirit. In his revealing work on the role of missionary print culture in the Treaty of Waitangi, D. F. McKenzie argued that missionaries considered printing as "the one instrument thought essential to give instant and local effect to universal literacy as the principal means to personal salvation." He noted how Bible reading eventually became a "new source of imagery in song and story" as well as a source for economic and political critique for the Maori. For Anglicans, this bookish imagery extended to the ritual manual of the Book of Common Prayer, which served as a guide for when to pray, when to sing, when to stand, and when to just sit and listen during a church service.[9] Making the printed word an article of faith whether in the form of a Bible or a treaty, the British Empire was built on a textual cosmology that claimed land through words on paper.

The printing press, however, was not a spiritual medium with one voice. For both missionaries and anti-colonial spiritual leaders, such as Gandhi, the printing press was a spiritual medium that spoke across distance, sending powerful words around the world. The Nisga'a shared this anti-colonial faith in the power of the printing press to assert their claims to a land that their creator had promised to them "since time immemorial." At the same time, they also continued to claim land through totem poles; as Nisga'a chief Azak put it to anthropologist Marius Barbeau in 1929, the totem pole was "just like a history writing" that told the story of Nisga'a families, territories, and traditions.[10]

The Burning of the Iron Pulpit

In 1883, the London-based Church Missionary Society sent the Irish-born James McCullagh to the Nass Valley to establish an Anglican mission upriver from Metlakatla. A Tlingit word, "Nass" translates to "food depot," which accurately describes the plentiful eulachon and salmon in the river. The Nisga'a who live on the Nass also know the river by a different name: K'alii Aksim Lisims, or "the murky river." In the Nisga'a adaawak of Txeemsim the

FIGURE 31. Mary Melita McCullagh (b. 1885). Photograph courtesy of the Royal British Columbia Museum and Archives (B-07593).

trickster, not only did he bring light to the world but he also journeyed along the river sharing his wisdom with all those he met.[11]

The missionaries, for their part, saw the land through a biblical story that promised it not to the Nisga'a but to them. For example, the new editors of *Across the Rockies*, a monthly founded in London in 1910 to support Anglican missions across the province of British Columbia, crowed: "The prize is ours, a land flowing with milk and honey, truly a goodly heritage. The obligation is imposed upon us of this generation of winning this land in the name of our Blessed Lord."[12] Always taking seriously the "British" in British Columbia, these editors drew confidence that this promised land was theirs to win thanks to both God and King.

James and Mary McCullagh arrived on the Nass River late in the summer of 1883. Mary gave birth to their daughter, Melita, in 1885, and the family lived side by side with their Nisga'a neighbors. Nisga'a men, women, and children taught the McCullaghs to speak their language; Mary, James,

FIGURE 32. James McCullagh (1907). From *North British Columbia News* (McCullagh tribute issue, August 1921). Photograph courtesy of the Archives of the Provincial Synod of British Columbia and Yukon.

and Melita taught them English in return (figs. 31–32). In 1893, McCullagh received his first printing press, a gift from the Church of England's Society for the Promotion of Christian Knowledge. Likely an Albion, the press was a one-ton mass of iron that journeyed from England and became his trusted companion.[13]

The eager missionary learned to use the press along with a group of young Nisga'a men whom he called—in print—"McCullagh's Indian Boys." In the Nisga'a understanding of community, most of these young men were among those expected to take up chiefly names as they grew older. Two of these printers, Paul Mercer and Charles Morven, would also take up roles as clergy in the Anglican Church. Together, McCullagh and the Nisga'a printers published translations of the Bible into Nisga'amk̲, the Nisga'a language, as well as school primers, hymnals, and chats—perky encouragements—for the scattered white settlers of what McCullagh thought of as his parish. They

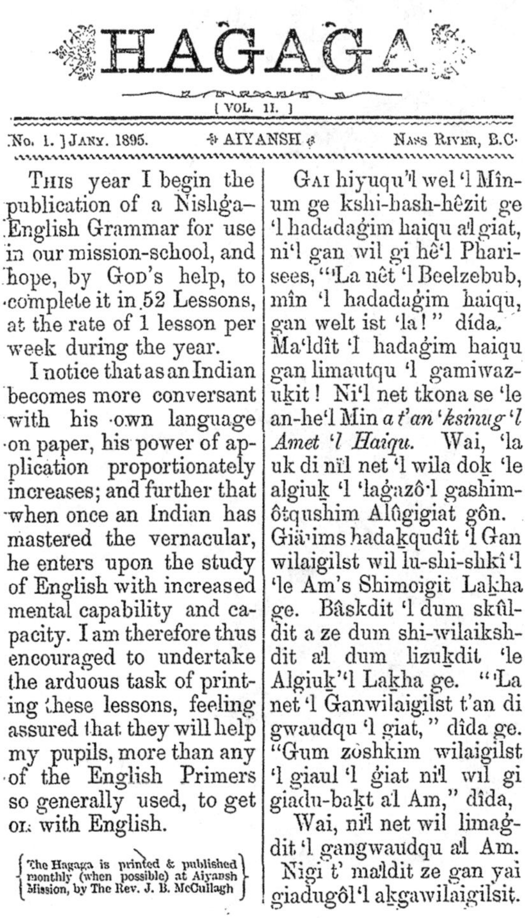

HAGAGA

[VOL. II.]

No. 1.] JANY. 1895. AIYANSH NASS RIVER, B.C.

THIS year I begin the publication of a Nishga–English Grammar for use in our mission-school, and hope, by GOD's help, to complete it in 52 Lessons, at the rate of 1 lesson per week during the year.

I notice that as an Indian becomes more conversant with his own language on paper, his power of application proportionately increases; and further that when once an Indian has mastered the vernacular, he enters upon the study of English with increased mental capability and capacity. I am therefore thus encouraged to undertake the arduous task of printing these lessons, feeling assured that they will help my pupils, more than any of the English Primers so generally used, to get on with English.

{The Hagaga is printed & published monthly (when possible) at Aiyansh Mission, by The Rev. J. B. McCullagh}

GAI hiyuqu'l wel 'l Mînum ge kshi-bash-hêzit ge 'l hadadaġim haiqu a'l giat, ni'l gan wil gi hê'l Pharisees, "'La nêt 'l Beelzebub, mîn 'l hadadaġim haiqu, gan welt ist 'la!" dída. Ma'ldît 'l hadaġim haiqu gan limautqu 'l gamiwazukit! Ni'l net tkona se 'le an-he'l Min *a t'an 'ksinug 'l Amet 'l Haiqu.* Wai, 'la uk di nïl net 'l wila dok 'le algiuk 'l 'laġazô'l gashimôtqushim Alûgigiat gôn. Giä'ims hadakqudît 'l Gan wilaigilst wil lu-shi-shkî 'l 'le Am's Shimoigit Lakha ge. Bâskdit 'l dum skûldit a ze dum shi-wilaikshdit a'l dum lizukdit 'le Algiuk''l Lakha ge. "'La net 'l Ganwilaigilst t'an di gwaudqu 'l giat," dîda ge. "Gum zoshkim wilaigilst 'l giaul 'l ġiat ni'l wil gi giadu-bakt a'l Am," dîda,

Wai, ni'l net wil limaġdit 'l gangwaudqu a'l Am.

Nigi t' ma'ldit ze gan yai giadugôl'l akgawilaigilsit.

FIGURE 33. *Hagaga*, vol. 2, no. 1 (January 1895). Photograph courtesy of the Royal British Columbia Museum and Archives (NWp 970.81 H 141).

also published *Hagaga: The Indian's Own Newspaper*, a bilingual English-Nisga'amk̲ newspaper, remembered now for its role in publishing the Indian Land Committee's strong views against white settlement of Nisga'a land, often mediated via McCullagh's commentary and interviewing techniques (fig. 33).[14]

In addition to *Hagaga*, McCullagh and the Nisga'a printers founded several other newsletters printed in Aiyansh, including the *Caledonia Interchange* and the *Trail Cruiser*. For McCullagh, publishing "local color" on his printing press was essential for missions both to white men and to the Nisga'a: "The Indians would benefit indirectly; for, while they might be indifferent in regard to what I printed for them and just take it for granted, they will never rest until they know every word of what I am saying to the white man. I shall print as time allows little CHATS by the way and mail the same with a type-written, friendly epistle to each [white] man just to say 'How do you do?' or 'Keep your pecker up,' etc." For McCullagh, the printing press was an everyday means of community building among the dispersed, mostly male, settlers moving to the Nass Valley. In a 1913 appeal to settlers in the *North British Columbia News*, McCullagh even hinted at a barter system, exchanging preaching for printing: "Meanwhile, you will have to put up with canned preaching, but I promise you they shall be good and fresh, straight from my own printing press. And this reminds me, if any of you want a little printing done I shall be glad to help you out."[15] McCullagh truly lived through a textual cosmology that saw words on paper as a medium for gifts of the spirit.

In May 1910, *Hagaga* featured an interview between McCullagh and three chiefly members of the Nisga'a Land Committee, A. M. Nahnegh, S. A. Zeedawit, and J. S. Nakmauz. The men clearly stated their objection to white settlement of their land, referring to both the "King's law" and biblical examples of justice to press their claim:

> We want to be free on our own land. We don't want to be restricted to the reserve. If we want to make a salmon trap in a certain stream, we expect to be free to do it—just as our ancesters [*sic*] did. If we want to cut timber for building purposes or firewood, we do not expect to have to go and buy a license to do so. We have always made these demands; we never will admit that our ancesters possessed no right or title to these lands simply because there was no White man on hand to give them a title: From time immemorial they inhabited these lands, they took possession of them, they held them against all enemies, they divided them up into family estates, and each family held its own estate against every other, and passed it on by tradition to the next heir, who always had to establish his title in public by means of the law known as the "Yuqu." And now the White man comes along and says to the Indian, "Who are you? What are you doing here? Get out!" We see what the reserve means—it is intended to be a prison-house for us.

Not convinced that the Canadian government walked and talked the true law of the King, the Nisga'a insisted that God was on their side: "We believe our case to be strong because God hates injustice. We know He is on our side because we are oppressed. We can put our case into His hands, but the government cannot commit their policy to Him. God says, 'Cursed is he that removeth his neighbor's landmark.'"[16] Combining the authority of the "Yuqu," or settlement feast (what the law would call the potlatch), with the law of the King and of God, the Nisga'a argument layered traditional, church, and colonial authority and sent it out into the world from their printing press.

A few months later, when a fire swept through the mission house in

September 1910, McCullagh's first iron pulpit melted in the blaze. He was plunged into a dark night of the soul. Writing of his first press with intimate affection, he attributed to the machine human and spiritual powers:

> The loss of my printing outfit and my books touches me closer than the loss of the buildings. I felt as though a lifelong colleague in my work had been suddenly taken away from me. One evening in the Church, while keeping vigil there, I asked the Lord about the printing press, but received no definite assurance. The people were at the time assembled in the town hall at a supper given by one of the chiefs, and the subject of my printing press formed the basis of their postprandial conversation. The dish went round and 65 dollars were collected on the spot. This was handed to me next day, and I received it as the Lord's answer to my inquiry.[17]

Whether the chief's supper was a traditional feast McCullagh does not say. He does, however, divinely triangulate the Nisga'a gift to give the credit to the Christian god, and not to Nisga'a generosity provoked by feasting. Donations from the Nisga'a, the Society for the Propagation of Christian Knowledge, and lay supporters in England funded the purchase of the community presses, but McCullagh preferred to think of them as gifts directly to him from God.

Not long after the fire, a disease struck Aiyansh, yet another scourge in a long series of colonial-era epidemics. In response, the Nisga'a turned again to their tradition of *yukw*, or settlement feasts, to mark the passing of their kin. McCullagh despaired over the double blow of what he considered to be a backsliding revival of feasting and the loss of his printing press. He retreated into the church for solitary, nocturnal conversations with his god (fig. 34). In these midnight prayer vigils, McCullagh pleaded and argued until he became convinced that God wanted him to ask for another iron pulpit. He did so in an appeal to readers through the *North British Columbia News* (fig. 35).[18]

The loss of his printing press challenged McCullagh's certainty about his holiness and his mission, but also heightened his faith in the text as a tool of transformation. During his 1910 vigil in the wake of the fire, he robed himself in his vestments and confessed his fears to God that his work had come to naught:

> It was 7 p.m. on a dark December night, the temperature fifteen or more degrees below zero, and the whole village had gone up to the feast. . . . I proceeded alone to the Church, where I put on my robes and entered the chancel, my solitary light looking like a ghostly star in the piled-up gloom. . . . Very fully

FIGURE 34. Holy Trinity Church, Aiyansh (ca. 1900). Photograph courtesy of the Royal British Columbia Museum and Archives (B-07594).

> did I realize that this was not just taking things to the Lord in prayer. I cannot well describe it or define the act, but I understood, and I knew the Lord would understand that, as His servant, I had come to the end of the ordinary means and resources placed in my hands. It was a wonderful passage in one's ministerial and spiritual life, and would be kept secret as well as sacred in my own breast if it were not that the glory of God demands the telling.[19]

Retrospectively narrating the events to his reader, McCullagh faced the dilemma of Christian testimony, displaying a twinge of self-consciousness for revealing such spiritually intimate details. He quickly patched over his worries with recourse to God's demand for testimony.

FIGURE 35. James McCullagh's "Iron Pulpit." From *North British Columbia News* (July 1914). Photograph courtesy of the Archives of the Provincial Synod of British Columbia and Yukon.

McCullagh then described a process of mystical reading in which God quizzed him on biblical interpretations. Despite not always providing the right answer, McCullagh was cleansed of doubt: "The Lord answered me fully and questioned and examined me closely on every point, all by means of the written Word, the Spirit applying it and throwing light upon it in my soul. I replied too, and pleaded also the written Word. But some of my pleadings were denied and plainly shown to me to be based on false assumptions. . . . There was no doubt left in my mind—the enemy was already driven back, beaten, discomfited!" Practicing what he saw as a kind of spiritual warfare, McCullagh considered his prayer and God's biblical response via "the written word" to have directly transformed from afar the behavior of the Nisga'a, causing them to abandon feasting.[20]

McCullagh chose a particularly textual ritual of repentance for each of his parishioners. After a personal interview with him in the church, he required them to stand up in front of the congregation to read aloud their individual confessions: "Each penitent had an interview with me in the vestry before the Service, and a list was drawn up for public announcement, together with a short statement from each, of his or her intention to lead a new life. This was read after the sermon, from the chancel steps, the penitents standing before me. The congregation was then asked to unite with me in prayer for the strengthening of these weak brethren. Sometimes the nature of a case demanded public admonition or some definite instruction, and these were delivered there at the time." Christmas arrived with "the wayward flock safely folded again," but nevertheless McCullagh refused to allow the church to be decorated in its customary finery, insisting instead that the "purple hangings" of Good Friday mourning be displayed.[21] McCullagh tried to force Christmas itself into submission.

This ritual of repentance was a process of reconciliation in the Christian sense: the Nisga'a confessed to their priest and he absolved them of their sins. The Christian ritual was overlaid with colonial legal force, since McCullagh was both priest and magistrate. He judged them for their supposed sins in the eyes of God as well as for their breaking of the anti-potlatch law in the eyes of the state.

The act of a person reading aloud his or her confession in a church is profoundly different from the experience of telling stories at a feast. Writing about present-day Ts'msyen traditions, Margaret Seguin Anderson and Tammy Anderson Blumhagen argue that Ts'msyen people have an aversion to confessional disclosure that stems in part from the protocols of the feast. In contrast to an overt confession of sins, the Ts'msyen feast offers the ritual and social space in which one can address one's shame or guilt without necessarily explicitly stating it: "When someone is publicly shamed s/he might 'wash' by giving a feast and distributing property, but once this is done it 'shuts the mouths' of the witnesses, and closes the topic for good."[22] In a way then, the feast is the opposite of the confessional—instead of an individual disclosure of wrongdoing, the gesture that soothes discord is a communal ritual of gift giving.

In addition to the feast, the totem pole also posed cosmological challenges for McCullagh. His biographer provided one final example of a material proof for the spiritual conversion of the Nisga'a after the fire in the mission house: "Very wonderful were some of the answers received for petitions offered at the throne of grace. A leading heathen chief named Nis Yog, at Gitlakdamiks, openly abjured heathenism and avowed his faith in the Lord Christ. He proved the reality of his new confession by cutting down his totem pole. In doing so he said: 'No man has talked to me about this, but the Spirit of God has put it into my heart this day.'" This was a new confession with potentially devastating social and political consequences: for "Nis Yog" to cut down his totem pole was to cut down the story of his house of Niysyok, part of the Wolf Clan, and its testament to the Niysyok claim to terrority.[23] If the anti-potlatch law sought to deny Indigenous peoples the ability and right to claim and transfer political leadership and territorial jurisdictions, the missionary who encouraged the felling of totem poles also sought to banish adaawak in order to rewrite history and the future. Totem poles are not built to last forever—old ones are meant to decay in their own time, as new ones are built to keep the story alive. But to chop down a totem pole was an act of violence to family, clan, and story.

But perhaps the testimony of Niysyok—who is called Peter Niosyog in a 1927 photograph by anthropologist Marius Barbeau (fig. 36)—can be read in another light, as Nicholas May suggests. Niysyok, at least according to McCullagh's biographer, shared with McCullagh a conviction of the power of the spirit to change the world: his drastic step to cut down his totem pole did not come about because of any "talking" from McCullagh but was directly inspired by the "Spirit of God." According to May, in the wake of the disease that had struck the community, Niysyok's felling of his totem was a gesture to halt the dying, thus pursuing "a very Nisga'a end, namely the preservation of one's House."[24] He still wore the chiefly authority of his name in 1927, and the House of Niysyok still exists today.

Totem poles and their complex significance for the Nisga'a continued to pose interpretive challenges for missionaries. Oliver Thorne, the missionary who succeeded McCullagh at Gitlakdamiks in 1921, also prematurely claimed victory over the totem pole. In the January 1922 issue of the *North British Columbia News*, he described Chief Timothy Derrick's use of a cut-up pole for the foundation posts of his new house: "I will get you a picture of Timothy's house with the totems supporting it like a lot of idols. It is a sign that the totem has lost what significance it ever had, when a chief will cut up his family totem into short lengths for props for his house."[25] The promised picture seems not to have made it to the newspaper, but a Marius Barbeau photograph from 1927 suggests that even when placed on their sides as fenceposts, totem poles told striking stories (fig. 37).

Though McCullagh urged the Nisga'a to cut down their totem poles, he did not necessarily profit from selling them to museums. In both 1905 and 1911, William and Charles Newcombe, a father-and-son team of collectors who worked for museums including the British Museum, the Royal Ontario Museum, and the Field Museum in Chicago, offered him payment for totem poles. In 1911, he politely refused, not out of moral scruples, but for more pragmatic reasons: "No individual Indian has the exclusive right over a totem pole, and although many of the Indians would, perhaps, like to sell, yet they are deterred by fear of the other members of the crest." Ever ingenious, he had a solution that involved not money but a kind of barter exchanging one

FIGURE 36. Peter Niosyog wearing his chief headdress, Gitlardamks (Gitlakdamix) (1927). Photography by Marius Barbeau. Photograph courtesy of the Canadian Museum of History (69682).

form of memorial for another: "I have an idea that if the pole were exchanged for a grave-stone it would solve the problem." McCullagh knew that totem poles continued to have meaning for the Nisga'a, even if he didn't want them to.[26]

McCullagh took explicit ritual steps to make testimony into an individual-

FIGURE 37. Totem pole turned into fence post, Aiyansh (1927). Photography by Marius Barbeau. Photograph courtesy of the Canadian Museum of History (69657).

ized, not clan-based process, in both Christian and legal senses of testimony. When a Nisga'a man or woman confessed in the presence of McCullagh, he or she offered a testimony before the power of the Christian god and the power of the Canadian state. Even the Indian agent noted how eagerly McCullagh used this combined spiritual and political power: "He is as familiar with their language and characteristics as a native; he has been, and is to-day, a power among these people; he has been their truest friend, guardian and protector, but in dealing out justice in his capacity as magistrate he has no mercy for the offender." When attacking the potlatch or the totem pole, McCullagh was trying to shift the Nisga'a storytelling self away from communal adaawak and into individual confession mediated through the written word.[27]

Stories for Cash

McCullagh and Du Vernet, like all Protestant missionaries, were under a constant burden to read, write, and publish. Shaped by what Gail Edwards has called "textual communities," missionaries in British Columbia were expected to write frequent and eloquent testimonies of their exploits well laced with biblical references, to read books and carry them on their travels, and, for the university-educated, to have knowledge of Greek and Latin.[28] McCullagh, though not university-trained, liberally sprinkled his prose with French and Greek; Du Vernet jotted in Greek and Hebrew in his notebooks. When missionaries, Du Vernet and McCullagh included, sent a telegram to CMS headquarters in London, the telegraphic address was none other than "testimony."

A missionary's success depended on his or her ability to tell a good story, especially in print. They had to compel their readers—both adults and children—to cultivate zeal, ardor, and an overwhelming love for the supposed "heathen," which would then ideally impel the reader to give generous and continued donations.[29] Physically speaking, a missionary testimony, whether from the Pacific northwest or the central hills of India, usually had to be written or typed on paper and then travel via a postal system to the "sending country," which in the case of the CMS was England. The story was then printed in newsletters and journals by missionary supporters in England, and mailed monthly or semiannually to audiences of adults and children throughout the Commonwealth. Some missionaries, McCullagh included, sought to bypass this publication cycle to retain more local control and local color, but even McCullagh depended on and cultivated publishing relationships with missionary societies in the metropole.

Printed and reprinted again and again, missionary writings circulated in an international network of print culture that was crucial to maintaining the financial solvency of their work. Part of a system which Christopher Bracken has cleverly called "postal colonial," Christian missionary testimony traveled through the mail in an exchange of stories for cash. As with the social complexity of the feasting system, the exchange involved in missionary testimony was never a "direct ask." One of McCullagh's greatest supporters in England, Mrs. Foquett, facilitated the stories-for-money exchange most delicately: "She did not ask people directly for money, but she used to transcribe McCullagh's long letters home, sending them round the circle of her friends and, except for the prayers that followed them, leaving these to make their own appeal to the hearts of the readers." In addition to circulating McCullagh's testimonies, Mrs. Foquett also gifted him with a "precious Jaeger dressing-gown," a classic English-designed, camel's hair robe, which blanketed McCullagh as he left Aiyansh as a sick, elderly man in 1920. In return for her considerable support, McCullagh gifted Mrs. Foquett by naming a street after her in the village of Aiyansh.[30]

The missionaries were not the only ones extracting stories for money on the northwest coast. Where missionaries gathered stories as "spiritual" resources, anthropologists collected them as "ethnographic data." Anthropologists such as Franz Boas and Edward Sapir visited Prince Rupert and the Nass Valley to record stories and Indigenous languages, document petroglyphs, and collect artifacts. They also paid their "informants" to write down their stories and send them to New York or Ottawa, and took advantage of the travel schedules of their Indigenous correspondents. For example, Edward Sapir gathered some of his Nisga'a "terms of relationship"—or the words the Nisga'a used to establish bonds of kinship in their community—from Nisga'a leaders visiting Ottawa in 1920 on "tribal business." Active in the Nisga'a land movement, Chief C. B. Barton of Kincolith and Chief P. C. Calder of Lakkalzap both consulted with Sapir while in Ottawa to argue their cause.[31]

The line between the spiritual and the ethnographic story was sometimes hard to draw. In 1887, McCullagh described for readers of the *Church Missionary Gleaner* how "Indian medicine men" on the Nass River diagnosed and cured the problem of another medicine man who had "inadvertently swallowed [a] sick man's soul at dinner!" A quick cycle of circulation followed: republished in an Alaskan newspaper in 1888, McCullagh's story caught the eye of an editor in the *Journal of American Folklore* who reprinted it again in 1889. More than twenty years later, McCullagh's tale of the medicine men, at once mocking and ethnographic, was selected by the legendary anthropologist James Frazer as an example of "the perils of the soul" and included in the third volume of *The Golden Bough*. Frazer the anthropologist chided McCullagh the missionary for lacking clarity in his account, but cited him nonetheless. Once in print, stories about Indigenous people circulated as evidence for both missionaries and anthropologists who sought to embed the souls of "native races" in their own textual accounts.[32]

Just as anthropologists sought to record Indigenous languages, so too did missionaries try to testify and write in more than one language. They were expected by their English-speaking superiors to deliver sermons in the Indigenous language of their mission, and their colleagues tested them on their competence. In 1883, when sent out by the CMS to Aiyansh, McCullagh received specific instructions: "It is always your principal object to set forth before them the wonderful words of God in their own tongue wherein they were born." This requirement of linguistic competency meant that missionaries were highly dependent on Indigenous teachers, including women such as Odille Morison, the Ts'msyen translator from Metlakatla.[33]

Missionaries acted with linguistic competence and incompetence in various ways. CMS Secretary Rev. Baring Baring-Gould, ensconced in faraway London, was a man with an upper-class name and a great deal of power over the CMS missionaries. He chastised William E. Collison, the missionary who had made innovative use of lantern slides, for his poor grasp of the Haida language. Du Vernet gently suggested to Baring-Gould a solution to this problem: "Mr. Collison seems to speak the Haida language fairly well. It seems almost a pity that when he can speak the Coast dialects so well (Tsimshian, Nishga, Kitkshian) that he should be in the one mission in the diocese where there is a totally different language."[34] Despite Du Vernet's wise counsel, Baring-Gould refused to post Collison to a mission where he could make use of his fluency.

For his part, Frederick Du Vernet seems not to have learned Sm'algyax, Nisga'amk̲, or Haida with any fluency. Since he arrived on the northwest coast at the beginning of large-scale white settlement and was appointed as a bishop who traveled among people who spoke many different Indigenous languages, perhaps language learning seemed impractical to him. He did, however, seem to appreciate linguistic diversity, translating words from various Indigenous languages in his notebooks and repeatedly requesting funds from the missionary societies in London and Toronto to support a Japanese-speaking missionary for the Japanese community in Prince Rupert. Noting that he could not count on local donations "owing to the strong feeling against the Asiatics getting a stranglehold over this Province," he reported with pride that in 1918, Mr Z. Higashi and his wife had set up a Japanese mission in Prince Rupert. By 1923, Du Vernet had secured funds to purchase land for the St. Andrew's Japanese Mission Hall, drawing in part from a bequest that his sister Fanny Gibbons had left him in her will (fig. 38).[35]

FIGURE 38. Japanese mission, Prince Rupert (ca. 1923). Du Vernet is in the middle row, standing fourth from the left. Photograph courtesy of the Diocese of Caledonia Archives.

The Cost of White Work

Nisga'a and missionaries both found whiteness to be a useful but hazardous categorization, whether protesting settlement or bifurcating missions between "Indians" and "whites." As Du Vernet put it plainly in a "history of the diocese" published in *Across the Rockies* in 1912: "There were only these three churches [Port Essington, Port Simpson, and Atlin] for white people when the present Bishop came to the diocese in 1904." The other churches, it went without saying, were for "Indians." In early twentieth-century British Columbia, the government project of taking Indigenous land and peopling it with white settlers had radically changed the field of missionary labor.[36] In drawing the line between missions of "white work" and "Indian work" and differentially valuing the two, the church underscored the story of the white possessive, but it also was sending a message to its supporters in eastern Canada and England.

The pressure to gain donors within the Diocese of Caledonia intensified as its "racial mission" slowly shifted to one of cultivating whiteness. For most of the nineteenth century, Anglican missionaries and bishops in British Columbia were paid by two British missionary societies, both of which spanned the empire. The Society for the Propagation of the Gospel (SPG), with its high church orientation, considered bishops to be essential to missionary endeavor—no missionaries could practice without a bishop who was leader of the flock and treasurer in chief. The SPG paid for missions by giving a "block grant" to the bishop, who would then disperse the funds to his diocese, to Indigenous missions or settler churches. By contrast, the Evangelical, low church Church Missionary Society (CMS) paid missionaries directly and wanted its money to go only to the conversion of so-called heathens. In the racialized cosmology of the CMS, this meant only Indian work and not white work would be supported.[37]

These different models of funding had important consequences for Du Vernet's job as chief accountant, in addition to being chief pastor, of the diocese. The SPG block grant could go to the greatest need, as decided by the bishop. For example, if the Nisga'a of Aiyansh had raised all the necessary money to build their Holy Trinity Church—which they did—the bishop could funnel SPG money to a new settler church along the railway instead (fig. 39). By contrast, the CMS "was distinctively an organization for preaching the Gospel to the heathen and not a Pastoral Aid Society."[38] If the missionaries were too successful and all the so-called heathens became Christians,

FIGURE 39. Construction of Holy Trinity Church, Aiyansh (ca. 1890s). Photograph courtesy of the Royal British Columbia Museum and Archives (B-07648).

the CMS could remove itself from northern British Columbia and spend its money elsewhere.

As McCullagh and Du Vernet regularly pointed out in great detail in their articles in church and missionary association publications, the Diocese of Caledonia was undergoing a financial crisis because its missionaries had been too successful—or more accurately, because they had told an overly convincing success story of their conversion of the Nisga'a, Ts'msyen, and Haida (their stories of converting the Gitxsan were never as triumphantly certain). McCullagh often made declarations that would suggest the goal of the CMS had been achieved: in 1905, he boasted to his supporters in England that "*there is not a heathen left on the Naas at this date*!"[39]

McCullagh's main response to ongoing financial pressures was to establish his own local publishing empire with the help of the Nisga'a printers and to develop a flurry of new transatlantic publishing networks. While on furlough in England in 1907, he founded yet another newsletter focused on his work, to be published and distributed by a group of supporters in England called the Nishga Union. This newsletter, *Aiyansh Notes*, featured McCullagh as its main correspondent. Prominent in almost every newsletter were tales of McCullagh's missionary labors in the form of letters, poems, or articles written by him.

McCullagh was well aware of the power of stories and his own need for producing them as a missionary. Explicitly conscious of rhetorical suasion, McCullagh crafted a narrative of his challenges and triumphs framed by the grace of God that depended on a confessional kernel of "personality." Reflecting on the qualifications of a preaching missionary, he asked: "Can he be convincing and at the same time entertaining? Can he elicit sympathy, without appealing for it? Can he infuse the spirit of sacrifice and show the glory of it? His story is only a means to an end and, be it long or short, unique or commonplace, he must reach that end—must reach it by force, by the force of his own personality. Poor missionary! He may never have given a thought to his little bit of personality, and yet—what would his story be without it?"[40] McCullagh hit the dilemma of confessional production on the nose: how to revel in sacrifice and glorify the Lord without losing one's self in the process.

McCullagh insisted that a missionary—even one with personality—must not work for worldly glory but as a slave to Christ. Describing his need to spend long nights writing and translating—since the days were too filled with "interruptions from the Indians"—McCullagh exulted, "I slaved and slaved. Yes, I glory in the word Slave of Jesus Christ. Paul exclaimed with joy *doulos eimi* [I am a slave], and it is with joy and thankfulness for the privilege that I also cry *doulos eimi*. It rings like music in my ears; it thrills me; it buoys me up amid the waves of discouragement, more than does the hope of glory. I crave not for glory." McCullagh, however, comfortably wielded power, if not glory, as both missionary and magistrate for Aiyansh and surrounding communities.[41]

While satisfying McCullagh's seemingly inexhaustible need to share the details of his life with the world, *Aiyansh Notes* did not please Bishop Du Vernet or the other missionaries in the diocese. In 1909, Du Vernet requested that the Nishga Union expand the paper into the *North British Columbia News*, to avoid a narrow focus on Aiyansh, McCullagh's mission, in particular.[42] The market grew even more crowded when yet another new London-based missionary publication, *Across the Rockies*, was founded in 1910. Established by the new British Columbia Church Aid Society, which was supported by the high church SPG, the newsletter was to provide coverage of the entire mission field of British Columbia. *Across the Rockies* hoped to further tame McCullagh's charisma and the dominance of Caledonia as a magnet for British donations by making the Diocese of Caledonia just one of five dioceses featured in the paper.

Not surprisingly, Frederick Du Vernet, holding the stature of bishop, made

FIGURE 40. Rev. Jocelyn Perkins, editor. From *Across the Rockies* (October 1912). Photograph courtesy of the Archives of the Provincial Synod of British Columbia and Yukon.

more frequent appearances in the high church *Across the Rockies* than he did in the *North British Columbia News*. The January 1912 issue of *Across the Rockies* referred to him using his full episcopal title and his honorary degree—"Bishop, The Right Rev. Frederick Herbert Du Vernet, D.D."—and featured him wearing his bishop's robes on the front cover. With Du Vernet's episcopal authority on display, *Across the Rockies* retold the story of Caledonia as a place not only of "Indian" conversion but also of white settlement, within British Columbia as a new land of settlement and promise.[43]

The correspondence between the treasurers of the two papers displayed the bitter rivalry between the newsletters. J. Robinson, a low church layman based in Surrey, England, was the treasurer of the Caledonia-focused *North British Columbia News*, and Jocelyn Perkins, the sacrist of Westminster Abbey, worked on the more broadly focused *Across the Rockies* (fig. 40). In a series of letters in 1914, the two Anglicans exchanged insults, each accusing the other of deception and bad management of funds that verged on corruption. By the 1920s, however, they were in agreement that it was the British Columbia clergy who were the real problem, as Perkins complained that they "played ducks and drakes with our money all over the place." Though Perkins and

Robinson did not openly criticize McCullagh, they were both particularly troubled by Bishop Du Vernet himself, in part because he refused to play the role of what historian Anna Johnston calls a "missionary celebrity." Perkins, who met Du Vernet on a journey to Prince Rupert, remarked cryptically after his death: "It is not for me to criticize the action or lack of action of the late Archbishop, but I confess that his attitude has always been incomprehensible to me."[44] Their liturgical differences overcome by their frustration with this Canadian-born archbishop, Perkins and Robinson's newfound harmony coalesced in the face of the enigma that was Frederick Du Vernet.

From its early days, Prince Rupert was a multicultural magnet. Since the mid-nineteenth century, northwestern British Columbia had seen several waves of what might be called migrant workers coming to its coasts and valleys, in search of gold, copper, fish, and work on the railway. Japanese families were common in the canneries along the coast, Chinese men came to build the railways, and the paper mills attracted both Japanese workers and "Hindus," according to Du Vernet. As Du Vernet noted, these groups were racialized and discriminated against by white settlers, who were not characterized as migrant workers. Instead, settlers were described as men, sometimes accompanied by wives, who came to "preempt" land—to build a house and farm plots of land, thereby "improving" it. These settlers hailed from Scotland, England, Scandinavia, Germany, and other parts of Europe; many had spent some time in Canadian settlements farther east before moving west. With a long history of anti-Asian discrimination and exclusion in addition to a history of Indigenous dispossession, British Columbia was a "white man's province" along several lines of color.[45]

From the beginning of his episcopate, Du Vernet raised questions about the viability of separating Christians out by categories of race. In a 1906 letter to Baring-Gould, CMS secretary, he wrote: "Our Synod will assemble Aug. 21, among the Lay Representatives there will be some of our native Christians. No difference is made. From this time forward, on the coast at least, our native people will be mingling more and more with the white people. The testing time is coming. We are anxious but hopeful." In a 1908 summary of the work of the diocese, he was more forthright: "It is not wise to draw the line too sharply between the White and the Indian work, and it is an inspiring sight to see men of different races worshipping the same God all together and in the same way."[46] Despite his insistence, his managers in the missionary societies in England and Toronto continued to require Du Vernet to submit separate records of his work divided by race.

Though he too turned on occasion to racist tropes of "heathens" and "savages," Du Vernet's rhetoric of mingling was decidedly less triumphalist than that of missionaries who had arrived on the northwest coast decades earlier. Consider the title of a memoir written by longtime CMS missionary William Henry Collison and published in 1915: *In the Wake of the War Canoe: A Stirring Record of Forty Years' Successful Labour, Peril and Adventure amongst the Savage Indian Tribes of the Pacific Coast, and the Piratical Head-Hunting Haidas of the Queen Charlotte Islands, B.C.* Hoping to "stir" the emotions of his readers far from the Pacific coast, Collison's memoir was an emotional appeal that depended on his having truly "been there," in the flesh—in labor, peril, and adventure.

At the end of his forty-year career as a missionary, it is somewhat curious that Collison would choose the sensational title of *In the Wake of the War Canoe* for his memoir. By 1915, Collison, together with Du Vernet, McCullagh, and his own son, William E. Collison, among others, had successfully established many Anglican churches among the Haida, the Ts'msyen, and the Nisga'a. As historian Nicholas May has shown, Nisga'a Anglicans were often eager and dedicated evangelists themselves, marching together to other Nisga'a, Ts'msyen, and Gitxsan villages to spread the gospel. Nisga'a evangelism, however, was "not the selfless act it was so often portrayed to be by the missionaries who came from afar and their hagiographers. Nineteenth-century Nisga'a discovered, or more precisely rediscovered in their taking up of evangelism, that collective engagements with the supernatural had a way of re-energizing all involved."[47] While McCullagh and Collison often focused their energies on the conversion of an individual soul, Nisga'a evangelists worked as collectives on collectives.

The racist excess of Collison's "savage" title, when contrasted with his lived experience of Indigenous people who worked alongside him, may have been a desperate bid to tell a story that downplayed the role of white settlers in the region. He could not, however, avoid mentioning whiteness in his conclusion: "We rejoice that the evangelisation of the Indian tribes has been effected before the inrush of the white population. And the foundation has been laid, the only sure foundation, on which to build up a new nation in this fair land of promise."[48] The promised land or the land of promise, either way the foundation was neither sure nor fair, as the Nisga'a and Ts'msyen repeatedly asserted.

Finding Men and Money

Money was frequently at the heart of Du Vernet's tensions with his colleagues over how to tell the story of Caledonia to the wider world. Du Vernet's insistence that McCullagh turn the local *Aiyansh Notes* into a broader diocesan newsletter to spread the "news" on a wider scale remained a sore spot with McCullagh, who had raised considerable funds through his vanity newsletter. Similarly, Du Vernet's tensions with his predecessor, William Ridley, the first bishop of Caledonia, circled back to the question of cash for stories. In a letter to lawyers in Victoria, he criticized Ridley's accounting practices: "On account of his wonderful power of graphic description both spoken and written [Bishop Ridley] was constantly receiving gifts of money for his work. The fact that all this money did not come through the channel of the Church Missionary Society but much of it was given to him direct to do with it as he saw best in the interests of the work does not make this private."[49] The lure of profiting from confessional production was tempting for a missionary, for whom it was so easy to appeal for donations to a "good cause."

Compared to McCullagh, Du Vernet's style of testimony in missionary print sources called more quietly to his audience, made less use of the first-person voice, and hardly ever recounted stories of his interactions with his family. His public reportage on the far-flung missions in the Diocese of Caledonia took on a rather remote air, in part because he regularly wrote about himself in the third person as "the Bishop." Later in life, however, once he began testifying to his scientific discoveries of radio mind, he took up the authority of the first person more regularly, writing with enthusiasm and confidence of his experiments with Alice, in both secular and church newspapers.

Du Vernet also differed from McCullagh when it came to relationships fostered through the medium of print. In Great Britain, McCullagh was a minor missionary celebrity who thought of the British—including both the English and the Protestant Irish—as his people. His furloughs allowed him to travel home to share his "magnetic personality" at missionary exhibitions and in church services and raise sizable sums in the process thanks to his "racy Irish humour when telling an anecdote." As Du Vernet put it more mildly: "His gift of pictorial description and his fervid Irish eloquence captured his audiences when home on deputation work."[50] Even with faith in his iron pulpit, McCullagh knew that printed appeals from a distance had to be paired with oral stories delivered in person to rouse sufficient donations.

With the British missionary societies withdrawing their support, McCullagh and Du Vernet scrambled to find more channels for British donations to make their way to British Columbia. Du Vernet hoped that the new British Columbia Church Aid Society would be less focused on mission defined by conversion and open to a broader mandate. He wrote of his financial worries in the society's 1911 yearbook: "Our Indian work is being maintained as usual, but our veteran missionaries cannot go on for ever. With every resignation of a C.M.S. missionary, the burden of the work is being thrown more upon the Canadian Church. It is a most serious question how we shall be able to find men and money to keep on this good work, but we must trust and go forward."[51] Both McCullagh and Du Vernet put a good deal of their trust in the printed word as a channel for finding men and money. The military recruitment, and by 1917 conscription, of World War I made the task of securing ministers even more difficult.

Though focused on finding men, Du Vernet commented often on the conundrum of women in missionary life. Du Vernet wrote to a colleague in 1914 bemoaning his failed attempt to place a young man as a priest in a parish: "It needs a man of no mean ability to handle both Railway men and pioneer farmers. I was well pleased with Buck and tried hard to secure him for this Diocese but his mother wants him nearer home." While some mothers and wives pulled men away from the remote life of the church missionary, others joined in as utterly necessary co-laborers in "the work." Women, such as teacher and deaconess E. J. Soal, had long served as CMS missionaries in the region, but Du Vernet was driven in his search for a "man of mature judgment" to minister to churches in Indigenous missions and white settlements. He regularly noted that neither single men nor single women could be sent out alone to Indigenous missions. A woman could be paired with a female counterpart, but a man required a wife, presumably to avoid unseemly sexual innuendo. Though sounding disheartened at times by the lack of clergymen in a "young man's country," Du Vernet was hopeful that "the tide will turn. No country in the world has more attractions for returning soldiers than British Columbia with its boundless resources and its spirit of freedom."[52] Aware of and attentive to the women, the Japanese, the Chinese, and the Indigenous people living all around him, Du Vernet imagined British Columbia as a land promised to white men.

Du Vernet knew that CMS support for the Caledonia bishopric would come to an end upon his retirement or death, whichever came first. He also knew that CMS money would dry up when all the old-timer missionaries—John Henry Keen, William Henry Collison, and James McCullagh—retired or died. The Diocese of Caledonia was supposed to become self-supporting, and generous offerings from Nisga'a and Ts'msyen Christians helped. But the diocese also depended on the Toronto-based Missionary Society of the Church of England in Canada (MSCC), a homegrown organization that Du Vernet had helped establish when he lived in Toronto. The MSCC would send out block grants to the dioceses for their work, but also expected each diocese to contribute to the central mission fund, to support Canadian missionaries working around the world. As the MSCC collaborated more intensively with the Dominion government to establish residential schools for Indigenous children, it put more pressure on missionary dioceses to accept these schools as a means of income. Du Vernet was well aware that the choices the MSCC was making came at the expense of Indigenous children and their families; he also knew, as we will see, that Nisga'a, Ts'msyen, and Haida parents vehemently opposed the systematic removal of their children from their care.

Unrest on Account of the Land

James McCullagh played multiples roles in the Nass Valley: as a missionary and priest, he saw himself as the messenger of God; as the magistrate, he was the enforcer of state law and could send people to the "lockup"; and as an erstwhile fisheries officer, he traveled the waterways in the employ of the state. As the local printer with imperial connections, he told stories of the Nass Valley on a global stage. Du Vernet, as his bishop, both encouraged and constrained McCullagh in his work, noting that McCullagh practiced what might seem to some to be "a strange mingling of the Law and the Gospel."[53] McCullagh used all his roles to pursue his unyielding desire to make Nisga'a men and women into Christians in part by forcing them to give up feasting and cutting down their totem poles. At the same time, he worked together with the Nisga'a as they tried to use the Bible, the law, their *yukw*, and the printing press to keep maps of settlement from recasting their valley.

The printing press was busy in the months before the mission house fire in 1910, printing both missionary texts and Nisga'a protests about white settlement of the land. In the first issue of the *North British Columbia News*, a 1909 letter from McCullagh translated the anti-colonial struggle of the Nisga'a into a question of pathos: "At present our Indians are slightly unsettled in view of the rapid opening up of the country, and are feeling sore at the idea of the lands over which they have roamed all their lives—masters of all they surveyed—being taken from them and fenced off against them by strangers. But I believe that when the settlement actually takes place they will see it is all in the way of better days. It is the old story, and has a very pathetic aspect for those who have hearts that can feel."[54] For McCullagh, the old story of a people "feeling sore" at the dispossession of their lands could be rewritten as a story with the foregone conclusion that the land had been promised to others.

Despite his attacks on the potlatch and totem poles, and his determined support of settler colonialism, McCullagh was sensitive to the importance of face-to-face storytelling for Nisga'a protocols and political organization. He understood that distance media, such as the printing press, could not entirely replace proximate media, such as oral stories that required people to gather at a more intimate scale. He argued strenuously that other settlers needed to think beyond the "White man's point of view" to take into consideration Nisga'a protocols about public, proximate storytelling. For example, in the 1910 "Interview with the Land Committee," printed in *Hagaga* before the fire, McCullagh contrasted the significance of the building of the railway for settlers and for Nisga'a: "To the White man it seems merely an affair of shovelling earth for the Grand Trunk Railway line to run through, and disturb the interments of an Indian cemetery. To the Indian, such exhumation and reinterment are a very serious business. I have often found the simple repair of an ordinary grave-fence to be beyond the means of those concerned. It cannot be done privately as we would do it. There must be a public feast, a public speech, and the rank and social standing of everyone present recognized by a suitable gift."[55] In other words, the railway company's disrespect of the graves and spirits of Nisga'a ancestors required repair through a public feast with appropriate protocols of storytelling.

Storytelling protocols, however, did not rule out the power of print for the Nisga'a. The same month that McCullagh's "Interview with the Land Committee" was published in *Hagaga*, the skillful printers among the Nisga'a used the printing press to convey the Land Committee's resistance to white settlement of their lands (fig. 41). Their conflict with settler Joshua Priestley still unresolved, they turned to the press to amplify their concerns. On May 17, 1910, the Nisga'a printers published a flyer that expanded their specific conflict with Priestley into a universal declaration of "Indian protest against White settlers coming into the Aiyansh Valley, Naas River, British Columbia" (fig. 42).[56]

Citing the 1763 Royal Proclamation of King George III, the eight Nisga'a chiefs who signed the document argued what their ancestors had long articulated orally and in printed letters and petitions sent to newspapers and government officials. The Nisga'a had inhabited their lands from time immemorial and had never ceded them to the Crown or anyone else: "WE DO THEREFORE, standing well within our constitutional rights, forbid you to stake off land in this valley, and do hereby protest against your proceeding further into our country with that end in view—until such time as a satisfactory settlement be made between the representatives of the Crown and ourselves."[57] Nine days later, the document had found its way down the coast to Victoria, arriving at the office of the superintendent of the Provincial Police on May 26, and by the next day, at the office of the attorney general of British Columbia. The printed protest traveled fast and far.

FIGURE 41. Printing office, Aiyansh (ca. 1906). Photograph courtesy of the Royal British Columbia Museum and Archives (NA-39400).

McCullagh and Du Vernet both found themselves in an awkward position of warily supporting the Nisga'a protest. Du Vernet's articles and letters display his developing anxieties about how whiteness was becoming increasingly powerful in the lives of the Nisga'a and Ts'msyen. The Indian Act and successive land commissions such as the McKenna-McBride Commission enabled white men to take Indigenous land. And with the rise of the Indian Residential Schools, increasingly supported by the MSCC in Toronto, the partnership of church and state was working to steal Indigenous children. In his charge to the Caledonia Synod of 1909, which several Indigenous Anglicans attended, Du Vernet made this clear:

> It cannot be denied that there is much unrest on account of the land question, and this unrest has hindered spiritual work. It was inevitable that the inrush of settlers taking up land over which the natives have been accustomed to hunt should cause agitation, but I cannot help feeling that much of this fric-

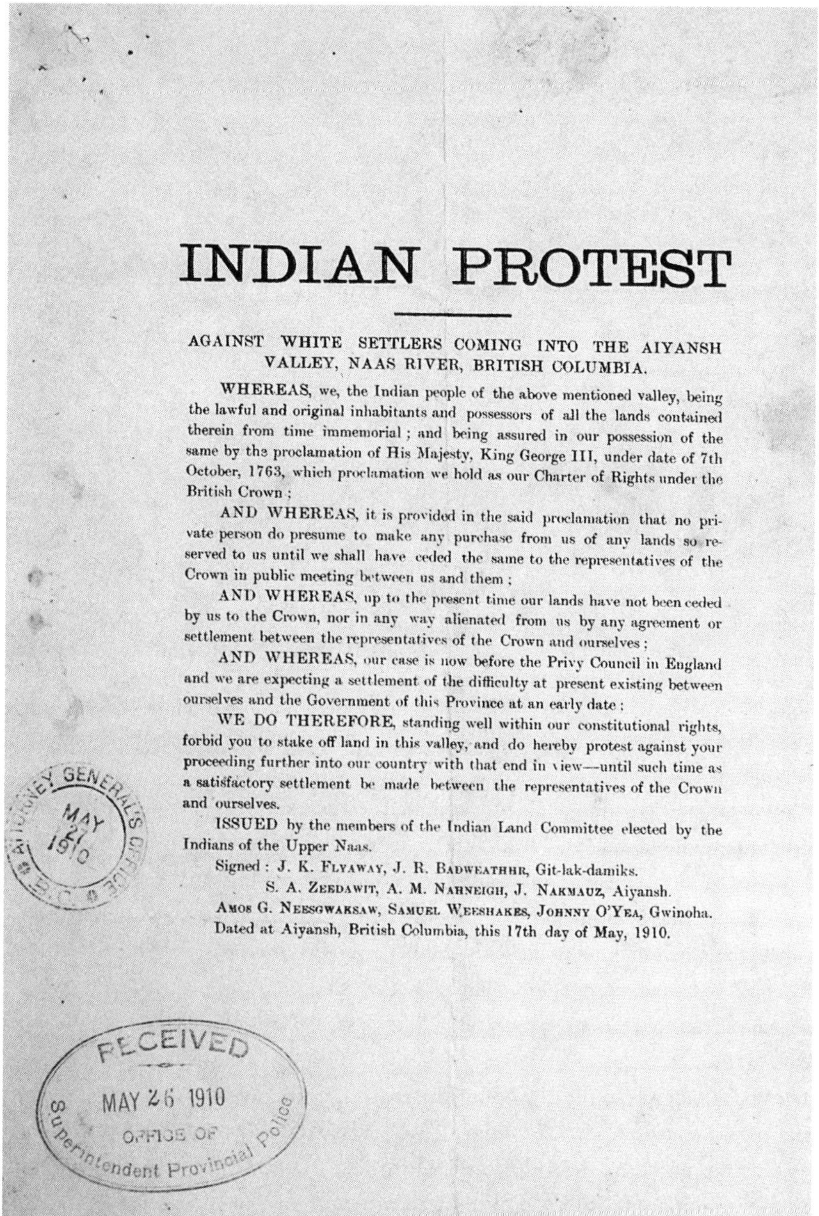

INDIAN PROTEST

AGAINST WHITE SETTLERS COMING INTO THE AIYANSH VALLEY, NAAS RIVER, BRITISH COLUMBIA.

WHEREAS, we, the Indian people of the above mentioned valley, being the lawful and original inhabitants and possessors of all the lands contained therein from time immemorial; and being assured in our possession of the same by the proclamation of His Majesty, King George III, under date of 7th October, 1763, which proclamation we hold as our Charter of Rights under the British Crown;

AND WHEREAS, it is provided in the said proclamation that no private person do presume to make any purchase from us of any lands so reserved to us until we shall have ceded the same to the representatives of the Crown in public meeting between us and them;

AND WHEREAS, up to the present time our lands have not been ceded by us to the Crown, nor in any way alienated from us by any agreement or settlement between the representatives of the Crown and ourselves;

AND WHEREAS, our case is now before the Privy Council in England and we are expecting a settlement of the difficulty at present existing between ourselves and the Government of this Province at an early date;

WE DO THEREFORE, standing well within our constitutional rights, forbid you to stake off land in this valley, and do hereby protest against your proceeding further into our country with that end in view—until such time as a satisfactory settlement be made between the representatives of the Crown and ourselves.

ISSUED by the members of the Indian Land Committee elected by the Indians of the Upper Naas.

Signed: J. K. Flyaway, J. R. Badweathhr, Git-lak-damiks.
S. A. Zeedawit, A. M. Nahneigh, J. Nakmauz, Aiyansh.
Amos G. Neesgwaksaw, Samuel Weeshakes, Johnny O'Yea, Gwinoha.
Dated at Aiyansh, British Columbia, this 17th day of May, 1910.

FIGURE 42. *Indian Protest*, flyer printed at Aiyansh (1910). Photograph courtesy of the Royal British Columbia Museum and Archives (GR-0429, 2561/10).

FIGURE 43. Anglican Diocese of Caledonia Synod (1909). Du Vernet is seated in front; Alice, his daughter, is standing behind him to the left; and Stella Du Vernet is to the left of Alice. Photograph courtesy of the Diocese of Caledonia Archives.

> tion might have been avoided had there been a better understanding between the Dominion and Provincial Governments in regard to the Indians, and had there been at the outset a formal treaty. While it is true that the Dominion Government has dealt liberally with the Indians looking well after their interests, yet the natives do not understand this. They were not properly consulted when the reserves were set apart. They do not see that the money spent upon their education, etc., has any connection with the surrender of their lands.[58]

Du Vernet sought to disabuse the government of its mistaken view that spending on education and residential schools was somehow a substitute for treaties. Surrounded by his family and white coworkers—but none of the Indigenous participants—in a group photograph of the 1909 synod, Du Vernet sits with his hands folded in his lap, confidently episcopal (fig. 43). Three years later at the 1912 synod, however, he attracted critics for his warning to the Nisga'a not to accept help in their land struggle from "outsiders."

In 1913, a group calling itself the Conference of the Friends of the Indians of British Columbia, which included Anglican clergy and laypeople from Vancouver and Toronto, published a three-page pamphlet with the title *Bishop*

Du Vernet and the Indians. Incensed by Du Vernet's claim during the 1912 synod that "outside agitators" were riling up the Nisga'a, the Friends of the Indians demanded an explanation for his comments. The group's pamphlet paraphrased Du Vernet's words: "He criticized us upon the alleged grounds that we had adopted the policy of stirring up the Indians by sending them letters urging them to take action to defend their rights by circulating petitions among them, by summoning delegates to meet in conference, and by collecting money from Indian villages." Then they quoted back at him his own 1909 charge to his synod, to show that Du Vernet had himself supported the Nisga'a Land Committee's political action to resolve the land question.[59]

The Friends of the Indians had a good point. Du Vernet and McCullagh had often voiced their support for the Indian Land Committee and had repeatedly noted the injustice of the lack of a treaty. They knew well that the Nisga'a and the Ts'msyen had articulated their grievances themselves, both in person and in print, long before lawyers and clergy came to them from "outside." The sophisticated analysis of the significance of the Royal Proclamation of 1763 voiced by the Indian Land Committee was a collective enterprise that may have involved some lawyers. But as the protest flyer and the printed *Hagaga* interview attest, Nisga'a printers put the arguments on the page themselves (fig. 44). Their printing labor provided the material means for turning textual and oral sources to the service of the Land Question:

> Since 1763 no government of Canada has considered itself free to dispossess the Indians of their lands without agreement and compensation. Mr. Justice Gwynne in 1856 agreed that the Indians possess territorial rights akin to those asserted by Sovereign Princes—that none of their land can be alienated save by treaty made publicly between the Crown and them.
>
> Q [McCullagh]. How do you know all this? I am a White man and yet I had no idea of what you are telling me—how do you know?

The Nisga'a chiefs replied that they based their argument on a speech given by the governor-general Lord Dufferin on a visit to British Columbia in 1876. They also had the assistance of a lawyer, Arthur O'Meara, a Wycliffe College graduate and former missionary to the Yukon, who helped them continuc their ancestors' argument against the fiction of the white possessive.[60]

McCullagh's surprise, perhaps feigned, that he knew none of this history even though he was a white man, is a significant remark. McCullagh turned neither to the law of the King nor to the Ten Commandments to support the case for dealing "fairly" with the Indian Land Question. Instead, he considered equity to be based in whiteness itself: "Any discussion of the Indian

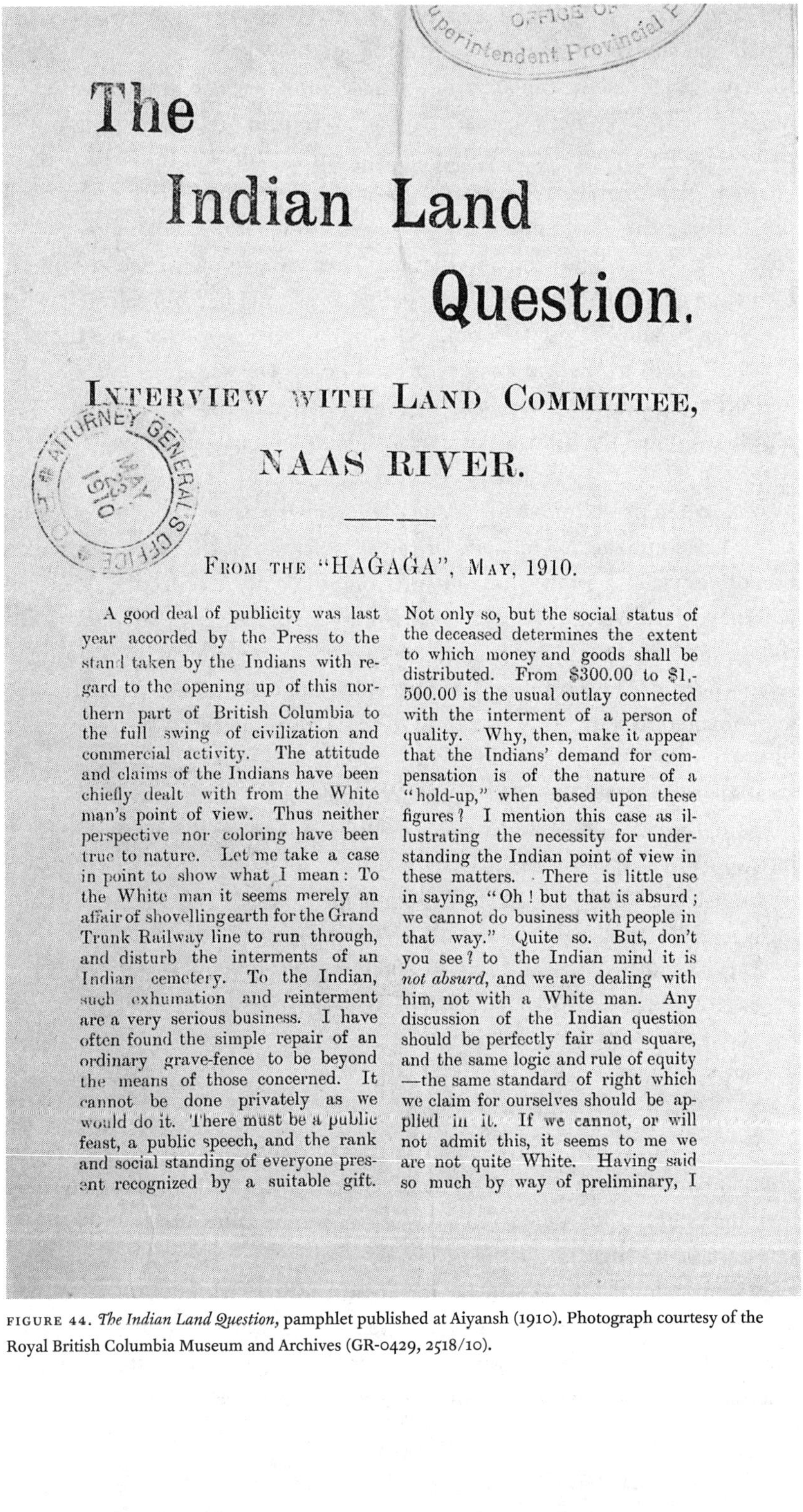

OFFICE OF Superintendent Provincial P

The Indian Land Question.

Interview with Land Committee, Naas River.

ATTORNEY GENERAL'S OFFICE MAY 23 1910

From the "HAĠAĠA", May, 1910.

A good deal of publicity was last year accorded by the Press to the stand taken by the Indians with regard to the opening up of this northern part of British Columbia to the full swing of civilization and commercial activity. The attitude and claims of the Indians have been chiefly dealt with from the White man's point of view. Thus neither perspective nor coloring have been true to nature. Let me take a case in point to show what I mean: To the White man it seems merely an affair of shovelling earth for the Grand Trunk Railway line to run through, and disturb the interments of an Indian cemetery. To the Indian, such exhumation and reinterment are a very serious business. I have often found the simple repair of an ordinary grave-fence to be beyond the means of those concerned. It cannot be done privately as we would do it. There must be a public feast, a public speech, and the rank and social standing of everyone present recognized by a suitable gift. Not only so, but the social status of the deceased determines the extent to which money and goods shall be distributed. From $300.00 to $1,500.00 is the usual outlay connected with the interment of a person of quality. Why, then, make it appear that the Indians' demand for compensation is of the nature of a "hold-up," when based upon these figures? I mention this case as illustrating the necessity for understanding the Indian point of view in these matters. There is little use in saying, "Oh! but that is absurd; we cannot do business with people in that way." Quite so. But, don't you see? to the Indian mind it is *not absurd*, and we are dealing with him, not with a White man. Any discussion of the Indian question should be perfectly fair and square, and the same logic and rule of equity—the same standard of right which we claim for ourselves should be applied in it. If we cannot, or will not admit this, it seems to me we are not quite White. Having said so much by way of preliminary, I

FIGURE 44. *The Indian Land Question*, pamphlet published at Aiyansh (1910). Photograph courtesy of the Royal British Columbia Museum and Archives (GR-0429, 2518/10).

FIGURE 45. Building the mission house, Aiyansh (1912). Photograph courtesy of the Royal British Columbia Museum and Archives (E-00967).

question should be perfectly fair and square, and the same logic and rule of equity—the same standard of right which we claim for ourselves should be applied in it. If we cannot, or will not admit this, it seems to me we are not quite White."[61] Du Vernet and McCullagh both knew that the Indian Land Question had to be answered through treaties that acknowledged the legitimacy of Indigenous sovereignty. While McCullagh named whiteness as a moral ground for equity, Du Vernet grew increasingly vocal about the virtues of spiritual mingling as a solution to racial, spiritual, and class strife.

One peculiar printed artifact from Aiyansh helps show why unrest grew in the Nass Valley in 1913. The Nisga'a rebuilt the burned-out mission house in the summer of 1912, this time making it large enough to accommodate many visitors (fig. 45). Then in 1913, at the encouragement of McCullagh and Du Vernet, a large influx of new settlers from eastern Canada and Europe arrived to claim homesteads along the Nass River. McCullagh's second wife, Eleanor, recalled later that many of them came to stay in the mission house and in other homes—perhaps even Nisga'a homes—for Christmas celebrations that same year (fig. 46). Thanks to Eleanor, who with the help of two unnamed Nisga'a men had saved from the fire a small proof press (a machine used to print small numbers of a text for the purpose of corrections), McCullagh printed a "souvenir" booklet of the Christmas festivities marking the "first 'White' Xmas" of the new settlers.[62]

FIGURE 46. New mission house, built after the fire (ca. 1914). Photograph courtesy of the Royal British Columbia Museum and Archives (NA-04006).

The booklet included within it a map of over fifty settlers' plots of land and documentation of their formation of the Nass Valley Agricultural Association, with Rev. James B. McCullagh elected as honorary president (fig. 47). In addition to accounts of Holy Communion at 8:00 a.m. on Christmas Day, the settler-hosted Christmas Day and Boxing Day banquets, and a reciprocal Nisga'a-hosted dinner and concert, the souvenir booklet featured a sermon and many poems from McCullagh. It also included an address by Chief Andrew Mercer, a frequent spokesman for the Indian Land Committee, including during the conflict with settler Joshua Priestley and in letters to the editors of local newspapers.[63]

Andrew Mercer's speech at the Boxing Day banquet expressed his vision for what would lead to harmonious relations along the Nass River, beginning with a historic appeal to affection:

> For the first time in the history of the Indian people the Whiteman has admitted us within the bounds of a common social friendship with himself. At this season of the year it is very appropriate to emphasise this feature of a common friendship. The pleasure afforded us by the presence here to-night of all the White settlers is very real. We are glad to see them, and to sit down to table with them. We have no hostile feelings against the Settlers, and we believe they have none against us. It is true there are questions at issue between ourselves and the government of the country: we have grievances, and our feelings in regard to them are more or less bitter; but we have learned to distinguish between things

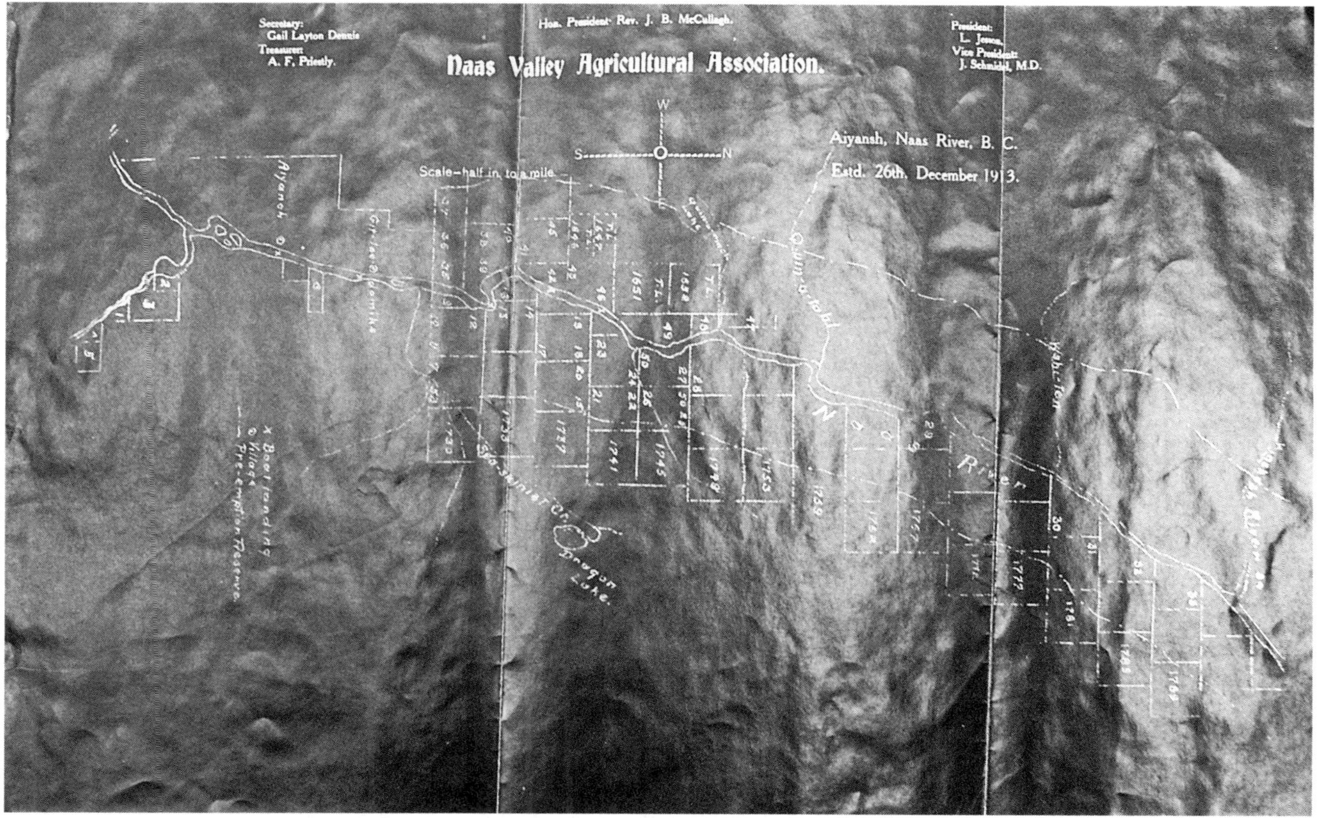

FIGURE 47. Map of Naas Valley Agricultural Association settler land plots. From a souvenir booklet printed by James B. McCullagh at Aiyansh: *Souvenir Booklet: Nass Valley Agricultural Association* (1913). Photograph courtesy of the Royal British Columbia Museum and Archives (NWP 970.7 M133).

> that differ, and the Settler is not responsible for any injustice done to us. Therefore we desire that a very real friendship should subsist between ourselves and the Settlers now resident in the valley. This cannot be done on a one-sided disposition of heart: it must be mutual to exist at all.

A call to reconciliation and to reparation, Mercer's speech insisted that a mutual disposition of heart required restitution on the part of the settlers and their government: "*We are not aliens!* We are here in our own native land—the land where our fathers were born, lived and died. If you, in developing the country, deprive us of our original means of subsistence, so that of necessity we are compelled to sell our labour as you do for a living, it is manifestly unfair that any discrimination should be made against us. On the contrary, there is by right a certain consideration due to us from you, which should be given without asking." Concluding in a gesture of hospitality, Mercer invited all the settlers to a Nisga'a-hosted dinner and concert the next night, promising that "several items on the programme will deal with the Indian life of the past which we trust you will find interesting."[64] McCullagh recorded Mercer's invitation, but did not include an account in the booklet of the Nisga'a festivities.

Embedding the settler map in the booklet of the Christmas celebrations, McCullagh tried to embed the territory of the Nisga'a within a Christian, colonial cosmology. Andrew Mercer's charge of discrimination, however, echoes the earlier assertiveness of the Nisga'a petitions "against white settlers coming into the Aiyansh Valley" printed on the mission press. To what degree Mercer's speech was edited by McCullagh is hard to know, but this was not the first time that the Aiyansh printing press had printed multiple voices, both celebrating and questioning colonial settlement.

Spiritual Realities

McCullagh's spiritual despondency in the wake of the fire that destroyed his first press, as well as Du Vernet's frustration over McCullagh's dedication to his printing presses, can be partly explained by the two men's different temperaments, the pressures of missionary finances, and the Indigenous land movement. But their conflicts were also shaped by their contrasting spiritual dispositions as to how the printed word was an Anglican medium for the spirit. While Du Vernet was emerging as a liberal Anglican open to the scientific theories of his day, McCullagh took a path known as holiness, which for some Anglicans became a road to a Pentecostal style of worship. Both men were dedicated to the Bible as a guide for living, but they came to interpret its words in radically different ways.[65]

For six years after the mission house fire, McCullagh appealed to his Nisga'a parishioners, to British supporters, and again to the Society for the Promotion of Christian Knowledge to give him the funds for a second iron pulpit:

> Three machines will be requisite—a platen press (a Chandler & Price, 14½ × 22 inside chase), a paper cutter and a wire stitcher with a sufficient supply of type and "furniture," paper, etc. It almost takes my breath away to mention what I think the whole would cost, but I will take hold of my faith with both hands and put it to the fence—$1000! You put your money into this, and I put my life into it—as much as remaineth. We will go shares in the sacrifice and by and by we will share in the joy.

McCullagh used the printing press as a metaphorical, material, and spiritual medium to hammer away at Nisga'a traditions of communication, quite literally calling it his "big gun."[66] But he did not rely on print alone.

Just as Nisga'a chiefs Barton and Calder traveled to Ottawa to bring urgency to their written petitions to the Canadian government, so too did McCullagh travel to England to bring his message to the center of missionary power. As his biographer Joseph Moeran contended: "McCullagh had no private income; but God did not let His servant's prayers go unanswered nor his passion for souls waste itself in vain desire. During his first furlough in 1890 a large amount of interest was awakened by the wonderful story he told in public, enhanced as it was by his magnetic personality and his fervent appeals to the conscience and sympathies of those who listened to him." On this trip to England, he brought with him Nisga'a clothing and masks and was photographed dressed as a "medicine man" at a missionary exhibition in Manchester (fig. 48). This picture became synonymous with the man and was subsequently used as a gold engraving on the cover of his 1923 biography (fig. 49). Perhaps fittingly, a 1957 children's book combines the image of McCullagh dressed as a medicine man with a mishmash of "Indian" stereotypes, none of which represent Nisga'a cultural forms.[67] Recycled once more, the 1890 photograph now stands as a large poster reproduction in the Nisga'a Museum at Laxgalts'ap with an explanation of McCullagh's forceful and domineering approach to conversion.

On his second trip to England, for his furlough of 1907, McCullagh left the Nass Valley as a grieving widower. His wife, Mary, had died in 1900 after eating a "bad can of salmon," leaving behind her fifteen-year-old daughter, Melita. Mary provoked more written reflection from her husband in death than

FIGURE 48. McCullagh dressed as a "medicine man" (1890). From *North British Columbia News* (August 1921). Photograph courtesy of the Archives of the Provincial Synod of British Columbia and Yukon.

she had in life. James was particularly surprised to learn that many of the Nisga'a men and women were very fond of Mary: "I never thought that the quiet, unobtrusive life and work of the dear patient worker had made such a deep impression on the callous Indian, and there by the side of her grave I silently gave God thanks for her and her good example. Thus closed the chapter of a quiet, meek and lowly life, diffidently consecrated to Christ and His service. She ever felt her little all was very little indeed, but she was faithful in that little; she was not little in her faithfulness and devotion; she was great." Whether callous or tender, the Nisga'a (who are rarely given names in McCullagh's account) saw something in Mary McCullagh that her husband had missed. They built a zinc-lined coffin for her and decorated her grave with white shells arranged in the shape of a cross.[68]

McCullagh's biographer, Joseph Moeran, also focused on the littleness of English Mary's life next to the blazing glory of her Irish husband when recounting her death: "She was one of those quiet retiring natures that shone

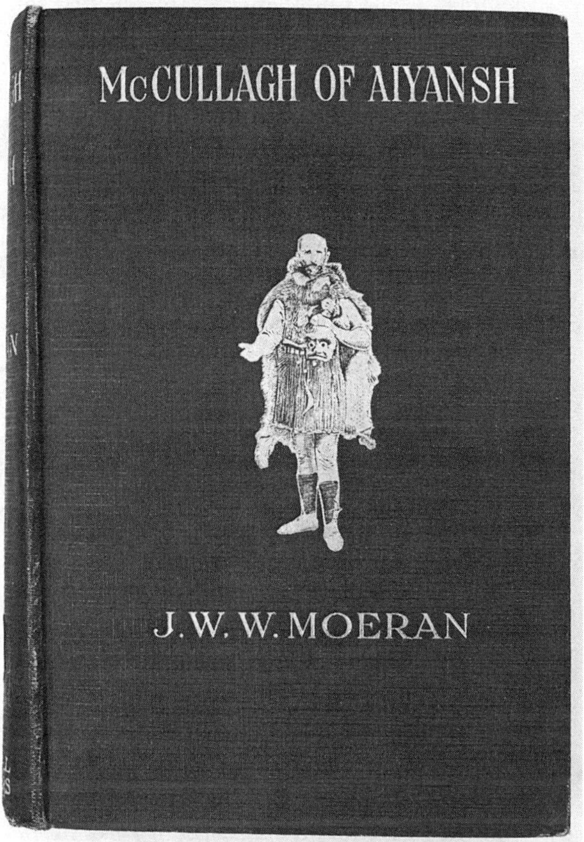

FIGURE 49. Cover of J. W. W. Moeran, *McCullagh of Aiyansh* (1923).

with a very subdued light beside the brilliant gifts and intense fervour of the man for whose sake she had given up the comforts of an English home with her own people. The monotony of her life may be gauged from the fact mentioned in one of her husband's journals that at one time 'for four years she did not see the face of a white sister of any degree or class.'" Monotony, characterized by Moeran as the lack of white faces and by her husband as the "earthly dullness" of "material labour," supposedly drained Mary's life of color and care.[69]

Melita, Mary's daughter, tells a different story of her mother in the biography. Living with Nisga'a neighbors and raising her daughter may not have been monotonous drudgery for Mary: "The Indians dearly loved my mother, and have never forgotten her. When anyone was sick and father was away she would see to them, sometimes being called up in the night to go to them; also she made soup and jellies for them when they were ill. My mother taught me everything; being an only child she could not bear to part with me. At the age of thirteen I played the organ at the Church Service for the first time, thanks to my mother's patient teaching, singing all the hymns and chants in the Indian language."[70] Teaching Melita the Anglican liturgy in the Nisga'a language, Mary raised her daughter and lived her life in a spirit of mingling. The pages of printed and handwritten texts that remain to record the life and times of James McCullagh are overwhelming; to a lesser extent, the same can be said for Frederick Du Vernet. The printed words that carry memories of their wives, Mary McCullagh and Stella Du Vernet, are few and far between.

Unlike McCullagh, Du Vernet did not feel the need to travel to England to be refreshed by the spirit. In a 1918 typewritten letter to Miss Emmeline Crump, the secretary-treasurer of the Church of St. John the Evangelist Women's Auxiliary of London, Ontario, he thanked her warmly for embroidered Communion linens donated by her Church Needlework Committee for the settler church in Pouce Coupe, east of the Rocky Mountains. Then he reminisced about his early visits to the region:

> I shall never forget the first Communion Service I held in that district before Mr. Kerr arrived. I had nothing with me except what a kind settler could provide—a plain napkin, a plate, a glass tumbler, and some saskatoon wine, as they could not even find any raisins out of which to extract some juice of the vine, and yet never have I known a more spiritual service with the Real Presence of Christ in our midst. I had travelled miles on foot with a pack-sack on my back and so did not even have my robes with me, only a short coat, which high prospector's boots on my feet needed for walking. It is such scenes which teach us to value the spiritual realities more. To the best of my knowledge it was the first administration of the Holy Communion in that part of the county.[71]

Emphasizing his plain spirituality, he also noted the "firsting" achieved by his settler Communion service, before he had his kit of traveling silverware (fig. 50).

Du Vernet declined to travel to England to serve as an in-the-flesh reminder of the missionary cause even when he was archbishop. But his words and numbers traveled there. He was in constant communication by mail with the English supporters of the Diocese of Caledonia, letting them know in great detail the specifics of the land purchases, the mission boats, and the missionaries they helped support. With the increasing bureaucratization and expansion of missionary organizations, he had to send regularly to London and Toronto detailed charts filled with statistics regarding payroll, expenses, income from offerings, and numbers of baptisms and confirmations. Du Vernet's refusal to visit England likely stemmed in part from his

FIGURE 50. Frederick Du Vernet's traveling Communion case. Courtesy of the Diocese of Caledonia Archives.

commitment to a more fully Canadian church. As a cleric born in Canada, Du Vernet was rare among early Anglican missionaries to British Columbia, most of whom, like McCullagh, came from Great Britain.

By Means of the Written Word

While on his 1907 furlough in England, McCullagh not only founded *Aiyansh Notes* but also married his second wife, Eleanor, who returned to the Nass Valley with him and went on to give birth to four children. *Aiyansh Notes* included many pictures of McCullagh and his growing family, as well as the family dog. In that summer of 1907, James and Eleanor spent their honeymoon enjoying spiritual refreshment at the legendary Keswick Convention in Cumberland in the hills of northwest England. The Keswick Convention was an interdenominational evangelical tent meeting organized every summer by Anglican clerics. More genteel than a Methodist camp meeting, Keswick held out the holiness promise that Christians willing to fully give themselves to Jesus Christ could achieve sanctification—the complete wiping away—of their sins.[72]

Holiness advocates sought to break free of what they took to be a hidebound—literally, overly bookish—Christianity. They yearned for what they hoped would be a more spontaneous faith that freely allowed the spirit of God to enter into a Christian; they were strongly criticized by other Protestants as coming dangerously close to the heretical idea that a sinner could somehow be perfected in this mortal life. Keswick participants, mostly middle to upper class and white, were thrilled to be part of a mass gathering of prayerful yet moderate Christians. As McCullagh put it in a 1907 article in *Aiyansh Notes*: "From 19th to 31st July there was Keswick (we neither could nor would have missed Keswick for anything)."[73] Taking his new bride to a tent revival was McCullagh's idea of a good honeymoon; hopefully for her sake, Eleanor agreed.

The Keswick experience depended on a strong commitment to the power of oral storytelling. One of the rules for attending Keswick was that participants should "lay aside for the time all reading except for the Bible" so that only biblical passages echoed in their heads when they amassed in large crowds to listen to preachers from various Protestant denominations. These were described as "solemn services where men and women humbly listen to the voice of God as it speaks to them through the lips of His honoured servants. In the holy stillness of the tents, as the truths of the Bible are unfolded, the heart is wonderfully responsive, and the words spoken fall on receptive soil." There was to be no discussion, no debate, and no controversy: just listening to the stories from the mouths of men, as women could only speak during women's gatherings. As participants gathered outdoors, the hills also conveyed the message: "In those mountain solitudes many a believer has, for the first time, come face to face with God, and from that time on the life has been glorified with a new purpose."[74]

Keswick was a "religious festival" that required a participant to pass on the gifts received: "He must bear his testimony to the saving and the keeping power of Jesus Christ and strive with all his might to lead his fellow-men into the same path of willing and glad obedience. There is no room for sloth in the service of the Heavenly King." Though the sanctified were supposed to spread the word, the organizers of Keswick were not publicity hounds, according to one supporter: "Keswick is firmly established and is a power for righteousness and holiness greater than is generally believed, for the movement never advertises itself, and makes no attempt to bring itself before the public." Despite this modesty, this supporter then went on to note that the Keswick Convention published its own weekly newsletter, *The Life of Faith*, ran a bookstall, and had its own publisher, Marshall Brothers. A seasonal gathering in which stories were told, relationships were rekindled, spiritual orientations were renewed, and some money changed hands, Keswick was a religious festival with more than one similarity to a northwest coast feast.[75]

If Keswick was his spiritual fountain, the Bible was the book that anchored McCullagh's soul. He wanted it to hold his converts in place too. Reading it, translating it, and dallying with it in prayer, McCullagh also drew from the Bible for every sermon. Just as Nisga'a and Ts'msyen storytellers depended on their listeners to understand the storied depth of a figure such as Raven, or Weeget, so too did missionaries count on their audiences to know their Bibles and to be able to read stories of the mission within the frame of familiar biblical passages or characters.

McCullagh saw his translation of biblical texts into the Nisga'a language as a channel of imperial holiness. Writing of the response to his 1917 translation of Paul's Letter to the Romans, McCullagh made great claims for the power of the letter on his Nisga'a hearers: "First [they had] a great sense of disappointment as to the man SELF; and secondly, a great and new joy in the man CHRIST JESUS! I may truly say that the whole Indian conception of eternity has been changed, and I am now eager to make that change permanent by printing the Epistle." Written to guide the men and women who gathered in small house churches in first-century Rome, Paul's letter drove home the point that his mission included converting the Gentiles, and insisted that men and women tame their bodies in the service of not "sin" but "holiness." Paul was seeking a change of material and spiritual life that McCullagh recognized as in keeping with his own work. The reward for a life so changed would last forever: "For the wages of sin is death; but the gift of God is eternal life through Jesus Christ our Lord" (Romans 6:23 [KJV]). That James McCullagh was convinced that printing a letter written in Greek by a Jewish man in the Roman Empire could completely transform the Nisga'a sense of eternity showed his commitment to the remarkable power of the gospel on paper. As he wrote in the *North British Columbia News* of October 1914, "You cannot rest in the Lord apart from the written Word. This Word, as Queen Victoria pointed out to an African chief, is the secret of England's greatness. And she was right: the HOLY BIBLE is the anvil on which our world-wide Empire has been forged and it is God Himself who has in all the days of our history wielded the hammer."[76]

McCullagh's translation of the Letter to the Romans was never sent back to England for printing by the Bible Society. The river swallowed it up. A great flood churned over the Aiyansh settlement in 1917, destroying the mission house for a second time. The printing press survived, but McCullagh's translated epistle did not. By the time the waters had receded, the Nisga'a had left the Christian settlement of Aiyansh behind, moving back across the river to Gitlakdamiks, taking the missionary and his family with them.

Frederick Du Vernet shared McCullagh's love of print and even his love of Paul, but his books took him on a very different spiritual journey. Delighted to report in his charge to the Synod of Caledonia in 1909 that a Canadian Anglican hymnal would soon be published, he compared this publication feat to the earlier establishment of a homegrown Canadian missionary society:

> As one who holds strongly that if our Canadian Church is to meet the needs of our Canadian people it must have an identity of its own, and not be simply a slavish copy of the revered Church of the motherland, with its entirely different environment, I hail with joy the production of a Canadian hymn book, which I earnestly hope will soon be used throughout this vast Dominion. We have now one Missionary Society for the whole Canadian Church instead of a dozen as in England. Soon we shall have one hymnbook instead of half a dozen as at present. This will help bind us together.[77]

Aiming a dig at McCullagh's multiplying private mission guilds in England, Du Vernet hoped that the Anglican hymnal would bind the nation as truly Canadian.

Just as Du Vernet often advised against drawing a sharp line between Indigenous and white, so too did he hesitate to make strong declarations about the relative holiness of others. Du Vernet read the work of Wesleyan biblical scholar Joseph Agar Beet, an Englishman deemed a heretic by many of his fellow Methodists for the way he questioned the doctrine that non-Christians would go to hell after death. In his reading of Beet's *Holiness as Understood by the Writers of the Bible*, Du Vernet underlined the last four words of this sentence: "Thus the holy man, and he only, lives a life strictly in accordance with the dictates of his reason." Du Vernet added in his own hand "Live for Jesus," underscoring Agar's point that to do so, one needed to bring together body and mind.[78]

By the time he reached his "radio mind" stage, Du Vernet had embraced the affective power of the press in a mode that sounded more like a media-positive humanitarian than a missionary-journalist: "When some dire calamity comes upon a suffering community through famine, earthquake, or conflagration, the public press is seen fulfilling its mission of light, and sympathetic offerings flow in from all parts of the world, to give denial to the popular belief that the greed of gain is the master-passion of man." While McCullagh was feeling the indwelling of the spirit at Keswick, Du Vernet was reading a supposedly heretical biblical scholar from Manchester who offered a mind-based definition of holiness: "And wherever mind is directed towards the Great Source of Mind, there is Holiness."[79]

Without traveling across the ocean, Du Vernet's spiritual journey was moving him toward a liberal Anglicanism espoused by men such as Agar, and women such as Lily Dougall, whose books were also on Du Vernet's shelves. These books helped lead Du Vernet to a spirituality of the written word that focused not only on a vertical dialogue with God but also on a collective conversation: "The possibility of God speaking to us through His written Word and His indwelling Spirit, and the possibility of our speaking to God through earnest prayer and quiet meditation become to us an intense reality when we believe firmly in the possibility of thought exchange between mind and mind."[80] For Du Vernet, spiritual reality became radio mind.

A Band of Printers Persists

In his handwritten notebooks, Du Vernet recorded two poignant transitions in McCullagh's presence in the Nass Valley. Describing a conversation with McCullagh as he lay dying in the Prince Rupert Hospital, Du Vernet cast his troublesome colleague in a sympathetic light:

> Rev. J. B. McCullagh who had labored among the natives for over 37 years was carried in a box to a big war canoe on the river. Rev McCullagh said to me (Mar. 5 1921 in the hospital P.R.) that it was like a man alive in his coffin attending his own funeral. All the Indians gathered on the riverbank. Crying + weeping and singing as the canoe pushed off. "God be with you 'till we meet again." He spoke to me of his natural pleasure and joy in the country. He knew every stick and stone. No credit he said to himself as he loved the valley. He gave not only his life but his love. When he spoke of the last time he went to Aiyansh and looked round he broke down and sobbed.[81]

Du Vernet also recorded in his notebook that by 1923, two years after McCullagh died, a group of seven young men ran the McCullagh Memorial Press in a new building in Gitlakdamiks they had named McCullagh Hall. The new print shop was built out of the lumber recycled from the torn-down Trinity Church, where the Nisga'a men and women had been forced by McCullagh to repent of their feasting. The "Indian boys" were now married men in Du Vernet's account: "1921. McCullagh Hall on hill at Gitlakdamiks. Printing press in this building in charge of Committee of seven young men (married). Paul Mercer, William J. Mercer, Anthony Adams, Stephen Eli, Moses James, Benjamin Munro(?), Cuthbert Morven (son of Charlie M.). Band of students and Printers."[82] These men still printed the *Trail Cruiser*, among other documents.

One of this band of printers, Paul Mercer, would go on to be not only the first Nisga'a Anglican priest but also a leader of the Nisga'a land movement, which eventually led to the Nisga'a Treaty at the turn of the millennium.[83] The printing press was a colonial spiritual medium that became an affordance for conversion and resistance, for prayer and for feasting, for division and solidarity. Though some have argued that print is a solitary medium, using a printing press was never really a solitary endeavor. Anyone who has ever worked a printing press knows how difficult, or even impossible, it is to operate one alone; a printing press works best with collective labor, regardless of religious affiliation.

Every gift of testimony demands a countergift in a cycle of reciprocity by which, to use Marcel Mauss's terms, giving away one's spiritual essence through a story is an exchange with unpredictable consequences. In his account of the "potlatch papers," the printed laws, letters, and stories that made the potlatch illegal, Christopher Bracken argues that the colonial naming of the "potlatch," as effected by government officials, missionaries, and anthropologists, was in itself a kind of treacherous gift. Bringing stasis and uniformity to feasting traditions that differed along the northwest coast, the potlatch papers were combined with maps to legitimate the Canadian seizure of Indigenous land. Through the printed Indian Act, the Canadian state attacked the spiritual political power of Indigenous ceremonies by reducing them to a monetary exchange. The law was oblivious to the fact that money changed hands in Christian rituals of sharing too, mediated by a newsletter or an offering plate, inspired by a stirring hymn.[84]

Marcel Mauss hoped, in writing *The Gift*, that reflection on the potlatch might ameliorate the greed-inspired excesses of capitalism and individualism that he saw around him in Europe in 1923. Though his text is still widely read, he would clearly be disappointed in its contemporary effects. Similarly, McCullagh's biographer Joseph Moeran, who also published his book in 1923, was confident that spreading McCullagh's life story after his death would reciprocate the gifts that McCullagh received from supporters over the years. That is, the story of the missionary's conversions of the Nisga'a would regift grace back to a spiritually bereft Europe: "The grace of God which made a new creation of the Red Indian on spiritual, ethical and material lines, is the one thing also needed by the white races on both sides of the Atlantic. Nothing else can cure the moral cancer which is sapping the life out of Europe."[85] The "white races" needed to take the spiritual essence of the "Red Indian" after—or because—they had taken their land.

The gifts of the missionary exchange were unpredictable, to say the least. As I learned on a visit to the Nisga'a Nation in 2012, McCullagh and his writings are remembered by some, but not with fondness. I found no memory of Du Vernet whatsoever. Feasts are alive and well, and even sometimes sacral ized in Anglican churches on the northwest coast. Totem poles are enjoying a revival as both historical artifacts and newly carved histories, and are themselves mediated in new ways. A prominent Nisga'a leader, the late Rod Robinson, can be found on many websites speaking eloquently about how totem poles "embody the mythology, the culture, and the spirituality of the Nisga'a nation . . . proclaiming the history to the world of who we are. Why we are this way, where did we come from and why it's very important that it be perpetuated into the future."[86] At his death, Robinson was both a canon of the cathedral in Prince Rupert—the church that Du Vernet helped build—and a recipient of the Order of Canada in recognition of his role in the long fight to establish Nisga'a land rights. His life was celebrated by a funeral in the Anglican Holy Trinity Church in Gitlakdamiks/New Aiyansh and by a settlement feast at the Nisga'a Nation's Recreation Centre.

While totem poles have undergone a revival as a storytelling technology in the past decades, the printing press is not faring quite as well. Printing presses have now joined totem poles in some museums, inviting visitors to reflect on earlier practices of building community through communication. The iron pulpit was never simply a tool to print letters on the page. A mass of iron that required collective labor to operate and maintain, the press was a many-voiced medium that could trumpet Christian conversion on one page and protest white settlement on the next.

7
Frequencies for Listening

Radio found its way to the northernmost reaches of the Pacific coast in slow waves. First ship-to-shore radio transmission became standard for the shipping industry—including in Prince Rupert harbor—but popular radio broadcasting took longer to emerge. In the early 1920s, home radio sets were still a new technology, limited to amateur enthusiasts and enterprising teenagers who made their own. Just as he was with the camera, Frederick Du Vernet was an early adopter of the radio: he had a store-bought short wave set in his own home by the 1920s. And just as the photograph and the printing press had earlier provoked spiritual desires and utopian dreams, so too did the radio.[1] A machine that enabled someone to hear a voice from afar and to broadcast their own in return extended the story from the mouth past the point of proximity. Carrying voices from a distance tuned to a frequency for listening, the radio was an aural and oral medium perfect for storytelling.

The first ever voice transmission over radio occurred on the shores of Massachusetts on Christmas Eve in 1906, when inventor Reginald Fessenden played "O Holy Night" on his violin and read from the Bible, speaking into the continuous wave radio set that would carry his holiday message out to the ships at sea. Fessenden, like Du Vernet, hailed from the Eastern Townships of Quebec, and was also the son of an Anglican minister; perhaps this goes some way to explaining the Christian sentimentality of his first broadcast. Almost two decades later, on February 11, 1924, the *Prince Rupert Daily News* reported with excitement that the "very latest thing in radio transmission" would be coming to town the next week, when a continuous wave radio set costing $7,000 would be installed at the wireless station on Digby Island, across the bay from the city of Prince Rupert. While it was placed on a hilltop that later became known as "CBC Hill" in celebration of the beloved Canadian public broadcaster, the radio's arrival on the land was considered newsworthy in itself.[2]

Digby Island had long been hailed as a powerful site of communication across distance and between worlds. As Du Vernet knew well, according to Ts'msyen creation stories, the island was the place where Weeget—or Txeemsim—first brought light to the world. After taking the golden ball of light from the Chief of the Heavens, Weeget landed at the village of Kanagatsiyot. Nisga'a stories relate that Txeemsim wandered down the Nass River as a trickster "full of human failings," but also as a spiritual being who taught the people the Ayuukhl Nisga'a: laws, protocols, and codes of conduct embedded in tales of spirits, animals, and people.[3] Txeemsim was an especially powerful being at the center of stories that told of the connections between spiritual and earthly worlds.

After years of Indigenous peoples of the northwest coast trying to present the laws of their land in a language and medium that the colonizers could understand—sending printed petitions and live delegations to various levels of government, including to Queens and Kings, and hiring lawyers to help them argue their case—the Indian Land Question remained unanswered. Successive waves of federal and provincial land commissions had carved up Indigenous territory into reserves, even though there were still no Indigenous treaties with Canada west of the Rocky Mountains. But the Nisga'a and Ts'msyen continued to use petitions, hoping somebody would listen. In 1917, they sent a joint petition to Prime Minister Borden protesting military conscription, arguing that they were not citizens under the Indian Act, and therefore not part of the democratic process of law-making that could authorize the state's right to conscript them. Haida parents also turned to petitions in the matter of the education of their children; they demanded local schooling for their children, stating clearly how the system of residential schools was a disaster for their children's lives and their own.[4] Du Vernet joined in their appeals, but not enough church and government officials had ears to hear.

The same month that the radio arrived in Prince Rupert, radio mind also made an appearance. According to the *Prince Rupert Daily News*, on February 18, 1924, Archbishop Frederick Du Vernet gave an evening "demonstration of radio mind."[5] A group of about twenty eager young people had gathered after church in the apartment above the newspaper's offices to watch Du Vernet exhibit the power of thought transference. Holding his Chevreul pendulum—this time a key tied to a pencil held above a lettered sheet of paper—the archbishop selected volunteers from the audience to take turns relaxing their

PLATE 1. Frederick Verner, *On Rainy River at Long Sault* (1873). Photograph courtesy of the National Gallery of Canada.

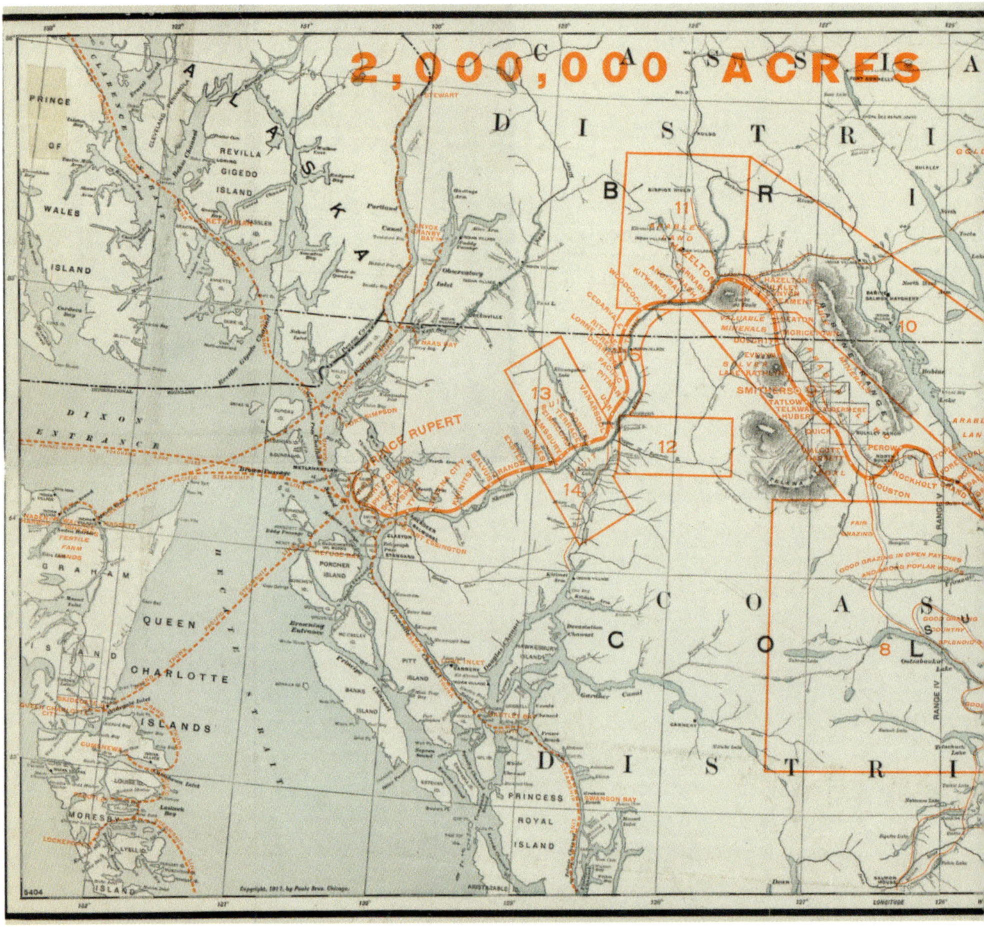

PLATE 2. *Map of the Central Section of British Columbia: Shewing the County Served by the Grand Trunk Pacific Railway* (Chicago: Poole Brothers, 1911). Photograph courtesy of the Map and Data Library, University of Toronto (G3572.C4 P3 1000 1911 B-2 Rare).

MAP OF
THE CENTRAL SECTION
OF
BRITISH COLUMBIA
SHEWING THE COUNTRY SERVED
BY THE
GRAND TRUNK PACIFIC RAILWAY
APPROXIMATE SCALE OF LAND MILES
1 Canoe River Country
2 Fraser River Valley
3 Peace River Country
4 Stuart Lake Country
5 Nechako Valley
6 Blackwater Country
7 Endako Valley
8 Ootsa Lake Country
9 Bulkley Valley
10 Babine Country
11 Kispiox Valley
12 Copper River Country
13 Kitsumgalum Valley
14 Lakelse Valley
15 Skeena Valley Bench Lands
16 Grande Prairie
17 Pouce Coupe
LINES UNDER CONSTRUCTION
LINES PROJECTED
RICULTURAL LAND
CARIBOO
ALBERTA
GRANDE PRAIRIE
AGRICULTURAL LANDS
AGRICULTURAL LAND
ARABLE LAND
PRINCE GEORGE
MC BRIDE
MOUNT ROBSON
JASPER PARK
BIG GAME HUNTING
FISHING
GOLD
GOLD QUARTZ
MAP LIBRARY
JAN 25 1966
DEPT. OF GEOGRAPHY
UNIVERSITY OF TORONTO

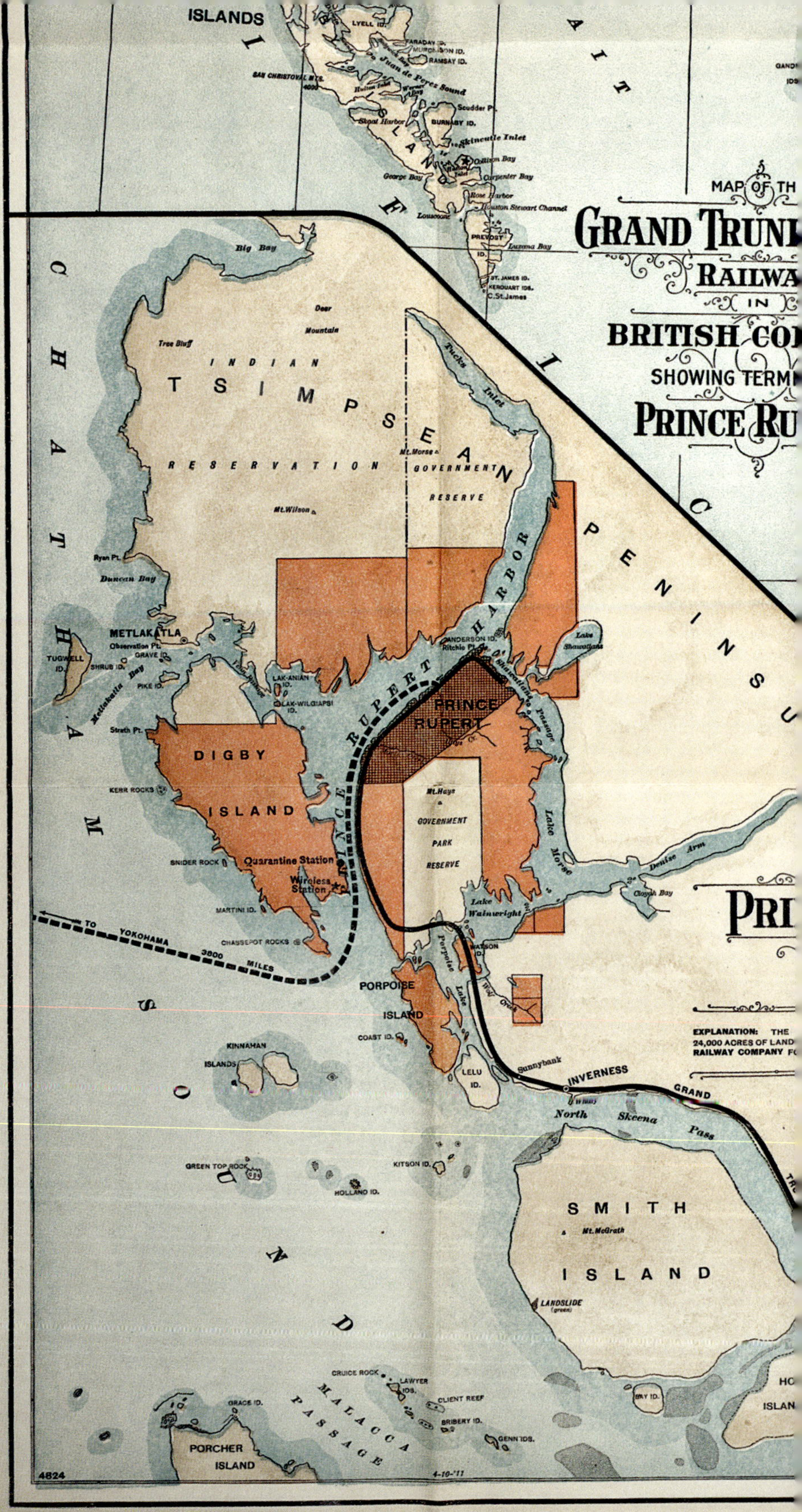
MAP OF TH
GRAND TRUNI
RAILWA
IN
BRITISH CO
SHOWING TERM
PRINCE RU
PRI
EXPLANATION: THE
24,000 ACRES OF LAND
RAILWAY COMPANY F
ISLANDS
LYELL ID.
Juan de Perez Sound
SAN CHRISTOVAL MTS.
Skincutle Inlet
Carpenter Bay
Rose Harbor
Houston Stewart Channel
PREVOST ID.
C.St.James
Big Bay
Tree Bluff
Deer Mountain
INDIAN
TSIMPSEAN
RESERVATION
Mt.Morse
GOVERNMENT
RESERVE
Mt.Wilson
PENINSU
Tucks Inlet
HARBOR
RUPERT
PRINCE
PRINCE RUPERT
Ryan Pt.
Duncan Bay
METLAKATLA
Observation Pt.
GRAVE ID.
TUGWELL ID.
SHRUB ID.
PIKE ID.
Metlakatla Bay
Strath Pt.
LAK-ANIAN ID.
LAK-WILGIAPSI ID.
ANDERSON ID.
Ritchie Pt.
Lake Shawatlans
Shawatlans Passage
DIGBY
ISLAND
KERR ROCKS
SNIDER ROCK
Quarantine Station
Wireless Station
MARTINI ID.
CHASSEPOT ROCKS
TO YOKOHAMA 3800 MILES
Mt.Hays
GOVERNMENT PARK RESERVE
Lake Morse
Lake Wainwright
Denise Arm
Clough Bay
PORPOISE
ISLAND
Porpoise Lake
Wolf Creek
COAST ID.
KINNAHAN ISLANDS
LELU ID.
Sunnybank
INVERNESS
GRAND
North Skeena Pass
CHATHAM
SOUND
GREEN TOP ROCK
KITSON ID.
HOLLAND ID.
SMITH
Mt.McGrath
ISLAND
LANDSLIDE
CRUICE ROCK
LAWYER IDS.
CLIENT REEF
BRIBERY ID.
GENN IDS.
MALACCA PASSAGE
GRACE ID.
PORCHER ISLAND
BAY ID.
4824
4-10-'11

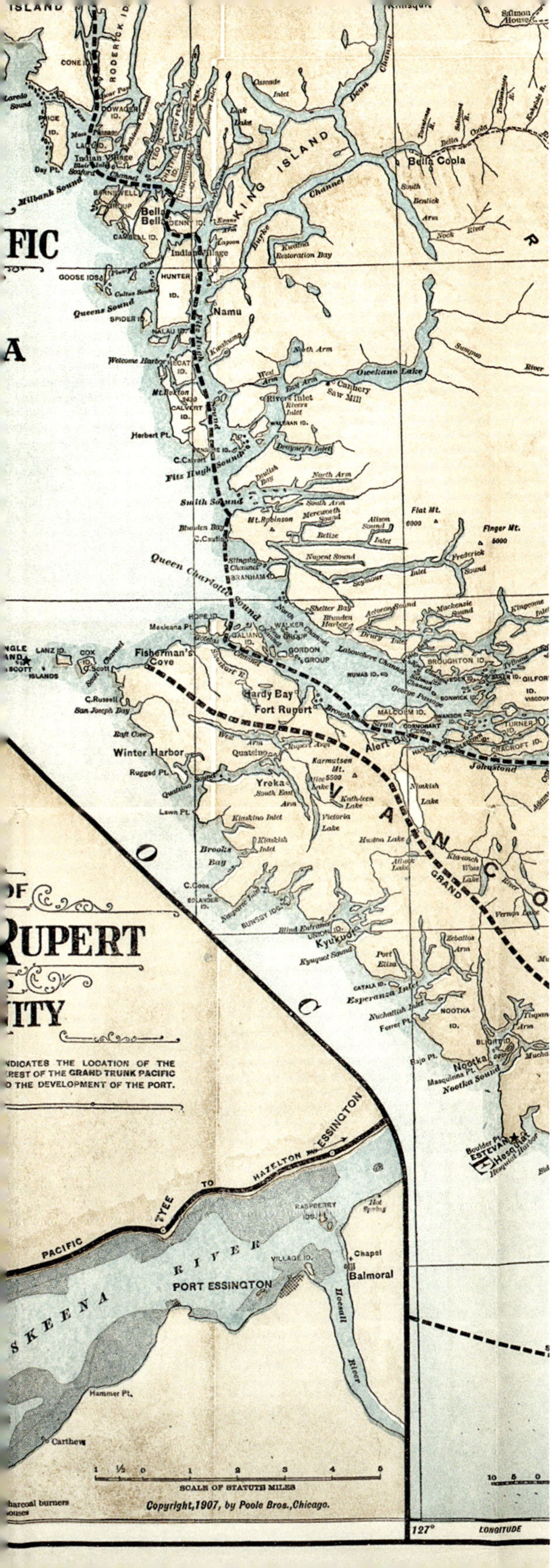

PLATE 3. *Map of the Grand Trunk Pacific Railway in British Columbia Showing Terminus at Prince Rupert Harbor* and *Map of Prince Rupert and Vicinity* (Poole Brothers, 1907). From *Prince Rupert, British Columbia: The Pacific Coast Terminus of the Grand Trunk Pacific Railway* (Montreal: Grand Trunk Pacific Railway Company, 1911). Photograph courtesy of Thomas Fisher Rare Book Library, University of Toronto.

PLATE 4. Wedding couple (ca. 1910s?). Lantern slide. Photograph courtesy of the Diocese of Caledonia Archives.

PLATE 5. Indian Land Committee, Aiyansh (ca. 1910?). The man on the far right is likely Andrew Mercer. Lantern slide. Photograph courtesy of the Diocese of Caledonia Archives.

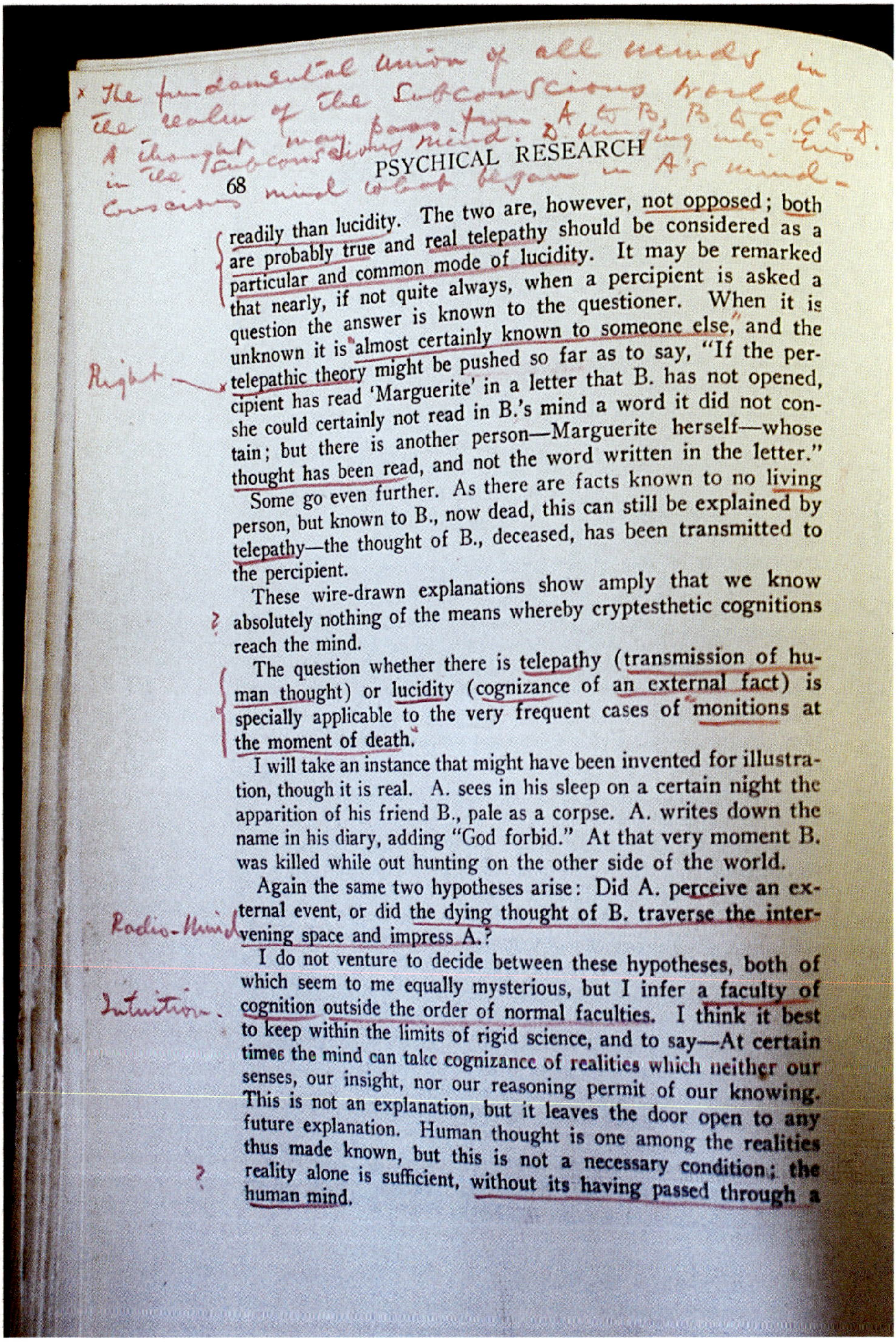

readily than lucidity. The two are, however, not opposed; both are probably true and real telepathy should be considered as a particular and common mode of lucidity. It may be remarked that nearly, if not quite always, when a percipient is asked a question the answer is known to the questioner. When it is unknown it is almost certainly known to someone else, and the telepathic theory might be pushed so far as to say, "If the percipient has read 'Marguerite' in a letter that B. has not opened, she could certainly not read in B.'s mind a word it did not contain; but there is another person—Marguerite herself—whose thought has been read, and not the word written in the letter."

Some go even further. As there are facts known to no living person, but known to B., now dead, this can still be explained by telepathy—the thought of B., deceased, has been transmitted to the percipient.

These wire-drawn explanations show amply that we know absolutely nothing of the means whereby cryptesthetic cognitions reach the mind.

The question whether there is telepathy (transmission of human thought) or lucidity (cognizance of an external fact) is specially applicable to the very frequent cases of monitions at the moment of death.

I will take an instance that might have been invented for illustration, though it is real. A. sees in his sleep on a certain night the apparition of his friend B., pale as a corpse. A. writes down the name in his diary, adding "God forbid." At that very moment B. was killed while out hunting on the other side of the world.

Again the same two hypotheses arise: Did A. perceive an external event, or did the dying thought of B. traverse the intervening space and impress A.?

I do not venture to decide between these hypotheses, both of which seem to me equally mysterious, but I infer a faculty of cognition outside the order of normal faculties. I think it best to keep within the limits of rigid science, and to say—At certain times the mind can take cognizance of realities which neither our senses, our insight, nor our reasoning permit of our knowing. This is not an explanation, but it leaves the door open to any future explanation. Human thought is one among the realities thus made known, but this is not a necessary condition; the reality alone is sufficient, without its having passed through a human mind.

PLATE 6. Du Vernet's marginalia. From Charles Richet, *Thirty Years of Psychical Research* (1923). Photograph courtesy of the Diocese of Caledonia Archives.

minds and then sending a word, letter by letter, to his own serene mind. The key successfully bobbed above the correct letter every time, the newspaper reported, causing a wave of concern for the youthful audience: "The effect of this was very apparent for, when it became clear that all our thoughts were broadcasted like a radio message and had an effect on the thoughts and actions of others it became doubly important that the thoughts should be of the right kind." For the young people, to confess their sins had once required words, but now the archbishop could (slowly) read their minds.

Nevertheless, the archbishop's young audience was fascinated, according to the newspaper: "So interested were they that after the talk the young people gathered around His Grace and questioned him more closely in regard to many points that had not been quite clear and also as to the possible relationship between thought transference and spiritualism." In 1924, the *Prince Rupert Daily News* published many articles about radio, celebrating it for its practical uses and speculating about radio's more imaginative possibilities. The newspaper also noted, in its coverage of the February 1924 demonstration, that while the older people of Prince Rupert largely ignored the "great truth" proven by Du Vernet's scientific demonstrations of radio mind, he had many admirers from afar: "He received many letters from all over the continent in regard to the matter and wherever he went people were keen to ask questions and look for demonstrations." He had ready answers to their questions, answers he authorized with reference to both science and the spirit.

Meeting Radio Mind

I first met Frederick Herbert Du Vernet in a castle high on a hilltop overlooking the Schwabian Alps in southern Germany. I was on my sabbatical year at the University of Tübingen, working in a room with a view of the Neckar River. This was the very room where in 1869 Friedrich Miescher discovered a chemical in white blood cells that he called the nuclein—a find that set the stage for the later discovery of DNA as the key to the story of every human being's genetic past and present.

As I sat at my desk, paging through photocopies of the Anglican *Canadian Churchman* that I had lugged with me all the way from Toronto for a book I was writing on Christianity and healing, I came across a tantalizing headline in the edition from November 23, 1922: "Reality in Religion." The article, written by Archbishop Du Vernet, a man I had never heard of before, began with a metaphor drawn from media: "The gramophone disks of old religious phrases are still being used because of their familiar music, but we are anxiously waiting for new records which will better express our inmost convictions." Those old disks, Du Vernet said, were filled with the "barren metaphysics of theology," an overly philosophizing way of thinking that had held sway over a vital "spiritual religion" for far too long. For Du Vernet, spiritual religion was an energetic form of Christianity that looked not to "dead doctrine" for its proof, but to Christ's imperative to love God and one's neighbor. Thankfully, in his view, "the outlook for spiritual religion was never brighter than it is today because the highest thinking of the age tends to identify ultimate reality with spiritual energy." He was, in short, a cosmic optimist.

Looking further, I found another article from August 30, 1923, that also turned to media to generate spiritual reflection: "The Psychology of the Motion Picture." Here, Du Vernet pondered the psychological implications of the new medium of the moving picture: "What will be the effect upon the rising generation of habitually watching the pantomime of life rather than plunging into the reality of life itself?" In the early age of cinema, the consequences of a life lived virtually were already causing worry among the older generation. The church, Du Vernet advised, would do well to learn from the psychology of the motion picture, by focusing less on the *will* and instead appealing to the *imagination*. Citing the apostle Paul's "profound truth" regarding the need to fill one's thoughts with true, pure, and gracious things, Du Vernet urged the church to take seriously the imaginative power of suggestion whether in movie theaters or church services.[6]

An issue from the next month, dated September 13, 1923, did not disappoint. There, I found an article entitled "Divine Healing" in which the archbishop introduced his idea of "radio mind," by which he meant the telepathic transference of a thought from one person's conscious mind to the subconscious mind of another. The most potent form of radio mind was rooted in a belief in God, according to Du Vernet: "This is the most powerful suggestion known to modern science because it brings the subconscious mind into touch with the Infinite so that the late[n]t energy of the soul is quickened into 'newness of life.'" Citing again the apostle Paul and the authority of science, Du Vernet heralded radio mind as a tool that could not only heal but also clear away the "mists of prejudice and superstition." Radio mind achieved its clarifying power through harnessing vibrations moving through the air.

The excitement continued. For the November 1 issue, Du Vernet contributed an article with the intriguing title "Telepathic Testimonies." The editors placed the article beside another piece very critical of Christian Science, a religion that also extols a form of distant healing through mental effort.[7] In

"Telepathic Testimonies," Du Vernet cast himself as a scientist reporting on his experiments in radio mind and shared several corroborating testimonies sent to him by his readers. The testimonies ranged from the trivial to the tragic: clergymen whose wives were able to communicate with them telepathically, succeeding in getting them to phone home or to pick up needed groceries; mothers who vividly saw the deaths of their soldier sons at the front, at the very time that their sons were killed. These testimonies, Du Vernet contended, were added proof that "thought radiation" was neither superstitious nor magical, a fact that his experiments had demonstrated: "The vast majority of people are slaves to the thought that the same body cannot be in two different places at the same time, but this law applies only to a material body, and mind energy is a spiritual entity, where it acts there it is, regardless of distance in space." I paged through further issues hoping to find more of Du Vernet, but it was late in the day and I had to return to my baby who needed me in the flesh, so our first meeting came to an end.

Radio mind! Who was this man and what was he doing writing with such wild optimism about the spiritual effects of new media in the *Canadian Churchman*, the relatively staid and conservative national newspaper of Canadian Anglicans? Though I hadn't discovered anything quite akin to the beginnings of DNA, I felt a thrill of discovery—I had found a mystic of mediation at the highest echelons of the Anglican Church. Combining his excitement over the innovations of radio technology with what psychology was newly revealing about the complexity of human consciousness, Du Vernet saw himself as opening up a new spiritual frequency for all. As he told his diocesan synod in 1923: "Psychology as the science of human behaviour as dependent upon human mind is furnishing the Church with a scientific method of relating spiritual truths to the lives of men, women, and children, according to their age, sex, and race. Religion can now become a reality to all sorts and conditions of people, where before it was generally supposed that only the favoured few of a mystical temperament could ever become the saints of God."[8] Not simply a vertical path of prayer from petitioner to God, radio mind was a vision of mystical communication at once collective and unconscious.

Though most psychologists today likely would not recognize Du Vernet as a participant in the history of their discipline, in the early twentieth century the lines between spiritual and psychological exploration were not so firmly set. They were bound by one word—psyche—that had roots in both the apostle Paul's views of human nature and the science of the mind. As a scaling up of telepathy on a cosmic scale, radio mind riffed on the work of Frederick Myers and William James and, by extension, the ideas of Sigmund Freud. All engaged with the Society for Psychical Research, these three early psychologists each worked with narratives and testimonies of patients or "case studies" as their pathway to understanding the psyche.[9]

Now banished to the realm of the paranormal, psychic research in the early twentieth century was a viable—albeit risky—line of scientific investigation. Frederick Du Vernet claimed his own stake in the field by way of a theory of mediation that was mystical and muscular, spiritual and scientific. As Roger Luckhurst has shown, psychologists and psychic researchers based in London drew heavily on testimony from the "imperial margin"—stories of the uncanny or supernatural that came from British colonies in India or Africa. Du Vernet joined this tradition of colonial testimony within the history of psychology.[10]

When I returned to the *Canadian Churchman* the next day, I had to read nearly a year's worth of issues before I found "The Psychology of Resting," a short piece printed August 21, 1924, in which Du Vernet appealed to readers to cultivate the benefits of a "restful mind" in a rushing age. With motorcars and flying machines speeding up the pace of life, Du Vernet argued, "the vital energy of our race is not able to keep up with the mechanical progress of our age." Recommending a daily half hour of "systematic muscular relaxation," Du Vernet urged his readers to "drop the idea of rest deep into the subconscious mind." With the muscles and the mind at rest, he advised the relaxed Christian to then call on the Lord to "claim the promise of perfect peace." In closing, he cited not Paul, but the American Quaker poet and abolitionist John Greenleaf Whittier: "Take from our souls the strain and stress, And let our ordered lives confess, The beauty of Thy peace."[11]

An Anglican clergyman so openly advocating the techniques of what might in other contexts be called mental science or New Thought was not entirely original. Other clerics, such as Episcopalian Elwood Worcester of the Boston-based Emmanuel Movement, had also experimented with psychotherapeutic healing techniques paired with Christian practices. Fears of the consequences of rapid technological change in both transportation and telecommunications exercised many people's minds at the time.[12] But an archbishop from the upper reaches of the Pacific northwest who testified with such verve and confidence to his own discovery (and christening) of a form of mystical communication he called radio mind struck me as delightfully unexpected, and even bizarre.

After the August 1924 article, the trail stopped. Several issues of the *Canadian Churchman* later, I read that Archbishop Du Vernet had died of a stroke on October 22, 1924, after several months of being bedridden with high blood pressure and an enlarged heart. I found myself saddened to learn of his death; radio mind had caught my imagination and would not let go.

A Late-Style Archbishop

Du Vernet came to radio mind as he entered his "late style," to use a term Edward Said deployed to think about musicians and writers at the end of their lives. Said sought to understand how creative artists, late in life, develop "new idioms," often by breaking from their communities of practice in "a sort of deliberately unproductive productiveness going *against*. . . ." Said saw late style as a kind of "exile" or alienation that opened a path for men and women with deep experience of the world—people who in an Indigenous context would be called elders—to lead others to see the world in a new way.[13]

Du Vernet was a man growing old, confronting mortality. He was living a constrained life of bed rest after years of vigorous travel around his diocese on foot and by canoe, steamer, dogsled, and, eventually, train and motorcar. But he had not lost his energy for conversion via testimony. In an article he wrote for the *Vancouver Province* in 1923, he proudly relayed a story of having convinced a "university professor" of the power of "inter-mental action," adding: "My desire is to have as many people as possible, by my method, convince themselves of the fact and then make an intelligent and beneficial use of the power of mental radiation." His idiom of radio mind was a new testimony of the spirit that was a "going against" orthodox Anglican views of Jesus Christ as "the one Mediator" to God.[14]

Under doctor's orders, Du Vernet had been forced to miss the 1920 Lambeth Conference, a worldwide gathering of Anglican bishops held in England usually once a decade under the leadership of the archbishop of Canterbury. The conference of 1920 was a busy one, out of which emerged resolutions encouraging missionaries in the colonies to give "the widest freedom to indigenous workers" to grow the church according to their own "national character," while acknowledging that sometimes this might entail establishing racially segregated churches. The bishops agreed that women should be given more roles and responsibilities in church work and should be paid fairly; they also forbade the use of "unnatural" means of contraception. Attempting to both encourage and curtail social change, the bishops were at cross-purposes on many issues.[15]

The bishops of the Lambeth Conference of 1920 also had sharp words for those Anglicans engaged in psychical research and those experimenting with Spiritualism, Christian Science, and Theosophy. While the bishops were "prepared to expect and welcome new light from psychical research upon the powers and processes of the spirit of man," they were adamant that Christians must believe in the incarnated Christ—God become man—as the real pathway to spiritual truth. They urged Anglicans not to be misled by untested hypotheses about psychic research: "Such scientific researches have confessedly not reached an advanced stage, and we are supported by the best psychologists in warning our people against accepting as final theories which further knowledge may disprove, and still more against the indiscriminate and undisciplined exercise of psychic powers, and the habit of recourse to seances, 'seers', and mediums." Grouping together Theosophy and psychic research as a misbegotten quest for false knowledge, the bishops declared these views to be "irreconcilable with the Christian faith as to the person and mission of Christ and with the missionary claim and duty of the Christian religion as the message of God to all mankind."[16] For an archbishop supervising missions in the far reaches of Canada to be won over to psychic research would have shocked the men gathered at Lambeth.

Whether or not Du Vernet's attendance at the Lambeth Conference would have made a difference to his late style, or to the bishops' resolutions on psychic research, it is likely that a lecture on spiritual radio would not have been well received. The city of Victoria, however, was another matter. Du Vernet first delivered his theory of radio mind as a series of lectures at St. Saviour's Church in Victoria, and the *Canadian Churchman* articles were then published between 1920 and 1924. During this same period, he published frequent articles in the *Montreal Daily Star*, the *Vancouver Province*, and the *Prince Rupert Daily News*, many of which were posthumously republished in 1927 as *Out of a Scribe's Treasure: Brief Essays in Practical Religious Thinking*.[17]

Many of his newspaper writings dealt explicitly with political topics ranging from income inequality to social justice, and in these articles, he bemoaned the "three mountain peaks" of capitalism: "excessive inequality in the distribution of wealth"; "insecurity of labour in employment"; and "exclusion of labour from any control in industry." He prophesied: "Sooner or later [these peaks] will dominate the landscape of the world." Du Vernet increasingly took up a radio mind–style socialism in his writings: "Since this life of God in the souls of men flows from one and the same source, it follows of necessity that wherever there is true religion it will tend to bind men of all classes, races, and nations together as ministering members of the one great family of God."[18] Urging universal harmony at once mystical and political, he hoped that telepathy would lead to sympathy, justice, and understanding around the world. Just how it would do so, he never quite spelled out.

Du Vernet's writings resound with themes articulated by social justice and human rights activists today: "Social justice requires to render to each man according to his capacity and to each capacity according to its work; but this does not lessen the equal right of all men, worthy or unworthy, to the opportunity to live a life worth living." He argued that new immigrants must be protected from the "tyranny of the majority" through both constitutional and spiritual means. And he championed not only a minimum wage but also maximum limits on interest: "If social control of the minimum wage of the worker is possible, social control of the maximum rate of interest for the investor is equally feasible." He also wrote about schools as the "gymnasium of democracy" where children should learn to play fair, to work together, to stand up to bullies, and to care for each other's welfare.[19]

To understand Du Vernet's late-style mix of spiritual politics and scientific experiment, and to tell this climactic chapter in the story of radio mind, the radio itself provides a fitting metaphor. Three different frequencies coursed through the last decade of Du Vernet's life, with more and less static, interference, and clarity. On one frequency, he was oriented by a growing commitment to unity across diversity. He worked hard to overcome divisions between high church and low church Anglicans and went even further to argue that all Protestant churches in Canada should unite. He urged wealthy capitalists to respond fairly to the valid concerns of the working class, and he questioned racialized hierarchies of "Indian" and "white." On the second frequency, he came to attune himself to psychic science through his experiments with spiritual radio and his voracious reading of philosophers of the mind, including Henri Bergson and William James.

The third frequency carried messages that Du Vernet had learned from listening to Indigenous parents opposed to sending their children to residential schools. He did not write about parents' concerns in his newspaper editorials, but instead channeled their objections in letters he wrote to church and government officials in Ottawa and Toronto. Sometimes this included presenting Indigenous parents' petitions for the opening of local boarding schools for their children, as in the case of Haida parents at Massett. Growing increasingly alarmed that his appeals went unheard, or even ignored, Du Vernet deplored the greed and "evils" of a residential school system that continued to grow in scale, wrenching more and more children from their parents and their land in order to both "civilize" and "Christianize" them. Adjusting the dial between these three frequencies reveals the intensity, inconsistency, and failure of radio mind as a tool of healing in the midst of the piercing violence of family annihilation, cultural genocide, and church and state deceit that was the residential school system.

The Frequency of Unity

Frederick Du Vernet never wanted to be an archbishop. At the same synod in Prince Rupert in 1909 during which he argued for a formal treaty for the Indigenous peoples of the northwest coast, Du Vernet dismissed as ridiculous the idea of instituting an archbishop for British Columbia. Addressing the ten male missionaries, the eleven "lady missionaries," and the five members of the laity gathered in Prince Rupert, he argued: "We do not need a third legislative body with power to enact coercive canons under the rule of an unnecessary Archbishop presiding with ludicrous dignity over an Upper House with two or three bishops."[20] Within six years, however, his fellow bishops elected him as the metropolitan of the Ecclesiastical Province of British Columbia, making him the Lord Archbishop of Caledonia (fig. 51). He accepted the role, but refused to sign his name as "Archbishop" and avoided the naming practices that would dub him "Frederick Caledonia." Nevertheless, people regularly called him by the honorific title of "Archbishop" or "Your Grace."

FIGURE 51. The Most Reverend F. H. Du Vernet, Archbishop of Caledonia (ca. 1915). Photograph courtesy of The General Synod Archives, Anglican Church of Canada (P7805-2).

After a lifetime of building bridges within his church, and having the regard of his peers as an eloquent speaker who was full of grace, Du Vernet was a sensible choice for the first metropolitan of the new Ecclesiastical Province of British Columbia. Realigned to better fit with provincial and territorial boundaries, Caledonia and its sister dioceses now lodged more seamlessly into the map of Canada. Du Vernet considered this rationalizing of the diocesan maps to be a good thing, so that Anglicans could collectively have some stronger effect on provincial laws related to "vital problems" such as "land tenure, mining claims, liquor licenses, school matters, hospital boards, women's rights, marriage regulations, divorce courts, etc."[21] After his consecration as archbishop in 1915, Du Vernet continued to work toward soothing breaches among his fellow Anglicans and sorting out the relationship between his church and the state.

The secret to unity across theological divides of "churchmanship," according to Du Vernet, was the "frank recognition of these differences." Before coming to British Columbia, he had already unified the various Canadian Anglican missionary societies into the Missionary Society of the Church of England in Canada, with its headquarters in Toronto. And he was in the middle of trying to unite—without suppressing—competing Evangelical and Anglo-Catholic seminaries into what would eventually become the Vancouver School of Theology. Alarmed in 1909 by the possibility that the Anglican seminary in Vancouver would only include high church views, which were more popular in the south of the province, Du Vernet rooted Anglican liturgical differences in the land: "We have no intention of allowing others to force upon us an extreme type of churchmanship which is not suited to the sturdy unconventional North, which loves the ritual of the snow-capped mountains, the music of the waterfalls, and all the freshness and freedom of pioneer life. We should be false to the sacred charge that God has given us to add our contribution of a simple, earnest, spiritual type of religion to the common life of the Church if we chose 'compromise for the sake of peace' instead of 'comprehension for the sake of truth.'"[22] Du Vernet insisted that unity did not mean that spiritual differences would be erased, and he used the land as his witness.

Both versions of Anglican churchmanship established their own theological colleges in Vancouver—the Evangelical Latimer Hall and the high church St. Mark's. Combined as two teaching colleges within the Anglican Theological College in 1912, they maintained their different identities under the presidency of Du Vernet, who led from afar in Prince Rupert. For example, in a 1913 issue of the *North British Columbia News*, CMS Secretary Henry Elliott Fox, a canon of St. Paul's Cathedral in London, wrote glowingly of the contributions that the Evangelical Latimer Hall could make to a highly gendered Christian unity within British Columbia: "It is a fine type of Christianity which is being developed out there. Men are manly and women womanly. Christians are broad-minded enough to regard the denominational differences which at home we set up as barbed-wire barriers, rather as varying uniforms in the one great Army of the one great Commander-in-Chief. The main danger in a new country is from the race for wealth, the rush after speculative schemes, the absorbing stimulus and the strain of competing secularities." Du Vernet shared Fox's fears that competing secularities—in the form of real estate speculation, liquor, and greed—were greater challenges than liturgical divides.[23]

Du Vernet's approach to resolving deep theological divisions by recognizing them and moving on was reminiscent of his earlier conciliatory approach to the enmity between the Wycliffe and Trinity Colleges in Toronto. In 1920, after countless letters and several time-consuming trips up and down the coast, Du Vernet succeeded in establishing a fully unified Anglican Theological College in Vancouver. Though based in Prince Rupert, he served as the president of the college until his death, a testament to his ability to bridge divides even from a distance. Du Vernet was especially delighted that the new school would eventually be built in the heart of the new Point Grey campus of the University of British Columbia, signaling its strong connection to secular higher education. Known as the "University Endowment Lands," since they were gifted to the university by the government, this location too was Indigenous land, whether or not Du Vernet knew it. The Vancouver Theological College was built on unceded Musqueam territory, a place still called Elk̲sn in the Coast Salish language.[24]

Du Vernet's commitment to unify people—to bring them together across common purposes, and not to divide them over differences—well qualified him as a leader in a church that was itself divided over ritual preferences, political convictions, and land. Some Anglicans were deeply committed to high church modes of smells and bells in their liturgies, while others insisted on the plainest of Communions to better become one with Jesus. Some Anglicans were among the wealthiest elites in the Dominion and wanted to maintain the status quo, while others argued for the state to play more of a role in repairing the yawning gap between the rich and the poor at a time of growing labor strife. Some Anglicans thought it was time to stop drawing lines between "white work" and "Indian work," while others thought that the color line was not only necessary but also natural. As the church increasingly focused on the "sacred enterprise" of residential schools as a priority for the Indian work, many lay Anglicans likely remained ignorant of the fact that their fellow church members, including Nisga'a, Haida, and Ts'msyen Christians, were petitioning the government to acknowledge their sovereign rights to their land and to keep their children close to home.[25]

Spiritual Conditions

Du Vernet was a spiritual pioneer in many senses, including as a mystic of mediation and as a settler who claimed Indigenous land. Writing in the *North British Columbia News* in 1917, he mused, "Environment has its effect on church life. In a new, wild country like this, traditional churchgoing has lost its power." His traveling schedule intensified once he extended his "spiritual jurisdiction" to the region of the Peace River in northeastern British Columbia, as when he opened a church in Pouce Coupe in 1915. Distraught by what he saw to be rampant land speculation in the Peace River Valley, Du Vernet did not comment on ongoing conflicts over Indigenous sovereignty in this region, which was part of the Treaty 8 territory of Athapaskan-speaking Indigenous nations.[26] He knew from his long journeys along the coast and into the inland valleys that what he called spiritual religion would not be expressed through a weekly piety of traditional Sunday churchgoing. Unlike Indigenous peoples, the dispersed settlers had few stories embedded in the land to give them spiritual guidance, and they had little in the way of religious community, save for a wandering bishop who dropped by every so often.

The "lonely" settlers whom he visited on his travels through the diocese welcomed Du Vernet as a pragmatic pastor. In the words of a local newspaper, Du Vernet's "spiritual ministration calls for much pioneering effort. The Bishop, however, is ready at all times to sling a pack on his back, and cheerfully tramp to any portion of his district where no other means of transportation is available." The writer was particularly impressed by his skill with a hammer: "When occasion offers the Bishop can show that he is no mean carpenter, as during his brief stay at Chilco, he made a temporary lectern, a prayer desk, and communion table, for the new church out of rough lumber."[27] Du Vernet ministered through a vocation of presence, literally trying to tramp the land into an Anglican diocese by way of his own footsteps.

Du Vernet's journeys on Indigenous land gave a spiritual sanction to colonial settlement; his support for formal treaties between the Dominion government and Indigenous peoples did not mean that he questioned "pioneering" or the agricultural transformation of the land. His colonial vision had markedly socialist tones, as in a letter to a newspaper back in eastern Canada in which he urged public spending on better roads and increased taxes to curb speculation and to benefit the spiritual welfare of settlers:

> Gathering these people together, we had the first service they had had since their arrival there three years ago. See the crime of the speculator! No school for these people! No church! Because the very best of land all round them which might have dozens of families living on it, is held by some selfish, greedy land-grabber who has done nothing whatever for the country's good. A rich man in Vancouver, a widow in Nova Scotia are holding this region back. I have heard the bitter cry of these settlers. I have seen the rich soil waiting for the plough. God intended this land for production, not for speculation.[28]

Hearing in one ear the bitter cry of the settlers who wanted schools for their children, Du Vernet heard in the other one similar anguished petitions from Indigenous parents. At a certain frequency, he understood that both these cries were related to the underlying fact of colonial dispossession and capitalist speculation. But he never quite put the two together.

Unity in the midst of diversity was a theme that carried over into Du Vernet's public role as a city leader, which included serving as the president of the ministerial association that brought together clergy from Prince Rupert's Christian churches. On the occasion of the death of King Edward in 1910, Du Vernet gave a speech before a gathering in Prince Rupert: "We have met together with representatives of all races and nationalities in our midst; all creeds and all churches, all classes rich and poor, young and old. The meeting is for one common purpose; to pay our tribute of respect to the late King Edward and to lay the wreath of immortelles of Prince Rupert upon the royal coffin." Du Vernet may have been accurate in enumerating the diversity of people gathered to recognize the King's death, which judging from photographs of the time included Indigenous participants. For example, one depicts an Empire Day celebration in 1911 featuring an audience that included the finely uniformed Nisga'a brass band. Another marks the visit of the Duke of Connaught in 1912 for which a contingent from Metlakatla erected an arch decorated with cedar boughs (figs. 52–53).[29]

Around the same time, Du Vernet also weighed in on the working lives of the residents of the new city. Writing to the *Prince Rupert Empire* in support of early closing laws for shops and especially for bars, Du Vernet reflected: "While I am an individualist to a certain degree I am enough of a socialist to say to myself, 'It is my duty to sacrifice my personal liberty in such a trifling matter as this in order that I may give others a chance.' We want our young men and young women working in shops and stores to have a little of the

FIGURE 52. Indian Band, Empire Day celebrations, Prince Rupert (1911). Photograph courtesy of the Prince Rupert City and Regional Archives (LP984-29-1759-392).

FIGURE 53. Metlakatla's "Arch of Welcome" for the visit of the Duke of Connaught to Prince Rupert (1912). Photograph courtesy of the Prince Rupert City and Regional Archives (Phylis Bowman Collection, P985-29-2397).

personal freedom which we value so highly. We want them to have the long summer evenings free to enjoy themselves in a healthy manner, instead of cooped up in a store." He was not a bishop with his nose buried in a Bible, or with his eyes on a plum promotion back east. He listened to the people around him and intervened in public affairs by writing letters to editors and officials, giving speeches, and, eventually, publishing articles in newspapers across the country. For example, at a meeting of the Prince Rupert Ministerial Association on January 13, 1913, "Bishop Du Vernet gave a short address, noting the gradual improvement in Spiritual Conditions in spite of lack of Moral Sense, Irreverence, Indifference, there were signs of hope in the rounding up of separate units, and we are on the eve of a great movement and the Building up of a great city." His optimism for the slow improvement of spiritual conditions came despite his ongoing frustration with illegal liquor sales in hotels and with problems of "white slaves," likely a reference to white women sex workers in the city.[30]

In the last years of his life, working on radio mind must have been a welcome distraction from the demands of his day job. Because of his illness, he was no longer able to travel to Toronto for the General Synod and the annual meeting of the Missionary Society of the Church of England in Canada (MSCC). These meetings had given him the chance to appeal in person to his colleagues for financial support and to impress upon them his strong views about everything from temperance to residential schools. Asking by letter for bits and pieces to cover the costs of his far-flung missions, Du Vernet was faced with the impossible task of accounting for the budgets of the "Indian work" and the "white work" down to the penny. He confessed to be at a loss, especially in places like Hazelton, where the time of "mingling" between settlers and Indigenous Christians had continued. Even the Cathedral Church of St. Andrew's featured Sundays when Indigenous Christians ran the services, music and all, with Haida chief Alfred Adams and Nisga'a chief Paul Mercer both giving sermons.[31]

Writing on April 23, 1924, to Canon Sydney Gould, the general secretary of the MSCC and also a Wycliffe-trained missionary, Du Vernet explained, "I am recovering from a somewhat severe illness and am scarcely fit yet to grapple with Statistics but I am endeavouring to get the Indian Estimate Sheet to you by May 1st. As to the White Work Statement for 3 years, this involves a vast amount of work. It is almost impossible in some of our missions to divide White and Indian contributions, for example in Hazelton the congregation giving through the Offertory Collections place their money in the same plate—no distinction between White and Indian." It was just as difficult for him to racially account for the salaries of the ministers in the diocese, since they too went back and forth between settler and Indigenous churches based on the rhythms of seasonal work in the canneries. His daughter, Alice, began to serve as his secretary and traveling companion, helping him with the overwhelming task of collating the statistics. But he knew quite well that even their combined efforts to account for race were an illusory performance of precision.[32]

Du Vernet also continued to grapple with the problem of not having enough ordained clergy to go around. In the same letter, he noted, "Several Indian missions are crying out for a resident ordained clergyman. I keep things going by promising to do my best for them, and sending them a clergyman for a season, removing him for White Work when they leave their village for the canneries." With a rising note of desperation in his letters to church leaders in Toronto, Du Vernet was a man feeling the stress of watching over the land and people his church had placed under his spiritual jurisdiction.

That the archbishop was required to quantify his spiritual work through classifications of race and records of cash flow was evidence that the story of missionary labors was increasingly mediated through the dehumanizing tool of colonial accounting.[33] The earlier stories of savage heathens, which had been dehumanizing in their own manner, had given way to ledger books by which residential schools for Indigenous children came to seem both Christian and profitable to many church leaders. From Du Vernet's perspective as a man who had traveled, in the flesh, to all the places he described in his letters and articles, unity was a movement that he could encourage but not control.

The Frequency of the Spirit

In the midst of his earthly efforts to unify his church and city, Du Vernet scaled up his search for unity to a cosmic plane. He turned not to legislation or church lobbying but to scientific experiment to find a spiritual current that would bind together across distance people, spirits, and the energy of love. In a chatty letter published in 1921 in *Across the Rockies*, and directed to Mrs. Satow, an English supporter of the Diocese of Caledonia, Du Vernet described himself thus: "I am feeling better, but the Doctor says I am a cracked cup, good for some years of service, but can stand no strain. This means no more tramps with a pack on my back. As I was a great walker and found this the best way of getting over a pioneer country in certain spots it is a [trial] to be told, 'Your life must be more circumscribed.'"[34] Constrained by his body's fragility, he turned ever more avidly to the exploration of psychic research.

In his bedridden hours, Du Vernet poured over his library of books, reading works by Henri Bergson, William James, Charles Richet, George Coe, and Josiah Royce, along with other (now) lesser-known philosophers of mind and psychic researchers. Luckily for me, he wrote, underlined, and drew on the pages of many of his books, leaving behind a record of his engagement with these authors. Du Vernet's marginalia reveal an active reader who "argue[d] with the text" and who clearly perceived himself to be part of a broader psychological conversation.[35] That a missionary-bishop in the northwest corner of the American continent felt that he was part of the discipline of psychology shows that this new science of the mind spoke to theologically oriented readers, often in a particularly gripping manner.

Many early twentieth-century psychologists were deeply involved with psychic research and made liberal use of the concept of the spirit.[36] They understood spirit to be channeled through the matter of the body and the mind, and sometimes even through the elements of the earth. In crafting his own late-style blend of matter, mind, and spirit, Du Vernet depended on these more legitimate scientists to ground his claims for radio mind as a technique for healing both bodies and societies. Ironically, perhaps, reading "orthodox" scientists who had taken a psychic turn gave him the tools to develop a spirituality that was increasing "unorthodox" in Anglican terms.

As I combed for evidence of these psychological influences upon Du Vernet's own psychic research, I came to think of searching in an archive as akin to the action of a diviner's rod, also known as the practice of dowsing. When I first stood in front of the Archbishop Du Vernet Caledonia Diocesan Library, two glass-fronted cases of dusty books in the basement that houses the archives of the Anglican Diocese of Caledonia, I ran my eyes along the bookshelves and came across Charles Richet's 1923 book *Thirty Years of Psychical Research*. Richet, a Nobel Prize winner in medicine, president of the Society for Psychical Research in 1905, and the man who coined the word "ectoplasm," had this to say about the divining rod: "The history of the divining rod is pertinent to our subject. For, if natural forces (underground water and metals) exercise an unknown action upon the subconscious mind, there must be unknown vibrations that awaken cryptesthetic sensibility; and we are brought back to the metaphysic that deals with the unknown vibrations of things." For Richet, "cryptesthesia" meant a "hidden sensibility" by which humans perceived things without knowing how they did so. Sometimes taking the form of telepathy, or "mental transmission" from one mind to another without speech, cryptesthesia was at the center of Richet's theory of the mind.[37]

The divining rod operates not by trickery or fraud, according to Richet, nor is it the effect of magic. Instead, the divining rod is an instrument by which the human subconscious and nervous system can feel the effects of the mysterious geophysical forces that Richet called "rhabdic force," or the "force that emanates from metals, sheets of water, and metallic salts." Coming from deep within the land and waters to shape human practice, rhabdic force would one day be explicable by scientific means, insisted Richet. The force of the land and water, for Richet, was paired with the power of memory, which he called "pantomnesia." Reading Richet's book, Du Vernet underlined this neologism and part of its definition: "we do not absolutely forget anything once it has been impressed on our senses." In searching for language to explain his theories of the human mind, Richet did not accept the terms "supernatural" or "spiritual." Instead, he used the term "metaphysic," as Du Vernet noted, to describe phenomena caused by the "intervention of either an extraneous power, or of an unknown faculty of the human mind." Du Vernet managed to lay his hands on Richet's 1923 book quite quickly and proceeded to read it critically through the lens of his own theory of radio mind (plate 6). He also evaluated Richet, mostly unfavorably, against the writings of Henri Bergson, a philosopher who also served as president of the Society for Psychical Research, in 1913, the same year Richet won his Nobel Prize.[38]

Throughout the margins of Richet's book, Du Vernet castigated his "wrong theory of mind energy" as if it showed a lack of metaphysical courage for being unwilling to utter the word "spiritual." For example, Richet wrote, "Wireless telegraphy has shown us that messages can be transmitted through space; it is therefore possible that by analogous but invisible mechanism to which our instruments and senses are insensitive, the brain may be affected without being able to perceive anything either of the transmitter or the receiver." In keeping with his own choice of technological analogy for the mysteries of mental transmission, Du Vernet wrote in the margin: "Why not radio mind?" He both concurred with and critiqued Richet's conclusions, marking up the text with his red pencil: "Experiments on normal persons indicate both telepathy and lucidity, and both are probable, however feeble and imperfect they may be. It follows that the thought of one man is mysteriously linked to that of others. We are not isolated, but are in some obscure connection with our fellows. . . . Is it permissible to compare this collective emotion to the mental transmission observable in the experiments detailed above?" In the margin, Du Vernet staked his claim: "My article expressing the same written long before this book was published F.H.D."[39] With the disquiet of a writer fearing that his writing has been plagiarized, or at least that his thoughts have been scooped, Du Vernet used marginalia to attest to his own discoveries.

As I searched the bookcases that housed what had been Du Vernet's library, which I had not even known existed before venturing to Prince Rupert, I felt what Richet might have called rhabdic force: I had a hunch, or even a compelling sense, that Henri Bergson's book *Mind-Energy* had to be there somewhere. As usual when one is looking for something, I couldn't find it on the first attempt. But once I said with certainty that I knew it had to be there, what did I see? A faded copy of *Mind-Energy*, its interior heavily annotated by Du Vernet's red pencil. I gave a cry of joy and knew my long journey had been richly rewarded.

The volunteer archivist helping me and my research assistants was at once puzzled and amused by the excitement we displayed for the bookshelves, which he did not consider to really be part of the archive. When we found not only Bergson and Richet but also William James's *The Principles of Psychology* (both volumes), George Coe's *The Psychology of Religion*, Josiah Royce's *The Philosophy of Loyalty* and *The Problem of Christianity*, and several collections on prayer, socialism, education, and labor rights, we became even more animated. I realize, of course, that my searching for *Mind-Energy* in Du Vernet's library did not make it appear; it would have lain there whether or not I had made the journey. But I might have entirely ignored the bookshelf had I not been interested in tracing these scholarly influences on Du Vernet as he developed his own curious metaphysics of radio mind. Du Vernet's annotation just within the front cover of *Mind-Energy* summed up his view: "The destiny of matter is to become the manifestation of spirit. A regulative ideal."

We set out to photograph every annotation in Du Vernet's hand, as if his red pencil marks and hand-drawn pointing finger could reveal him to us. In our excitement, we were similar to many recent historians of North American "spirituality," who thrill over drawing unexpected lines of influence as they trace the contours of spirituality and politics in the twentieth century, focusing on lineages and intersections that are unusual and even suppressed.[40] Finding Henri Bergson on the shelf was the thread that unraveled the mystery of radio mind for me.

Du Vernet was profoundly shaped by his reading of *Mind-Energy*, the 1920 English translation of *L'Energie Spirituelle*. Across the copious marginalia that he left in his books, Henri Bergson and mind energy are consistent themes. Within many of the books in his library that were published between 1855 and 1923, including works by Charles Richet, Noah Porter, George Coe, Seth Pringle-Pattison, and Josiah Royce, Du Vernet wrote marginalia related to Bergson's *Mind-Energy*. Since his copy of *Mind-Energy* was published in 1920, this means that he likely read or reread these other books sometime between 1920 and 1924. Book historian Heather Jackson, in her reading of the margi-

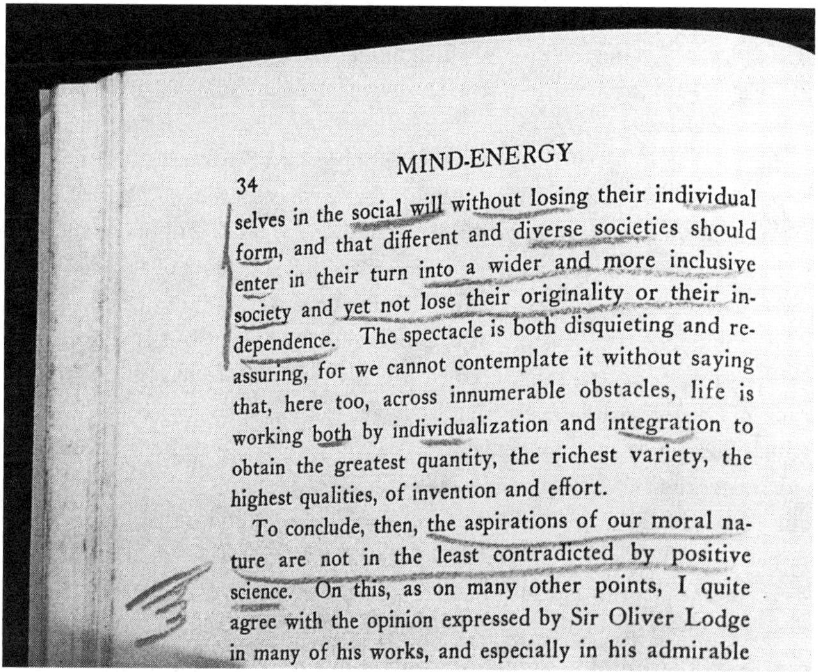

MIND-ENERGY

34

selves in the social will without losing their individual form, and that different and diverse societies should enter in their turn into a wider and more inclusive society and yet not lose their originality or their independence. The spectacle is both disquieting and reassuring, for we cannot contemplate it without saying that, here too, across innumerable obstacles, life is working both by individualization and integration to obtain the greatest quantity, the richest variety, the highest qualities, of invention and effort.

To conclude, then, the aspirations of our moral nature are not in the least contradicted by positive science. On this, as on many other points, I quite agree with the opinion expressed by Sir Oliver Lodge in many of his works, and especially in his admirable

FIGURE 54. Du Vernet's marginalia. From Henri Bergson, *Mind-Energy* (1920). Courtesy of the Diocese of Caledonia Archives.

nalia of T. H. White, another man fascinated with psychology (and especially Freud), aptly characterized the intimate and analytical traces he left behind in the margins of his books: "The record of a dip into the contents of his unconscious mind, it acted at the same time as a vindication of his faith in Freud."[41] Throughout his marginalia, Du Vernet vindicated Bergson's theories in part by confidently associating radio mind and mind energy as companion projects bound by their commitment to morality and science (fig. 54).

Bergson was a French philosopher drawn to questions of memory, time, and matter, and who worked in conversation with scientists and scientific theories of his day. In his earlier work *Creative Evolution*, he introduced the concept of élan vital—or life force—arguing that a quasi-mystical element pushed forward the creativity and change endemic to human evolution. Du Vernet read *Creative Evolution*, but perhaps from a borrowed book, as he took copious notes on the text in the back pages of his copy of *Mind-Energy*. Thanks to these books and others, Bergson is credited with reviving the philosophy of vitalism, which argued that "living phenomena" could not be fully explained by mechanistic sciences. He insisted that "the 'vital principle' might indeed not explain much, but it is at least a sort of label affixed to our ignorance, so as to remind us of this occasionally, while mechanism invites us to ignore that ignorance."[42] Through a kind of epistemological humility, Bergson sought to make space for mysticism—and eventually for his understanding of God—in a scientific worldview.

Bergson has enjoyed a renaissance among scholars in recent years, perhaps because his vitalism fits well with the "new materialism," a theoretical movement that infuses the material, including the land, with an agency not unlike that found in Indigenous cosmologies. In a rereading of Bergson, Mathew Scherer considers Bergson through the lens of questions of "church and state," "modern secularism," and "conversion." Scherer roots his argument in Bergson's focus on the "force of life" as it is manifested in a continual cycle of creativity and novelty that is always infused with "layers of the past," which Bergson framed by the concept of "duration." He argues that Bergson challenges the view of conversion as a sharp break with the past: "Where the authorized image of conversion posits a stark choice and transition from old to new, from 'religious' to 'secular' for example, Bergson suggests that the new emerges continuously from the old, and that the old presses into and coexists within the new as the source of novelty, that the interaction between the distinct layers of a crystalline structure is more fundamental than their separation."[43] Scherer's hopeful Bergsonian revision of conversion as a transition that honors the past is sharply tested in the case of missionaries desiring to convert the "heathen" or the colonial state seeking to civilize—through dispossession—the "Indian." The very fact, however, that many Indigenous people embraced aspects of Christianity at the same time that they reasserted their sovereignty since time immemorial suggests the merits of understanding life as an ongoing process of duration, change, and creativity in which the past remains.

Du Vernet was not reading Bergson to develop a theory of secularism and conversion, or to better understand his own ongoing worries about the relation of church and state. He read Bergson through *Mind-Energy*, one of Bergson's most popular books. *Mind-Energy* curiously goes unmentioned (or unmentionable?) in many serious scholarly treatments of Bergson, perhaps because of the way in which it distinctly popularized psychic interests. Bergson, a French Jew with an abiding interest in Christianity, shared with Du Vernet a combination of mystical enthusiasm and pragmatic public action; he wrote with care about both psychic research and the League of Nations. One of his more accessible books, perhaps because most of the chapters were originally lectures delivered orally, *Mind-Energy* included Bergson's ruminations on telepathy, dreams, the soul, and what would now be called cognitive science.[44]

Consistent with his argument that vitalism was a science-friendly approach to morality, memory, and the spiritual, Bergson charged science with the task of taking intuition seriously: "How could there be disharmony between our intuitions and our science, how especially could our science make us renounce our intuitions, if these intuitions are something like instinct,—an instinct conscious, refined, spiritualized,—and if instinct is still nearer life than intellect and science?" Armed with Bergson's spiritual energy, Du Vernet turned to his bookshelf, well stocked with a remarkably wide-ranging set of philosophical, psychological, and theological texts. For example, he rallied Bergson to argue against philosopher Josiah Royce, in the margins of Royce's *The Problem of Christianity*. Royce claimed: "Direct telepathy, if it ever occurs at all, is a rare and . . . a wholly negligible fact." Du Vernet's red pencil countered in the margin: "Fully established. Basic notion of Mind Energy." Royce had read Bergson, or at least knew of his ideas through reading William James's *A Pluralistic Universe*, published in 1909.[45] According to Du Vernet, however, Royce had not read Bergson correctly.

Mind-Energy had a pragmatic bent to its mysticism that Du Vernet shared, as it sought to clarify how "energy" could change, or heal, the world. Bergson argued that élan vital could pass between bodies, through "healing by suggestion or . . . by the influence of mind on mind." Du Vernet's marginalia in Charles Richet's *Thirty Years of Psychical Research* concurred, citing the authority of his own tests with the Chevreul pendulum: "My experiments prove that the conscious mind energy of one person can penetrate the subconscious mind of another person and produce nervous effects with muscular reactions."[46] To argue that mind energy affected the muscles was a bold testimony that sought to fulfill the destiny of matter by spiritualizing it, using the rhetoric and affect of science.

Once he had read Bergson, Du Vernet's writing became fully saturated with spiritual energy. No longer filtering his arguments primarily through biblical metaphors, he turned increasingly to what he took to be scientific examples and authority as foil for his testimony. With high hopes that the German method of historical criticism would reveal the history of the Bible and its composition, Du Vernet also embraced the philosophical school of pragmatism: "The philosophy of common-sense leads us to make much of the testimony of experience." Like Bergson, he remained cautiously critical of science, and held a privileged space for that which science could not explain: "Spiritual energy, whether it be in the form of vital energy, mental energy, or personal energy, cannot be cut up into little pieces and measured, even with the most minute index, or weighed, even with the most delicate balance." At the same time, he also accused dogmatic Christian theology of a tendency to cut up what was, for him, truly spiritual: "In the name of common-sense why should practical people be forced to hold intellectually, on threat of excommunication, some hair-splitting theological definition which does not produce the slightest effect upon character and life?"[47] Du Vernet was in the throes of a late-style critique of all the forces of inequality, ineptitude, and pettiness that he could name.

Du Vernet was also reading William James, the philosopher and psychologist who would become a founding figure in the academic study of religion. He was particularly interested in James's ideas of the brain as physical matter and of the soul as a unity across brains, marking this sentence in his copy of volume 1 of *The Principles of Psychology*: "The soul would be thus a medium upon which . . . the manifold brain-processes combine their effects." Taking the medium of the soul even further, James noted cautiously that the "phenomena of thought transference, mesmeric influence and spirit control . . . are being alleged nowadays on better authority than ever before." Du Vernet bypassed the caution, underlining "thought transference" and adding in the margins "the interpenetrations of minds."[48]

Scaling up the soul, Du Vernet also marked James's conjecture about the possibility of a world soul, drawing a pointing hand next to this sentence: "I find the notion of some sort of an anima mundi thinking in all of us to be a more promising hypothesis in spite of all its difficulties, than that of a lot of absolutely individual souls." After this cosmic speculation, James changed direction quite abruptly, noting that the word "soul" was not appropriately scientific, so after more than three hundred pages, he would no longer use it. Nevertheless, he encouraged his reader to "feel free to believe" as he could neither prove nor disprove the existence of the soul, an admission that Du Vernet studiously underlined.[49] For Du Vernet, the anima mundi eventually led to God, but a God who no longer quite resembled the Evangelical Father-God of his youth.

Du Vernet also tackled the second volume of James's *Principles of Psychology*, penciling in "Mind Energy" beside a passage where James conceded that hypnosis confirms the probability of "emanations" proceeding from human minds. Where James and Bergson might waver on whether the concept of the soul implies the existence of a god, Du Vernet was convinced, frequently equating the "universe" with "God." Though I have no evidence that Du Vernet read James's Gifford Lectures published as the *Varieties of Religious Experience* in 1912, my guess is that he did. For James, the evidence of religious experience was rooted in testimony and storytelling.[50] For Du Vernet, testimony from experience became increasingly useful and prominent as he explored the possibilities of radio mind.

To bolster his convictions about the soul and the spirit, Du Vernet turned to another Gifford Lecturer, the philosopher and self-described rational theist Andrew Seth Pringle-Pattison, a scholar of Hegel and Kant. Taking his pencil to Pringle-Pattison's essay in an edited collection entitled *The Spirit: The Relation of God and Man, Considered from the Standpoint of Recent Philosophy and Science*, Du Vernet noted his call for human beings to strive to live with a "nature attuned to the divine." Defining the spirit as "the illuminative presence of God operative in every soul which He has created," Pringle-Pattison stressed the "naturalness" of spiritual illumination.[51] The crossing of the domains of the natural and the spiritual was the ground of radio mind.

Du Vernet noticed how another essay in the volume, entitled "God in Action" and written by Lily Dougall, seconded this natural bent: "The hypothesis of this essay is that God is all-powerful to produce good in His own way by educating, not by compelling, living spirits that each have their own degree of freedom; by using the organising power of life as His instrument, not by overriding nature." One of the rare female authors on Du Vernet's bookshelf, Dougall was a Canadian-born writer who ran a liberal Anglican salon from her home in England. Du Vernet marked up her essay carefully, noting her discussion of Frederick Myers's distinction between the subconscious and conscious mind and her assertion that Christianity needed to embrace psychology, lest it repeat the mistakes of earlier church responses to scientific discoveries: "No astronomical discovery is of as much importance to the world as any really forward step in the knowledge of the human mind; but the ecclesiastical mind, as such, often appears even more averse to the psychological knowledge of to-day than it was to the astronomy of the Renaissance."[52] Perhaps in direct response to the Lambeth bishops so opposed to psychic research, Dougall's essay was very much on the same page as Du Vernet.

Dougall and Du Vernet drew on the rhetoric of a scientific spirit not only to defend psychic research against the Lambeth bishops but also as a response to holiness and Pentecostal spiritual currents that were growing inside and outside of their church. For example, Dougall handily reinterpreted a holiness-inspired story told by the evangelist Dwight Moody about the power of prayer into evidence for telepathy. Similarly, Du Vernet's red pencil marks concurred with another article in *The Spirit*, written by C. A. Anderson Scott, a professor of New Testament at Cambridge University, in which Scott sought to historicize the events of Pentecost as described in the book of Acts in order to challenge the Pentecostal view of the spirit. Where Pentecostals understood that the Holy Spirit descended in a flaming blaze to bestow gifts of healing and speaking in tongues upon the apostles, Scott downplayed these gifts to foreground the description in Acts in which the faithful "sold their possessions and goods, and parted them to all men, as every man had need" (Acts 2:45 [KJV]). Scott mused: "Judging by the analogy of Pentecost, we should have to be prepared also for consequences that might be described as revolutionary, whether in thought or in organisation. The Spirit is sovereign where He dwells, though His witness to the individual has always to be checked by His witness to the community. Even the doctrine of private property went up in that flame."[53] This very Anglican balance between the individual and the community is one that Du Vernet articulated often, at the same time that he lived with the knowledge that the doctrine of private property was contested not only by the sovereign spirit but also by the Indian Land Committee.

Du Vernet's marginalia reveal that he was reading as a Christian socialist open to scientific discovery and yet committed to the possibilities of the spirit. These books, which must have traveled quickly from their origins in London and New York to his Pacific coast home, were utterly necessary to his development as a mystic of mediation. Reading narratives of discovery that were more akin to meditations on the human spiritual condition than to lab reports based on empirical observations, Du Vernet followed their example. Literalizing telepathy through the letters of the Chevreul pendulum, he labored to document the reality of radio mind not via charts and statistics but by testimony and story.

Family Matters

In addition to signaling the universality of the human family, radio mind was also a personal family affair for Du Vernet. As he wrote in "The Law of Harmony" in the *Montreal Daily Star* on February 3, 1923: "The best recorded examples of spontaneous thought transference, in contrast to scientific experiments, are between mother and son, husband and wife, also between two brothers, two sisters, two intimate friends, or two lovers." Alice was critical to the success of their shared scientific experiments. In a piece called "Inter-Mental Action" printed in the *Vancouver Province* on January 26, 1923, Du Vernet wrote, "When receiving [thought transference] on one occasion a hundred miles away from my daughter I could tell the exact moment when her mind energy penetrated my subconscious mind by a slight swerving of the pendulum as it swung on the 'start' index." Father and daughter were mystics of mediation together (fig. 55).

On another occasion, Frederick reported in the same article, he and Alice had prearranged a time for a radio mind transmission while he was far from

FIGURE 55. Frederick and Alice Du Vernet at the Anglican Diocese of Caledonia Synod (1909) (detail of fig. 43). William H. Collison is standing at left. Photograph courtesy of the Diocese of Caledonia Archives.

home. When distracted by unexpected visitors, Alice forgot their appointment but received the transmission via her subconscious nonetheless: "When she suddenly became conscious of her oversight this gave her a mental shock so that she was in a highly sensitive state when she held the pendulum in her hand. As the subconscious mind never forgets the slightest detail the memory of my message impinged upon her nervous system and directed aright the swinging pendulum." Alice's ability to store up a message to receive it after the fact brought Frederick to a new declaration that radio mind was constrained neither by time nor space:

> After a critical survey of all the experimental data which I have carefully gathered I feel justified in announcing that there is now scientific proof of the stu-

> pendous fact that inter-mental action is independent of space and time. The bearing of this profound truth upon health and happiness, inspiration and fellowship, prayer and prophecy, peace and good-will must be evident to all deep thinkers. The past lives in us. The future overshadows us. We both influence others and are influenced by them regardless of distance. Millions of minds are inter-acting. We are in touch with the Infinite for the Mind of God is independent of both space and time.

Sending him newspapers, hiking with him in the mountains, helping him with his letters, validating his experiments, Alice was not only a spiritual medium but also a co-laborer in the field of spiritual energy. They likely needed each other's support; one newspaper article briefly mentions the possibility that Du Vernet's experiments with a pendulum could attract "ridicule," and it must have happened more than once.[54]

Alice made another cameo appearance in an essay Du Vernet called "The Principle of Publicity," in which he argued for the moral and psychological value of transparency and disclosure. Advising his readers of the virtue of sharing stories that told of the everyday or weighed on one's conscience, he drew an example from what must have been his own experience as a father: "In after years when the grown-up daughter sits by the side of the parent's bed and tells of the evening party, there is still the beautiful application of this vital principle."[55] Turning the "principle of publicity" into a moral imperative for everyone, children, politicians, and bankers alike, Du Vernet believed in the therapeutic and political power of a story shared side by side.

Though his wife, Stella, does not appear in his stories of radio mind, his son, Horace, played a compelling role in one telepathic testimony. Far from home in a Vancouver hospital, Horace lay close to death. In Du Vernet's telling, he prayed for his son, knowing with "scientific certainty that, regardless of the distance, my mind energy was penetrating his subconscious mind as he lay in the hospital very weak and highly susceptible to mental influence." Horace recovered, and later recounted to his father that at the deepest point of his illness, a thought compelled him: "'I must live for the sake of my wife and children.' This auto-suggestion, stimulated from afar, dropped into his subconscious mind, and there revived the latent energy of his soul."[56] Convinced that the energy of the soul was a physical medium that could be aroused by the spirit, Du Vernet continually painted radio mind as a force for good. What might happen should a spurned lover or an angry parent abuse the power of radio mind to hurt those people who were particularly "susceptible" to mind energy was not something he considered in print.

Colonial Spirituality

The concept of spirituality, like that of religion, has always been deeply intertwined with colonialism. Regardless of what champions of spirituality over against religion might claim, it is just as institutionalized and historically embedded as the category of religion. What are the destructive and productive effects of the word "spirituality," and what has been done in its name? How does the very word amplify the power of the English language itself, while also providing space for the critique of that power?

As an English word used in early anthropological writings, "spirit" often brought along with it the non-English words that it stood in for: *mana*, *Geist*, *esprit*, *manitu*, *orenda*, *chi*, *prana*. Or the Ts'msyen word *halaayt*, which can mean "spiritual power," "shaman," or "shaman's dance."[57] Scholars have often chosen to use these words, especially *mana*, without translation in English, which raises the question, are these "subaltern" terms that have been appropriated, or are these terms so powerful that no translation can do them justice?

One of the earliest scholars in the anthropological tradition, Edward Tylor, devoted considerable thought to the question of the "spirit" and the "spiritual." In his classic 1871 text *Primitive Culture* (which I did not find on Du Vernet's bookshelf), Tylor provided a vast compendium of the spirit and its appearances around the globe. He argued that even the educated elite in late nineteenth-century Europe and North America were not immune to the spirit, as evidenced by their enthusiasm for Spiritualist mediums who served as channels for the living to speak to the dead. Taking a satirical approach, Tylor asserted that "the world is again swarming with intelligent and powerful disembodied spiritual beings, whose direct action on thought and matter is again confidently asserted as in those times and countries where physical science had not as yet so far succeeded in extruding these spirits and their influences from the system of nature."[58] Tylor would likely have included Du Vernet among the crowd of the spiritually excited, despite Du Vernet's claims to have "scientifically" proven the power of radio mind over physical matter.

Tylor did not entirely let off the hook those scientifically enlightened beings who had successfully extruded the spirit. In Tylor's evolutionary view, the word "spirit" tied the "thought of the savage to its hereditary successor, the thought of the philosopher. Barbaric philosophy retains as real what civilized language has reduced to simile."[59] Putting aside for a moment the racist evolutionism in Tylor's language, we see that his point was one of similarities: the philosopher, despite his enlightenment, could not let go of the spirit. Du Vernet, as a missionary and a self-declared scientist, did not consign the spirit to simile. His insistence on the reality of the spirit would place him with the "savages" in Tylor's evolutionary terms—those who were unable or unwilling to extract the spirits from nature.

The Frequency of Listening

The rhabdic force of finding Bergson on the bookshelf and my subsequent communing with Du Vernet through his marginalia give me pause. How does my luck in finding written links to James, Bergson, and Royce allow me to put my Pacific philosopher-mystic in an orbit much headier and historically prominent than his literally parochial colleagues? What stories did I miss—or not find—on the shelves of the bookcases or in the carefully stored file boxes of the archives? The most difficult stories to find are those that relate how Du Vernet's spiritual imagination was shaped by his relationships with Ojibwe, Ts'msyen, Nisga'a, Haida, and other Indigenous peoples. What effects did their spiritual conditions and practices of spiritual communication have on radio mind?

Finding his library relatively intact, thanks to the care and foresight of his wife, Stella, was a great gift to my research. The books allowed me to develop a rich sense of what Du Vernet meant when he referred to the "highest thinking of the age." This text-based historical research, however, does little to reveal the lines of influence of the Ts'msyen, Nisga'a, and Haida people who played a prominent role in Frederick Du Vernet's work and life. He spent twenty years trying to convert them to Christianity and encouraging white settlement in the region. At the same time, he tried to thwart the disastrous trend of residential schools. In light of this, might his late-in-life radio mind experiments with his own homemade divining rod, the Chevreul pendulum, be a mode of turning matter into spirit that had its parallels in the Ts'msyen concept of halaayt? Overlapping with the English words "spirit power," "shaman," "priest," and "seer," halaayt was a means by which a human being could hold spiritual power through engaging with the natural world.[60] If spiritual energy, as Du Vernet understood it, was truly universal, did halaayt also access it in a way that he could recognize and even accept?

In the last four years of his life, when he wasn't thinking about and experimenting on radio mind, Du Vernet was overwhelmed by the state of his diocese and province. One of the issues that troubled him the most was the rise of "boarding schools" for Indigenous children. What became known as "residential schools," these were places to which Indigenous children were often forcibly taken by police, where they were not allowed to speak their own languages, and where because of unsanitary conditions, lack of food, violence, and despair, they often grew ill or died. Residential schools were one of the most lethal forms of an alliance between church and state in the history of Canada (and the United States, as reading Louise Erdrich's *Love Medicine* reveals). Paid for by the state, while staffed and operated by Catholic, Anglican, Methodist, Presbyterian, and United churches, residential schools were a "national crime."[61]

From his early years in Prince Rupert, Du Vernet was a harsh critic of the system of "Indian education" and tried to convince his colleagues in Toronto to support a plan for day schools, which would not remove children from their families. He knew well that the issue of residential schools was related to the Indian Land Question and that the fortunes of the church were tied to both. At the same time that the British-based missionary societies were slowly withdrawing their funds, Indigenous Christians were giving less to church offerings and more to support lawyers assisting with the land movement.[62] In the wake of these financial pressures, the churches saw a way to attract government funding through the per capita system whereby they were paid per child in attendance at their schools.

Already in a 1908 letter to CMS Secretary Baring Baring-Gould in London, Du Vernet emphasized the different responsibilities of government and church as they related to schooling and the government purchase of Indigenous land: "These schools are Government Schools. The INDIANS are wards of the Dominion Government. In return for lands surrendered the Dom. Gov. undertakes to educate the Indian children. At first the Missionary Societies were doing this as far as they could, but by degrees the Government came forward erecting School Buildings, paying Grants. But these grants have been too small to do the work effectually. The per capita system has led to many evils." Consistently pointing to the health dangers of the schools, which packed in as many children as possible under the incentives of the per capita model, Du Vernet noted that among the evils of the system were the frequent deaths of children from tuberculosis in the ill-equipped schools, including at the Anglican Metlakatla Industrial School, which had closed by 1908.[63]

Du Vernet likely learned of the evils of the per capita model not only from observing the Metlakatla school and hearing from Indigenous parents but also from reading Dr. Peter Bryce's scathing 1907 report on the state of residential schools in Canada. The chief medical officer for the Department of Indian Affairs (and brother of the Presbyterian minister who had excavated a Rainy River mound), Bryce's report clarified the evils of the per capita system in great detail. A few of his Anglican colleagues joined with Du Vernet in protesting the schools, but the bishops from dioceses where the income from residential schools propped up their budgets won the day.[64]

While critical of residential schools, Du Vernet did believe in high school and industrial school education for "advanced" Indigenous students. He also believed that the church had something "spiritual" to teach to Indigenous children: "We ask only for the privilege of imparting religious instruction to our Indian children. The Government is responsible for their secular education." Clearly worried that Baring-Gould was not getting the message, he spoke plainly, directly tying the money that the government had received for selling surrendered Indigenous lands to money it should be spending on education: "It is a mistake for the Missionary Societies to go on relieving the Government of the work it is bound to do. The sale of Indian lands has brought in millions of dollars. I sometimes wonder if the C.M.S. Secretaries ever see the Annual Report of the Department of Indian Affairs."[65] With such a frank rebuff to CMS Secretary Baring-Gould, Du Vernet showed that four years into his episcopate, the issue of Indigenous education was already alarming him.

Despite Du Vernet's assertion that the Dominion government was obliged to pay for Indigenous day schools out of the monies it had received from selling land supposedly surrendered by Indigenous peoples, he knew the matter was not so simple. As James McCullagh wrote of the situation in Aiyansh in the *North British Columbia News* in April 1913, "The Indians have rejected the offer of the Indian Department to erect a day school, on the ground that the acceptance of these benefits would prejudice their case *re* Indian Land Question. They take the stand that a full and complete settlement should be arrived at before receiving these benefits, and that, by their acceptance of them in the past they tacitly acknowledged a satisfactory settlement which had never been made." Without a government-funded school, Paul Mercer, a Nisga'a man active in the church and with the printing press, took it upon himself to teach the children of Aiyansh in his grandfather's house.[66]

Perhaps with Paul Mercer as an inspiration, Du Vernet rooted his clear separation between duties of the state and those of the church in part in a conviction that Indigenous Christians should become self-sufficient, as he wrote in a letter to his Toronto colleague Canon Gould: "The Indian work has got into a rut and it must be lifted out of this rut. The C.M.S. made a great mistake in doing too much for the Indians. Let the M.S.C.C. adopt a new and vigorous policy, leaving to the Government what the Government is responsible for, and insisting upon the spiritual side of the work with a wise method of making the Indians depend more upon themselves."[67] Du Vernet's strict division between spiritual work and government responsibility was also informed by his awareness that Indigenous parents had their own stake in the matter of their children's education.

In 1921, at the urging of Haida parents who wanted a local boarding school at Massett that their children could attend when they were away for fishing seasons, Du Vernet sent a letter, on behalf of the Executive Committee of the Anglican Synod of the Diocese of Caledonia, to ask the MSCC to establish two boarding schools. The committee's letter stated that the Indigenous peoples of the diocese "belong to five different tribes, and that strong prejudices exist between them, and moreover the long distances between Settlements, and also differences of Climatic conditions are such, that we believe that their educational interests would be best cared for by the establishment of two Boarding Schools." The MSCC declined to support this plan. In 1922, Du Vernet once again supported a "co-operative plan," backed by all four Indian agents in the diocese, which would see the government establish one boarding school at Prince Rupert, which the churches would not administer. Instead, each church would supply Christian education for students in their denominations. The MSCC, by then fully committed to a program of strictly Anglican residential schools paid for with government support, did not support this plan either.[68] At this point, Du Vernet seemed to be losing heart, both literally and in spirit.

Forced to curtail his travel around the diocese because of his illness, he grew increasingly reflective—and angry—about the approach of both church and government to Indigenous education. In November 1922, the same month he published "Reality in Religion" in the *Canadian Churchman*, Du Vernet wrote a letter to Thomas B. R. Westgate, the acting secretary of the MSCC and a fellow Wycliffe graduate, recalling the development of his views on Indian education:

> High up officials in the Indian Department when here said openly that as long as the Indian Department can get the Churches to take the responsibility of education of the Indian children the Dep[a]rtment is only too glad. To use the exact words "It is a matter of economy." Eighteen years ago when I came to this Diocese, I adopted the attitude that the Indian Department was solely responsible for the education of the Indian children and the Churches for their spiritual teaching. By degrees the Department accepted my position. . . . The Indian Day Schools in this Diocese are doing most efficient work, and it is not costing the Anglican Church a single dollar. The Bishop still can recommend a teacher, but the teacher is appointed by the Government.

Du Vernet's argument for the day schools partly arose from a philosophy of church-state cooperation through separation, as well as from frugality. But his views also came from what Haida, Ts'msyen, and Nisga'a parents told him of the fatal effects of residential schools: "Again, when we had our Industrial School at Metlakatla we found that the Indians in the interior would not send their children down to the damp coast to catch tuberculosis and die. Nearly every Naas river boy who went to Alert Bay Industrial School came back to die [in] a few years, so they gave up sending there (after our Metlakatla Industrial School was closed)."[69] Nisga'a parents made choices about their children's education, and Du Vernet noticed.

Du Vernet ended his letter to Westgate with a frank assessment of both the cruelty and the foolishness of the per capita system of funding for residential schools, lambasting his church's misguided "hobby" of developing residential schools to attract government money: "I heard a former Indian Agent deliberately state that 75% of the girls who passed through one of the Boarding Schools on this coast are in the cemetry [*sic*], and yet the enormous cost compared with the Indian Day Schools, which allow for a more natural life. I cannot understand why the M.S.C.C. is devoting so much time and energy to Boarding Schools and so little to the Indian Missions from whence the children must come and to which they must return." That Du Vernet considered the "mission" a place to which a child would return means that he understood, in part, that their homes were a place of value to Indigenous peoples, and not a place they sought to abandon through educational achievement. The "natural life" of the Indian day school also included the ability of a child to go home after school and to continue being cared for by her family, to speak in her own language, and to hear the stories of her ancestors and spirits.

In August 1923, just a month before his first definition of radio mind was published in the *Canadian Churchman*, Du Vernet tried one last time to convince church officials in Toronto to establish a boarding school at Massett, on Haida Gwaii, again at the urging of Haida parents. Given a petition signed by the five men of the Haida council, including Chief Alfred Adams, a leader in the Indigenous land movement who had conducted services in St. Andrew's Cathedral in Prince Rupert, he passed it on to Canon Gould in Toronto. The Haida petition appealed at once to bonds of parental affection and to the Haida's good faith efforts at participating in both church and market:

> Our Bands are increasing, and we are compelled to send some of our children many hundreds of miles from home, to obtain an education, far from the Church and their Homes. We send them at a tender age, and cannot see them

> for many years. Parting from our children, for eight or ten years, is a hardship. Why should we have to send our children to Chilliwhack, when small Bands of Indians have Boarding Schools, elsewhere? Surely the Church, and the Government, will realize our need of a Boarding School, in the great Northern country. We are considered progressive Indians, by many people, and we are anxious for our children to become educated. We cannot stay at home, supporting our children, to send them to Day Schools. We must earn our living, and theirs, which closes the Day Schools, many months in the year.[70]

Agonized by the long separation from their young children, the Haida parents wanted a school on their own terms and on their own land.

In his letter to Gould accompanying the Haida petition, Du Vernet emphasized to his Toronto colleague the importance of the petition as a plea from parents who cared for the well-being of their children and who suffered from being separated from them. He suggested a hybrid day school and boarding school plan to fit the seasonal needs of Haida parents: "Beginning in this way it might work out towards a boarding school at least during certain months when parents are away. It is a mistake to releave [*sic*] the Indian parents of all responsibility for their children." Du Vernet's awareness of the generational effects of severing ties between parent and child is echoed in critical analyses of the residential school system today. At the same time that he was experimenting and writing about the power of thoughts to travel across great distance, he was insisting on the importance of bodies in proximity.

Du Vernet did not need radio mind to reach this conclusion. He knew the importance of parents caring for their children already in 1909, when he sent an appeal to the secretary of the Department of Indian Affairs in Ottawa and a copy to Samuel Blake of the MSCC in Toronto. Even back then he argued for a "hybrid" plan flexible enough to meet parents' needs based on the fishing seasons: "The Day School is all that the ordinary child needs, and the parents will not feel the separation as in the case of a distant boarding school. 'My child might as well be dead' said one mother bitterly when she found she could not get her child back for eight years." Insisting, as he would again later, that "it is a mistaken policy for the Government to releave [*sic*] the parents from the duty of providing for their children," Du Vernet argued strongly against residential schools on both pragmatic and emotional grounds: "Why should the Government take children away from their parents and clothe and feed them, when these parents live in good houses, earn good wages &c.?" As a father and a bishop who traveled throughout the diocese, Du Vernet knew well the ties of family and the toll of distance.[71]

When reading Du Vernet's prolific public writings about radio mind contrapuntally—to borrow another useful musical concept from Edward Said—with his bishop's letters about residential schools, it becomes clear that Du Vernet separated these two areas of his writing life. For Said, a contrapuntal reading juxtaposes a view from the perspective of a colonial metropole with the absent or obscured perspective from the colonized territory.[72] In Du Vernet's case, to read his "scientific" radio mind writings contrapuntally with his "episcopal" residential school letters—both of which are the writings of a colonial man in the colonies—is to juxtapose two aspects to the same man that he seemingly kept apart.

In an explication of radio mind published in the *Prince Rupert Daily News* in January 1924, Du Vernet made a rare reference to Indigenous spiritual mediation. Du Vernet insisted that "the unity which exists in the subconscious realm is a primitive unity. This is proven by the fact telepathy prevails among young children, and primitive races before they have an intelligent understanding of the human mind."[73] This line alone might be enough to condemn his ideas to the hopelessly racist traditions of missionary and anthropological thought, except for the fact that Du Vernet celebrated telepathy as itself an intelligent way to understand the human mind.

Moving on to give an example of a mother quieting her crying baby with her "soothing thought," he also tells this story pulled from the local past: "Many years ago an important event which occurred among the Indians of the Upper Naas River was intuitively known by some of the Indians of Metlakatla on the coast, so that when the messenger arrived he found that the news was there before him." Du Vernet knew how difficult it could be to travel up and down the Nass River, and how interdependent people had to be to survive. On his last trip to Aiyansh in the fall of 1923, his motorboat could not make it up the river and twenty-six Nisga'a men had to haul the boat over the rapids. Perhaps with an awareness of how the Nisga'a knew the river—and many other aspects of life on the northwest coast—much better than he did, he counseled humility in his reader: "Because this unity of mind energy is a primitive unity, we must not, in our pride of intellect, despise it. . . . There is a beyond which is within." In a late-style twist, he closed the article by suggesting that "all men of genius," including great musicians and poets, have the power of radio mind.

Why didn't Du Vernet bring radio mind or even "social justice" to bear on his arguments against residential schools more directly? For all his bluster and scientific spirit, perhaps he realized that telepathy—or radio mind—was not a remedy for the violence and alienation of residential schools. Despite his many letters, Du Vernet was not able to convince the government officials and church leaders living far away in Toronto and Ottawa of the devastation they created by pulling children away from their families. For these officials, looking at "Indian children" from a distance, the residential school seemed the perfect solution to their task of "civilization." The church and government officials knew about the pain and anguish that they were causing, because their own colleagues told them clearly, with words that they ignored. A believer in the power of communication, a father who clearly appreciated having his daughter close by, Du Vernet heard the torment and anger voiced by Indigenous parents and children; perhaps radio mind was his meager solution when nothing else had worked.

Radio mind is an ambivalent example of what Said identified as the heart of late style: "Late style is what happens if art does not abdicate its rights in favour of reality."[74] Du Vernet boldly proclaimed telepathic testimonies and the scientific contribution of radio mind in the face of a church that could have deemed him a heretic and a scientific community that would have likely called him a flake. He found his late style by using the margin as a medium when reading the philosophy and psychology of his day. His late style also came at the end of a long journey on Indigenous land, during which he met many Nisga'a, Ts'msyen, Haida, and other Indigenous people face-to-face. At the same time that he was writing on the cosmic scale of radio mind, he stood close to and recorded the anger, pain and even terror of parents whose children had been stolen away by the Canadian state through the channel of his church.

8
Truths and Reconciliations

After a life of walking the land and navigating the waters, Frederick Herbert Du Vernet died at his home overlooking Hecate Strait on October 22, 1924. At sixty-four years old, he had visualized death and was ready for it. His musings about passing from the "twilight zone" to "life after death," also the title of his article in the *Montreal Daily Star* from March 31, 1923, sought to prepare his readers for the time when their own souls would take flight:

> As our mind energy leaves our material body at death we shall feel like a bird escaping from its cage. At first we shall not be fully conscious of what we are, or where we are. We have been so long dependent upon our physical senses for evidence that we shall need a little time to realize that the ultimate reality of the universe is spiritual energy. We shall find many points of resemblance between our dream-life now and our life after death. For example, we shall be amazed at the way in which, without apparent effort, we can pass from scene to scene, and from memory to memory. Possibly our life here would have been better had we known that our subconscious mind never forgets.

With shades of Txeemsim, the trickster who became a bird to fly to the heavens so as to bring light—and a new perspective—to the world, Du Vernet's mind energy was a traveling spirit.

Du Vernet's faith in the restorative power of dreams and memories—that people would find comfort and not terror in the idea that after death they would never forget any moment of their existence—was both tenacious and naïve. In the same article, Du Vernet counseled his readers that life after death would be a "fellowship of the spirit" that was not to be feared: "According to St. Paul, our vital spirit will clothe itself in an ethereal body as well adapted to a spiritual environment as our present body is to a material world. What more than this could we wish? Flesh and blood cannot enter the realm of the spiritual. Psychology indicates that Christianity declares that the Energy of the Mind cannot be buried in the Tomb of Death." Soaked in Pauline metaphors and Bergsonian concepts, Du Vernet bound together psychology and Christianity with defiant confidence in the last years of his life.

As his heart weakened, Du Vernet's compulsion to testify to his newfound wisdom, backed by the empirical experiments he conducted with Alice, grew stronger. The *Montreal Daily Star* received his last article just twenty-four hours after he died. "The Pathway of Psychology" is one of his more pragmatic essays, advising the church that it must learn from psychology, just as educators and salespeople have done. According to the archbishop, most ministers ignored the four signposts along this pathway: "Arrest attention! Create interest! Arouse desire! Induce decision!" Lost in their own pedantry and piety, preachers bored their congregations instead of engaging them with the help of the latest science of the mind. In an unusually pessimistic tone, he concluded: "The Holy Spirit never violates our mental constitution but cooperates with our latent energy. It is not too much to say that nine-tenths of what passes for religion in our country has no scientific relationship to the daily behaviour of the men and women who attend our churches."[1] A parting shot at a church that did not seem to be listening to him whether it came to radio mind or residential schools, his last words written for publication in a Montreal newspaper conveyed the same frustration he demonstrated in his private letters to church leaders in Toronto.

Remembering the Late (Style) Archbishop

On the day of Frederick Du Vernet's funeral, the Cathedral Church of St. Andrew's could not contain the "throng of mourners": Anglican dignitaries from around the province, the clergy of the diocese, parishioners, neighbors. Two pews were reserved for "representative natives gathered from the villages," one for the workers in the Japanese mission, and one for clergy from the "sister churches" of Prince Rupert.[2] He collected unity in diversity even after his death.

The accolades written in commemoration of the archbishop followed a curious pattern. Obituaries and reminiscences published in church papers and newsletters repeatedly praised him as a beloved and tireless worker for the church and lamented that he died prematurely, worn down by the physical demands of his episcopal responsibilities. They were significantly silent, however, on his investigations of radio mind. By contrast, articles in secular newspapers in Vancouver, Victoria, Prince Rupert, and Montreal all proclaimed his greatness as a bishop, a Canadian, and an intellectual whose writings on psychology and politics had brought him a degree of renown nationally and internationally. In the words of the front-page headline in the *Prince Rupert Daily News* on the day of his death: "Archbishop Du Vernet Died Early This Morning Closing Active Career: Famous Divine Was Scholar and Student as Well as Active Worker in Cause of Religion and Humanity." At the end of his life, Du Vernet was not a missionary celebrity, but he was a spiritual personality.

The year after Du Vernet's death, there was still no bishop to give a "charge"—an oral address—to the Caledonia Synod. There was also no money. The Church Missionary Society (CMS) had fully withdrawn its financial support; bishops in the East had scuttled a plan for the national church to fill in the gaps. Archdeacon George Rix organized the synod gathering, writing a letter to his fellow clergymen in lieu of giving a speech. He had kind words for Du Vernet, imagining him giving "higher service" in the afterlife:

> The Diocese of Caledonia suffered an irreperable [*sic*] loss in the death of the late greatly beloved Archbishop Du Vernet. . . . As for the care and love of God in removing our chief pastor from his strenuous field of labor to the higher service which today he is giving there is no doubt. . . . Our most pleasing discovery is that the name and personality which we so greatly revered and loved was so generally appreciated throughout the whole church in Canada. The memory of his faithful service, his deep spirituality and his gentle Christlike character, will certainly prove an inspiration to clergy and people of Caledonia to higher standards of character and service. As Administrator during these past months, I have begun to realize what a burden of anxiety he carried in the manning of the field, in the happiness of the men and the supply of money to carry on the work.

On his way to becoming the third bishop of Caledonia, George Rix consistently praised his predecessor and lamented his passing. He pointed out the enormity of Du Vernet's responsibilities to keep the church solvent and functioning: "A task that the strongest men might shrink from and as a matter of fact, it proved more than the Bishop could long endure, for as a comparatively young man he died . . . leav[ing] in Caledonia Diocese, a monument to his energy and faith."[3] But Rix said nothing about radio mind.

Jocelyn Perkins, editor of *Across the Rockies*, was considerably less charitable in a 1925 editorial in which he mourned the "terrible state of things" in the wake of the archbishop's death and the consequent loss of CMS funding for his episcopal seat: "It seems a pity that steps could not have been taken before now to place this Bishopric of Caledonia upon a secure financial basis, but then it must be remembered that the War and post-War conditions have produced in the Far West a very complicated state of things. Doubtless, Archbishop Du Vernet felt that the times were wholly unpropitious for raising any large sums of money for this purpose so far as the Far West was concerned."[4] Politely casting aspersions on the late archbishop mere months after his passing for being a poor fundraiser, Jocelyn Perkins continued his mistrust of colonial bishops from his perch in Westminster Abbey.

Soon after Du Vernet's death, the Missionary Society of the Church of England in Canada (MSCC) in Toronto published a pamphlet to help raise funds for the Caledonia bishopric, which included admiring words from the primate—the highest Anglican bishop in the country—who described the search for "a worthy successor to take up the mantle of the late Dr. Du Vernet, who loved the work of God in Caledonia and gave himself so unreservedly to it." But again, the primate made no mention of radio mind, what Du Vernet considered to be the culmination of his life's work. In his words: "Perhaps this is the greatest contribution I have to make to the cause of Science. The supposed barrier of space between two minds can be effectually annihilated by the power of the imagination working through the fundamental union of all souls in the realm of the subconscious world."[5] In remembering Du Vernet's life as an archbishop most of his colleagues chose to forget his contributions to the cause of science.

Later histories and accounts also eclipsed the story of radio mind. In 1942, Walter Rushbrook, a Canadian-born priest and the captain of the *Northern Cross*, a mission boat that Du Vernet had launched in 1914, wrote a personal reminiscence of his bishop. With a quality of detail that suggests he either had enjoyed long conversations with Du Vernet while adrift at sea or had access to stories from someone like Stella, Rushbrook portrayed Du Vernet as a progressive, pragmatic, and deeply spiritual man: "While his Churchmanship was sound and his services bright and soulful, there was no catering to silly, foolish and expensive unnecessary frills and furbelows. He was a nourisher of hungry souls—not an aesthetic entertainer. He was outstandingly a man's man, powerful in intellect, gentle in manners, affable in social contact, capable as a chairman—of smaller gatherings or the important Diocesan or Provincial Synods." Perhaps his portrait of the manly, soulful bishop of "outstanding spiritual fitness" and "capable social leadership" was in direct contrast to the showmanship of James McCullagh, but it is hard to know. Rushbrook made no mention of the Irish missionary who had been his colleague, just as he said nothing about spiritual radio.[6]

The eulogies in secular newspapers, however, loudly lauded Du Vernet's psychological achievements on the edges of spiritual consciousness. In the front-page *Prince Rupert Daily News* article on the day of his death, the writer, who was undoubtedly a friend of Du Vernet's, recounted his "long and brilliant career," noting that he had died "peacefully" at his home earlier that morning: "Of simple and modest demeanor despite his intellectual attainments, his ministrations were welcome and looked for by even the smallest congregations of his extensive diocese. Ever abhorrent of personal glory or self esteem, the late Archbishop's modest personality was always apparent." Recapping his career, the writer described how when Du Vernet arrived in the diocese his job "was devoted mainly to the Indians." By 1924, however, "the main work of the church in the diocese is among white people and there are seventeen clergymen in the district whose congregations are white." Shifting the diocese to "white work" was one of the monuments to Du Vernet's "energy and faith"; helping build the new city of Prince Rupert from its literal foundations, he enabled patterns of settlement and resource extraction that dispossessed the Indigenous peoples of their land.

The *Prince Rupert Daily News* writer did not stop with Du Vernet's settler churchmanship. The tribute also celebrated his late-style researches as "a deep student of psychology" and explained how his psychological and political writings

> were sought for and published in all parts of Canada. His serious illness of the last several months did not prevent his further researches and it was only a few weeks ago that the last contributions from his pen were published. The Archbishop was a man whose mind advanced far ahead of his physique, which in itself was necessarily robust to meet the demands of his ecclesiastical duties which took him far afield. It was perhaps with a feeling of premonition that one of the last writings penned from his sick bed pointed out that the mind could not advance too far ahead of the body without results disastrous to the human frame.

As his body became tired and immobilized, he kept on writing with a steady hand, in the margins of his books, in newspapers, and in letters to church officials.

The *Prince Rupert Daily News* saw fit to reprint a memorial published in the *Victoria Colonist*, which also focused on the significance of Du Vernet's late-style writings:

> There have been few dignitaries of the Anglican Church better known in Canada. The Archbishop made himself known by his writings. He was an apostle of peace and goodwill among men and he felt that it was his duty to go outside the scope of his immediate See to tell the thoughts that were in him. Though he believed in the value of publicity, he sought it not vain-gloriously because he was modest and humble in all his dealings with mankind. . . . During the last few years public attention had been directed to him more than ever before because of the theories he put forward on the subject of thought transference. He believed implicitly in these and felt it was right to inform all within his range of the discoveries he had made.

The writer in the *Colonist* recognized something that most of Du Vernet's clerical colleagues did not see or would not say: that by the end of his life his testimony of the spirit no longer fit within the traditional confines of Anglican creeds, but he was compelled to share it anyway. Writers for both church and secular newspapers did agree on one thing: Du Vernet had died too young. As the *Colonist* writer lamented: "He will be remembered with reverence but diluted with sorrow in that one of his attainments could not have been spared for a longer period to spread a beneficial doctrine of spiritual good will."[7]

Du Vernet's writings were indeed sought after: within three years of his passing, two edited collections of his writings had been published, one in the United States and one in Canada. *Spiritual Radio*, introduced by Episcopalian rector A. J. Gayner Banks, might well have already been underway when Du Vernet was alive, as it was published in 1925 by the Society of the Nazarene in Mountain Lakes, New Jersey. Stella sent along some of the articles and had a handsome hardbound copy in her possession already that same year (fig. 56). Collecting twelve articles previously published in the *Canadian Churchman* and elsewhere, the volume highlighted Du Vernet's claims about the healing dimensions of spiritual radio in keeping with Gayner Banks's interests—he later went on to cofound the healing-focused Order of St. Luke.[8]

Casting Du Vernet as a "prophet and seer" in a long Christian lineage, Gayner Banks set spiritual radio in a wider tradition of "sacramental philosophy—that every outward and visible achievement of science adumbrates some inward and invisible spiritual reality." Comparing Du Vernet's insights to Scottish evangelist and scientist Henry Drummond, author of the wildly popular 1883 book *Natural Law in the Spiritual World*, as well as to the apostle Paul and the Swedish scientist-mystic Emanuel Swedenborg, Banks made grand claims for the book and the man: "'Spiritual Radio' is vindicating the work of the great Mystics of Christian history; it is demonstrating that the 'Interior Life' is not limited to the seclusion of the cloister but produces a

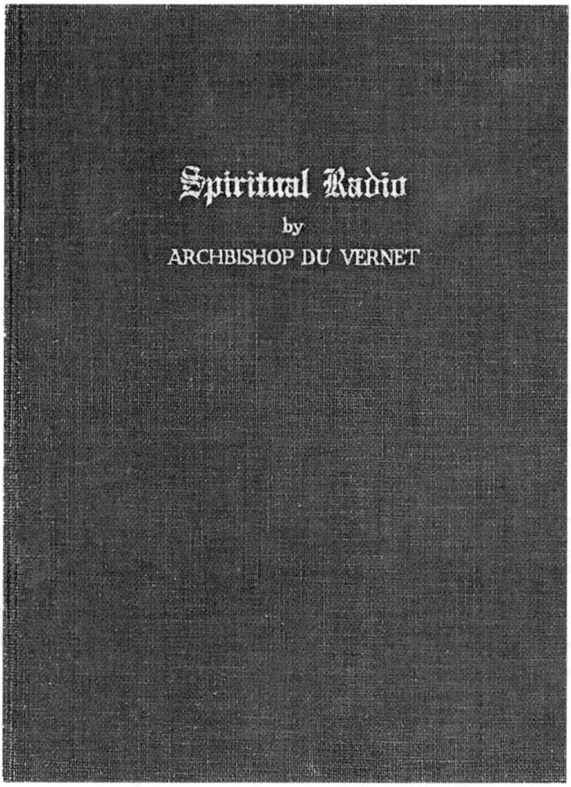

FIGURE 56. Stella Du Vernet's copy of *Spiritual Radio* (1925). Courtesy of the Diocese of Caledonia Archives.

robust type of Christian manhood and womanhood that makes for leadership and achievement in the marvelous age in which our lot is cast."[9] The back pages recommended an eclectic list of books—including volumes on healing and the spirit by Anglican writers Percy Dearmer and Lily Dougall—setting Du Vernet within a canon of liberal experimentalists.

Two years later, Robert Connell, an Anglican rector in Victoria, published *Out of a Scribe's Treasure: Brief Essays in Practical Religious Thinking* with the respected Ryerson Press of Toronto. Du Vernet had given a series of lectures, "Spiritual Radio: Modern Psychology as Related to Religious Truth," at Connell's parish, St. Saviour's Church, in the early 1920s. Connell likely met Du Vernet through their shared work to bridge theological divides in the formation of the Vancouver Theological College (fig. 57). A Christian socialist, Connell later became a leader in the Co-operative Commonwealth Federation, a political party borne from a coalition of socialists, farmers, and labor activists, which would go on to become the New Democratic Party of Canada.[10]

Where others emphasized how Du Vernet "made himself known by his writings," Connell highlighted his gifts of oratory: "The Archbishop was

FIGURE 57. Frederick Du Vernet (*seated third from left*) and Robert Connell (*standing second from left*), at Anglican Theological College in the last year of Du Vernet's life, 1924. Photograph courtesy of the Archives of the Provincial Synod of British Columbia and Yukon.

trained in the old Evangelical school of Anglican theology, and with all his burning desire to utilize modern psychology in the interests of religious thought and practice he never lost the trembling earnestness of that school, either in writing or speaking. It was still, you felt, the old message of power, though expressed in modern terms. But his positive attitude towards religion in its various past and present manifestations bred in him an open-hearted tolerance that found a ready response in the hearts of Canadian men and women of varying creeds and churches."[11] With echoes of the magnetic power of McCullagh's Irish charm, Du Vernet's "trembling earnestness" was deployed to a new gospel of spiritual energy, as he conveyed the old message of power as a story both from the mouth and through the organs of the press.

In what must have been something of a celebrity coup, Connell managed to secure H. D. A. Major, the principal of Ripon Hall in Oxford and editor of the liberal Anglican journal *Modern Churchman*, to write the foreword for the book. Fresh off his Noble Lectures at the Memorial Church of Harvard University in 1925–1926, which became his most recognized book, *English Modernism*, Major was one of the best-known Anglican clerics of his day. Himself a "colonial" cleric, having grown up in New Zealand and attended seminary there, Major celebrated Du Vernet's "élan vital": "It was in January, 1924, that I was first impressed by a vigorous and striking utterance of Archbishop Du Vernet. It seemed so unlike what might be expected from an ordinary Anglican archbishop abroad. . . . When I turned to 'Crockford' it appeared, *mirabile dictum* [wonderful to relate] that this *vox clamantis in deserto* [voice crying in the wilderness] was a Canadian Anglican, a pure product of Canadian church life, and that his diocese was supported by the Church Missionary Society. Truly the spirit bloweth where it listeth."[12] Major pointed out what few people would say in print: Du Vernet's radio mind was a bizarre spiritual political undertaking for an Evangelical Anglican archbishop engaged in missionary work.

As the man providing the seal of approval for Du Vernet's writings, Major was a bold choice since he had just survived the threat of a heresy trial in England. Described by later commentators as a "panentheistic" thinker who was convinced that God is "in the cosmos," Major had a liberal's openness to higher criticism of the Bible, theories of evolution, and the idea that God works through the "natural world" rather than via the miraculous. This tenor of his thinking shines through in his endorsement of Du Vernet: "It is this note of optimism and adventure which forms the deep undertone of the late Archbishop's pilgrim chant. He comes to us as the exponent of a dynamic, not a static religion—communion with an ever-present, life-giving Spirit, not the profession of some hoary dogmatic tradition."[13]

With his eclectic set of commitments, it is not a surprise that in 1922, Major was accused by a fellow cleric of heresy on two counts: first, denying the church's teachings about bodily resurrection, or the idea that after death the body, and not just the spirit, would be resurrected; and second, "importing the teaching of a heathen mystic (Gautama) into the Christian religion without warrant of reason or of observed fact."[14] Major responded with vehemence that he was not bringing the Buddha into the church. He also defended his approach to the afterlife with detailed reference to the Bible, the Church Fathers, and more recent theologians.

On the matter of what survives after death, his answer made use of the vague term "personal identity" to blur the line between the material body and the spirit, and to narrowly avoid the charge of heresy: "The form which the doctrine of the resurrection assumes in my mind is the survival of death by a personality which has shed its physical integument for ever. By survival I need hardly add that I mean full survival of all that constitutes whatever is essential to a human personality, in short all that is meant by the term 'personal identity.'" In the end, Major was successful in convincing a group of Oxford theologians that he was not challenging the doctrine that held that when Christians were resurrected after death, both their bodies and their spirits would travel to heaven.[15]

Major's convictions about the resurrection of a "personality" were very similar to those uttered by Du Vernet: "Flesh and blood cannot enter the realm of the spiritual." But Du Vernet did not take refuge in vague terms: "Personal identity does not lie in material particles but in spiritual personality which thinks and remembers, loves and chooses."[16] Read in light of most Anglican theology of his day, Du Vernet's views on how the material body passes through the "twilight zone" to the spiritual beyond would have been enough to have him deemed a heretic. His interests in psychic research, a line of inquiry into the spirit proscribed by the bishops at the 1920 Lambeth Conference, would have confirmed his heresy in the minds of many clerics.

When compared to the practice of believing in the bodily resurrection—the idea that dead people would rise again in all their pulsing corporality—perhaps radio mind seems not so odd. Is the belief that heaven will be filled with the bodies of the resurrected any more unusual than the conviction that human spirits will fly like birds after death, just as they do in dreams? In light of Du Vernet's heterodox teachings, it is particularly surprising that the *Canadian Churchman* published his radio mind speculations with no comment added. Perhaps it would have been too difficult to reject the essays of an archbishop; perhaps someone on the editorial staff found him a kindred spirit. In articles remembering him after his death, however, the *Canadian Churchman* drew little attention to his psychological interests. One brief article in 1926 on "The Women's Page" of the August 12 issue of the *Canadian Churchman* noted that Edwin Moss, a priest from Ladysmith, British Columbia, had been inspired by Du Vernet's "demonstrations of 'Radio Mind'" to form a "League for the Direction of Purer Thought" aimed at channeling the "thought of mankind" for the good of the world. A later article described the 1928 installation of a stained glass window dedicated to Du Vernet's memory at St. John's, West Toronto, his first parish. Recounting in some detail his boyhood, education, and career, the article left unmentioned his late-style meditations, except to say that even after suffering a paralytic stroke, his "brain and pen [were] still active" for months afterward.[17]

A more recent collection of Frederick Du Vernet's writings edited by his son's daughter-in-law, Sylvia DuVernet, took a different approach. Sylvia argued that Frederick was "syncretistic" in at least two directions: one, that he supported a mix of Indigenous and Christian spiritual practices, and two, that he mixed Theosophical and Christian thought. Never having met Du Vernet, but an eager recipient of family lore and a diligent collector of his writings, Sylvia wrote *Portrait of a Personality* as a self-published combination of family memoir, collected writings, and historical reflection. She raised the possibility that since anthropological records from the time when Du Vernet was bishop showed that "shamans" still practiced on the Skeena River, in an area of his diocese where he spent his summers, he must have been neither "personally [nor] religiously offended by shamanic practice." Aligning his radio mind writings to certain tenets of Theosophy, she suggested that his "mode of thought" could be put under a "metaphysical umbrella."[18] Frederick Du Vernet, however, did not have the power to stop shamans, or *halaayt*, from healing the sick or casting their thoughts, even if he had wanted to. Gitxsan halaayt did not necessarily understand themselves to be under his spiritual jurisdiction. And Du Vernet never articulated his work as Theosophical or Spiritualist—he cast his lot with psychology and the apostle Paul, over and over again. Nevertheless, Sylvia's provocative reading and research in honor of her husband's ancestor, like Stella's library, has been a great gift to my own research.

Stella and Alice

Frederick died with "fifty one hundred fifty two dollars and forty-nine cents" to his name, almost half of it in real estate: a Crown grant on the Nass River, a piece of land at Kitwanga on the Skeena, which was intersected by the Grand Trunk Pacific Railway, and eight lots in Prince Rupert. In his will, written already in 1908, he gave everything he had to his "beloved wife Stella." Of the $2,500 he left in cash and investments, she spent almost $900 on his hospital bills and funeral costs. Luckily for Stella, she had also bought some Prince Rupert real estate with her own money, so she had funds to fall back on.[19]

Stella offered a most eloquent testimony to her husband's spiritual experimentation, by endowing a library in his name with the goal of keeping his eclectic collection of books together. This gesture, along with her careful inscription of her name and the date on the first page of her copy of *Spiritual Radio*, suggests that she loved both him and his mind energy. She took care with the books that had inspired him and claimed as her own a copy of the unusual book that bore his name. For the next four years, she lived as a widow with her daughter, Alice, still at her side; Horace had moved to Greenville, South Carolina, just before his father's death, after trying for a few years to establish himself as a farmer, a postmaster, and even a justice of the peace near Kitwanga.[20]

Stella passed away on December 10, 1928, at the age of seventy-eight. Outliving her husband who was ten years her junior, she was buried next to Frederick in the Fairview Cemetery. According to Walter Rushbrook, upon Stella's death, the *North British Columbia News* described her as a "real mother to the clergy, and indeed to the hundreds of young men who were trying to establish themselves in this new land." He called her a "splendid helpmeet of the Bishop" and noted that she was the first president of the Women's Auxiliary of the Diocese of Caledonia, a voluntary organization of laywomen dedicated to church and community work.[21] Her willingness to support the publication of *Spiritual Radio* shows that her help extended into his spiritual experiments.

At the age of thirty-five, Alice Du Vernet had lost her father and her radio mind companion, with whom she had been sharing spiritual energy for years. She must have played some role in gathering his papers for publication in *Out of a Scribe's Treasure* and *Spiritual Radio*, but neither editor mentions her. She also tried her best to gather the numbers her father left behind. In a 1925 letter to Archdeacon George Rix, the administrator of the diocese after her father's death, she listed all the sources she had compiled to complete several years of statistical reports for the General Synod, demonstrating that she also had an adept knowledge of her father's bureaucratic labors. Finding that a "report that Father was working on when taken ill after Easter was all there was to go on," she cobbled together his reports on "Indian Missions" to the MSCC and forms sent in by the clergy, calculating statistics along the way. In closing her letter, she requested that Rix return the completed form to her, so that she could "type-write the copy to go to the General Synod."[22] This was likely a task she had done for her father for years.

Five years after her father's death, and a few months after the death of her mother, Alice married James Byers Gibson in St. Andrew's Cathedral. A clergyman her father had placed in the diocese, Gibson had become the rector of St. Andrew's, and in 1945, he became the fourth bishop of Caledonia. Alice, who was forty years old at the time of her wedding, had lived her life in service to the church by way of her father for most of that time. When she was fifteen, she sent the Toronto newspapers to her father far away in Metlakatla during his first year as a bishop. As a young woman, she typed up his reports, kept track of the mail, and joined in the experiments by which they sought to prove the power radio mind. She was his trusted assistant, and to his credit, he paid her a small wage. Now, as the wife of a clergyman in the cathedral her father built, she would continue to serve the church.

Even the *North British Columbia News* noticed her hard work, commenting on how her new husband would benefit from her years of experience: "The marriage of Miss Du Vernet to Rev. J. B. Gibson, will, we believe, prove a very happy alliance, and her years of close fellowship in the work of her father, the Late Archbishop, will doubtless be of great value to her husband."[23] Passing

Alice's expertise from the office of her father to the benefit of her husband, the newspaper did not specify which kinds of close fellowship—secretarial or telepathic—it meant.

In July of 1952, at sixty-three years old, almost the same age her father was upon his death, Alice and her husband were killed when their car plunged off a cliff on a treacherous mountain road. Her death prompted a *Vancouver Province* newspaper columnist to recall for his readers Frederick and Alice's experiments with the Chevreul pendulum almost thirty years earlier:

> At 10 o'clock of a Monday morning, Feb. 19, 1923, a lady in Prince Rupert sent a message through the medium of thought transference to her father in the living-room of his host's house on Robson street [in Vancouver]. And Canada and the world had another long-distance proof of the experiments carried out by an English Church cleric and his daughter. The girl was the daughter of the late Archbishop H.F. [*sic*] Du Vernet, first [*sic*] bishop of Caledonia. Thursday she was killed in an auto accident near Prince Rupert, along with her husband, also Bishop of Caledonia, Rt. Rev. James Byers Gibson. Long a student of psychology, the late Bishop Du Vernet had plenty of opportunity to test his theories and studies when making lone trips in the wilds of his diocese.[24]

Not given the dignity of her own name when remembered upon her death, in the public record Alice's identity was subsumed by those of her husband and father, and by the story of radio mind.

Bodies, Spirits, and Stories

What did Du Vernet mean when he wrote, "Personal identity does not lie in material particles but in spiritual personality which thinks and remembers, loves and chooses"?[25] Did it matter if spiritual personality inhered in the body of a woman or the body of a man? Were the material particles of Indigenous and white people given the same freedoms to inhabit and exercise their personal identities? In early twentieth-century British Columbia, and even today, the material particles of one's body were not irrelevant to the scope of one's freedom to think and to remember, to love and to choose. The body itself was, and is, a medium of power, the site where telepathy happened and from which testimony sprung. But the body was also the frame by which people were coded and governed in a Christian colonial system structured by race, sex, money, and ritual.

Only those who seldom feel the constrictions that come with their material particles can so boldly assert their insignificance. In Du Vernet's day, white skin was a seal of citizenship that brought with it the right to own land and to take the land of people called "Indians"; "red" skin was the mark of subjection.[26] In Du Vernet's church, the color line was also the bottom line: whether money flowed from the missionary desire to convert the heathen or the Dominion of Canada's drive to assimilate the Indigenous child, the "Indian work" was a lucrative business for the church. Du Vernet was able to see the stark effects of the fetishization of skin color in his midst. He tried to challenge it by urging church officials to open themselves to "mingling" and to Indigenous authority in the church. Without using the word "racism," he disputed its force when he warned his colleagues that their greedy excitement over residential schools demeaned and denied the bonds of Indigenous parents and their children.

Even though he was celebrated as a "man's man," Du Vernet came to a modest endorsement of women's rights. In Du Vernet's church, the material particles of being a man were a fundamental requirement to hold sacramental power as a bishop or a priest. No matter what she thought or remembered, loved or chose, a woman could never enter into the chain of authority of apostolic succession that extended through the past, bishop to bishop, man to man, to collapse into the body of Christ himself. She could not mediate the spiritual power of the Eucharist, sprinkle the water of baptism, or lay consecrating hands on the head of a man to help transform him into a bishop. She could play an auxiliary role as helpmeet, but hers was never a role of glorious, or even modest, leadership. Stella's views on the enfranchisement of women, however, must have won him over, as by the end of his life he, too, supported women's suffrage and the idea of women taking on leadership roles in their communities, if not in their churches.[27]

It is also noteworthy that he worked with Alice to explore the power of spiritual energy. Not adhering to the usual division of labor in which the woman was the "medium" for the spirits, whether in séances or automatic writing, Frederick and Alice took turns as the sender and receiver of their telepathic messages. As a bishop in the Anglican Church in the early twentieth century, Du Vernet was a medium for God in a way that only a (usually white) man, consecrated by the hands and prayers of three other white men, could be. As a scientist of radio mind, however, he was setting in motion a traveling circuit of spiritual energy that anyone in the whole world could mediate, regardless of "age, sex, and race," if they simply relaxed their bodies and let radio mind do its work.[28]

On the same day that Du Vernet died and was eulogized on the front page of the *Prince Rupert Daily News*, the newspaper also ran a short piece on an inside page entitled "Indians Claim All Land in B.C.: No Treaty Ever Made and No Compensation Given for Property Taken." The Nisga'a Indian Land Committee had joined with other Indigenous nations to form the Allied Indian Tribes and, together with the Friends of the Indians, had taken their claim once more to the federal government. A few years later, the government would amend the Indian Act yet again to make it illegal for Indigenous people to hire lawyers, as a way of halting the land movement.[29] While their archbishop had taken to new media to open up his spiritual imagination, the Nisga'a were using the medium of print to build a wider political movement.

As a matrilineal people, the Nisga'a understood the significance of the body for gendered spiritual political power differently from missionaries such as James McCullagh and Frederick Du Vernet. Women were at the heart of clans, even if they were not always the chiefs sought out by colonial officials or missionaries as the "true" leaders. Though missionaries and the Dominion of Canada called them heathens and wards of the state, Nisga'a and Ts'msyen people did not concur with these names and their implications. While they may have taken on the names of "Indian" and "chief" as they built a collective movement to fight the dispossession of their land across the new province, they did not forget the names of their clans, unpronounceable and unrecognizable to colonial officials (but not necessarily to missionaries). Often bestowed on men, these names could also be held by women. For example, Niysyok, the man who cut down his totem pole on the Nass, held a name that in the nineteenth century had also been held by a woman.[30]

Du Vernet put the body at the center of radio mind, despite his preference for the spiritual over the material. Markings on the paper of the Chevreul pendulum were merely visible proof of the body—mind, nerves, muscles—in a state of relaxation, acting as a medium. But spiritual energy did not travel to a body in isolation, in a vertical relation to God. Instead, people were to share their spiritual energy with each other, mind to mind, to somehow work collective transformations on the world.[31] We can travel past the bounds of our bodies, he claimed, by way of our minds and spirits working together.

As an episcopal shaman—a bishop who opened new pathways for spirits traveling outside the body—Du Vernet took his place beside other colonial spiritual practitioners who vouched for telepathy as a tool of healing. As Juan Obarrio has written of Liberato and Jacobo, two Toba shamans from Argentina who became Anglican priests at the hands of British missionaries in the mid-twentieth century, they too were "materialised spirits" who saw "ideas travelling as communications through the airways." Obarrio points out how the figure and concept of the shaman, along with that of the cannibal, has been the "absolute alterity" of colonial imaginations, in which "the firm yet agitated body of the shaman was the space where modernity located its dread and its desire."[32] To understand Frederick's spiritual radio as a medium for a shamanic Christianity raises the specter of appropriating Indigenous traditions. But if the shaman is always already a colonial construct, then perhaps the name fits him quite well.

Juan Obarrio's poetic description of the shaman does sound uncannily like the practitioner of radio mind: "A poignant presence that trespasses the boundaries of the world of the alive, talks to animals, fl[ies] with the eagles, stops the flux of time, heals the sick, gives political advice and invokes the dead ancestors." Obarrio's shamans, whom he recognizes are mediated through his own writing, share their poignancy with Du Vernet. So too does Obarrio himself: "Memory is not an individual device. . . . Memory is a structure that works by itself, through subjects. Across all of us. Memory remembers." Granting similar agency to memory, with a very Bergsonian flair, Du Vernet declared: "Character is largely founded upon memory which conserves for us the experience of the past to guide us as we face the future." Thinking for so long about this man, walking in the places where he walked, and reading his words over and over again, sometimes I, too, feel that "something remembers in me," to borrow Juan Obarrio's words.[33]

It is perhaps not so surprising, or uncanny, to find that two Indigenous Anglican shamans from a remote region of Argentina—at least when mediated by an anthropologist who has a knack for making connections across time and space—sound so similar to an Anglican archbishop living in what some consider to be the edge of the world. The Toba of Argentina, like the Ts'msyen of the northwest coast, were described by both missionaries and anthropologists alike as "cannibals" and as "shamans," the two categories of alterity that have most sharply distinguished the Christian from the heathen, and the white from the Indigenous person, in missionary and anthropological writings. As William Duncan worried when he tried to bring Anglicanism to Metlakatla more than a century and a half ago, how could he know whether the Metlakatlans could tell the difference between cannibalism and the act of ingesting the body and blood of Jesus in the Eucharist? As James McCullagh reported and James Frazer repeated, the shaman who mistakenly swallowed the soul of his patient made a story worthy of circulating in a print culture that accrued authority to them as missionary and anthropologist.

When Bishop Ridley kicked Duncan out of the CMS for withholding the sacrament of Eucharist from the Ts'msyen Christians (and for holding on to the land), he opened up a portal of spiritual mingling—exchanging rituals and exchanging stories—that went in more than one direction.[34] In Ridley's wake, Frederick Du Vernet, by the end of his life, fostered a sacramental mysticism of mediation in which he trespassed boundaries of the alive and the dead, looked forward to flying like a bird, overcame time and space, promised to heal the sick, proffered political advice, and invoked dead ancestors, most often the apostle Paul.

As he counseled his clergy in his 1923 bishop's charge to the synod: "Concentration of mind is necessary to efficacy in prayer. Shakespeare taught us this when he made the King of Denmark say:—'My words fly up, my thoughts remain below, Words without thoughts never to heaven go.'"[35] Embodying and advocating a spiritual mingling that sounded more shamanic than evangelical, Du Vernet's journey to radio mind was the conversion of the missionary himself, from missionary-bishop to episcopal shaman.

Curricula and Conversion

Canada was made by remapping the land with new stories and names that tried to suppress those told and held by Indigenous people. Photographs, maps, printing presses, and radio were all media for the spiritual invention of the nation. With both cardinal and spiritual compasses guiding them, pulled by the magnetic force of the earth and the energetic force of the spirit, missionaries were eager users of any new medium they could deploy to tell their stories to Indigenous people. Telling and eliciting testimonies with the help of both law and the Bible, their work of colonization and Christianization seemed to them to evoke an inevitable narrative of conversion that would erase the stories of people already in and of the land.

Throughout this remapping, however, multiple visions of the spirit have always been at play, sometimes faintly resembling each other, sometimes one obscuring the other altogether. Frederick Du Vernet was a man who loved the rivers and forests of his adopted home, copying into his notebook a verse from a hymn to America: "I love thine inland seas / Thy groves of giant trees / Thy rolling plains / Thy rivers mighty sweep / Thy mystic canyons deep / Thy mountains wild & steep / All thy domains."[36] He also seems to have genuinely cared for many of the people he met and befriended, whether Jeremiah Johnston on the Rainy River or Alfred Adams in Massett. By the end of his life, he came to envision a world governed by spiritual laws that were shaped by his interactions with these people, as well as by his visions of a powerful energy that was at the core of each human being and that flowed everywhere in the universe. At the same time, he lived within and helped create a world that was governed by earthly laws, which worked according to principles of division and extraction, in which lands and people were severed from the past and from each other, through railways, Indian Acts, hydrographic surveys, and residential schools.

I regularly pass by the red sandstone building of Wycliffe College, Du Vernet's alma mater, on my bicycle route to work. A college that trained most of the Canadian-born Anglican missionaries who went west in the nineteenth century, including many of the men who became principals of Anglican residential schools, Wycliffe was oriented by a curriculum of conversion.[37] Wycliffe College was also the place where Du Vernet was first introduced to the study of psychology within a nineteenth-century Christian context, and where he became a strong missionary activist, as editor of the *Canadian Church Missionary Gleaner*.

After being taught by and becoming family with Simon Gibbons, the Inuit priest, the next time that Du Vernet encountered Indigenous people in a meaningful way was when he set off from Wycliffe on his missionary tour of the Rainy River. Talking face-to-face with Ojibwe men, women, and children, he saw that the Ojibwe cared for their children and for the graves of their dead. A seed of doubt was planted in his missionary confidence. The old women and the chiefs told him a story of the land and spirits that resisted his own. When he left Ontario for good, and met more Indigenous men and women who spoke to him frankly and wrote him letters and petitions, including Andrew Mercer and Alfred Adams, that seed grew. By the end of his life, he testified to a very different spirit of conversion, which resembled Indigenous understandings of traveling spirits much more than Anglican ones.

Today, Wycliffe College is also the alma mater of Mark MacDonald, the first national Indigenous bishop in the Anglican Church of Canada. An episcopal seat established by the Anglican Council of Indigenous Peoples in 2005, the position of national Indigenous bishop rewrites the map, adhering to no diocesan boundaries, in acknowledgment that "Indigenous people coexist with the land and it is the artificial diocesan boundaries that cross over Indigenous territories."[38] MacDonald, a Wyandotte priest who has lived and worked just south of Manidoo Ziibi, has been participating in retelling the story of missionary conversion.

In the spring of 2016, he visited the Nass River, hosted by the Nisga'a at the Laxgalts'ap Community Centre. The Anglican First Nations Diocese of Caledonia invited him, along with the Anglican primate and the current bishop of Caledonia, to come to the Nisga'a Nation to reiterate the church's apology for its role in residential schools. They wanted to hear the apology not via a website, or through a piece of paper, but directly from the mouths of the church leaders. While there, he participated in a ritual commemorating the times when the missionaries insisted on the burning of masks and the chopping of totem poles. There was Nisga'a dancing and a luncheon, speeches and a Eucharistic service. And with echoes of the Christmas celebration of 1913 in the Nass Valley, the master of ceremonies was a man named Andrew Mercer, Sim'oogit Wisin Xbiĺtkw.[39]

No matter what new media technologies may emerge, the body remains a necessary medium for communication. Stories from the mouth, in which a storyteller speaks directly into the ears of the audience, his or her voice carried across the air, resound differently than those one can read or receive over wires or through transmitters. For settlers in Canada and the United States, being with Indigenous people on their own ground—even when that ground feels like home—and hearing their stories face-to-face requires learning new modes of listening.

Taking Du Vernet's words with me to the Rainy River First Nations and to the Nisga'a Nation has opened up new stories, new relationships, and new ways to mediate the past. Telling the story of radio mind has required the help of many people, including those I have come to know on visits to archives, to First Nations, and in my classroom: from Andrew Mercer who wrote letters to the editor in 1911 to Art Hunter who has talked with me and my students at Kay-Nah-Chi-Wah-Nung. The curriculum of conversion will not be fully remedied by a curriculum of reconciliation, but a new cycle of stories must begin somewhere, rooted in relationships of talking and listening.

Nations are defined by the stories they tell in laws and maps, in schools and books, in intimate circles and via broadcasts radiating across the land. Fully grasping the importance of the social imaginary of stories means respecting their power as medicine that can hurt and can heal. Perhaps "radio mind" seems a quaintly outmoded technological metaphor, whatever one thinks of its spiritual reality. We live in a time when some of the most powerful ways of imagining the mind and its powers are oriented by fever-pitch tales of neural networks, machine learning, and artificial intelligence, in which computers will fast outpace human beings' embodied capacities to listen to and think with each other.

But even today's stories of the mind in the digital age must be situated in human bodies and communities that live on the land. The software that guides many people through their days and connects them virtually to each other does not bring either healing or justice without people to act and listen. The hardware that makes up laptops and cell phones depends on critical minerals, which are often mined on Indigenous land, leaving poisonous contaminants behind. Once thrown out in a quick cycle of obsolescence, the laptops and cell phones become mountains of toxic waste, often shipped across the ocean to countries where the poor comb through the rubble to extract the valuable minerals once again, and are poisoned in the process. Words such as "cyberspace" or "the cloud" create a seemingly floating digital "space" that obscures the material and relational nature of these storytelling technologies; they may provide a bird's-eye view of the world, but they obscure the reality that even the virtual world feeds off the land.

Any story of the mind worth listening to—or reading—acknowledges that the land is the ground of human existence. Without caring for the land and for each other, no manner of cognitive, technological innovation will save us. Inspired by Henri Bergson's hope that spiritual energy could be a creative source of change rooted in the mind, in memory, and in collective action, Frederick Du Vernet told a story of radio mind that was optimistic and flawed. By placing his story on the Ojibwe, Ts'msyen, Nisga'a, and Haida lands on which he journeyed, I have sought to show that when thinking about the stories that have created and continue to sustain Canada, his vision is worth remembering for both its failings and its hope.

Acknowledgments

While following the path of Frederick Du Vernet's journey, I have enjoyed the company of many fellow travelers along the way. Without the support, guidance, and critical insights of these people, this book would never have found its way to paper. Many of them saved me from errors, but none of them are responsible for any that might remain. I am particularly grateful to people from the Rainy River First Nations and the Kay-Nah-Chi-Wah-Nung Historical Centre, an area visited by Du Vernet in 1898. Art Hunter offered his deep knowledge of his nation's and his family's history over the course of several visits to the Rainy River. Art's hospitality opened the way for me and my students to meet elders Dorothy Medicine and Willie Wilson, as well as his brothers Al Hunter and Joe Hunter, all of whom shared their perspectives on Du Vernet's account of his time on the river. At the Kay-Nah-Chi-Wah-Nung Historical Centre, Tara Montague, Mylo Smith, Loraine Cochrane, and Doreen Hunter have been generous with their time and their expertise.

I am also thankful for the support I received when visiting the Nisga'a Nation. Nita Morven, cultural research analyst in the Ayuuk̲hl Nisg̲a'a Department of the Nisg̲a'a Lisims Government, has been particularly collegial, sharing both documents and her own considerable historical and linguistic knowledge. I also thank Deanna Nyce, president of the Wilp Wilxo'oskwhl Nisga'a Institute, for encouraging conversations. I am also grateful to Bishop John Hannen for sharing his long experience of the Diocese of Caledonia with me, and to National Indigenous Anglican Bishop Mark MacDonald for recounting his more recent experiences in the region.

Many museums and archives were indispensable sites for my research, both as repositories for papers, photographs, and artifacts, and as places to think about how to remember missionaries and their troubling legacies.

I have many people to thank for their help. Cliff Armstrong, the volunteer archivist at the Diocese of Caledonia Archives in Prince Rupert, British Columbia, opened up Du Vernet's papers and library to my research assistants and me with generosity and good humor. What we found there made it possible to tell the story of radio mind. Laurel Parsons and Nancy Hurd at the General Synod Archives of the Anglican Church of Canada first led me to Du Vernet's remarkable 1898 "Diary of a Missionary Tour," which continues to be a central focus of my research. For their helpfulness and their commitment to their work, I also thank Melanie Delva of the Archives of the Provincial Synod of British Columbia and Yukon (Anglican); Jean Eiers-Page of the Prince Rupert City and Regional Archives; Kelly-Ann Turkington of the Royal British Columbia Museum and Archives; Janet Hathaway of Archives and Special Collections at the University of King's College; Dan Mark of Archives Hemmingford; Sylvia Lassam, the Rolph-Bell Archivist of the Trinity College Archives; Maureen Matthews of the Manitoba Museum; Lori Nelson and Lynn Halley at the Lake of the Woods Museum in Kenora; Rilla Race of the Chapple Museum; Trudy Nicks of the Royal Ontario Museum; and Rachel Klassen and Isabelle Charron of Library and Archives Canada. Douglas Fast, a cartographer, helped visualize Du Vernet's journey in his elegant maps.

My students and research assistants have been with me at every stage of this process. Amy Fisher, then a PhD student, and Sarina Annis, then an undergraduate, traveled to British Columbia with me twice to visit archives in Prince Rupert, Vancouver, and Victoria. Their skill at negotiating archives and their brilliance at making connections among the voluminous materials we found made it possible for me to write. Their shared excitement and despair at what we learned in these places heartened me many times over. Sarina's research, funded by the University of Toronto Excellence Award and focused on the nineteenth-century philosophers we found amid Du Vernet's library, helped frame my own argument. The Story Nations team accompanied me to Rainy River First Nations for two consecutive summers, as we worked to tell the story of Du Vernet's "Diary of a Missionary Tour" in a digital form. My PhD students, Judith Brunton, Meaghan Weatherdon, Kaleigh McLelland, and Annie Heckman, have shown great dedication and spirit in our travels and ongoing work. I am very grateful to my undergraduate students who joined these trips and worked on the project as part of the Research Opportunities Program and Research Excursion Program, including Russell Turner, Tamim Mansour, and Erin Ray. Keith Garrett, also supported by a University of Toronto Excellence Award, unearthed some important sources at the last minute. Audrey Rochette, who is now a graduate student in her own right, and her mother, Shishigo Gijig, traveled with us to Manidoo Ziibi in 2016. Their shared knowledge of Ojibwe history and language transformed our visit—Chi Miikwec!

Magdalene Klassen made important discoveries in archives in Quebec and Ontario, including the discovery of Simon Gibbons, Du Vernet's Inuit tutor and brother-in-law. Magdalene also read an earlier version of the manuscript; her knack for catching the "dead spots" in my prose kept me striving for clarity. I am also grateful to research assistants who have helped in the later stages of the book, including Megan Harvey, who scoured microfilm reels; Artemisia Robins, who made several maps and charts; and Orvis Starkweather, who helped with the family tree. In a heroic last push to finish the book manuscript with its many illustrations and maps, Greg Fewster, Annie Heckman, and Suzanne van Geuns were remarkably patient and adept. Roxanne Korpan also offered helpful suggestions and corrections, and took the lead on conceiving and compiling the index, with assistance from Magdalene Klassen. Students in several of my classes also read and commented on portions of the book, and I thank the students in Mediascapes and in North American Religions.

Writing this book has widened my circle of colleagues both in Toronto and elsewhere. I am especially grateful for my continued collaborations with Monique Scheer of the University of Tübingen and Benjamin Berger of the Osgoode Hall Law School at York University, with whom it is such a pleasure to think and teach. Paul Bramadat of the Centre for Studies in Religion and Society at the University of Victoria first invited me to present this research as the John Albert Hall Lectures at the Centre for Studies in Religion and Society (CSRS) at the University of Victoria. The opportunity to develop these chapters first as four oral presentations to an audience in British Columbia made me think very carefully about what I had to say and how I wanted to say it. I am very thankful to the CSRS, and especially to Paul for the trust he put in me, and for his continued collegiality and friendship. At the University of Victoria, several scholars have generously commented on my research and pointed me in new directions; I particularly thank Avigail Eisenberg, John Borrows, John Lutz, James Tully, Hamar Foster, and Wendy Wickwire. I thank Julie Cruikshank of the University of British Columbia, Susan Neylan of Wilfrid Laurier University, and Daniel Midena of the University of Queensland for helpful conversations. Nicholas May, now a postdoctoral fellow at the University of British Columbia, has shared with me his fascinating research on Nisga'a Christianity with candor and sincerity, and very generously read and commented on earlier versions of this manuscript. Near the end of my writing, Maureen Atkinson kindly shared with me her vast knowledge of British Columbia's radio history.

The community of scholars brought together in the Global Seminars in Media, Religion, and Culture became a formative testing ground for this research; I am profoundly grateful to Birgit Meyer and Stewart Hoover for inviting me to seminars at the University of Ghana in Accra and the University of Hyderabad, where I began to conceive of this project as in the orbit of religion and media. Birgit's generous invitations to Utrecht helped me move further in this direction. Elsewhere, Courtney Bender, Winnifred Fallers Sullivan, Michael McNally, Kathryn Lofton, Paul C. Johnson, Sally Promey, Judith Weisenfeld, John Lardas Modern, Heather Curtis, Matthew Engelke, Elizabeth Shakman Hurd, Kate Bowler, Elizabeth McAlister, and David Morgan have been critical intellectual companions as I wrote this book.

At the University of Toronto, I am blessed with colleagues who are brilliant and collaborative, many of whom have provided ongoing critical inspiration for my work, both as we teach together and in more informal ways. I thank Ruth Marshall, Simon Coleman, Kevin O'Neill, Ajay Rao, Natalie Zemon Davis, Michael Wayne, J. Barton Scott, Kyle Smith, Amira Mittermaier, Karen Ruffle, John Marshall, Amanda Goodman, John Kloppenborg, Robert Gibbs, Heidi Bohaker, Nicholas Terpstra, Cara Krmpotich, David Cameron, Suzanne Akbari, Jill Carter, Thomas Keymer, Andrea Most, Will Robins, Linda Hutcheon, Edward Chamberlin, and many others, for their enthusiasm and wisdom. The Honourable Frank Iacobucci graciously shared with me his perspective on the Indigenous Residential Schools Settlement Agreement. Marcel Fortin, the head librarian of the Map and Data Library at the University of Toronto, generously fed me maps to help me think and tell this story. I also thank Fereshteh Hashemi, Marilyn Colaço, Christopher Pugh, and Irene Kao at the Department for the Study of Religion for their help along the way.

I am lucky to have a second academic home at the University of Tübingen, Germany, where my research has been supported in my role as Distinguished Visiting Professor in the Anthropology of Modern Religion at the Ludwig-Uhland-Institute für Empirische Kulturwissenschaft, as well as during a sabbatical as a returning Humboldt Fellow at the Institut für Ethnologie. In addition to Monique Scheer, I thank Gabriele Alex and Roland Hardenberg, and other colleagues, students, and staff at both of these departments for their ongoing support and their interest in my work.

These chapters were presented in earlier versions at many universities and conferences, and I want to acknowledge the importance of queries and comparisons raised by audience members at many sites, including the following: the Religion Department at Syracuse University; the Material and Visual Cultures of Religion Project at Yale University; the Department of Religion at Columbia University; the Religion Department at Haverford College; the

Faculty of Law at McGill University; the Museum of Archaeology and Anthropology at the University of Cambridge; the Chester Ronning Centre for Religion and Public Life at the University of Alberta; the Department of Religious Studies at Memorial University; the Material Economies of Religion in the Americas project; the Book History and Print Culture Program, the Department of Anthropology, and the Department for the Study of Religion at the University of Toronto; the International Society for Intellectual History; the American Academy of Religion Annual Meeting; the American Society for the Study of Religion; the American Society of Church History; the British Columbia Studies Conference; the Religion and Diversity Project at the University of Ottawa; the Social Science Research Council; the American Anthropological Association Annual Meeting; the Society for the Anthropology of Religion; and the International Association for the History of Religion.

This book was made possible by the financial support of many organizations dedicated to sustaining and cultivating research in the humanities. I am very grateful to the Social Sciences and the Humanities Research Council of Canada, both for an individual Standard Research Grant and for its support of the University of Ottawa's Religion and Diversity Project, directed by Lori Beaman, which helped fund my research with the Kay-Nah-Chi-Wah-Nung Historical Centre. I am especially thankful to the Alexander von Humboldt Foundation based in Germany, which has been supporting my research since 2004 in various ways, awarding me the Anneliese Maier Research Award for 2015–2020, held at the University of Tübingen with Monique Scheer as my host. The generosity of the Humboldt Foundation is unparalleled. I am honored to be part of a national organization so committed to the idea that the best scholarship thrives when researchers from around the world can work side by side that it funds scholars from outside its borders. The Maier Award provided a generous subsidy for the illustrations in the book. My research has also been supported by many of my communities closer to home at the University of Toronto: Victoria College, the Department for the Study of Religion, the Faculty of Arts and Science, and the Jackman Humanities Institute, where my year as a fellow in residence first brought the idea of this book to life.

At the University of Chicago Press, I am thankful to Alan Thomas for urging me to write this book as a story, and for letting me use so many illustrations to do so. Along the way, his frank suggestions for what worked and what did not were both gracious and welcome. Randy Petilos guided me through the late stages of the manuscript and illustrations with patience and consideration. Two anonymous reviewers for the press offered critique and encouragement that helped me better articulate the point of this project.

Kelly Finefrock-Creed was a remarkably astute and thorough copyeditor, and I am grateful to her for the many improvements that she made to the story. I also thank other staff at the press, including designer Isaac Tobin, production controllers Skye Agnew and Lauren Reese, and two promotions managers, Katryce Lassle and Brian Carroll.

I am thankful to many friends and family for supporting me both as a writer and as a mother. When I needed a last-minute traveling companion on the road to Rainy River, Barbara Burkholder changed her plans and hopped on a plane and into a rental car to travel with me on my first visit to Kay-Nah-Chi-Wah-Nung. Maggie MacDonald sees me through every up and down, scholarly and otherwise. Ruth Marshall reads my work and shares her own, changing mine for the better. Lorraine and Oliver Sutherns have, as always, shared the pleasures and challenges of parenting and work. Susanne and Florian Seiberlich have given me a much-appreciated home away from home in Tübingen, offering not only home-cooked meals but also a sounding board for how to translate these stories of Canada in a different land. My mother, Susanna Klassen, has traveled alongside me to care for my children while I worked on this book, as well as stayed home to do so when I went away; she has helped me fulfill my responsibilities in so many ways. John Klassen, my father, and Vicki Sharp, his partner, who now live across from Du Vernet's former church in Toronto, are profoundly supportive, as are my brother Joel and his family. Michael Dore is always interested in my stories. My uncle, Ernst Klassen, shared with me his many years of experience living and working with Indigenous people in some of the very same places as Du Vernet; his own mystical curiosities have inspired my work.

Finally, I thank my husband and daughters for living with Frederick Du Vernet in our lives for so many years. They traveled with me to Du Vernet's birthplace in Quebec and to the Nisga'a Nation and Haida Gwaii. They listened as I recounted every twist and turn as I pieced together his story. John Marshall, my husband and colleague, read every word of the manuscript; as always, he took great care to help me make it better in his prudent and insightful manner. My daughters, each in their own way, are in these pages. Magdalene, who is becoming a historian who tells stories of her own, worked through the writing and thinking in every chapter with me. Isabel, who first asked me to tell her stories from my mouth, has been a steadfast companion on the journey. And Georgia, who carried on the tradition of requesting stories from my mouth, gave me the gift of listening and asking for more, thereby teaching me the difference that a story, its telling, and its teller could make.

This book is for my children.

Notes

Archives, Museums, and Historical Centers Consulted and/or Visited

Archives and Special Collections, King's College, Halifax, Nova Scotia
Archives Hemmingford, Hemmingford, Quebec
Archives of Manitoba, Winnipeg, Manitoba
Archives of Ontario, Toronto, Ontario
Archives of the Anglican Diocese of Montreal, Montreal, Quebec
Archives of the Provincial Synod of British Columbia and Yukon (Anglican), Vancouver, British Columbia
Ayuukhl Nisga'a Department, Nisga'a Lisims Government, Gitlaxt'aamiks, Nisga'a Nation, British Columbia
Bibliothèque et Archives Nationale du Québec, Montreal, Quebec
Canadian Museum of History, Gatineau, Quebec
Diocese of Caledonia Archives, Prince Rupert, British Columbia
Fort Frances Museum and Cultural Centre, Fort Frances, Ontario
General Synod Archives of the Anglican Church of Canada, Toronto, Ontario
Haida Heritage Centre at Kay Llnagaay, Skidegate, Haida Gwaii, British Columbia
Kay-Nah-Chi-Wah-Nung Historical Centre, Rainy River First Nations, Ontario
Lake of the Woods Museum, Kenora, Ontario
Library and Archives Canada, Ottawa, Ontario
Manitoba Museum, Winnipeg, Manitoba
Map and Data Library, University of Toronto, Toronto, Ontario
Minnesota Historical Society, St. Paul, Minnesota
Missisquoi Historical Society, Quebec
Museum of Northern British Columbia, Prince Rupert, British Columbia
National Gallery of Canada, Ottawa, Ontario
Nisga'a Museum, Laxgalts'ap, Nisga'a Nation, British Columbia
Northern British Columbia Archives, University of Northern British Columbia, Prince George, British Columbia
Prince Rupert City and Regional Archives, Prince Rupert, British Columbia

Royal British Columbia Museum and Archives, Victoria, British Columbia
Thomas Fisher Rare Book Library, University of Toronto, Toronto, Ontario

Chapter 1

1 Frederick H. Du Vernet, "Inter-Mental Action," *Vancouver Province*, January 26, 1923, Du Vernet Clippings File, Archives of the Provincial Synod of British Columbia and Yukon, Vancouver, BC; Bill Dunford, in *Vancouver Province*, July 26, 1952, Du Vernet Clippings including Newspapers, Archives of the Provincial Synod of British Columbia and Yukon, Vancouver, BC.

2 Frederick H. Du Vernet, "The Communion of the Mind," *Spiritual Radio* (Mountain Lakes, NJ: Society of the Nazarene, 1925), 47. For an in-house history of the diocese, see Hugh McCullum and Karmel Taylor McCullum, *Caledonia: 100 Years Ahead* (Toronto: Anglican Book Centre, 1979).

3 The strait was named after the HMS *Hecate*, a British paddlewheel sloop used in the 1860s to survey the lands and waters of what came to be called British Columbia. "Hecate Strait," BC Geographical Names, accessed January 17, 2016, http://apps.gov.bc.ca/pub/bcgnws/names/38500.html. On the biodiversity of the region, see George F. MacDonald, "Coast Tsimshian Pre-contact Economics and Trade: An Archaeological and Ethno-Historic Reconstruction" (paper for Metlakatla/Lax Kw'alaams Land Claim File, submitted to Ratliff & Co. by 6347371 Canada Inc., July 15, 2006), http://faculty.arts.ubc.ca/menzies/documents/macdonal_g.pdf. See also Stephen Watkinson, "Life after Death: The Importance of Salmon Carcasses to British Columbia's Watersheds," *ARCTIC* 53, no. 1 (2000): 92–96.

4 Susan Marsden, "Adawx, Spanaxnox, and the Geopolitics of the Tsimshian," *BC Studies: The British Columbian Quarterly*, no. 135 (2002): 101–35 (quotations, 103). See also Margaret Seguin Anderson, "Lest There Be No Salmon: Symbols in the Traditional Tsimshian Potlatch," in *The Tsimshian: Images of the Past, Views for the Present*, ed. Margaret Seguin Anderson (Vancouver: University of British Columbia Press, 1984), 110–36; Marius Barbeau, William Beynon, John J. Cove, and George F. MacDonald, *Tsimshian Narratives* (Ottawa: Education and Cultural Affairs Division, 1987); Robert Budd and Roy Henry Vickers, *Raven Brings the Light* (Madeira Park, BC: Harbour, 2013); Marie-Françoise Guedon, "An Introduction to Tsimshian World View and Its Practitioners," in Anderson, *The Tsimshian*, 137–59; Nisga'a Tribal Council, *Nisga'a: People of the Nass River* (Vancouver: Douglas & McIntyre, 1993), 15, 108. Spelling varies among the three related languages of the Nisga'a, Ts'msyen, and Gitxsan. As much as possible, I have tried to use the orthography appropriate to the nation I am discussing. I thank Nita Morven for her advice on this issue.

5 The words "Indian," "Indigenous," "Aboriginal," and "First Nation" all have specific legal and historical uses, and are all problematic for different reasons. Generally, I use the names of specific nations (e.g., Nisga'a Nation) when possible, and otherwise use the term "Indigenous" to describe the collectivity of peoples and nations with territorial sovereignty that precedes, and persists in parallel to, the Canadian nation-state. I use the term "Indian" when it is deployed in historical and legal sources (including Canada's still extant "Indian Act" legislation). I use "Aboriginal" only when in a quotation. "First Nations" refers to specific

Indigenous governments under Canadian law. For more on this question, see Taiaiake Alfred and Jeff Corntassel, "Being Indigenous: Resurgences against Contemporary Colonialism," *Government and Opposition* 40, no. 4 (September 1, 2005): 597–614.

6 Gauri Viswanathan, *Outside the Fold: Conversion, Modernity, and Belief* (Princeton, NJ: Princeton University Press, 1998), 30; Frederick H. Du Vernet, "The Pathway of Psychology," in *Out of a Scribe's Treasure: Brief Essays in Practical Religious Thinking* (Toronto: Ryerson, 1927), 95. For other accounts of Spiritualism, psychic research, and colonial doubt among Protestants, see Georgina Byrne, *Modern Spiritualism and the Church of England, 1850–1939* (Suffolk, UK: Boydell & Brewer, 2010); Gillian McCann, *Vanguard of the New Age: The Toronto Theosophical Society, 1891–1945* (Montreal: McGill-Queen's University Press, 2012); Christopher G. White, *Unsettled Minds: Psychology and the American Search for Spiritual Assurance, 1830–1940* (Berkeley: University of California Press, 2009); Peter van der Veer, *Imperial Encounters: Religion and Modernity in India and Britain* (Princeton, NJ: Princeton University Press, 2001).

7 Eden Robinson, *The Sasquatch at Home: Traditional Protocols and Modern Storytelling* (Edmonton: University of Alberta Press, 2012), 31; Powell and Elders, quoted in ibid., 13. See also Leanne Simpson, "Stories, Dreams, and Ceremonies—Anishinaabe Ways of Learning," *Tribal College* 11, no. 4 (2000): 26–29.

8 Thomas King, *The Truth about Stories: A Native Narrative* (Toronto: House of Anansi Press, 2003), 32, 92.

9 King, *The Truth about Stories*, 26.

10 J. Edward Chamberlin, *If This Is Your Land, Where Are Your Stories? Finding Common Ground* (New York: Random House, 2004), 2. See also J. Edward Chamberlin, *The Banker and the Blackfoot: A Memoir of My Grandfather in Chinook Country* (Toronto: Knopf Canada, 2016).

11 The Ojibwe are part of a larger Indigenous cultural and linguistic grouping called the Anishinaabeg whose territories range from the Great Lakes to the eastern Canadian Prairies. For the most part, I use the term "Ojibwe" here, in keeping with the common practice of the Kay-Nah-Chi-Wah-Nung Historical Centre and the Rainy River First Nations. For more reflection on the limits and usefulness of the term "Ojibwe," see Maureen Matthews, *Naamiwan's Drum: The Story of a Contested Repatriation of Anishinaabe Artefacts* (Toronto: University of Toronto Press, 2017), 275n2.

12 Simone de Beauvoir wrote: "One is not born, but rather becomes, woman." Simone de Beauvoir, *The Second Sex* (New York: Vintage Books, 1953), 319. See also Marshall McLuhan, *Understanding Media: The Extensions of Man* (Abingdon, UK: Routledge Classics, 2001), 9.

13 John Barker, "Missionary Ethnography on the Northwest Coast," in *Anthropology's Debt to Missionaries*, ed. Vinson Sutlive, Leonard Plotnicov, and Paula Brown, Ethnology Monographs 20 (Pittsburgh, PA: University of Pittsburgh Department of Anthropology, 2007), 17.

14 Frederick H. Du Vernet to Owsley Robert Rowley, April 9, 1908, Owsley Robert Rowley Anglican Episcopal Correspondence Collection, University of King's College Archives, Halifax, NS. On the doctrine of discovery, see Robert J. Miller, Jacinta Ruru, Larissa Behrendt, and Tracey Lindberg, *Discovering Indigenous Lands: The Doctrine of Discovery in the English Colonies* (Oxford: Oxford Univer-

sity Press, 2012). On the Dominion of Canada, see H. V. Nelles, *A Little History of Canada* (Toronto: Oxford University Press, 2004), 114.

15 Donovan Giesbrecht, "Metis, Mennonites and the 'Unsettled Prairie,' 1874–1896," *Journal of Mennonite Studies* 19, no. 1 (2001): 103–11. I thank my cousin Kholiswa Stower for sharing her reflections on our family history with me.

16 Truth and Reconciliation Commission of Canada, *The Final Report of the Truth and Reconciliation Commission of Canada*, vol. 1, *Canada's Residential Schools: The History, Part 1, Origins to 1939* (Montreal: McGill-Queen's University Press, 2016), 3. For a wider discussion of testimony in truth and reconciliation commissions, see Rosanne Kennedy, Lynne Bell, and Julia Emberley, eds., *Decolonising Testimony: On the Possibilities and Limits of Witnessing*, Humanities Research, vol. 15, no. 3 (Canberra: Australian National University Press, 2009).

17 Truth and Reconciliation Commission of Canada, *Final Report of the Truth and Reconciliation Commission of Canada*, vol. 1, *Summary: Honouring the Truth, Reconciling for the Future* (Toronto: James Lorimer & Company, 2015), 199.

Chapter 2

1 Adele Perry, "The State of Empire: Reproducing Colonialism in British Columbia, 1849–1871," *Journal of Colonialism and Colonial History* 2, no. 2 (2001), https://doi.org/10.1353/cch.2001.0028.

2 Robert Vipond, *Making a Global City: How One Toronto School Embraced Diversity* (Toronto: University of Toronto Press, 2017), 58.

3 For more information, see William Westfall, *Founding Moment: Church, Society, and the Construction of Trinity College* (Montreal: McGill-Queen's University Press, 2002); H. V. Nelles, *A Little History of Canada* (Toronto: Oxford University Press, 2004), 114; Martin L. Friedland, *The University of Toronto: A History*, 2nd ed. (Toronto: University of Toronto Press, 2013).

4 Peter Karsten, *Between Law and Custom: "High" and "Low" Legal Cultures in the Lands of the British Diaspora—the United States, Canada, Australia, and New Zealand, 1600–1900* (Cambridge: Cambridge University Press, 2002), 207. See also Eric Ross Arthur and Stephen A. Otto, *Toronto, No Mean City* (Toronto: University of Toronto Press, 1986); Westfall, *Founding Moment*.

5 For a history of the neighbourhood, see Jon Harstone, *Between the Bridge and the Brewery: A History of the Trinity-Bellwoods Neighbourhood in Toronto* (Toronto: Trinity Bellwoods Neighbourhood Association, 2005).

6 Simcoe is discussed in Westfall, *Founding Moment*, 16–19; and William A. Spray, "Saunders, John," in *Dictionary of Canadian Biography*, University of Toronto/Université Laval, 2003–, accessed November 8, 2015, http://www.biographi.ca/en/bio/saunders_john_6E.html.

7 Harstone, *Between the Bridge and the Brewery*, 8, 12–13; Enemikeese, *The Indian Chief: An Account of the Labours, Losses, Sufferings, and Oppression of Ke-Zig-Ko-E-Ne-Ne (David Sawyer), a Chief of the Ojibbeway Indians in Canada West* (Toronto: Coles, 1974), 151–53; A. Rodney Bobiwash, "The History of Native People in the Toronto Area: An Overview," in *The Meeting Place: Aboriginal Life in Toronto*, ed. Frances Sanderson and Heather Howard-Bobiwash (Toronto: Native Canadian Centre of Toronto, 1997), 18–19.

8 For a discussion of the unsettling and incommensurable challenges of decoloni-

zation as a practice that "requires the abolition of land as property and upholds the sovereignty of Native land and people," see Eve Tuck and K. Wayne Yang, "Decolonization Is Not a Metaphor," *Decolonization: Indigeneity, Education & Society* 1, no. 1 (2012): 26.

9 Alan Wilson, *The Clergy Reserves of Upper Canada*, Canadian Historical Association Booklets 23 (Ottawa: Canadian Historical Association, 1969), 3.

10 Alan Lauffer Hayes, *Anglicans in Canada: Controversies and Identity in Historical Perspective* (Chicago: University of Illinois Press, 2004), 66. See also William Katerberg, *Modernity and the Dilemma of North American Anglican Identities, 1880–1950* (Montreal: McGill-Queen's University Press, 2001).

11 S. H. Blake to Rev. Canon Jeffrey, 1911, Canadian Church Mission Society, accession no. M74-7, General Synod Archives of the Anglican Church of Canada, Toronto, ON (hereafter cited as "Archives of the Anglican Church of Canada").

12 Wycliffe College, *The Calendar of Wycliffe College in Affiliation with the University of Toronto, 1885–1886* (Toronto: Wycliffe College, 1885), 7.

13 Owsley Robert Rowley, *The Anglican Episcopate of Canada and Newfoundland* (London: A. R. Mowbray & Co., 1928), 2, 1.

14 First Story Toronto, "Exploring the Aboriginal History of Toronto!," *First Story Blog*, accessed April 26, 2016, https://firststoryblog.wordpress.com/aboutfirststory/.

15 Frederick H. Du Vernet to Owsley Robert Rowley, April 9, 1908, Owsley Robert Rowley Anglican Episcopal Correspondence Collection, University of King's College Archives, Halifax, NS. See also "One Archbishop Enough for Canada: Bishop Du Vernet Says Common Use of Title Cheapens It," *Toronto Sunday World*, April 21, 1914, 12.

16 Edward W. Said, *On Late Style: Music and Literature against the Grain* (New York: Pantheon Books, 2006), 7.

17 For histories of new forms of mediation and their imaginaries, see Lisa Gitelman, *Always Already New: Media, History and the Data of Culture* (Cambridge, MA: MIT Press, 2008); Lisa Gitelman and Geoffrey B. Pingree, eds., *New Media, 1740–1915* (Cambridge, MA: MIT Press, 2004); John Durham Peters, *Speaking into the Air: A History of the Idea of Communication* (Chicago: University of Chicago Press, 1999).

18 For more on the history of Loyalists, see Maya Jasanoff, *Liberty's Exiles: American Loyalists in the Revolutionary World* (New York: Knopf Doubleday, 2012).

19 Official Languages and Bilingualism Institute (OLBI), "The Arrival of the Loyalists in Canada," Site for Language Management in Canada, accessed November 8, 2015, https://slmc.uottawa.ca/?q=arrival_loyalists.

20 T. Watson Smith, "The Slave in Canada," *Collections of the Nova Scotia Historical Society* 10 (1899): 85 (quotation). For more biographical details, see Jacob Ellegood Sr., "The Loyalist Collection: Jacob Ellegood Papers" [catalogue record], MIC-Loyalist FC LFR.E4J3P3, Harriet Irving Library University of New Brunswick, accessed November 12, 2015, https://loyalist.lib.unb.ca/node/4709; Robin W. Winks, *The Blacks in Canada: A History* (Montreal: McGill-Queen's University Press, 1997), 44.

21 Smith, "The Slave in Canada," 105; Spray, "Saunders, John"; Winks, *The Blacks in Canada*, 108–9. For Ellegood's will, see the digital version of R. Wallace Hale, "Early New Brunswick Probate, 1785–1835" [catalogue record], Provincial Archives of New Brunswick, accessed November 8, 2015, http://archives

.gnb.ca/Search/MC3706/Details.aspx?culture=en-CA&abstract=7933&section=FreemanSlave.

22 For a 1782 report by Abraham Du Vernet on munitions at the Detroit garrison, as well as speeches by Thayendanegea, see Michigan Pioneer and Historical Society, *Historical Collections: Haldimand Papers*, vol. 20 (Lansing, MI: Robert Smith & Co., 1892), 4, 646. On Brant's role in the Revolutionary War, see Jasanoff, *Liberty's Exiles*.

23 On Henry Du Vernet's role in building the canals, see Robert Ferguson Legget, *Ottawa River Canals and the Defence of British North America* (Toronto: University of Toronto Press, 1988).

24 On Robert and Neville Parker, see Philip Buckner, "Parker, Robert," and "Parker, Neville," in *Dictionary of Canadian Biography*, University of Toronto/Université Laval, 2003–, accessed November 8, 2011, http://www.biographi.ca/en/bio/parker_robert_9E.html, http://www.biographi.ca/en/bio/parker_neville_9E.html; Lorenzo Sabine, *Biographical Sketches of Loyalists of the American Revolution: With an Historical Essay*, vol. 2 (Boston: Little, Brown and Company, 1864), 149. On Frederick Du Vernet's invention, see "The Origin of the Screw Propeller," *United Service Magazine*, 1870.

25 J. Douglas Borthwick, *History of the Diocese of Montreal, 1850–1910* (Montreal: J. Lovell, 1910), 86; Chris Massiah and R. J. Bradley, *The Quebec Railway Statutes: A Compilation of All Railway Charters Granted, with the Amendments Thereto, Up to and Including the Session of 1883: With a Copious Alphabetical Index* (Quebec City: A. Coté, 1883), 147.

26 Margaret M. Bruchac, "Earthshapers and Placemakers: Algonkian Indian Stories and the Landscape," in *Indigenous Archaeologies: Decolonising Theory and Practice*, ed. Claire Smith and H. Martin Wobst (New York: Routledge, 2005), 60.

27 For discussion of the Royal Proclamation and its significance for Indigenous land, see Colin G. Calloway, *The Scratch of a Pen: 1763 and the Transformation of North America* (New York: Oxford University Press, 2006); John Borrows, "Wampum at Niagara: The Royal Proclamation, Canadian Legal History, and Self-Government," in *Aboriginal and Treaty Rights in Canada: Essays on Law, Equality, and Respect for Difference*, ed. Michael Asch (Vancouver: University of British Columbia Press, 1997), 155–72. On Missisquoi, see Bruce Dudley Walker, "The County of Missisquoi in the Eastern Townships of the Province of Quebec (1770s–1867)" (MA thesis, McGill University, 1974), 34. For the 1776 map, see Jonathan Carver, *A New Map of the Province of Quebec: According to the Royal Proclamation, of the 7th of October 1763* (London: Printed for Robt. Sayer and John Bennett, 1776), facsimile courtesy of the Map and Data Library, University of Toronto, also available at the Library of Congress, https://www.loc.gov/item/74694799/. Joseph Bouchette's 1831 map of the region, *Lower & Upper Canada . . . With A Large Section of the United States*, also features a small insert map of the "British Dominions in North America," including what would become British Columbia. The map is available at the Map and Data Library, University of Toronto Library, G.3410 1831 B6, and online at http://www.davidrumsey.com/luna/servlet/detail/RUMSEY~8~1~3256~340003:Map-of-the-Provinces-of-Lower-&-Upp.

28 Anne Drummond, "Gender, Profession, and Principals: The Teachers of Quebec Protestant Academies, 1875–1900," *Historical Studies in Education* 2, no. 1 (1990): 59–71; Clarenceville Academy, *Catalogue of Clarenceville Academy, Canada-East,*

1849 (Edmonton: University of Alberta Libraries, 1849), microform, https://archive.org/details/cihm_93780.

29 Walter Rushbrook, "Archbishop F. H. Du Vernet, D.D.," 1942, accession no. 210 C3, Diocese of Caledonia Archives, Prince Rupert, BC. Rushbrook's account has Du Vernet quoting John 6:37.

30 For an Anglican perspective on Simon's life, see Leonard F. Hatfield, *Simon Gibbons, First Eskimo Priest: The Life of a Unique Clergyman and Church Builder* (Hantsport, NS: Lancelot Press, 1987).

31 Hatfield, *Simon Gibbons*; Frederick H. Du Vernet to Canon Gould, MSCC, May 23, 1923, accession no. GS75-103, box 51, file 4, Archives of the Anglican Church of Canada. I am grateful to Magdalene Klassen-Marshall for her research that discovered Simon Gibbon's role in Du Vernet's life.

32 Sylvia Du Vernet, *Portrait of a Personality: Archbishop Frederick Herbert DuVernet* (Toronto: Sylvia Du Vernet, 1987), 13 (quotation); Henry J. Morgan, *The Canadian Men and Women of the Time: A Handbook of Canadian Biography of Living Characters* (Toronto: William Briggs, 1912), 359; Rowley, *Anglican Episcopate of Canada and Newfoundland*, 137.

33 Du Vernet is mentioned frequently in Dyson Hague, *The Jubilee Volume of Wycliffe College* (Toronto: Wycliffe College, 1927).

34 Emily J. Manktelow, "The Rise and Demise of Missionary Wives," *Journal of Women's History* 26, no. 1 (2014): 135–59; Myra Rutherdale, *Women and the White Man's God: Gender and Race in the Canadian Mission Field* (Vancouver: University of British Columbia Press, 2003), 140.

35 Jesse Edgar Middleton, *The Municipality of Toronto: A History* (Toronto: Dominion Publishing Company, 1923), 3:97.

36 A young maid experiencing sexual harassment from her employer, a member of the wealthy and prominent Massey family, had shot him. For more on the Massey murder trial, see Charlotte Gray, *The Massey Murder: A Maid, Her Master and the Trial That Shocked a Country* (New York: Harper Collins, 2013).

37 Canadian Church Missionary Association Constitution, ca. 1895, Canadian Church Mission Society, accession no. M74-7 2580, Archives of the Anglican Church of Canada.

38 Arthur and Otto, *Toronto, No Mean City*, 207.

39 For more on changing approaches to missionary work among Anglicans, see Hayes, *Anglicans in Canada*; Rutherdale, *Women and the White Man's God*.

40 Frederick H. Du Vernet, "Canadian C.M.S Department," *New Era* 1, no. 5, 1902, 20.

41 Du Vernet, "Canadian C.M.S Department," 21.

42 Du Vernet, *Portrait of a Personality*, 18. See also a description of an address by Du Vernet in which he argued that Christianity did not adequately address the concerns of working class people: "Alumni Throng Wycliffe Halls," *Toronto Daily Mail and Empire*, October 5, 1899, 6.

43 Frederick H. Du Vernet, "Diary of a Missionary Tour," Monday, July 11, 1898, accession no. M81-41, Archives of the Anglican Church of Canada.

44 Ronald Niezen, *Spirit Wars: Native North American Religions in the Age of Nation Building* (Berkeley: University of California Press, 2000), 223. For a contemporary account, see George Mercer Dawson, *To the Charlottes: George Dawson's 1878 Survey of the Queen Charlotte Islands*, ed. Douglas Cole and Bradley John Lockner (Vancouver: University of British Columbia Press, 1993).

45 Charles Taylor, *Modern Social Imaginaries* (Durham, NC: Duke University Press, 2004), 23.

46 Truth and Reconciliation Commission of Canada, *Final Report of the Truth and Reconciliation Commission of Canada*, vol. 1, *Summary: Honouring the Truth, Reconciling for the Future* (Toronto: James Lorimer & Company, 2015).

47 Jeremy Webber, *The Constitution of Canada: A Contextual Analysis* (London: Bloomsbury Publishing, 2015), 263.

Chapter 3

1 Pauline Hillaire, *A Totem Pole History: The Work of Lummi Carver Joe Hillaire* (Lincoln: University of Nebraska Press, 2013), xxi.

2 For a range of examples of courts depending on textual evidence, see John Borrows, *Drawing Out Law: A Spirit's Guide* (Toronto: University of Toronto Press, 2010); Antonia Curtze Mills, *"Hang Onto These Words": Johnny David's Delgamuukw Evidence* (Toronto: University of Toronto Press, 2005); Cheryl Suzack, "The Transposition of Law and Literature in Delgamuukw and Monkey Beach," *South Atlantic Quarterly* 110, no. 2 (2011): 447–63. For a discussion of diverse grounds for the credibility of stories about people, nations, and religions, see Leanne Simpson, "Stories, Dreams, and Ceremonies—Anishinaabe Ways of Learning," *Tribal College* 11, no. 4 (2000): 26–29; Michael Warner, "Publics and Counterpublics," *Public Culture* 14, no. 1 (2002): 49–90; Sidonie Smith and Julia Watson, *Reading Autobiography: A Guide for Interpreting Life Narratives* (Minneapolis: University of Minnesota Press, 2010); Tomoko Masuzawa, *The Invention of World Religions; Or, How European Universalism Was Preserved in the Language of Pluralism* (Chicago: University of Chicago Press, 2005).

3 Anthony F. Beavers, "In the Beginning Was the Word and Then Four Revolutions in the History of Information," in *Luciano Floridi's Philosophy of Technology: Critical Reflections*, ed. Hilmi Demir (Dordrecht, Neth.: Springer, 2012), 85–103.

4 For analyses of the diverse consequences of changes in communication technologies, including spiritual and environmental effects, see Bonnie Mak, *How the Page Matters* (Toronto: University of Toronto Press, 2011); Lisa Gitelman and Geoffrey B. Pingree, eds., *New Media, 1740–1915* (Cambridge, MA: MIT Press, 2004); Jeffrey Sconce, *Haunted Media: Electronic Presence from Telegraphy to Television* (Durham, NC: Duke University Press, 2000); Bev J. Clark and Todd J. Sellers, *Rainy-Lake of the Woods: State of the Basin Report*, 2nd ed. (Kenora, ON: Lake of the Woods Water Sustainability Foundation, 2014); John Barker, "Tangled Reconciliations: The Anglican Church and the Nisga'a of British Columbia," *American Ethnologist* 25, no. 3 (1998): 433–51; John Corsiglia and Gloria Sniveky, "Knowing Home: Nisga'a Traditional Knowledge and Wisdom Improve Environmental Decision Making," *Alternatives Journal* 23, no. 3 (1997): 22; Hillaire, *A Totem Pole History*.

5 See Isabel Hofmeyr, "Inventing the World: Transnationalism, Transmission and Christian Textualities," in *Mixed Messages: Materiality, Textuality, Missions*, ed. Jamie S. Scott and Gareth Griffiths (New York: Palgrave Macmillan, 2005), 19–36.

6 John Durham Peters, *Speaking into the Air: A History of the Idea of Communication* (Chicago: University of Chicago Press, 1999), 9.

7 Peters, *Speaking into the Air*, 9.

8 Peters, *Speaking into the Air*, 77; Birgit Meyer, "Religious Sensations: Why Media, Aesthetics, and Power Matter in the Study of Contemporary Religion," in *Religion: Beyond a Concept*, ed. Hent de Vries (New York: Fordham University Press, 2009), 707; Webb Keane, *Christian Moderns: Freedom and Fetish in the Mission Encounter* (Berkeley: University of California Press, 2007), 18. See also Caroline Walker Bynum, *Christian Materiality: An Essay on Religion in Late Medieval Europe* (Cambridge, MA: Zone Books, 2011); Leigh Eric Schmidt, *Hearing Things: Religion, Illusion, and the American Enlightenment* (Cambridge, MA: Harvard University Press, 2000).

9 For a range of approaches to conflicts over mediation, see Jeffrey Glover and Matt Cohen, eds., *Colonial Mediascapes: Sensory Worlds of the Early Americas* (Lincoln: University of Nebraska Press, 2014).

10 Mary Longman, "Ancestors Rising: Aboriginal Art as Historical Testimonials," in *Decolonising Testimony: On the Possibilities and Limits of Witnessing*, ed. Rosanne Kennedy, Lynne Bell, and Julia Emberley, Humanities Research vol. 15, no. 3 (Canberra: Australian National University Press, 2009), 100.

11 Kennedy, Bell, and Emberley, *Decolonising Testimony*, 1. For perspectives of those who testified, see "Where Are The Children? Healing the Legacy of the Residential Schools," Where Are the Children?, accessed November 13, 2015, http://wherearethechildren.ca/en. For more analyses of TRC processes, see Kevin Lewis O'Neill, "Writing Guatemala's Genocide: Truth and Reconciliation Commission Reports and Christianity," *Journal of Genocide Research* 7, no. 3 (2005): 331–49; Naomi Angel, "Before Truth: Memory, History, and Nation in the Context of Truth and Reconciliation in Canada" (PhD diss., New York University, 2013).

12 Stimson quoted in Lynne Bell, "Buffalo Boy Testifies: Decolonising Visual Testimony in a Colonial-Settler Society," in Kennedy, Bell, and Emberley, *Decolonising Testimony*, 94; Adrian Stimson, "Used and Abused," in Kennedy, Bell, and Emberley, *Decolonising Testimony*, 71–80; Jeff Corntassel, Chaw-win-is, and T'lakwadzi, "Indigenous Storytelling, Truth-Telling, and Community Approaches to Reconciliation," *ESC: English Studies in Canada* 35, no. 1 (2009): 145; *OED Online*, s.v., "reconciliation," accessed June 20, 2017, http://www.oed.com/view/Entry/159781; Church of England, "Common Worship: Services and Prayers for the Church of England," 2000, https://www.churchofengland.org/prayer-worship/worship/texts.aspx.

13 Alexander R. Galloway, *Protocol: How Control Exists after Decentralization* (Cambridge, MA: MIT Press, 2004), 8; Umeek/E. Richard Atleo, *Principles of Tsawalk: An Indigenous Approach to Global Crisis* (Vancouver: University of British Columbia Press, 2011), 100. See also Eden Robinson, *The Sasquatch at Home: Traditional Protocols and Modern Storytelling* (Edmonton: University of Alberta Press, 2012). On confessional production in other contexts, see Kathryn Lofton, *Oprah: The Gospel of an Icon* (Berkeley: University of California Press, 2011); Pamela E. Klassen and Kathryn Lofton, "Material Witnesses: Women and the Mediation of Christianity," in *Media, Religion, and Gender: Key Issues and New Challenges*, ed. Mia Lövheim (New York: Routledge, 2013), 52–65; Ronald Niezen, "Digital Identity: The Construction of Virtual Selfhood in the Indigenous Peoples' Movement," *Comparative Studies in Society and History* 47, no. 3 (2005): 532–51.

14 Peter Brooks, *Troubling Confessions: Speaking Guilt in Law and Literature* (Chi-

cago: University of Chicago Press, 2000), 19. For more on confession, see Chloé Taylor, *The Culture of Confession from Augustine to Foucault* (New York: Taylor & Francis, 2008).

15 James J. O'Donnell, "Prolegomena," in *The "Confessions" of Saint Augustine*, ed. James J. O'Donnell (Oxford: Clarendon Press, 1992), Stoa Consortium, http://www.stoa.org/hippo/comm.html.

16 *The "Confessions" of Saint Augustine*, ed. James J. O'Donnell (Oxford: Clarendon Press, 1992), Stoa Consortium, http://www.stoa.org/hippo/.

17 O'Donnell, "Prolegomena."

18 *OED Online*, s.v., "confession," accessed August 7, 2017, http://www.oed.com/view/Entry/38779. See also Brooks, *Troubling Confessions*.

19 Sarah Rivett, *The Science of the Soul in Colonial New England* (Chapel Hill, NC: University of North Carolina Press, 2011), 217. On the intersection of categories and practices of law and religion, see John Borrows, *Canada's Indigenous Constitution* (Toronto: University of Toronto Press, 2010).

20 Michel Foucault, *The History of Sexuality*, vol. 1, *An Introduction*, Vintage Books (New York: Random House, 1990); Brooks, *Troubling Confessions*, 18. I discuss the colonial secular more fully in my contributions to Paul Christopher Johnson, Pamela E. Klassen, and Winnifred Fallers Sullivan, *Ekklesia: Three Inquiries in Church and State* (Chicago: University of Chicago Press, 2018), and in Pamela E. Klassen, "Fantasies of Sovereignty: Civic Secularism in Canada," *Critical Research on Religion* 3, no. 1 (2015): 41–56.

21 Judith P. Butler, *Giving an Account of Oneself* (New York: Fordham University Press, 2005), 21. See also Klassen and Lofton, "Material Witnesses."

22 Maurice Bucke, quoted in William James, *The Varieties of Religious Experience* (Cambridge, MA: Harvard University Press, 1985), 371. I have no evidence that Du Vernet and Bucke knew each other, but they were active within similar southern Ontario circles at the turn of the twentieth century. See also Michael Robertson, *Worshipping Walt: The Whitman Disciples* (Princeton, NJ: Princeton University Press, 2010).

23 Courtney Bender, "'Every Meaning Shall Have Its Homecoming Festival:' A Secular Age and the Senses of Modern Spirituality," in *Working with a Secular Age: Interdisciplinary Perspectives on Charles Taylor's Master Narrative*, ed. Guido Vanheeswijck, Colin Jager, and Florian Zemmin (Berlin: De Gruyter, 2016), 284. On the diverse effects of missionary practices in British Columbia, see John Sutton Lutz, *Makúk: A New History of Aboriginal-White Relations* (Vancouver: University of British Columbia Press, 2008); Susan Neylan, *The Heavens Are Changing: Nineteenth-Century Protestant Missions and Tsimshian Christianity* (Montreal: McGill-Queen's University Press, 2002).

24 Ruth B. Phillips, "'Dispel All Darkness': Material Translations and Cross-Cultural Communication in Seventeenth-Century North America," *Art in Translation* 2, no. 2 (2010): 173. See also Birgit Meyer, *Translating the Devil: Religion and Modernity among the Ewe in Ghana* (Edinburgh: Edinburgh University Press, 1999); Meyer, "Religious Sensations."

25 For a discussion of the work of Boas in conjunction with other anthropological practices of collecting stories, see Richard Bauman and Charles L. Briggs, *Voices of Modernity: Language Ideologies and the Politics of Inequality* (Cambridge: Cambridge University Press, 2003), esp. chap. 8.

26 Franz Boas, quoted in Charles Briggs and Richard Bauman, "'The Foundation

of All Future Researches': Franz Boas, George Hunt, Native American Texts, and the Construction of Modernity," *American Quarterly* 51, no. 3 (1999), 479. On bentwood boxes, also see Hilary Stewart, *Cedar: Tree of Life to the Northwest Coast Indians* (Vancouver: Douglas & McIntyre, 1995); Donald Ellis, Steven Clay Brown, and Bill Holm, *Tsimshian Treasures: The Remarkable Journey of the Dundas Collection* (Vancouver: Douglas & McIntyre, 2007). See also Robert Bringhurst's re-mediation of the Haida stories collected by one of Boas's students, which has provoked more controversies over appropriation: Robert Bringhurst, *A Story as Sharp as a Knife: The Classical Haida Mythtellers and Their World* (Vancouver: Douglas & McIntyre, 1999).

27 See Laura M. Stevens, *The Poor Indians: British Missionaries, Native Americans, and Colonial Sensibility* (Philadelphia: University of Pennsylvania Press, 2004).

28 See, for example, Matthew Hedstrom, *The Rise of Liberal Religion: Book Culture and American Spirituality in the Twentieth Century* (New York: Oxford University Press, 2013); Matthew Engelke, *God's Agents: Biblical Publicity in Contemporary England* (Berkeley: University of California Press, 2013); Klassen and Lofton, "Material Witnesses."

29 Askenootow, quoted in Winona Wheeler, "The Journals and Voices of a Church of England Native Catechist: Askenootow (Charles Pratt), 1851–1884," in *Reading Beyond Words: Contexts for Native History*, ed. Jennifer S. H. Brown and Elizabeth Vibert (Peterborough, ON: Broadview Press, 2003), 255; Margaret Seguin Anderson and Tammy Anderson Blumhagen, "Memories and Moments: Conversations and Re-collections," *BC Studies: The British Columbian Quarterly*, no. 104 (2010): 99. Also see Julie Cruikshank, *The Social Life of Stories: Narrative and Knowledge in the Yukon Territory* (Lincoln: University of Nebraska Press, 2000); Sophie McCall, *First Person Plural: Aboriginal Storytelling and the Ethics of Collaborative Authorship* (Vancouver: University of British Columbia Press, 2011); Lenora Ledwon, "Native American Life Stories and 'Authorship': Legal and Ethical Issues," *American Indian Quarterly* 21, no. 4 (1997): 579–93.

30 See Alan Corbiere and Crystal Migwans, "Animikii miinwaa Mishibizhiw: Narrative Images of the Thunderbird and the Underwater Panther," in *Before and after the Horizon: Anishinaabe Artists of the Great Lakes*, ed. David W. Penney and Gerald McMaster (Washington, DC: National Museum of the American Indian, 2013), 37; Patricia June Vickers, "Ayaawx (Ts'msyen Ancestral Law): The Power of Transformation" (PhD diss., University of Victoria, 2008); Bruce Granville Miller, *Oral History on Trial: Recognizing Aboriginal Narratives in the Courts* (Vancouver: University of British Columbia Press, 2012).

31 Leanne Simpson, "Anticolonial Strategies for the Recovery and Maintenance of Indigenous Knowledge," *American Indian Quarterly* 28, no. 3 (2004): 380. Also see Louis Bird and Susan Elaine Gray, *The Spirit Lives in the Mind: Omushkego Stories, Lives, and Dreams* (Montreal: McGill-Queen's University Press, 2007); Michael David McNally, *Honoring Elders: Aging, Authority, and Ojibwe Religion* (New York: Columbia University Press, 2009).

32 Ronald Niezen, *The Rediscovered Self: Indigenous Identity and Cultural Justice* (Montreal: McGill-Queen's University Press, 2009), 50; "Join in a Peaceful Revolution," Idle No More, accessed November 13, 2015, http://www.idlenomore.ca/.

33 This is not to say that there are not many Indigenous authors and bloggers who share personal stories, but to point to an ideal of a more proximate, face-to-face, mediation of stories. See the Nisga'a Lisims Government—Nisga'a

Nation Facebook page, accessed January 15, 2012, https://www.facebook.com/NLGNisgaaNation/. For examples of the significance of testimonials in a variety of Protestant settings, see Susan Harding, *The Book of Jerry Falwell: Fundamentalist Language and Politics* (Princeton, NJ: Princeton University Press, 2001); Heather Hendershot, *Shaking the World for Jesus: Media and Conservative Evangelical Culture* (Chicago: University of Chicago Press, 2004); R. Marie Griffith, *God's Daughters: Evangelical Women and the Power of Submission* (Berkeley: University of California Press, 2000); Tanya Erzen, *Straight to Jesus: Sexual and Christian Conversions in the Ex-Gay Movement* (Berkeley: University of California Press, 2006).

34 Neylan, *Heavens Are Changing*, 264. See also Douglas Cole and Ira Chaikin, *An Iron Hand upon the People: The Law against the Potlatch on the Northwest Coast* (Vancouver: Douglas & McIntyre, 1990); Paige Sylvia Raibmon, *Authentic Indians: Episodes of Encounter from the Late-Nineteenth-Century Northwest Coast* (Durham, NC: Duke University Press, 2005). For a discussion of the colonial production of the potlatch, see Christopher Bracken, *The Potlatch Papers: A Colonial Case History* (Chicago: University of Chicago Press, 1997). A more recent account of both anthropological theories of the potlatch and contemporary practice among northwest coast First Nations is that of Christopher F. Roth, who writes of the potlatch as a "coastal-wide system of international feasthall diplomacy that enabled northerly and southerly coastal peoples to recognize each other's sovereignty and legitimacy as societies of names." Christopher F. Roth, "Goods, Names, and Selves: Rethinking the Tsimshian Potlatch," *American Ethnologist* 29, no. 1 (2002): 144. See also "Potlatch Society (Martin Roth, Victoria and Albert Museum & Corrine Hunt) | DLD11," YouTube video, 10:05, posted by "DLDconference," February 1, 2011, https://www.youtube.com/watch?v=lxJjsSW1rWU.

35 Miss E. J. Soal, "Hazelton," *North British Columbia News*, July 1916, 27. Also see Cole and Chaikin, *Iron Hand*; Charlotte Coté, "Food Sovereignty, Food Hegemony, and the Revitalization of Indigenous Whaling Practices," in *The World of Indigenous North America*, ed. Robert Warrior (New York: Routledge, 2014), 239–62; Tina Loo, "Dan Cranmer's Potlatch: Law as Coercion, Symbol, and Rhetoric in British Columbia, 1884–1951," *Canadian Historical Review* 73, no. 2 (1992): 125–65. For a contemporary perspective, see the discussion of the history of the repatriated potlatch collection at U'mista Cultural Society: "The History of the Potlatch Collection," U'mista Cultural Centre, accessed August 10, 2011, http://www.umista.ca/exhibits/index.php.

36 Marcel Mauss, *The Gift: The Form and Reason for Exchange in Archaic Societies*, trans. W. D. Hall (Oxford: Routledge, 2002), 16.

37 Amos Gosnell, William Jeffrey, and Billy Williams, "A Plea for Potlatches" *Victoria Daily Colonist*, February 20, 1896. See also Daniel Raunet, *Without Surrender, without Consent: A History of the Nisga'a Land Claims* (Vancouver: Douglas & McIntyre, 1996). Many Continental theorists took up the potlatch as a ritual system that was good to think with, largely divorced from its historical or cultural contexts. These include Derrida, Bataille, and a mid-twentieth-century French journal titled *Potlatch*. David Graeber, for example, in an essay on the significance of "exchange" for studies of media, turns to what he calls the "Kwakiutl potlatch" to exemplify the social and symbolic importance of specific media to processes of exchange: "The medium served to define the recipient—it ennobled or degraded." David Graeber, "Exchange," in *Critical Terms for Media Studies*, ed.

W. J. T. Mitchell and Mark B. N. Hansen (Chicago: Chicago University Press, 2010), 223.

38 Jill Doerfler, Niigaanwewidam James Sinclair, and Heidi Kiiwetinepinesiik Stark, *Centering Anishinaabeg Studies: Understanding the World through Stories* (East Lansing: Michigan State University Press, 2013).

Chapter 4

1 This chapter draws slightly from a previous publication: Pamela E. Klassen, "Christianity as a Polemical Concept," in *A Companion to the Anthropology of Religion*, ed. Janice Boddy and Michael Lambek (London: Wiley-Blackwell, 2013), 344–62.

2 Frederick H. Du Vernet, "Diary of a Missionary Tour," July 18, 1898, accession no. M81-41, General Synod Archives of the Anglican Church of Canada, Toronto, ON. Providing reliable citations for the unpublished diary is a challenge. The handwritten version of the diary as found in the archive is out of chronological order, and Du Vernet did not provide explicit dates for every entry, although I have reconstructed the dates based on his account, and provide these dates in the notes. The most accessible way to read the diary and find the quotations I discuss is at storynations.utoronto.ca.

3 I am grateful to Al Hunter Jr. for telling me the name of the river, and to elder Dorothy Medicine for telling me the story of how Manitou Rapids got its name. In other sources, the name Gimiwani Ziibiing is used. See Robert Animikii Horton, "A Seventh Fire Spark: Preparing the Seventh Generation: What Are the Education Related Needs and Concerns of Students from Rainy River First Nations?" (MA thesis, Lakehead University, Thunder Bay, 2011), 5. On *manidoo* (pl. *manidoog*), see Ruth B. Phillips, "Things Anishinaabe: Art, Agency, and Exchange across Time," in *Before and after the Horizon: Anishinaabe Artists of the Great Lakes*, ed. David W. Penney and Gerald McMaster (Washington, DC: National Museum of the American Indian, 2013), 55. For histories of Treaty 3 and the region, see Anishinaabe Nation Grand Council Treaty #3, *"The Creator Placed Us Here": Timeline of Significant Events of the Anishinaabeg of Treaty #3* (Kenora, ON: Anishinaabe Grand Council Treaty #3, October 3, 2013); David T. McNab, "The Administration of Treaty 3: The Location of the Boundaries of Treaty 3 Indian Reserves in Ontario, 1873–1915," in *As Long as the Sun Shines and Water Flows: A Reader in Canadian Native Studies*, ed. Ian A. L. Getty and Antoine S. Lussier (Vancouver: University of British Columbia Press, 1983), 145–57; Sara J. Mainville, "Manidoo Mazina'igan: An Anishinaabe Perspective of Treaty 3" (MA thesis, University of Toronto, 2007); William E. Lass, *Minnesota's Boundary with Canada: Its Evolution since 1783* (Saint Paul: Minnesota Historical Society, 1980); Grace Lee Nute, *Rainy River Country: A Brief History of the Region Bordering Minnesota and Ontario* (St. Paul: Minnesota Historical Society Press, 1950).

4 George Bryce, "Among the Mound Builders' Remains," *Manitoba Historical Society Transactions*, 1, no. 18 (May 28, 1885), http://www.mhs.mb.ca/docs/transactions/1/moundbuilders.shtml. The Story Nations digital project is found at storynations.utoronto.ca.

5 On the 1970s archaeological dig, see Walter Andrew Kenyon, *Mounds of Sacred Earth: Burial Mounds of Ontario* (Toronto: Royal Ontario Museum, 1986).

Al Hunter is also a poet: Al Hunter, *Spirit Horses* (Wiarton, ON: Kegedonce Press, 2002); Al Hunter, *Beautiful Razor: Love Poems and Other Lies* (Wiarton, ON: Kegedonce Press, 2012).

6 On Ojibwe reception of missionaries, see Jennifer S. H. Brown, "'I Wish to Be as I See You': An Ojibwa-Methodist Encounter in Fur Trade Country, Rainy Lake, 1854–1855," *Arctic Anthropology* 24, no. 1 (1987): 19–31; Edmund F. Ely, *The Ojibwe Journals of Edmund F. Ely, 1833–1849*, ed. Theresa M. Schenck (Lincoln: University of Nebraska Press, 2012).

7 Anishinaabe Nation Grand Council Treaty #3, *"The Creator Placed Us Here,"* 6. The treaty, along with current discussion of its implications, can be found at the official website of the Grand Council Treaty #3: http://www.gct3.ca/ (accessed October 1, 2017). See also D. J. Hall, *From Treaties to Reserves: The Federal Government and Native Peoples in Territorial Alberta, 1870–1905* (Montreal: McGill-Queen's University Press, 2015), 50–52. The description of the area of Long Sault reserve can be found in Ontario Department of Mines, *Sixth Report of the Bureau of Mines* (Toronto: Warwick Bros and Rutter, 1896).

8 On waves of missionaries in the Rainy River area, see Brown, "'I Wish to Be as I See You.'"

9 For discussions of the Indian Act and various amendments, including their effects on the Rainy River Ojibwe, see Wendy Moss and Elaine Gardner-O'Toole, *Aboriginal People: History of Discriminatory Laws* (Ottawa: Government of Canada Publications, 1991), http://publications.gc.ca/Collection-R/LoPBdP/BP/bp175-e.htm#2.%20Restricted%20Right%20to%20Sell%20Agricultural%20Products (txt); Leo G. Waisberg and Tim E. Holzkamm, "'A Tendency to Discourage Them from Cultivating': Ojibwa Agriculture and Indian Affairs Administration in Northwestern Ontario," *Ethnohistory* 40, no. 2 (1993): 175–211; Joan A. Lovisek, Tim E. Holzkamm, and Leo G. Waisberg, "Fatal Errors: Ruth Landes and the Creation of the 'Atomistic Ojibwa,'" *Anthropologica* 39, no. 1–2 (1997): 133–45.

10 Keith D. Smith, *Strange Visitors: Documents in Indigenous-Settler Relations in Canada from 1876* (Toronto: University of Toronto Press, 2014), chap. 4. For a discussion of the resource issues, see Tim E. Holzkamm, Victor P. Lytwyn, and Leo G. Waisberg, "Rainy River Sturgeon: An Ojibway Resource in the Fur Trade Economy," *Canadian Geographer / Le Géographe Canadien* 32, no. 3 (1988): 194–205; Greg Keenan, David Parkinson, and Brent Jang, "Paper Trail: The Decline of Canada's Forestry Industry," *Globe and Mail*, December 5, 2014, http://www.theglobeandmail.com/report-on-business/economy/paper-trail-the-fall-of-forestry/article21967746/.

11 Waisberg and Holzkamm, "'A Tendency.'"

12 On community divisions stemming from memories of the amalgamation, see Horton, "A Seventh Fire Spark," 98.

13 The only extant publication from Du Vernet's trip is found in a reprint of a *Canadian Church Missionary Gleaner* article: Frederick Du Vernet, "The Mission Field," *Church Missionary Intelligencer* 24 (January 1899): 50.

14 Government of Canada, *Dominion of Canada Annual Report of the Department of Indian Affairs for the Year Ended 30th June 1898* [transcription], accessed August 7, 2017, http://www.bac-lac.gc.ca/eng/discover/aboriginal-heritage/first-nations/indian-affairs-annual-reports/Pages/item.aspx?IdNumber=11856.

15 On the "photographic event," see Christopher Pinney and Nicolas Peterson, *Photography's Other Histories* (Durham, NC: Duke University Press, 2003).

16 Jennifer S. H. Brown, "Mission Indian Progress and Dependency: Ambiguous Images from Canadian Methodist Lantern Slides," *Arctic Anthropology* 18, no. 2 (1981): 17–27 (Brown discusses the lantern slideshows of Egerton Ryerson Young, a Methodist missionary among the Ojibwe of northern Manitoba); Christraud M. Geary, "Missionary Photography: Private and Public Readings," *African Arts* 24, no. 4 (1991): 48–100; Gregory S. Jackson, *The Word and Its Witness: The Spiritualization of American Realism* (Chicago: University of Chicago Press, 2009), 74 ("spiritual sight"); Gerald Vizenor, foreword to *We Are at Home: Pictures of the Ojibwe People*, by Bruce White (Minneapolis: Minnesota Historical Society, 2008), ix ("imagic presence"). Katherine Long offers a fascinating discussion of a female missionary photographer tutored by photojournalist Cornell Capa: Kathryn T. Long, "'Cameras 'Never Lie': The Role of Photography in Telling the Story of American Evangelical Missions," *Church History: Studies in Christianity and Culture* 72, no. 4 (2003): 820–51. See also Richard Eves, "'Black and White, a Significant Contrast': Race, Humanism and Missionary Photography in the Pacific," *Ethnic and Racial Studies* 29, no. 4 (2006): 725–48.

17 Du Vernet, "Diary of a Missionary Tour," front matter, 1898. For more on the "voyageurs," see Carl Benn, *Mohawks on the Nile: Natives among the Canadian Voyageurs in Egypt, 1884–1885* (Hamilton, ON: Dundurn Press, 2009); Anthony P. Michel, "To Represent the Country in Egypt: Aboriginality, Britishness, Anglophone Canadian Identities, and the Nile Voyageur Contingent, 1884–1885," *Histoire Sociale / Social History* 39, no. 77 (2006): 45–77.

18 Du Vernet, "Diary of a Missionary Tour," July 19, 1898.

19 See Christopher Vecsey, *Traditional Ojibwa Religion and Its Historical Changes* (Philadelphia, PA: American Philosophical Society, 1983); Maureen Katherine Lux, *Medicine That Walks: Disease, Medicine and Canadian Plains Native People, 1880–1940* (Toronto: University of Toronto Press, 2001).

20 For more on spirit photography, see Louis Kaplan, *The Strange Case of William Mumler, Spirit Photographer* (Minneapolis: University of Minnesota Press, 2008); Clément Chéroux, *The Perfect Medium: Photography and the Occult* (New Haven, CT: Yale University Press, 2005).

21 Heike Behrend, "Photo Magic: Photographs in Practices of Healing and Harming in East Africa," *Journal of Religion in Africa* 33, no. 2 (2003): 133. For more reflection on the camera as a spiritually problematic tool, see Heike Behrend, "Seelenklau: Zur Geschichte eines interkulturellen Transfers," in *Seele: Multiple Räume*, ed. Johannes Bilstein and Matthias Winzen (Baden-Baden, Ger: Verlag für moderne Kunst Nürnberg, 2004); Janet A. Hoskins, "The Camera as Global Vampire? Tourism and Photography in Remote Areas," in *The Framed World: Tourism, Tourists and Photography*, ed. David Picard (Hants, UK: Ashgate Publishers, 2009), 151–68.

22 Louise Erdrich, *Books and Islands in Ojibwe Country* (Washington, DC: National Geographic, 2003), 5. On traditions of Anishinaabe art, past and present, see Penney and McMaster, *Before and after the Horizon*.

23 Maureen Ryan, "Picturing Canada's Native Landscape: Colonial Expansion, National Identity, and the Image of a 'Dying Race,'" *RACAR: Revue d'Art Canadienne / Canadian Art Review* 17, no. 2 (1990): 138–49 (esp. 145, 139). On Ojibwe approaches to images, including birchbark scrolls and photographs, see Erdrich, *Books and Islands in Ojibwe Country*; Basil Johnston, *The Manitous: The Spiritual World of the Ojibway* (New York: HarperPerennial, 1996); John Borrows,

Drawing Out Law: A Spirit's Guide (Toronto: University of Toronto Press, 2010); White, *We Are at Home.*

24 David Maxwell, "Photography and the Religious Encounter: Ambiguity and Aesthetics in Missionary Representations of the Luba of South East Belgian Congo," *Comparative Studies in Society and History* 53, no. 1 (2011): 38–74. See also International Mission Photography Archive (IMPA), USC Digital Library, University of Southern California Libraries, accessed December 31, 2016, http://digitallibrary.usc.edu/cdm/landingpage/collection/p15799coll123.

25 Frances Densmore, *Chippewa Customs* (Minneapolis: Minnesota Historical Society Press, 1929); Frances Densmore, "A Minnesota Missionary Journey of 1893," *Minnesota History* 20, no. 3 (1939): 310–13.

26 Roland Barthes, *Camera Lucida: Reflections on Photography*, trans. Richard Howard (New York: Hill and Wang, 1981), 88–89.

27 Barthes, *Camera Lucida*, 109.

28 Barthes, *Camera Lucida*, 84–85. On Barthes's understanding of Zen, see Avram Alpert, "Overcome by Photography: Camera Lucida in an International Frame," *Third Text* 24, no. 3 (2010): 331–39.

29 Walter Benjamin, "A Small History of Photography," in *One-Way Street and Other Writings* (London: NLB, 1979), 243. For more on Benjamin and photography, see Linda Haverty Rugg, *Picturing Ourselves: Photography and Autobiography* (Chicago: University of Chicago Press, 1997).

30 David Morgan, *Protestants and Pictures: Religion, Visual Culture and the Age of American Mass Production* (Oxford: Oxford University Press, 1999), 348; Matthew Engelke, *A Problem of Presence: Beyond Scripture in an African Church* (Berkeley: University of California Press, 2007).

31 Du Vernet, "Diary of a Missionary Tour," July 22, 1898.

32 Du Vernet, "Diary of a Missionary Tour," July 15, 1898.

33 Du Vernet, "Diary of a Missionary Tour," July 16, 1898.

34 Du Vernet, "Diary of a Missionary Tour," July 18, 1898.

35 *OED Online*, s.v. "soul," accessed August 7, 2017, http://www.oed.com/view/Entry/185083.

36 Maureen Matthews, *Naamiwan's Drum: The Story of a Contested Repatriation of Anishinaabe Artefacts* (Toronto: University of Toronto Press, 2017), 14; Johnston, *The Manitous*, 3 (quotation), 172. On the significance of lightning, see Alan Corbiere and Crystal Migwans, "Animikii miinwaa Mishibizhiw: Narrative Images of the Thunderbird and the Underwater Panther," in Penney and McMaster, *Before and after the Horizon*, 44.

37 Michael David McNally, *Honoring Elders: Aging, Authority, and Ojibwe Religion* (New York: Columbia University Press, 2009), 1, 44. See also Basil Johnston, *Ojibway Heritage* (Toronto: McClelland and Stewart, 1976).

38 Johnston, *The Manitous*, 2. I am grateful to Michael McNally for discussing prayer book translations with me (pers. comm., January 5, 2012). For more history of Ojibwe translations of the Bible and Book of Common Prayer, also see Theresa Schenck's introduction to *The Ojibwe Journals of Edmund F. Ely*; and Charles Wohlers, "Portions of the Book of Common Prayer in Ojibwe," accessed August 7, 2017, http://justus.anglican.org/resources/bcp/Canada/ojibwe.htm.

39 Du Vernet, "Diary of a Missionary Tour," July 15, 1898.

40 Du Vernet, "Diary of a Missionary Tour," July 30, 1898. Du Vernet had experienced a similar failure a few days earlier when he sought to photograph the

Ojibwe leader Great Hawk at Manitou Rapids, a reserve long opposed to Christian proselytization.

41 I am grateful to Michael McNally for pointing me to this interpretation.

42 Du Vernet, "Diary of a Missionary Tour," July 15, 1898.

43 Du Vernet was likely using a dry plate camera, with a shutter. I am grateful to Michael Robinson for sharing his expertise on early cameras.

44 Du Vernet, "Diary of a Missionary Tour," July 20, 1898.

45 Du Vernet, "Diary of a Missionary Tour," July 17, 1898.

46 Du Vernet, "Diary of a Missionary Tour," July 17, 1898.

47 Du Vernet, "The Mission Field," 50. For an Anishinaabe view on treaties, see Mainville, "Manidoo Mazina'igan."

48 Du Vernet, "Diary of a Missionary Tour," July 18, 1898.

49 See also the writings of Catholic missionary-anthropologist John M. Cooper, "The Northern Algonquian Supreme Being," *Primitive Man* 6, nos. 3–4 (1933): 41–111.

50 In this regard, see also Jennifer Brown's argument that Egerton Ryerson Young presented different versions of his views on missions in different media, with the images of his lantern slides being particularly "ambiguous." Brown, "Mission Indian Progress and Dependency."

51 Brown, "'I Wish to Be as I See You.'"

52 For Ojibwe reactions to photography at the same time in Minnesota, see White, *We Are at Home*.

53 For perspectives on religious pedagogy within the act of photography, see Geary, "Missionary Photography"; Christopher Pinney, *Camera Indica: The Social Life of Indian Photographs* (Chicago: University of Chicago Press, 1997). On psychagogy, see John S. Kloppenborg, "James 1:2–15 and Hellenistic Psychagogy," *Novum Testamentum* 52, no. 1 (2010): 37–71.

54 For a discussion of photography sovereignty, see Elizabeth Edwards, "Tracing Photography," in *Made to Be Seen: Perspectives on the History of Visual Anthropology*, ed. Marcus Banks and Jay Ruby (Chicago: University of Chicago Press, 2011), 179.

Chapter 5

1 "Welcome to the Metlakatla First Nation," Metlakatla First Nation, accessed April 7, 2014, http://www.metlakatla.ca/community/welcome-metlakatla-first-nation; Sylvia Du Vernet, *Portrait of a Personality: Archbishop Frederick Herbert DuVernet* (Toronto: Sylvia Du Vernet, 1987), 25.

2 See the inclusion of Abraham in G. E. Eyre and W. Spottiswoode, *A List of the Officers of the Army and of the Corps of Royal Marines* (London: British Stationary Office, 1778). I have been unable to discern whether Henry and Abraham were brothers or cousins, but I am convinced that they were related, not only because of their unusual last name, but also because Abraham named his first son Henry. To view Henry's map online, see Henry Duvernet, *Sketch of the River Miamis. The Sketch Taken in the Month of Novr. 1778 H. Duvernet 2d. Ltd. R. R. Ay* (Canada, 1778), Online MIKAN no. 4149332, 4 items, Library and Archives Canada, http://collectionscanada.gc.ca/ourl/res.php?url_ver=Z39.88-2004&url_tim=2015-11-26T03%3A02%3A27Z&url_ctx_fmt=info%3Aofi%2Ffmt%3Akev

%3Amtx%3Actx&rft_dat=4149332&rfr_id=info%3Asid%2Fcollectionscanada.gc .ca%3Apam&lang=eng.

3 Parks Canada, *Sainte-Anne-de-Bellevue Canal: National Historic Site of Canada Management Plan* (Ottawa: Government of Canada, 2005), http://www.pc.gc.ca /eng/docs/r/qc/annedebellevue/pd-mp/index.aspx. Henry Du Vernet's 1831 map is available online: see *Plan of the Vicinity of Ste Anne's Rapid at the West End of the Island of Montreal Showing Projections for Improving the Navigation at That Place by Henry DuVernet, Lieutt Coll Roy. Staff Corps. 8th of March 1831* (Canada, 1831), Online MIKAN no. 4128945, 2 items, Library and Archives Canada, http://collectionscanada.gc.ca/pam_archives/index.php?fuseaction=genitem .displayEcopies&lang=eng&rec_nbr=4128945&rec_nbr_list=4128945,4126649 ,4170739,4141402,4142884,4126326&title=Plan+of+the+vicinity+of+Ste+Anne %27s+rapid+at+the+west+end+of+the+island+of+Montreal+showing+projections +for+improving+the+navigation+at+that+place+by+Henry+DuVernet%2C+Lieutt +Coll+Roy.+Staff+Corps.+8th+of+March+1831.+%5Bcartographic+material%5D.+ &ecopy=n0010971&new_width=100.

4 Frederick H. Du Vernet, from a paper tucked into the "Notebook on Diocesan Affairs," 1904–1924, accession no. 203, Diocese of Caledonia Archives, Prince Rupert, BC (hereafter cited as "Diocese of Caledonia Archives"). This notebook is a collection of short histories of missions, lists of parishioners, and other miscellany handwritten by Du Vernet. It is unevenly paginated and largely undated.

5 Jean M. O'Brien, *Firsting and Lasting: Writing Indians Out of Existence in New England* (Minneapolis: University of Minnesota Press, 2010), xii, 57. See also Malcolm Lewis, *Cartographic Encounters: Perspectives on Native American Mapmaking and Map Use* (Chicago: University of Chicago Press, 1998). For the naming of Du Vernet Point, see Geographic Board of Canada, *Decisions of the Geographic Board of Canada since Issue of the Sixth Report to March 31, 1907* (Ottawa: Government of Canada, 1907), accession no. 77-36c, Diocese of Caledonia Archives.

6 Hugh Brody, *Maps and Dreams: Indians and the British Columbia Frontier* (Vancouver: Douglas & McIntyre, 1981).

7 Stephanie Pyne, "Mapping Indigenous Perspectives in the Making of the Cybercartographic Atlas of the Lake Huron Treaty Relationship Process: A Performative Approach in a Reconciliation Context," *Cartographica: The International Journal for Geographic Information and Geovisualization* 47, no. 2 (January 1, 2012): 92–104; Kapil Raj, *Relocating Modern Science: Circulation and the Construction of Knowledge in South Asia and Europe, 1650–1900* (New York: Palgrave Macmillan, 2007).

8 Frederick H. Du Vernet to Stella Du Vernet, February 6, 1905, accession no. 94/30, Diocese of Caledonia Archives.

9 For an account of the Metlakatla mission, see Jean Usher, *William Duncan of Metlakatla: A Victorian Missionary in British Columbia* (Ottawa: National Museums of Canada, 1974).

10 Hamar Foster, "Letting Go the Bone: The Idea of Indian Title in British Columbia, 1849–1927," in *British Columbia and the Yukon*, ed. Hamar Foster and John McLaren, vol. 6, *Essays in the History of Canadian Law* (Toronto: University of Toronto Press, 1995), 36.

11 For a range of perspectives on the history of Metlakatla, see Sir Henry Solomon Wellcome, *The Story of Metlakahtla* (London: Saxon & Co, 1887); Joanne MacDonald, "From Ceremonial Object to Curio: Object Transformation at Port Simpson and Metlakatla, British Columbia in the Nineteenth Century," *Canadian*

Journal of Native Studies 10, no. 2 (1990): 193–217; Adele Perry, "The Autocracy of Love and the Legitimacy of Empire: Intimacy, Power and Scandal in Nineteenth-Century Metlakahtlah," *Gender & History* 16, no. 2 (2004): 261–88; Susan Neylan, *The Heavens Are Changing: Nineteenth-Century Protestant Missions and Tsimshian Christianity* (Montreal: McGill-Queen's University Press, 2002). For Ts'msyen perspectives, see Peggy Brock, *The Many Voyages of Arthur Wellington Clah: A Tsimshian Man on the Pacific Northwest Coast* (Vancouver: University of British Columbia Press, 2011); and Kenneth Campbell and First Nations Education Council, *Persistence and Change: A History of the Ts'msyen Nation* (Prince Rupert, BC: Tsimshian Nation and School District 52, 2005).

12 Wellcome, *Story of Metlakahtla*, 173; Campbell and First Nations Education Council, *Persistence and Change*, 85.

13 For descriptions of Duncan's and Ridley's roles in the church, see Gail Elizabeth Edwards, "Creating Textual Communities: Anglican and Methodist Missionaries and Print Culture in British Columbia, 1858–1914" (PhD diss., University of British Columbia, 2001), 50; Neylan, *Heavens Are Changing*. I draw some of my discussion of Anglican "real estate" from Pamela E. Klassen, "God Keep Our Land: The Legal Ritual of the McKenna-McBride Royal Commission, 1913–1916," in *Religion and the Exercise of Public Authority*, ed. Benjamin L. Berger and Richard Moon (Oxford: Hart Publishing, 2016), 79–93.

14 See Foster, "Letting Go the Bone."

15 For perspectives on Christianity and the feasting system, see Tina Loo, "Dan Cranmer's Potlatch: Law as Coercion, Symbol, and Rhetoric in British Columbia, 1884–1951," *Canadian Historical Review* 73, no. 2 (1992): 125–65; Douglas Cole and Ira Chaikin, *An Iron Hand upon the People: The Law against the Potlatch on the Northwest Coast* (Vancouver: Douglas & McIntyre, 1990); Nicholas May, "Feasting on the AAM of Heaven: The Christianization of the Nisga'a, 1860–1920" (PhD diss., University of Toronto, 2013); Leslie Robertson, *Standing up with Ga'axsta'las: Jane Constance Cook and the Politics of Memory, Church, and Custom* (Vancouver: University of British Columbia Press, 2012); Jay Miller, "Tsimshian Ethno-Ethnohistory: A 'Real' Indigenous Chronology," *Ethnohistory* 45, no. 4 (1998): 657–74; Margaret Seguin Anderson, *The Tsimshian: Images of the Past, Views for the Present* (Vancouver: University of British Columbia Press, 1984).

16 James Benjamin McCullagh, *The Indian Potlatch: Substance of a Paper Read before C.M.S. Annual Conference at Metlakatla, B.C., 1899* (Toronto: Women's Missionary Society of the Methodist Church, 1899), 2.

17 McCullagh, *Indian Potlatch*, 19.

18 On land commissions and ongoing Ts'msyen resistance, see Anderson, *The Tsimshian*; Cole Harris, *Making Native Space: Colonialism, Resistance, and Reserves in British Columbia* (Vancouver: University of British Columbia Press, 2002).

19 Benedict Anderson, *Imagined Communities: Reflections on the Origin and Spread of Nationalism* (London: Verso, 1991); Jonathan Z. Smith, *Relating Religion: Essays in the Study of Religion* (Chicago: University of Chicago Press, 2004), 94 ("sacred spaces"); Jonathan Z. Smith, *Map Is Not Territory: Studies in the History of Religions* (Chicago: University of Chicago Press, 1993), 293, xiv.

20 Smith, *Map Is Not Territory*, xiv.

21 Smith, *Relating Religion*, 89 ("primitives"), 18 ("the white man"); Smith, *Map Is Not Territory*, 309 ("We need to reflect").

22 Aileen Moreton-Robinson, *The White Possessive* (Minneapolis: University of Minnesota Press, 2015); *OED Online*, s.v., "territory," accessed June 20, 2017, http://

www.oed.com/view/Entry/199601. Also see Stuart Elden, *The Birth of Territory* (Chicago: University of Chicago Press, 2013); David Turnbull and Helen Watson, *Maps Are Territories: Science Is an Atlas: A Portfolio of Exhibits* (Chicago: University of Chicago Press, 1989).

23 Audra Simpson, *Mohawk Interruptus: Political Life across the Borders of Settler States* (Durham, NC: Duke University Press, 2014), 191. For a range of approaches to critical Indigenous cartography, see Les Field, "Mapping Erasure: The Power of Nominative Cartography in the Past and Present of the Muwekma Ohlones of the San Francisco Bay Area," in *Recognition, Sovereignty Struggles, and Indigenous Rights in the United States: A Sourcebook*, ed. Jean M. O'Brien and Amy E. Den Ouden (Chapel Hill: University of North Carolina Press, 2013), 287–309; Irène Hirt, "Mapping Dreams/Dreaming Maps: Bridging Indigenous and Western Geographical Knowledge," *Cartographica: The International Journal for Geographic Information and Geovisualization* 47, no. 2 (2012): 105–20; Mark Palmer, "Theorizing Indigital Geographic Information Networks," *Cartographica: The International Journal for Geographic Information and Geovisualization* 47, no. 2 (January 1, 2012): 80–91.

24 James A. McDonald, "Bleeding Day and Night: The Construction of the Grand Trunk Pacific Railway across Tsimshian Reserve Lands," *Canadian Journal of Native Studies* 10, no. 1 (1990): 33–68; David Alexander Gamble and David Vogt, "'You Don't Suppose the Dominion Government Wants to Cheat the Indians?': The Grand Trunk Pacific Railway and the Fort George Reserve, 1908–12," *BC Studies: The British Columbian Quarterly*, no. 166 (2010): 55–72.

25 First signed in 1899, Treaty 8 was prompted by Indigenous resistance to the rushing onslaught of would-be gold miners. Like most British Columbians at the time, including cartographers who covered up the territory of Treaty 8 with their legends when making maps of the province, Du Vernet seemed hardly aware of this treaty. On the history of Treaty 8 and its maps, see Arthur Ray, "Treaty 8: A British Columbian Anomaly," *BC Studies: The British Columbian Quarterly*, no. 123 (1999): 49.

26 Du Vernet, "Notebook on Diocesan Affairs." For more on the specific legal history of reserves in British Columbia at this time, see Foster, "Letting Go the Bone," 61; Harris, *Making Native Space*, 355n2.

27 Du Vernet, "Notebook on Diocesan Affairs." On the significance of baptism and naming, see Edwards, "Creating Textual Communities," 274. I use the spelling *Massett*, and not the current *Masset*, in keeping with the contemporary usage in my sources.

28 Cole Harris, "Moving amid the Mountains, 1870–1930," *BC Studies: The British Columbian Quarterly*, no. 58 (1983): 28; Frederick H. Du Vernet to Stella Du Vernet, February 6, 1905.

29 Frederick H. Du Vernet, "History of Caledonia," February 6, 1905, p. 1, Du Vernet Correspondence re Historical Notes, accession no. 77-36a, Diocese of Caledonia Archives.

30 Du Vernet, "History of Caledonia," p. 4 (quotations). On Nisga'a interaction with missionaries, see May, "Feasting on the AAM of Heaven"; John Barker, "Tangled Reconciliations: The Anglican Church and the Nisga'a of British Columbia," *American Ethnologist* 25, no. 3 (1998): 433–51.

31 Frederick H. Du Vernet to Robert Whittington, February 8, 1906, Du Vernet Correspondence re Methodist Mission Land, accession no. 77-36c, Diocese of

Caledonia Archives. For Whittington's approach to missions, see R. Whittington, *The British Columbia Indian and His Future* (Toronto: Dept. of Missionary Literature of the Methodist Church, Canada, 1906), http://archive.org/details/britishcolumbiin00whitrich.

32 Du Vernet to Whittington, February 8, 1906.
33 Du Vernet to Whittington, February 8, 1906.
34 May, "Feasting on the AAM of Heaven," 124.
35 On the Kaien Island land grab, see Campbell and First Nations Education Council, *Persistence and Change*, 160. On the history of the GTP, see Frank Leonard, *A Thousand Blunders: The Grand Trunk Pacific Railway and Northern British Columbia* (Vancouver: University of British Columbia Press, 1996).
36 On the question of reversion, see Foster, "Letting Go the Bone."
37 George Morrow, *Report on Indian Affairs* (Ottawa: Department of Indian Affairs, 1906), 244–45.
38 Raj, *Relocating Modern Science*, 91; "Notes from Metlakahtla: Bishop Du Vernet Makes Canoe Trip of over 150 Miles," *Victoria Daily Colonist*, May 27, 1906.
39 Editors, "British Columbia: First Church at Prince Rupert," *Church Missionary Gleaner*, August 1907.
40 "An Act Further to Amend the Indian Act," 1895, National Aboriginal Document Database, http://epe.lac-bac.gc.ca/100/205/301/ic/cdc/aboriginaldocs/m-stat.htm.
41 Harlan I. Smith, "Archeological Remains on the Coast of Northern British Columbia and Southern Alaska," *American Anthropologist* 11, no. 4 (1909): 595.
42 Susan Marsden, "Adawx, Spanaxnox, and the Geopolitics of the Tsimshian," *BC Studies: The British Columbian Quarterly*, no. 135 (2002): 101–35.
43 For one account, see Conservative Party of British Columbia., ed., *The Case of Kaien Island* (Victoria, BC, 1906).
44 Frederick H. Du Vernet to Ernest Du Vernet, September 20, 1906, F2120-1-1-8, Archives of Ontario.
45 Leonard, *Thousand Blunders*, 129.
46 Frederick H. Du Vernet to Ernest Du Vernet, September 20, 1906.
47 Frederick H. Du Vernet to Ernest Du Vernet, September 20, 1906.
48 *Prince Rupert Empire*, December 14, 1907.
49 Foster, "Letting Go the Bone," 36. See Donald McKenzie's fascinating discussion of the role of Anglican missionary William Colenso in Maori treaty making: Donald Francis McKenzie, *Oral Culture, Literacy and Print in Early New Zealand: The Treaty of Waitangi* (Wellington, NZ: Victoria University Press, 1985).
50 Kim TallBear, "An Indigenous Reflection on Working beyond the Human/Not Human," *GLQ: A Journal of Lesbian and Gay Studies* 21, nos. 2–3 (2015): 230.
51 Du Vernet, "Notebook on Diocesan Affairs" ("two ends of steel"); Frederick Du Vernet quoted in "Editor's Notes," *Across the Rockies*, 1919, Archives of the Provincial Synod of British Columbia and Yukon, Vancouver, BC ("hard blow").
52 Frederick H. Du Vernet, handwritten reminiscence, n.d., Miscellaneous, Diocese of Caledonia Archives.
53 On the precarity of reserve boundaries and the pressures of the railway, see Anderson, *The Tsimshian*; Neil Sterritt, *Tribal Boundaries in the Nass Watershed* (Vancouver: University of British Columbia Press, 1998).
54 Frederick Du Vernet to Richard McBride, March 10, 1909, Official Correspondence Premier McBride, accession no. GR-0441, box 33, file 3, 83/09; Richard

McBride to Frederick Du Vernet, March 26, 1909, Official Correspondence Premier McBride, accession no. GR-0441, box 33, file 3, 83/09; S. Blackburn to Richard McBride, August 24, 1909, Official Correspondence Premier McBride, accession no. GR-0441, box 35, file 3, 377/09; Richard McBride to S. Blackburn, September 4, 1909, Official Correspondence Premier McBride, accession no. GR-0441, box 35, file 3, 377/09. All items are from the Royal British Columbia Museum and Archives, Victoria, BC (hereafter cited as "Royal British Columbia Museum and Archives").

55 Du Vernet, "Notebook on Diocesan Affairs."

56 Frederic Maitland, "The Crown as Corporation," *Law Quarterly Review* 17 (1901): 131 ("curious freak"); Perry Dane, "The Corporation Sole and the Encounter of Law and Church," in *Sacred Companies: Organizational Aspects of Religion and Religious Aspects of Organizations*, ed. Nicholas Jay Demerath (New York: Oxford University Press, 1998), 57 ("secular embodiment"), 58 ("extraordinary, irregular"). See also Frederic Maitland, "The Corporation Sole," *Law Quarterly Review* 16 (1900): 335–54; James B. O'Hara, "The Modern Corporation Sole," *Dickason Law Review* 93 (1988): 23–39. This section draws in part from Pamela E. Klassen, "Mentality, Fundamentality and the Colonial Secular; or How Real Is Real Estate?," in *Transformations of Religion and the Public Sphere: Postsecular Publics*, ed. Rosi Braidotti, Bolette Blaagaard, and Eva Midden (London: Palgrave Macmillan, 2014), 175–94.

57 Frederick H. Du Vernet to Crease & Crease, Barristers, Victoria, BC, August 17, 1909, Du Vernet Correspondence, accession no. 77-36b, Diocese of Caledonia Archives.

58 Frederick H. Du Vernet to Crease & Crease, Barristers, Victoria, BC, March 4, 1910, Du Vernet Correspondence, accession no. 77-36b, Diocese of Caledonia Archives; Kent McNeil, "Judicial Approaches to Self-Government since Calder: Searching for Doctrinal Coherence," in *Let Right Be Done: Aboriginal Title, the Calder Case, and the Future of Indigenous Rights*, ed. Hamar Foster, Heather Raven, and Jeremy Webber (Vancouver: University of British Columbia Press, 2007), 141 ("time immemorial").

59 Du Vernet, "Notebook on Diocesan Affairs," p. 210.

60 Joshua Priestley to Frederick Hussey, "Re against Land Claims," May 13, 1908, Attorney General Correspondence Inward, 1908, accession no. GR 0429, box 15, file 03, 2119/08 Royal British Columbia Museum and Archives.

61 Priestley to Hussey, "Re against Land Claims," May 13, 1908.

62 Alfred Carter to Frederick Hussey, "Nisga'a/Priestley Land Dispute," May 13, 1908, Attorney General Correspondence Inward, 1908, accession no. GR 0429, box 15, file 03, 2119/08, Royal British Columbia Museum and Archives.

63 Carter to Hussey, "Nisga'a/Priestley Land Dispute," May 13, 1908.

64 Carter to Hussey, "Nisga'a/Priestley Land Dispute," May 13, 1908.

65 Carter to Hussey, "Nisga'a/Priestley Land Dispute," May 13, 1908.

66 Andrew Mercer, "Indians' View of Land Question," *Prince Rupert Evening Empire*, January 22, 1912, in Du Vernet and Indian Affairs, Documents, accession no. 77-37/22, Diocese of Caledonia Archives.

67 On Houston and his struggles with the GTP, see Leonard, *Thousand Blunders*. See also R. Geddes Large, *Prince Rupert: A Gateway to Alaska* (Vancouver: Mitchell Press, 1960).

68 Du Vernet, handwritten reminiscence, n.d., Miscellaneous, Diocese of Caledonia Archives.

69 "Demonstration of Radio Mind," *Prince Rupert Daily News*, February 18, 1924; Frederick H. Du Vernet, "A Local Legend: For Open Meeting of Reading Club, May 12, 1924, The Golden Ball of Light" (Prince Rupert, BC, May 12, 1924), Du Vernet Correspondence re Historical Notes, accession no. 77-36a, Diocese of Caledonia Archives. This section draws in part from Pamela E. Klassen, "Fantasies of Sovereignty: Civic Secularism in Canada," *Critical Research on Religion* 3, no. 1 (2015): 41–56.

70 Du Vernet, "The Golden Ball of Light."

71 "Adaawak (Stories)," Nisga'a Lisims Government, accessed January 1, 2017, http://www.nisgaanation.ca/adaawak-stories; Odille Morison, "Tsimshian Proverbs," *Journal of American Folklore* 2, no. 7 (1889): 285–86. For more on Odille Morison, see Maureen L. Atkinson, "The 'Accomplished' Odille Quintal Morison: Tsimshian Cultural Intermediary of Metlakatla, British Columbia," in *Recollecting: Lives of Aboriginal Women of the Canadian Northwest and Borderlands*, ed. Sarah Carter and Patricia Alice McCormack (Edmonton, AB: Athabasca University Press, 2011), 135–56.

72 Atkinson, "The 'Accomplished' Odille Quintal Morison," 136, 142.

73 Charles Frederick Morison, "Reminiscences of British Columbia from 1862: By a Pioneer of the North-West Coast" (unpublished manuscript, ca. 1919), Imbert Orchard papers, box 2, file 9, Special Collections, University of British Columbia, Vancouver. I am very grateful to Maureen Atkinson for this reference.

74 "Du Vernet Point," BC Geographical Names, accessed August 25, 2014, http://apps.gov.bc.ca/pub/bcgnws/names/36558.html; AECOM, *Project Description: Prince Rupert LNG* (Burnaby, BC, 2013), https://a100.gov.bc.ca/appsdata/epic/documents/p402/d35568/1367597846227_cd923f726e6163a34f51cad80e3c4736296240fe17144d5b554ddd0f94716141.pdf; Harlan I. Smith, "The Man Petroglyph near Prince Rupert, or the Man Who Fell from Heaven," in *Essays in Anthropology: Presented to A. L. Kroeber in Celebration of His Sixtieth Birthday, June 11, 1936*, ed. Robert Harry Lowie (Berkeley: University of California Press, 1936), 309–14.

75 Other missionaries, such as Methodist Thomas Crosby, and anthropologists, including the Tsimshian ethnographer William Beynon, also conveyed versions of this story in the early twentieth century. Du Vernet likely read at least Crosby's version. Thomas Crosby, *Up and Down the North Pacific Coast by Canoe and Mission Ship* (Toronto: Missionary Society of the Methodist Church, 1914); William Beynon, *The Beynon Manuscript: The Literature, Myths and Traditions of the Tsimshian People* (Ann Arbor, MI: University Microfilm International, 1980); Marius Barbeau, William Beynon, John J. Cove, and George F. MacDonald, *Tsimshian Narratives* (Ottawa: Education and Cultural Affairs Division, 1987). For more-recent accounts, see Miller, "Tsimshian Ethno-Ethnohistory"; Marsden, "Adawx, Spanaxnox, and the Geopolitics of the Tsimshian"; Valerie Ruth Napoleon, "Ayook: Gitksan Legal Order, Law, and Legal Theory" (PhD diss., University of Victoria, 2009).

76 Recorded by Benyon, in Marius Barbeau, *Tsimsyan Myths: Illustrated* (Ottawa: Department of Northern Affairs and National Resources, 1961), 75; Wilson Duff, *Histories, Territories and Laws of the Kitwancool* (Victoria: Royal British Colum-

bia Museum, 1959); Zandra Wilson, "An Insider's Look at Tlingit Artist Preston Singletary," April 14, 2011, National Museum of the American Indian, accessed April 7, 2107, http://blog.nmai.si.edu/main/2011/04/an-insiders-look-at-tlingit-artist-preston-singletary.html; Robert Budd and Roy Henry Vickers, *Raven Brings the Light* (Madeira Park, BC: Harbour, 2013).

77 Patricia June Vickers, "Ayaawx (Ts'msyen Ancestral Law): The Power of Transformation" (PhD diss., University of Victoria, 2008), 171, 175, 195, 196.

78 Eden Robinson, *Son of a Trickster* (Toronto: Alfred A. Knopf, 2017), 15.

79 May, "Feasting on the AAM of Heaven," 199.

80 Perry Dane, "The Maps of Sovereignty: A Meditation," *Cardozo Law Review* 12, nos. 3–4 (1991): 1004, 1005.

Chapter 6

1 James Benjamin McCullagh, "Thanks and Appreciation," *North British Columbia News*, July 1914, 36.

2 Norman Etherington, "The Missionary Writing Machine in Nineteenth-Century Kwazulu-Natal," in *Mixed Messages: Materiality, Textuality, Missions*, ed. Jamie S. Scott and Gareth Griffiths (London: Palgrave Macmillan, 2005), 37–50; Frederick H. Du Vernet to Baring-Gould, Secretary CMS, December 20, 1906, *Church Missionary Society Archive*, sec. 4, *Missions to the Americas*, pt. 4, *British Columbia, 1856–1925* (Marlborough, UK: Adam Matthew Publications, 2002), microfilm.

3 Du Vernet to Baring-Gould, December 20, 1906.

4 On the growing unrest along the Nass River, see Hamar Foster, "We Are Not O'Meara's Children: Law, Lawyers, and the First Campaign for Aboriginal Title in British Columbia, 1908–28," in *Let Right Be Done: Aboriginal Title, the Calder Case, and the Future of Indigenous Rights*, ed. Hamar Foster, Heather Raven, and Jeremy Webber (Vancouver: University of British Columbia Press, 2007), 61–84. McCullagh uses the phrase "valley of eternal bloom" in his self-published booklet *Ignis: A Parable of the Great Lava Plain in the Valley of Eternal Bloom* (Aiyansh, BC, 1918). Hoping to raise money for fire extinguishers, he sent the booklet out on a "prospecting trip" in "pursuit of the nimble dime" (McCullagh, *Ignis*, 1). *Ignis* is available at https://archive.org/details/cihm_15537 (accessed September 8, 2017).

5 A. M. Nahnegh, S. A. Zeedawit, and J. S. Nakmauz, quoted in James Benjamin McCullagh, *The Indian Land Question: Interview with Land Committee, Naas River. From the 'Hagaga,' May 1910* [pamphlet] (Aiyansh, BC, 1910), pp. 2–3, Attorney General correspondence, 1872–1937, accession no. GR-0429, reel B9324, Royal British Columbia Museum and Archives, Victoria, BC (hereafter cited as "Royal British Columbia Museum and Archives"). I am grateful to Nicholas May for sharing this pamphlet with me. On the "white possessive," see Aileen Moreton-Robinson, *The White Possessive* (Minneapolis: University of Minnesota Press, 2015).

6 Anthony F. Beavers, "In the Beginning Was the Word and Then Four Revolutions in the History of Information," in *Luciano Floridi's Philosophy of Technology: Critical Reflections*, ed. Hilmi Demir (Dordrecht: Springer, 2012), 100. On the connections between Protestantism and print, also see Elizabeth L. Eisenstein, *The Printing Press as an Agent of Change* (Cambridge: Cambridge University

Press, 1980); Adrian Johns, *The Nature of the Book: Print and Knowledge in the Making* (Chicago: University of Chicago Press, 1998). On "textual healing," see Pamela E. Klassen, *Spirits of Protestantism: Medicine, Healing, and Liberal Christianity* (Berkeley: University of California Press, 2011).

7 See Benedict Anderson, *Imagined Communities: Reflections on the Origin and Spread of Nationalism* (London: Verso, 1991). On print culture, missions, and Indigenous people, see Sarah Rivett, *The Science of the Soul in Colonial New England* (Chapel Hill: University of North Carolina Press, 2011); Susan Neylan, *The Heavens Are Changing: Nineteenth-Century Protestant Missions and Tsimshian Christianity* (Montreal: McGill-Queen's University Press, 2002); Jean M. O'Brien, *Firsting and Lasting: Writing Indians out of Existence in New England* (Minneapolis: University of Minnesota Press, 2010).

8 Stuart McKee, "How Print Culture Came to Be Indigenous," *Visible Language* 44, no. 2 (2010): 161–86; James B. McCullagh, "Materializing the Spiritual, Spiritualizing the Material" *Caledonia Interchange*, vol. 1 (October 31, 1900): 1, available at http://eco.canadiana.ca/view/oocihm.8_04502_5/2?r=0&s=1 (accessed September 8, 2017).

9 Donald Francis McKenzie, *Oral Culture, Literacy and Print in Early New Zealand: The Treaty of Waitangi* (Wellington, NZ: Victoria University Press, 1985), 13. On Grouard, see Patricia Demers and Arok Wolvengrey, *The Beginning of Print Culture in Athabasca Country: A Facsimile Edition and Translation of a Prayer Book in Cree Syllabics by Father Émile Grouard, OMI, Prepared and Printed at Lac La Biche in 1883*, trans. Naomi L. McIlwraith and Dorothy Thunder (Edmonton: University of Alberta Press, 2010). On the Book of Common Prayer, see Gail Elizabeth Edwards, "Creating Textual Communities: Anglican and Methodist Missionaries and Print Culture in British Columbia, 1858–1914" (PhD diss., University of British Columbia, 2001), 283.

10 Isabel Hofmeyr, *Gandhi's Printing Press* (Cambridge, MA: Harvard University Press, 2013); J. K. Flyaway et al., *Indian Protest* [flyer] (Aiyansh, BC: Indian Land Committee, May 17, 1910), Attorney General Correspondence, accession no. GR-0429, folio 2561/10, Royal British Columbia Museum and Archives ("since time immemorial"); Daniel Raunet, *Without Surrender, without Consent: A History of the Nisga'a Land Claims* (Vancouver: Douglas & McIntyre, 1996), 127 ("just like a history writing").

11 "Heritage Sites," Nisga'a Lisims Government, accessed April 20, 2016, http://www.nisgaanation.ca/heritage-sites.

12 Editors, "Foreword!," *Across the Rockies*, July 1910, Archives of the Provincial Synod of British Columbia and Yukon, Vancouver, BC (hereafter cited as "Synod of British Columbia and Yukon").

13 I am very grateful to Stephen Sword and Nelson Adams, Massey College printer, for speculating with me about the printing presses of Aiyansh.

14 McCullagh, "Materializing the Spiritual." See also Nicholas May, "Feasting on the AAM of Heaven: The Christianization of the Nisga'a, 1860–1920" (PhD diss., University of Toronto, 2013), 99.

15 McCullagh, quoted in Moeran, *McCullagh of Aiyansh*, 191; James Benjamin McCullagh, "Aiyansh: Plans for New Work," *North British Columbia News*, July 1913, 40.

16 Nahnegh, Zeedawit, and Nakmauz, quoted in McCullagh, *The Indian Land Question*, 3, 4.

17 McCullagh, quoted in Moeran, *McCullagh of Aiyansh*, 179.
18 May, "Feasting on the AAM of Heaven," 146; McCullagh, "THANKS AND APPRECIATION," 33–36.
19 McCullagh, quoted in Moeran, *McCullagh of Aiyansh*, 183.
20 McCullagh, quoted in Moeran, *McCullagh of Aiyansh*, 185. Daniel Raunet, in his history of the Nisga'a land claim, also refers to this time of revival after the fire, but states that McCullagh "gave no explanation for this turnaround." Raunet, *Without Surrender, without Consent*, 126.
21 McCullagh, quoted in Moeran, *McCullagh of Aiyansh*, 185.
22 Margaret Seguin Anderson and Tammy Anderson Blumhagen, "Memories and Moments: Conversations and Re-collections," *BC Studies: The British Columbian Quarterly*, no. 104 (2010): 99. For more on Indigenous protocols related to life stories, see Julie Cruikshank, *The Social Life of Stories: Narrative and Knowledge in the Yukon Territory* (Lincoln: University of Nebraska Press, 2000); Sophie McCall, *First Person Plural: Aboriginal Storytelling and the Ethics of Collaborative Authorship* (Vancouver: University of British Columbia Press, 2011); Lenora Ledwon, "Native American Life Stories and 'Authorship': Legal and Ethical Issues," *American Indian Quarterly* 21, no. 4 (1997): 579–93.
23 Moeran, *McCullagh of Aiyansh*, 186. For a detailed reading of Niysyok's act, see May, "Feasting on the AAM of Heaven," 147–48. According to May, "Niysyok is a chiefly name of the head of the *wilp*, or House, of Niysyok that together with other Houses form the Gisk̲ansnaat Clan (People of the Hawthorn Bushes), which itself belongs to the Laxgibuu, or Wolf, tribe of the Nisg̲a'a." Nicholas May, "Life of Niysyok: Exploring Nisga'a Religious Lives through Biography of a Personage" (paper presented at the Berkshire Conference on the History of Women, Toronto, May 24, 2014), 2.
24 May, "Life of Niysyok," 6.
25 Oliver Thorne, "Flood and Frost at Aiyansh," *North British Columbia News*, January 1922, 42.
26 James Benjamin McCullagh to W. Newcombe, May 17, 1911, Newcombe Family Fonds, accession no. A10753, box 12, vol. 15, Correspondence Oct/Nov 1905, Royal British Columbia Museum and Archives. For his part, in 1950 Marius Barbeau celebrated Nisga'a pole carving as a great artistic tradition that "belongs to the past." Declaring totem poles to be a lost art helped him justify his busy traffic in collecting Nisga'a poles in the 1920s: three of the totem poles that he collected from Gitlakdamiks now stand in the Royal Ontario Museum in Toronto, around the corner from Wycliffe College. Marius Barbeau, *Totem Poles*, vol. 1 (Ottawa: Department of Resources and Development, Development Services Branch. National Museum of Canada, 1950), 1. For a Nisga'a poet's perspective on Barbeau's collecting, see Jordan Abel, *The Place of Scraps* (Vancouver: Talonbooks, 2013).
27 George Morrow, *Report on Indian Affairs* (Ottawa: Department of Indian Affairs, 1906), 239–40. For more on McCullagh's work as magistrate, see Moeran, *McCullagh of Aiyansh*; Neil Sterritt, *Tribal Boundaries in the Nass Watershed* (Vancouver: University of British Columbia Press, 1998); Douglas Cole and Ira Chaikin, *An Iron Hand upon the People: The Law against the Potlatch on the Northwest Coast* (Vancouver: Douglas & McIntyre, 1990); James Benjamin McCullagh, *The Indian Potlatch: Substance of a Paper Read before C.M.S. Annual Conference at Metlakatla, B.C., 1899* (Toronto: Women's Missionary Society of the Methodist Church, 1899).

28 Edwards, "Creating Textual Communities," 153.

29 For specific examples from missions in British Columbia, see Adele Perry, "Metropolitan Knowledge, Colonial Practice, and Indigenous Womanhood: Missions in Nineteenth-Century British Columbia," in *Contact Zones: Aboriginal and Settler Women in Canada's Colonial Past*, ed. Katie Pickles and Myra Rutherdale (Vancouver: University of British Columbia Press, 2005), 109–31; Myra Rutherdale, *Women and the White Man's God: Gender and Race in the Canadian Mission Field* (Vancouver: University of British Columbia Press, 2003). More broadly, see Felicity Jensz, "The Function of Inaugural Editorials in Missionary Periodicals," *Church History* 82, no. 2 (2013): 374–80; Hugh Morrison, "'Impressions Which Will Never Be Lost': Missionary Periodicals for Protestant Children in Late-Nineteenth Century Canada and New Zealand," *Church History* 82, no. 2 (2013): 388–93.

30 Christopher Bracken, *The Potlatch Papers: A Colonial Case History* (Chicago: University of Chicago Press, 1997), 27; Moeran, *McCullagh of Aiyansh*, 151, 216. On missionary testimonies and appeals more broadly, see Isabel Hofmeyr, "Inventing the World: Transnationalism, Transmission and Christian Textualities," in Scott and Griffiths, *Mixed Messages*, 19–36; Felicity Jensz and Hanna Acke, eds., *Missions and Media: The Politics of Missionary Periodicals in the Long Nineteenth Century* (Stuttgart, Ger.: Franz Steiner Verlag, 2013); Jensz, "Function of Inaugural Editorials"; Anna Johnston, "British Missionary Publishing, Missionary Celebrity, and Empire," *Nineteenth-Century Prose* 32, no. 2 (2005): 20–43.

31 Charles Briggs and Richard Bauman, "'The Foundation of All Future Researches': Franz Boas, George Hunt, Native American Texts, and the Construction of Modernity," *American Quarterly* 51, no. 3 (1999): 479–528; E. Sapir, "Nass River Terms of Relationship," *American Anthropologist* 22, no. 3 (July 9, 1920): 261–71.

32 McCullagh, quoted in "The Anmalga," *Church Missionary Gleaner*, August 1887, 91; "Record of American Folk-Lore: For Native Races," *Journal of American Folklore* 2, no. 4 (1889): 74–75; James George Frazer, *The Golden Bough: A Study in Magic and Religion, Taboo and the Perils of The Soul* (London: MacMillan, 1911), 76. For a broader history of missionary contributions to anthropology in the region, see John Barker, "Missionary Ethnography on the Northwest Coast," in *Anthropology's Debt to Missionaries*, ed. Vinson Sutlive, Leonard Plotnicov, and Paula Brown, Ethnology Monographs 20 (Pittsburgh, PA: University of Pittsburgh Department of Anthropology, 2007), 17.

33 CMS instructions, quoted in Edwards, "Creating Textual Communities," 254; Maureen L. Atkinson, "The 'Accomplished' Odille Quintal Morison: Tsimshian Cultural Intermediary of Metlakatla, British Columbia," in *Recollecting: Lives of Aboriginal Women of the Canadian Northwest and Borderlands*, ed. Sarah Carter and Patricia Alice McCormack (Edmonton, AB: Athabasca University Press, 2011), 135–56. For more on the linguistic abilities of missionaries in the region, see Marcus Tomalin, *And He Knew Our Language: Missionary Linguistics on the Pacific Northwest Coast* (Amsterdam: John Benjamins Publishing, 2011).

34 Frederick H. Du Vernet to Baring-Gould, Secretary CMS, June 19, 1906, *Church Missionary Society Archive*, sec. 4, *Missions to the Americas*, pt. 4, *British Columbia, 1856–1925* (Marlborough, UK: Adam Matthew Publications, 2002), microfilm. On language competence among missionaries, also see Edwards, "Creating Textual Communities," 253.

35 Frederick Du Vernet, quoted in Sylvia Du Vernet, *Portrait of a Personality: Archbishop Frederick Herbert DuVernet* (Toronto: Sylvia Du Vernet, 1987), 127; Frederick Du Vernet, "Notebook on Diocesan Affairs," 1904–1924, p. 190, accession no. 203, Diocese of Caledonia Archives, Prince Rupert, BC (hereafter cited as "Diocese of Caledonia Archives"). The "Notebook on Diocesan Affairs" is an unevenly paginated and largely undated collection of short histories of missions, lists of parishioners, and other miscellany handwritten by Du Vernet.

36 Frederick H. Du Vernet, "History of the Diocese of Caledonia," *Across the Rockies*, September 1912, Synod of British Columbia and Yukon. For more discussion of the social changes wrought by increased white settlement, see Adele Perry, *On the Edge of Empire: Gender, Race, and the Making of British Columbia, 1849–1871* (Toronto: University of Toronto Press, 2001); Perry, "Metropolitan Knowledge"; Sylvia van Kirk, "From 'Marrying-In' to 'Marrying-Out': Changing Patterns of Aboriginal/Non-Aboriginal Marriage in Colonial Canada," *Frontiers: A Journal of Women's Studies* 23, no. 3 (2002): 1–11.

37 Edwards, "Creating Textual Communities," 32–33. On the idea of "racial mission," see Carl Berger, *Sense of Power: Studies in the Ideas of Canadian Imperialism, 1867–1914* (Toronto: University of Toronto Press, 1971), chap. 9.

38 James Benjamin McCullagh, "The Valedictory," *Aiyansh Notes*, 1907.

39 McCullagh, quoted in Moeran, *McCullagh of Aiyansh*, 148. See also James Benjamin McCullagh, *The Aiyansh Mission: Naas River, British Columbia* (London: Church Missionary Society, 1907).

40 McCullagh, quoted in Moeran, *McCullagh of Aiyansh*, 197.

41 McCullagh, quoted in Moeran, *McCullagh of Aiyansh*, 229. See Cole and Chaikin, *Iron Hand*; E. Palmer Patterson, *Mission on the Nass: The Evangelization of the Nishga (1860–1890)* (Waterloo, ON: Eulachon Press, 1982).

42 Editor, "The Work of the Caledonia Diocesan Committee," *Across the Rockies*, April 1916, 68–70, Synod of British Columbia and Yukon.

43 *Across the Rockies*, January, 1912, cover, Synod of British Columbia and Yukon.

44 Jocelyn Perkins to J. Robinson, February 9, 1926, British Columbia and Yukon Church Aid Society Fonds, Letterbook, Synod of British Columbia and Yukon; Johnston, "British Missionary Publishing"; Jocelyn Perkins to J. Robinson, December 22, 1924, British Columbia and Yukon Church Aid Society Fonds, Letterbook, Synod of British Columbia and Yukon.

45 Frederick H. Du Vernet, "Caledonia Notes," *Across the Rockies*, January 1919, Synod of British Columbia and Yukon. For more on the diversity and inequities of settlement in British Columbia, see Renisa Mawani, *Colonial Proximities: Crossracial Encounters and Juridical Truths in British Columbia, 1871–1921* (Vancouver: University of British Columbia Press, 2010); Kamala Elizabeth Nayar, *The Punjabis in British Columbia: Location, Labour, First Nations, and Multiculturalism* (Montreal: McGill-Queen's University Press, 2012); Sarah Carter, "'Daughters of British Blood' or 'Hordes of Men of Alien Race': The Homesteads-for-Women Campaign in Western Canada," *Great Plains Quarterly* 29, no. 3 (2009): 267–86; Patricia E. Roy, *The Oriental Question: Consolidating a White Man's Province, 1914–41* (Vancouver: University of British Columbia Press, 2011).

46 Du Vernet to Baring-Gould, Secretary CMS, June 19, 1906; Frederick H. Du Vernet, "Diocese of Caledonia," Prince Rupert, BC, 1908, Du Vernet Corresponence re Historical Notes, accession no. 77-36a, Diocese of Caledonia Archives.

47 May, "Feasting on the AAM of Heaven," 206.

48 William H. Collison, *In the Wake of the War Canoe: A Stirring Record of Forty Years' Successful Labour, Peril and Adventure amongst the Savage Indian Tribes of the Pacific Coast, and the Piratical Head-Hunting Haidas of the Queen Charlotte Islands, B.C.* (London: Seeley & Service, 1915), 347.

49 Frederick H. Du Vernet to Crease & Crease, Barristers, Victoria, BC, August 17, 1909, Du Vernet Correspondence, accession no. 77-36b, Diocese of Caledonia Archives.

50 Moeran, *McCullagh of Aiyansh*, 197, 229 (Du Vernet quotation).

51 Frederick H. Du Vernet, "Annual Report," in *Yearbook* (Surrey, UK: British Columbia Church Aid Society, 1911), 41.

52 Frederick H. Du Vernet to Principal Vance, April 15, 1918, Letter Collection: Du Vernet, Most Rev. Frederick Herbert, 1860–1924 Correspondence 24/1, Synod of British Columbia and Yukon ("needs a man"); Frederick H. Du Vernet to Principal Vance, November 18, 1914, Letter Collection: Du Vernet, Most Rev. Frederick Herbert, 1860–1924 Correspondence 24/1, Synod of British Columbia and Yukon; Du Vernet, "Caledonia Notes" ("young man's country"). For a discussion of Du Vernet's masculine rhetoric, see Rutherdale, *Women and the White Man's God*, 10. Also see Rhonda Semple, "Missionary Manhood: Professionalism, Belief and Masculinity in the Nineteenth-Century British Imperial Field," *Journal of Imperial and Commonwealth History* 36, no. 3 (2008): 397; Michelle Tusan, "Gleaners in the Holy Land: Women and the Missionary Press in Victorian Britain," *Nineteenth Century Gender Studies* 6, no. 2 (2010), available at http://www.ncgsjournal.com/issue62/tusan.htm (accessed May 10, 2016).

53 Du Vernet, quoted in May, "Feasting on the AAM of Heaven," 177.

54 James Benjamin McCullagh, "Aiyansh," *North British Columbia News*, September 1909, vii.

55 McCullagh, *The Indian Land Question*, 1.

56 Flyaway et al., *Indian Protest*.

57 Flyaway et al., *Indian Protest*. For more on this Nisga'a protest, see Raunet, *Without Surrender, without Consent*; May, "Feasting on the AAM of Heaven." For more on broader Indigenous petitions and protests in British Columbia, see Megan Harvey, "Story People: Stó:lo-State Relations and Indigenous Literacies in British Columbia, 1864–1874," *Journal of the Canadian Historical Association* 24, no. 1 (2013): 51–88; Jim Aldridge, *Keeping Promises: The Royal Proclamation of 1763, Aboriginal Rights, and Treaties in Canada* (Montreal: McGill-Queen's University Press, 2015).

58 Frederick H. Du Vernet, quoted in "Anglican Synod: Prince Rupert, the See City, a Busy Spiritual Place this Week," *Prince Rupert Empire*, August 14, 1909, 4.

59 Friends of the Indians of British Columbia, *Bishop Du Vernet and the Indians* (Conference of the Friends of the Indians of British Columbia, 1913), pamphlet, accession no. 77-37/4, Diocese of Caledonia Archives.

60 McCullagh, *The Indian Land Question*, 4. On O'Meara, see Foster, "We Are Not O'Meara's Children."

61 McCullagh, *The Indian Land Question*, 1.

62 Eleanor McCullagh, quoted in Moeran, *McCullagh of Aiyansh*, 193, 175; James Benjamin McCullagh, ed., *Souvenir Booklet: Nass Valley Agricultural Association* (Aiyansh, BC: Aiyansh Press, 1913), p. 16, accession no. NWP 970.7 M133, Royal British Columbia Museum and Archives.

63 See, for example, Andrew Mercer, "Indians' View of Land Question," *Prince*

Rupert Evening Empire, January 22, 1912, in Du Vernet and Indian Affairs, Documents, accession no. 77-37/22, Diocese of Caledonia Archives.

64 Andrew Mercer, "The Indian Speech," in McCullagh, *Souvenir Booklet*, 17.

65 For more on the significance of the "world on paper," see Neil ten Kortenaar, *Postcolonial Literature and the Impact of Literacy: Reading and Writing in African and Caribbean Fiction* (Cambridge: Cambridge University Press, 2011); Sean Hawkins, *Writing and Colonialism in Northern Ghana: The Encounter between the LoDagaa and "The World on Paper"* (Toronto: University of Toronto Press, 2002).

66 McCullagh, "Thanks and Appreciation" ("three machines"); James Benjamin McCullagh, "An Interview with Myself," *North British Columbia News*, April 1915 ("big gun").

67 Moeran, *McCullagh of Aiyansh*, 150; Phyllis Matthewman, *James B. McCullagh*, Heroes of the Cross (Grand Rapids, MI: Zondervan, 1957).

68 McCullagh, quoted in Moeran, *McCullagh of Aiyansh*, 138.

69 Moeran, *McCullagh of Aiyansh*, 146; McCullagh, "Materializing the Spiritual."

70 Melita, quoted in Moeran, *McCullagh of Aiyansh*, 136.

71 Frederick H. Du Vernet to Emmeline Crump, January 11, 1918, Du Vernet Correspondence, accession no. 77-36e, Diocese of Caledonia Archives.

72 For a history of Keswick, see David W. Bebbington, *Evangelicalism in Modern Britain: A History from the 1730s to the 1980s* (New York: Routledge, 2003), 151–79.

73 McCullagh, "The Valedictory."

74 J. Kennedy MacLean, "The Keswick Convention," *Quiver* 45, no. 9 (1910): 802, 803.

75 MacLean, "Keswick Convention," 804. For a discussion of how a Keswick meeting was adapted in an African mission context, see Jason Bruner, "Keswick and the East African Revival: An Historiographical Reappraisal," *Religion Compass* 5, no. 9 (2011): 477–89.

76 McCullagh, quoted in Moeran, *McCullagh of Aiyansh*, 206; James Benjamin McCullagh, "Aiyansh," *North British Columbia News*, October 1914, 44.

77 Du Vernet, quoted in "Anglican Synod."

78 Joseph Agar Beet, *Holiness: As Understood by the Writers of the Bible: A Bible Study* (London: Hodder and Stoughton, 1901), 45. For a critique of Beet, see "Dr. Beet's 'Heresy,'" *Zion's Herald* 80, no. 23 (July 4, 1902): 709.

79 Frederick H. Du Vernet, "The Principle of Publicity," in *Out of a Scribe's Treasure: Brief Essays in Practical Religious Thinking* (Toronto: Ryerson, 1927), 120–21; Beet, *Holiness*, 45.

80 Du Vernet, "Thought Exchange," in *Out of a Scribe's Treasure*, 73.

81 Du Vernet, "Notebook on Diocesan Affairs." See also the account of Du Vernet's remembrance of McCullagh in Matthewman, *James B. McCullagh*, 94–95.

82 Du Vernet, "Notebook on Diocesan Affairs."

83 John Barker, "Tangled Reconciliations: The Anglican Church and the Nisga'a of British Columbia," *American Ethnologist* 25, no. 3 (1998): 433–51.

84 Bracken, *Potlatch Papers*, 127.

85 Moeran, *McCullagh of Aiyansh*, 231.

86 Rod Robinson's discussion of totem poles is available at "Teacher Resources," Ancient Villages & Totem Poles of the Nisga'a, accessed September 9, 2017, http://gingolx.ca/nisgaaculture/ancient_villages/resources.html. Also see Christopher F. Roth, "Goods, Names, and Selves: Rethinking the Tsimshian Pot-

latch," *American Ethnologist* 29, no. 1 (2002): 123–50; Deirdre Tombs, "Legendary Nisga'a Leader Leaves Legacy of Hope," *Aboriginal Multi-Media Society*, 8, no. 7 (2004), http://www.ammsa.com/node/27786.

Chapter 7

1 For the reminiscences of such a teenager after the fact, see Clarence Insulander, Dick Gordon with Clarence Insulander, April 1982, tape 216, CD 94, track 1, CBC/CFPR Radio Archives, Prince Rupert Archives, Prince Rupert, BC (hereafter cited as "Prince Rupert Archives"). Insulander founded the first radio station in Prince Rupert in 1936. I am very grateful to Maureen Atkinson for sharing her deep knowledge of Prince Rupert's radio history with me. See also Mary Vipond, *Listening In: The First Decade of Canadian Broadcasting, 1922–1932* (Montreal: McGill-Queen's University Press, 1992), 13; Michele Hilmes and Jason Loviglio, eds., *Radio Reader: Essays in the Cultural History of Radio* (New York: Routledge, 2002). On Du Vernet's radio, see Sylvia Du Vernet, *Portrait of a Personality: Archbishop Frederick Herbert DuVernet* (Toronto: Sylvia Du Vernet, 1987). On the spirituality prompted by media, see Lisa Gitelman and Geoffrey B. Pingree, eds., *New Media, 1740–1915* (Cambridge, MA: MIT Press, 2004).

2 Douglas A. Ferguson, "Editor's Remarks," *Journal of Radio Studies* 14, no. 1 (2007): 1–2; Christopher H. Sterling, "Fessenden, Reginald, 1866–1932," in *Biographical Encyclopedia of American Radio*, ed. Christopher H. Sterling (New York: Routledge, 2013), 136–40; "New Radio Is Almost Ready," *Prince Rupert Daily News*, February 11, 1924. See plate 3 for a map that includes Digby Island and the wireless station.

3 On Kanagatsiyot, see George F. MacDonald, "Coast Tsimshian Pre-contact Economics and Trade: An Archaeological and Ethno-Historic Reconstruction" (paper for Metlakatla/Lax Kw'alaams Land Claim File, submitted to Ratliff & Co. by 6347371 Canada Inc., July 15, 2006), http://faculty.arts.ubc.ca/menzies/documents/macdonal_g.pdf. For the quoted description of Txeemsim, see "Txeemsim (Superbeing)," Nisga'a Lisims Government, accessed March 24, 2016, http://www.nisgaanation.ca/txeemsim-superbeing. See also Patricia June Vickers, "Ayaawx (Ts'msyen Ancestral Law): The Power of Transformation" (PhD diss., University of Victoria, 2008).

4 See Katharine A. McGowan, "'Until We Receive Just Treatment': The Fight against Conscription in the Naas Agency, British Columbia," *BC Studies: The British Columbian Quarterly*, no. 167 (2010): 47–70; Alfred Adams et al., "Petition to Archbishop Du Vernet," in Frederick H. Du Vernet to Canon Gould, MSCC, August 8, 1923, accession no. GS75-103, box 51, file 4, General Synod Archives of the Anglican Church of Canada, Toronto, ON (hereafter cited as "Archives of the Anglican Church of Canada").

5 "Demonstration of Radio Mind," *Prince Rupert Daily News*, February 18, 1924.

6 Du Vernet is referring to Philippians 4:8.

7 I set Du Vernet's approach to healing in a broader historical context in Pamela E. Klassen, *Spirits of Protestantism: Medicine, Healing, and Liberal Christianity* (Berkeley: University of California Press, 2011). I am grateful to Laurel Zwissler, whose research assistance with this earlier book first pointed me to Du Vernet's *Canadian Churchman* writings.

8 Frederick Du Vernet, "Charge to the Synod of 1923," in Du Vernet, *Portrait of a Personality*, 121.

9 On nineteenth-century approaches to the psychological with reference to telepathy, see Roger Luckhurst, *The Invention of Telepathy, 1870–1901* (Oxford: Oxford University Press, 2002); Ann Taves, *Fits, Trances, and Visions: Experiencing Religion and Explaining Experience from Wesley to James* (Princeton, NJ: Princeton University Press, 1999).

10 Luckhurst, *Invention of Telepathy*, 147.

11 Whittier's poem "The Brewing of Soma" drew from Max Mueller's discussion of Vedic religion and argued against an overly sensual spirituality in any religious context.

12 On Elwood Worcester, see Klassen, *Spirits of Protestantism*, 78–82. For a wider discussion of spiritual hopes and fears stoked by technology, see Gitelman and Pingree, *New Media*; Jeremy Stolow, "Technology," in *Key Words in Religion, Media and Culture*, ed. David Morgan (New York: Routledge, 2008), 187–97.

13 Edward W. Said, *On Late Style: Music and Literature against the Grain* (New York: Pantheon Books, 2006), 7; Michael David McNally, *Honoring Elders: Aging, Authority, and Ojibwe Religion* (New York: Columbia University Press, 2009). I am grateful to Linda Hutcheon for pointing me to Said's writings on late style.

14 Frederick H. Du Vernet, "Inter-Mental Action," *Vancouver Province*, January 26, 1923, Du Vernet Clippings File, Archives of the Provincial Synod of British Columbia and Yukon, Vancouver, BC (hereafter cited as "Synod of British Columbia and Yukon"); Lambeth Conference, "Resolution 58—Spiritualism, Christian Science, Theosophy," 1920, Anglican Communion, accessed May 4, 2016, http://www.anglicancommunion.org/resources/document-library/lambeth-conference/1920/resolution-58-spiritualism,-christian-science,-theosophy-spiritualism.aspx.

15 Lambeth Conference, "Resolution 34—Missionary Problems," 1920, Anglican Communion, accessed May 4, 2016, http://www.anglicancommunion.org/resources/document-library/lambeth-conference/1920/resolution-34-missionary-problems.aspx; Lambeth Conference, "Resolution 54—The Positions of Women in the Councils and Ministrations of," 1920, Anglican Communion, accessed September 9, 2017, http://www.anglicancommunion.org/resources/document-library/lambeth-conference/1920/resolution-54-the-position-of-women-in-the-councils-and-ministrations-of.aspx; Lambeth Conference, "Resolution 68—Problems of Marriage and Sexual Morality," 1920, Anglican Communion, accessed September 9, 2017, http://www.anglicancommunion.org/resources/document-library/lambeth-conference/1920/resolution-68-problems-of-marriage-and-sexual-morality.aspx.

16 Lambeth Conference, "Resolution 56—Spiritualism, Christian Science, Theosophy," 1920, Anglican Communion, accessed May 4, 2016, http://www.anglicancommunion.org/resources/document-library/lambeth-conference/1920/resolution-56-spiritualism,-christian-science,-theosophy.aspx; Lambeth Conference, "Resolution 64—Spiritualism, Christian Science, Theosophy," 1920, Anglican Communion, accessed May 4, 2016, http://www.anglicancommunion.org/resources/document-library/lambeth-conference/1920/resolution-64-spiritualism,-christian-science,-theosophy-theosophy.aspx.

17 Du Vernet, *Portrait of a Personality*, 221; Frederick H. Du Vernet, *Out of a Scribe's Treasure: Brief Essays in Practical Religious Thinking* (Toronto: Ryerson, 1927).

18 Du Vernet, "Mutual Understanding," in *Out of a Scribe's Treasure*, 149–50; Frederick H. Du Vernet, "True Religion," *Montreal Daily Star*, September 4, 1920.

19 Du Vernet, *Out of a Scribe's Treasure*, 156–57 (from "Equality"), 163 (from "The Tyranny of the Majority"), 175 (from "The Rate of Interest"), 104 (from "Thoughts on Family and School").

20 Du Vernet, quoted in "Anglican Synod: Prince Rupert, the See City, a Busy Spiritual Place This Week, Bishop Du Vernet Deals with Intemperance and the Indian Situation," *Prince Rupert Empire*, August 14, 1909.

21 Frederick H. Du Vernet, "The Formation of an Ecclesiastical Province of British Columbia," *Across the Rockies*, February 1912, 44–45, Synod of British Columbia and Yukon.

22 Du Vernet, quoted in "Anglican Synod."

23 H. E. Fox, *North British Columbia News*, April 1913, 18. On "secularity" in British Columbia, see Lynne Marks, "Leaving God Behind When They Crossed the Rocky Mountains: Exploring Unbelief in Turn-of-the-Century British Columbia," in *Household Counts: Canadian Households and Families in 1901*, ed. Peter Baskerville and Eric W. Sager (Toronto: University of Toronto Press, 2007), 371–404; Tina Block, *The Secular Northwest: Religion and Irreligion in Everyday Postwar Life* (Vancouver: University of British Columbia Press, 2016).

24 Robert K. Burkinshaw, *Pilgrims in Lotus Land: Conservative Protestantism in British Columbia, 1917–1981* (Montreal: McGill-Queen's University Press, 1995), 29; Kwi Awt Stelmexw, "Oh The Places You Should Know," accessed May 11, 2016, http://ohtheplacesyoushouldknow.com.

25 Eric Taylor Woods, "A Cultural Approach to a Canadian Tragedy: The Indian Residential Schools as a Sacred Enterprise," *International Journal of Politics, Culture, and Society* 26, no. 2 (2013): 173–87.

26 Frederick H. Du Vernet, "A Short Survey of the Diocese of Caledonia," *North British Columbia News*, May 1917, 52–54; "Editor's Notes," *Across the Rockies*, January 1917, 50, Synod of British Columbia and Yukon. On Treaty 8, see Arthur Ray, "Treaty 8: A British Columbian Anomaly," *BC Studies: The British Columbian Quarterly*, no. 123 (1999): 5–58.

27 "Editor's Notes: New Church at Chilco," *Across the Rockies*, October 1916, 178 Synod of British Columbia and Yukon.

28 F. H. Du Vernet, "Beautiful Northern Valleys Held Back by Land Grabbers," *The World*, July 9, 1918, Clippings File, accession no. 92-19/17, Diocese of Caledonia Archives, Prince Rupert, BC (hereafter cited as "Diocese of Caledonia Archives").

29 Du Vernet, quoted in *Prince Rupert Optimist*, May 21, 1910; "Indian Band Empire Day Celebration Prince Rupert 1911" [photograph], n.d., LP984-29-1759-392, Prince Rupert Archives; "Indian's Welcome to Duke of Connaught, 1912" [photograph], n.d., P985-29-2397, Phylis Bowman Collection, Prince Rupert Archives.

30 Frederick H. Du Vernet, "Early Closing in Prince Rupert: Bishop Du Vernet Says Spirit of Age Favors Early Closing of Business Premises—A Letter Explaining His Views," *Prince Rupert Empire*, ca. 1910, Du Vernet Clippings File, Synod of British Columbia and Yukon; Prince Rupert Ministerial Association Minutes, January 13, 1913 ("irreverence"), and July 4, 1910 ("white slaves"), Book 994-37-MS #2855, Prince Rupert Archives.

31 "Natives Have Charge of Anglican Services: Music and Preaching Are of High

Order and of Interest to Congregations," *Prince Rupert Daily News*, September 17, 1923, Du Vernet Clippings File, Diocese of Caledonia Archives.

32 Frederick H. Du Vernet to Canon Gould, MSCC, April 23, 1924, accession no. GS75-103, box 51, file 4, Archives of the Anglican Church of Canada.

33 See Dean Neu, "'Presents' for the 'Indians': Land, Colonialism and Accounting in Canada," *Accounting, Organizations and Society* 25, no. 2 (2000): 163–84.

34 Frederick H. Du Vernet to Mrs. Satow, *Across the Rockies*, ca. 1921, Synod of British Columbia and Yukon.

35 Heather J. Jackson, *Marginalia: Readers Writing in Books* (New Haven, CT: Yale University Press, 2002), 140.

36 For several accounts of psychic researchers' perspectives on spirituality, see Christopher G. White, *Unsettled Minds: Psychology and the American Search for Spiritual Assurance, 1830–1940* (Berkeley: University of California Press, 2009); John Lardas Modern, *Secularism in Antebellum America* (Chicago: University of Chicago Press, 2011); Rhodri Hayward, "Demonology, Neurology, and Medicine in Edwardian Britain," *Bulletin of the History of Medicine* 78, no. 1 (2004): 37–58.

37 Charles Richet, *Thirty Years of Psychical Research* (New York: MacMillan, 1923), 233. For more on Richet, see M. Brady Brower, *Unruly Spirits: The Science of Psychic Phenomena in Modern France* (Springfield: University of Illinois Press, 2010); Régine Plas, "Psychology and Psychical Research in France around the End of the 19th Century," *History of the Human Sciences* 25, no. 2 (2012): 91–107. For her careful reading of Du Vernet's marginalia, I am very grateful to my research assistant, Sarina Annis. For further reflection on finding and crafting stories in the archive, see Natalie Zemon Davis, *Fiction in the Archives: Pardon Tales and Their Tellers in Sixteenth-Century France* (Stanford, CA: Stanford University Press, 1987).

38 Charles Richet, *Thirty Years of Psychical Research*, 236, 52. When citing Du Vernet's marginalia throughout this chapter, I am referring to his books, which are housed in the Diocese of Caledonia Archives, Prince Rupert. Underlining matches Du Vernet's own marks.

39 Charles Richet, *Thirty Years of Psychical Research*, 66, 53, 99.

40 See, for example, Leigh Eric Schmidt, *Hearing Things: Religion, Illusion, and the American Enlightenment* (Cambridge, MA: Harvard University Press, 2000); Leigh Eric Schmidt, *Heaven's Bride: The Unprintable Life of Ida C. Craddock, American Mystic, Scholar, Sexologist, Martyr, and Madwoman* (New York: Basic Books, 2010); Courtney Bender, *The New Metaphysicals: Spirituality and the American Religious Imagination* (Chicago: University of Chicago Press, 2010); White, *Unsettled Minds*; Joseph Kip Kosek, *Acts of Conscience: Christian Nonviolence and Modern American Democracy* (New York: Columbia University Press, 2011).

41 Jackson, *Marginalia*, 147.

42 Henri Bergson, *Creative Evolution*, trans. Arthur Mitchell (London: Macmillan, 1911); Monica Greco, "On the Vitality of Vitalism," *Theory, Culture & Society* 22, no. 1 (2005): 15–27 (Bergson quotation, 18).

43 Matthew Scherer, *Beyond Church and State: Democracy, Secularism, and Conversion* (Cambridge: Cambridge University Press, 2013), 100, 99. For wider discussion of Bergson, see Alexandre Lefebvre and Melanie White, *Bergson, Politics, and Religion* (Durham, NC: Duke University Press, 2012). For an Indigenous perspective on the "newness" of new materialism, see Kim TallBear, "An Indigenous Reflec-

tion on Working Beyond the Human/Not Human," *GLQ: A Journal of Lesbian and Gay Studies* 21, no. 2–3 (2015): 230–35.

44 For more on the range of Bergson's interests, see Lefebvre and White, *Bergson, Politics, and Religion*; Suzanne Guerlac, *Thinking in Time: An Introduction to Henri Bergson* (Ithaca, NY: Cornell University Press, 2006).

45 Henri Bergson, *Mind-Energy: Lectures and Essays*, trans. H. Wildon Carr (New York: Henry Holt, 1920), 34; Josiah Royce, *The Problem of Christianity: Lectures* (New York: Macmillan, 1913), 21; William James, *A Pluralistic Universe: Hibbert Lectures at Manchester College on the Present Situation in Philosophy* (New York: Longmans, Green, and Company, 1909).

46 Bergson, *Mind-Energy*, 99; Charles Richet, *Thirty Years of Psychical Research*, 105.

47 Du Vernet, "The Philosophy of Common Sense," in *Out of a Scribe's Treasure*, 3 ("the philosophy of"), 5 ("in the name of"); Du Vernet, "The Revolution of Thought," in *Out of a Scribe's Treasure*, 11 ("spiritual energy").

48 William James, *The Principles of Psychology* (New York: Holt, 1890), 1:181, 350.

49 James, *The Principles of Psychology* 1:346, 350.

50 William James, *The Principles of Psychology* (London: MacMillan, 1891), 2:611; James, *The Principles of Psychology*, 1:313; William James, *The Varieties of Religious Experience* (Cambridge, MA: Harvard University Press, 1985).

51 Andrew Seth Pringle-Pattison, "Immanence and Transcendence," in *The Spirit: The Relation of God and Man, Considered from the Standpoint of Recent Philosophy and Science*, ed. Burnett Hillman Streeter (New York: Macmillan, 1922), 15.

52 Lily Dougall, "God in Action," in Streeter, *The Spirit*, 40, 34; Joanna Dean, *Religious Experience and the New Woman: The Life of Lily Dougall* (Bloomington: Indiana University Press, 2007).

53 Dougall, "God in Action," 47; C. A. Anderson Scott, "What Happened at Pentecost," in Streeter, *The Spirit*, 154.

54 "Man but Unit of Universal Mind Says Archbishop," clipping with no date or newspaper title, Du Vernet Clippings File, Diocese of Caledonia Archive.

55 Du Vernet, "The Principle of Publicity," in *Out of a Scribe's Treasure*, 120–21.

56 Frederick H. Du Vernet, "The Communion of the Mind," in *Spiritual Radio* (Mountain Lakes, NJ: Society of the Nazarene, 1925), 50.

57 For the use of some of these words, see Émile Durkheim, *The Elementary Forms of Religious Life* (Oxford: Oxford University Press, 2001); Marcel Mauss, *The Gift: The Form and Reason for Exchange in Archaic Societies*, trans. W. D. Hall (Oxford: Routledge, 2002). On *halaayt*, see Vickers, "Ayaawx (Ts'msyen Ancestral Law)," 212n292.

58 Edward Burnett Tylor, *Primitive Culture: Researches into the Development of Mythology, Philosophy, Religion, Art, and Custom* (London: J. Murray, 1871), 129.

59 Tylor, *Primitive Culture*, 181.

60 Susan Marsden, "Adawx, Spanaxnox, and the Geopolitics of the Tsimshian," *BC Studies: The British Columbian Quarterly*, no. 135 (2002): 131–50; Margaret Seguin Anderson, "Sm'algyax Living Legacy Talking Dictionary," last updated April 2013, accessed May 11, 2016, http://web.unbc.ca/~smalgyax/; Marie-Françoise Guedon, "An Introduction to Tsimshian World View and Its Practitioners," in *The Tsimshian: Images of the Past, Views for the Present*, ed. Margaret Seguin Anderson (Vancouver: University of British Columbia Press, 1984), 137–59; Jay Miller, *Tsimshian Culture: A Light Through the Ages* (Lincoln: University of Nebraska Press, 2000), 23, 29.

61 For historical and fictional accounts of residential schools, see James Rodger Miller, *Shingwauk's Vision: A History of Native Residential Schools* (Toronto: University of Toronto Press, 1996); John S. Milloy, *A National Crime: The Canadian Government and the Residential School System, 1879 to 1986* (Winnipeg: University of Manitoba Press, 1999); Richard Wagamese, *Indian Horse* (Vancouver: Douglas & McIntyre, 2012). For accounts of residential schools in the United States, see Louise Erdrich, *Love Medicine*, rev. ed. (New York: Harper Collins, 1993); Brenda J. Child, *Boarding School Seasons: American Indian Families, 1900–1940* (Lincoln: University of Nebraska Press, 1998).

62 Frederick H. Du Vernet to Canon Gould, MSCC, September 9, 1922, accession no. GS75-103, box 51, file 4, Archives of the Anglican Church of Canada.

63 Frederick H. Du Vernet to Baring-Gould, Secretary CMS, April 2, 1908, *Church Missionary Society Archive*, sec. 4, *Missions to the Americas*, pt. 4, *British Columbia, 1856–1925* (Marlborough, UK: Adam Matthew Publications, 2002), microfilm; Mary Lee Stearns, *Haida Culture in Custody: The Masset Band* (Seattle: University of Washington Press, 1981), 63.

64 Eric Porter, "The Anglican Church and Native Education: Residential Schools and Assimilation" (MA thesis, University of Toronto, 1981), 60.

65 Du Vernet to Baring-Gould, Secretary CMS, April 2, 1908.

66 James B. McCullagh, "After Many Days: A Stirring Story from Aiyansh," *North British Columbia News*, April 1913, Synod of British Columbia and Yukon.

67 Frederick H. Du Vernet to Canon Gould, MSCC, July 27, 1915, accession no. GS75-103, box 51, file 4, Archives of the Anglican Church of Canada.

68 Frederick H. Du Vernet to Canon Gould, MSCC, March 5, 1921, accession no. GS75-103, box 51, file 4, Archives of the Anglican Church of Canada; Du Vernet to Canon Gould, MSCC, September 9, 1922. For more on Anglican approaches to residential schools, see Porter, "Anglican Church and Native Education"; Woods, "Cultural Approach to a Canadian Tragedy."

69 Frederick H. Du Vernet to Thomas B. R. Westgate, MSCC, November 10, 1922, xii, accession no. GS75-103, box 51, file 4, Archives of the Anglican Church of Canada. Westgate was a fellow graduate of Wycliffe College and also a former CMS Missionary posted in East Africa. Both a veteran of the Riel Rebellion and a prisoner of war in German East Africa in 1915, Westgate was a transnational colonial churchman. In the letter, Du Vernet thanks Westgate for sending on a copy of a letter from the infamous Duncan Campbell Scott, deputy secretary of the Department of Indian Affairs and a primary architect of the residential school system as an explicitly assimilative tool.

70 Alfred Adams et al., "Petition to Archbishop Du Vernet," in Frederick H. Du Vernet to Canon Gould, MSCC, August 8, 1923, accession no. GS75-103, box 51, file 4, Archives of the Anglican Church of Canada.

71 Frederick H. Du Vernet to S. H. Blake, MSCC, March 23, 1909, accession no. GS75-103, box 15, Archives of the Anglican Church of Canada.

72 Edward W. Said, *Culture and Imperialism* (New York: Vintage, 1994).

73 "Archbishop Du Vernet Gives an Explanation of the Scientific Fact of Thought Transference," *Prince Rupert Daily News*, January 21, 1924.

74 Said, *On Late Style*, 9.

Chapter 8

1 Frederick H. Du Vernet, "The Pathway of Psychology," in *Out of a Scribe's Treasure: Brief Essays in Practical Religious Thinking* (Toronto: Ryerson, 1927), 95.

2 C. B. Robinson, "The Late Archbishop Du Vernet: The Funeral," *North British Columbia News*, January 1925, 147 Archives of the Provincial Synod of British Columbia and Yukon, Vancouver, BC (hereafter cited as "Synod of British Columbia and Yukon").

3 George Rix to Caledonia Clergy, May 1926, Bishop George Alexander Rix Correspondence, accession no. 77-60, Diocese of Caledonia Archives, Prince Rupert, BC (hereafter cited as "Diocese of Caledonia Archives"); George Rix, "Report on the History of the Diocese of Caledonia," ca. 1928, accession no. 7736a, Diocese of Caledonia Archives.

4 Jocelyn Perkins, "Editor's Notes," *Across the Rockies*, January 1925, Synod of British Columbia and Yukon.

5 Primate of Church of England in Canada, *In the Diocese of Caledonia* (MSCC, ca. 1925), Pamphlet Collection, Diocese of Caledonia Archives; Frederick H. Du Vernet, "Radio-Mind," in *Spiritual Radio* (Mountain Lakes, NJ: Society of the Nazarene, 1925), 27–28.

6 Walter Rushbrook, "Archbishop F. H. Du Vernet, D.D.," 1942, pp. 1 and 3, accession no. 210 C3, Diocese of Caledonia Archives. For an example of another later history omitting mention of radio mind, see Hugh McCullum and Karmel Taylor McCullum, *Caledonia: 100 Years Ahead* (Toronto: Anglican Book Centre, 1979).

7 "Victoria Paper on Late Archbishop: Victoria Colonist Speaks of Him as the Apostle of Peace and Goodwill," *Prince Rupert Daily News*, November 4, 1924, Newspaper Clippings, Diocese of Caledonia Archives.

8 On the Order of St. Luke, see Pamela E. Klassen, *Spirits of Protestantism: Medicine, Healing, and Liberal Christianity* (Berkeley: University of California Press, 2011), 144–45.

9 Banks, introduction to Du Vernet, *Spiritual Radio*, 8–9, 4. On Henry Drummond's popularizing of a "biological" spirituality, see Anne Scott, "'Visible Incarnations of the Unseen': Henry Drummond and the Practice of Typological Exegesis," *British Journal for the History of Science* 37, no. 4 (2004): 435–54.

10 For a description of the lectures, see Sylvia Du Vernet, *Portrait of a Personality: Archbishop Frederick Herbert DuVernet* (Toronto: Sylvia Du Vernet, 1987), 221. On Connell, see Christine Price, "'A Very Conservative Radical': Reverend Robert Connell's Encounter with Marxism in the BC CCF" (MA thesis, Simon Fraser University, 2006).

11 "Victoria Paper on Late Archbishop"; Connell, preface to Du Vernet, *Out of a Scribe's Treasure*, v.

12 H. D. A. Major, foreword to Du Vernet, *Out of a Scribe's Treasure*, xi.

13 Major, foreword, xii. For descriptions of Major, see Mark D. Chapman, *Ambassadors of Christ: Commemorating 150 Years of Theological Education in Cuddesdon, 1854–2004* (Aldershot, UK: Ashgate, 2004), 112 ("panentheistic," "in the cosmos," "natural world").

14 Charles Edward Douglas, quoted in Lord Bishop of Oxford H. M. Burge, *The Doctrine of the Resurrection of the Body: Documents Relating to the Question of Heresy*

Raised against the Rev. H. D. A. Major, Ripon Hall, Oxford (Oxford: A. R. Mowbray & Co., 1922), 1.

15 Major, quoted in Burge, *Doctrine of the Resurrection of the Body*, 59. For a fascinating discussion of Christian views of bodily resurrection, see Caroline Walker Bynum, *Fragmentation and Redemption: Essays on Gender and the Human Body in Medieval Religion* (Cambridge, MA: Zone Books, 1992).

16 Frederick H. Du Vernet, "Life after Death," *Montreal Daily Star*, March 31, 1923; Du Vernet, "The Spirit of Easter," in *Out of a Scribe's Treasure*, 195.

17 "Would Form League for Purer Thought," *Canadian Churchman*, August 12, 1926; "Archbishop Du Vernet's Memory Honored," *Canadian Churchman*, n.d.

18 Du Vernet, *Portrait of a Personality*, 253, 217, 250. For a broader analysis of the "metaphysical tradition" in the United States, see Catherine L. Albanese, *A Republic of Mind and Spirit: A Cultural History of American Metaphysical Religion* (New Haven, CT: Yale University Press, 2006).

19 "In Probate on the Matter of the Will of the Estate of Frederick Herbert Du Vernet," February 3, 1925, Probate Files, 1910–1944, British Columbia Supreme Court, accession no. GR-1483, Royal British Columbia Museum and Archives.

20 Du Vernet, *Portrait of a Personality*, 7. I am grateful to Nicholas May for sharing with me his sources on Horace's status as justice of the peace.

21 Rushbrook, "Archbishop F. H. Du Vernet, D.D.," 5. See also Myra Rutherdale, "Maternal Metaphors in the Northern Canadian Mission Field," in *Canadian Missionaries, Indigenous Peoples: Representing Religion at Home and Abroad*, ed. Alvyn Austin and Jamie S. Scott (Toronto: University of Toronto Press, 2005), 47.

22 Alice F. Du Vernet to George Rix, August 2, 1925, Bishop George Alexander Rix Correspondence, accession no. 77-60, Diocese of Caledonia Archives.

23 "Prince Rupert," *North British Columbia News*, July, 1929, 341.

24 Bill Dunford, in *Vancouver Province*, July 26, 1952, Du Vernet Clippings File, Synod of British Columbia and Yukon.

25 Du Vernet, "The Spirit of Easter," in *Out of a Scribe's Treasure*, 195.

26 For a fuller discussion, see Glen Sean Coulthard, *Red Skin, White Masks: Rejecting the Colonial Politics of Recognition* (Minneapolis: University of Minnesota Press, 2014).

27 On women's suffrage, see Frederick Du Vernet, "Archbishop Du Vernet's Charge Delivered to the Synod of the Diocese of Caledonia," *North British Columbia News*, January 1919. On employment, see Du Vernet, "Occupational Psychology," in *Out of a Scribe's Treasure*, 169.

28 Frederick Du Vernet, "Charge to the Synod of 1923," in Du Vernet, *Portrait of a Personality*, 121. On the gendered division of labor within Spiritualism, see Alex Owen, *The Darkened Room: Women, Power, and Spiritualism in Late Victorian England* (Chicago: University of Chicago Press, 1989).

29 Hamar Foster, "We Are Not O'Meara's Children: Law, Lawyers, and the First Campaign for Aboriginal Title in British Columbia, 1908–28," in *Let Right Be Done: Aboriginal Title, the Calder Case, and the Future of Indigenous Rights*, ed. Hamar Foster, Heather Raven, and Jeremy Webber (Vancouver: University of British Columbia Press, 2007), 61–84.

30 For more on clans and gendered authority, see Nicholas May, "Feasting on the AAM of Heaven: The Christianization of the Nisga'a, 1860–1920" (PhD diss., University of Toronto, 2013); Nicholas May, "Life of Niysyok: Exploring Nisga'a

Religious Lives through Biography of a Personage" (paper presented at the Berkshire Conference on the History of Women, Toronto, May 24, 2014).

31 Frederick H. Du Vernet, "Telepathic Testimonies," *Canadian Churchman*, November 1, 1923.

32 Juan Obarrio, "Postshamanism (1999)," *Cultural Studies Review* 13, no. 2 (2007): 171, 168.

33 Obarrio, "Postshamanism (1999)," 182 ("poignant presence"), 185 ("memory"), 174 ("something remembers in me"); Du Vernet, "Conscious Memory," in *Out of a Scribe's Treasure*, 89 ("character").

34 For two perspectives on the mutual exchange of knowledge through ritual, see Susan Neylan, *The Heavens Are Changing: Nineteenth-Century Protestant Missions and Tsimshian Christianity* (Montreal: McGill-Queen's University Press, 2002); May, "Feasting on the AAM of Heaven."

35 Du Vernet, "Charge to the Synod of 1923," 122. Also see Du Vernet, "The Outlook for Religion," in *Out of a Scribe's Treasure*, 18–19.

36 Frederick H. Du Vernet, "Notebook on Diocesan Affairs" 1904–1924, accession no. 203, Diocese of Caledonia Archives. This notebook is a collection of unevenly paginated and largely undated short histories of missions, lists of parishioners, and other miscellany handwritten by Du Vernet.

37 On the role of Wycliffe College in the development of residential schools, see Eric Porter, "The Anglican Church and Native Education: Residential Schools and Assimilation" (MA thesis, University of Toronto, 1981).

38 The Anglican Council of Indigenous Peoples, *National Indigenous Bishop: A Step to a New Era* (Toronto: General Synod of the Anglican Church, 2006), http://www.anglican.ca/wp-content/uploads/2011/01/acip-nib.pdf.

39 I am grateful to Bishop MacDonald for telling me his story of this visit to the Nass Valley, and to Nita Morven for correcting my spelling. See also Anglican First Nations Council of Caledonia, "Reiteration of Anglican Church of Canada Apology to Nisga'a Indian Residential School Survivors," April 27, 2016, Nisga'a Lisims Government, accessed September 10, 2017, http://www.nisgaanation.ca/news/reiteration-anglican-church-canada-apology-nisgaa-indian-residential-schools-survivors.

Bibliography

Abel, Jordan. *The Place of Scraps*. Vancouver: Talonbooks, 2013. 283

Albanese, Catherine L. *A Republic of Mind and Spirit: A Cultural History of American Metaphysical Religion*. New Haven, CT: Yale University Press, 2006.

Aldridge, Jim. *Keeping Promises: The Royal Proclamation of 1763, Aboriginal Rights, and Treaties in Canada*. Montreal: McGill-Queen's University Press, 2015.

Alfred, Taiaiake, and Jeff Corntassel. "Being Indigenous: Resurgences against Contemporary Colonialism." *Government and Opposition* 40, no. 4 (September 1, 2005): 597–614.

Alpert, Avram. "Overcome by Photography: Camera Lucida in an International Frame." *Third Text* 24, no. 3 (2010): 331–39.

Anderson, Benedict. *Imagined Communities: Reflections on the Origin and Spread of Nationalism*. London: Verso, 1991.

Anderson, Margaret Seguin. "Lest There Be No Salmon: Symbols in the Traditional Tsimshian Potlatch." In *The Tsimshian: Images of the Past, Views for the Present*, edited by Margaret Seguin Anderson, 110–36. Vancouver: University of British Columbia Press, 1984.

———, ed. *The Tsimshian: Images of the Past, Views for the Present*. Vancouver: University of British Columbia Press, 1984.

Anderson, Margaret Seguin, and Tammy Anderson Blumhagen. "Memories and Moments: Conversations and Re-collections." *BC Studies: The British Columbian Quarterly*, no. 104 (2010): 85–102.

Angel, Naomi. "Before Truth: Memory, History, and Nation in the Context of Truth and Reconciliation in Canada." PhD diss., New York University, 2013.

Arthur, Eric Ross, and Stephen A. Otto. *Toronto, No Mean City*. Toronto: University of Toronto Press, 1986.

Anishinaabe Nation Grand Council Treaty #3. *"The Creator Placed Us Here": Timeline of Significant Events of the Anishinaabeg of Treaty #3*. Kenora, ON: Anishinaabe Grand Council Treaty #3, October 3, 2013.

Atkinson, Maureen L. "The 'Accomplished' Odille Quintal Morison: Tsimshian Cultural Intermediary of Metlakatla, British Columbia." In *Recollecting: Lives of Aboriginal Women of the Canadian Northwest and Borderlands*, edited by Sarah Carter and Patricia Alice McCormack, 135–56. Edmonton, AB: Athabasca University Press, 2011.

Barbeau, Marius. *Totem Poles*. Vol. 1. Ottawa: Department of Resources and Development, Development Services Branch. National Museum of Canada, 1950.

———. *Tsimsyan Myths: Illustrated*. Ottawa: Department of Northern Affairs and National Resources, 1961.

Barbeau, Marius, William Beynon, John J. Cove, and George F. MacDonald. *Tsimshian Narratives*. Ottawa: Education and Cultural Affairs Division, 1987.

Barker, John. "Missionary Ethnography on the Northwest Coast." In *Anthropology's Debt to Missionaries*, edited by Vinson Sutlive, Leonard Plotnicov, and Paula Brown, 1–22. Ethnology Monographs 20. Pittsburgh, PA: University of Pittsburgh Department of Anthropology, 2007.

———. "Tangled Reconciliations: The Anglican Church and the Nisga'a of British Columbia." *American Ethnologist* 25, no. 3 (1998): 433–51.

Barthes, Roland. *Camera Lucida: Reflections on Photography*. Translated by Richard Howard. New York: Hill and Wang, 1981.

Bauman, Richard, and Charles L. Briggs. *Voices of Modernity: Language Ideologies and the Politics of Inequality*. Cambridge: Cambridge University Press, 2003.

Beavers, Anthony F. "In the Beginning Was the Word and Then Four Revolutions in the History of Information." In *Luciano Floridi's Philosophy of Technology: Critical Reflections*, edited by Hilmi Demir, 85–103. Dordrecht, Neth.: Springer, 2012.

Bebbington, David W. *Evangelicalism in Modern Britain: A History from the 1730s to the 1980s*. New York: Routledge, 2003.

Beet, Joseph Agar. *Holiness: As Understood by the Writers of the Bible: A Bible Study*. London: Hodder and Stoughton, 1901.

Behrend, Heike. "Photo Magic: Photographs in Practices of Healing and Harming in East Africa." *Journal of Religion in Africa* 33, no. 2 (2003): 129–45.

Behrend, Heike. "Seelenklau: Zur Geschichte eines interkulturellen Transfers." In *Seele: Multiple Räume*, ed. Johannes Bilstein and Matthias Winzen. Baden-Baden, Ger.: Verlag für moderne Kunst Nürnberg, 2004.

Bell, Lynne. "Buffalo Boy Testifies: Decolonising Visual Testimony in a Colonial-Settler Society." In *Decolonising Testimony: On the Possibilities and Limits of Witnessing*, edited by Rosanne Kennedy, Lynne Bell, and Julia Emberley, 81–96. Humanities Research, vol. 15, no 3. Canberra: Australian National University Press, 2009.

Bender, Courtney. "'Every Meaning Shall Have Its Homecoming Festival:' A Secular Age and the Senses of Modern Spirituality." In *Working with a Secular Age: Interdisciplinary Perspectives on Charles Taylor's Master Narrative*, edited by Guido Vanheeswijck, Colin Jager, and Florian Zemmin, 283–304. Berlin: De Gruyter, 2016.

———. *The New Metaphysicals: Spirituality and the American Religious Imagination*. Chicago: University of Chicago Press, 2010.

Benjamin, Walter. "A Small History of Photography." In *One-Way Street and Other Writings*, 240–57. London: NLB, 1979.

Benn, Carl. *Mohawks on the Nile: Natives among the Canadian Voyageurs in Egypt, 1884–1885*. Hamilton, ON: Dundurn Press, 2009.

Berger, Carl. *Sense of Power: Studies in the Ideas of Canadian Imperialism, 1867–1914*. Toronto: University of Toronto Press, 1971.

Bergson, Henri. *Creative Evolution*. Translated by Arthur Mitchell. London: Macmillan, 1911.

———. *Mind-Energy: Lectures and Essays*. Translated by H. Wildon Carr. New York: Henry Holt, 1920.

Beynon, William. *The Beynon Manuscript: The Literature, Myths and Traditions of the Tsimshian People*. Ann Arbor, MI: University Microfilm International, 1980.

Bird, Louis, and Susan Elaine Gray. *The Spirit Lives in the Mind: Omushkego Stories, Lives, and Dreams*. Montreal: McGill-Queen's University Press, 2007.

Block, Tina. *The Secular Northwest: Religion and Irreligion in Everyday Postwar Life*. Vancouver: University of British Columbia Press, 2016.

Bobiwash, A. Rodney. "The History of Native People in the Toronto Area: An Overview." In *The Meeting Place: Aboriginal Life in Toronto*, edited by Frances Sanderson and Heather Howard-Bobiwash, 5–24. Toronto: Native Canadian Centre of Toronto, 1997.

Borrows, John. *Canada's Indigenous Constitution*. Toronto: University of Toronto Press, 2010.

———. *Drawing Out Law: A Spirit's Guide*. Toronto: University of Toronto Press, 2010.

———. "Wampum at Niagara: The Royal Proclamation, Canadian Legal History, and Self-Government." In *Aboriginal and Treaty Rights in Canada: Essays on Law, Equality, and Respect for Difference*, edited by Michael Asch, 155–72. Vancouver: University of British Columbia Press, 1997.

Borthwick, J. Douglas. *History of the Diocese of Montreal, 1850–1910*. Montreal: J. Lovell, 1910.

Bracken, Christopher. *The Potlatch Papers: A Colonial Case History*. Chicago: University of Chicago Press, 1997.

Briggs, Charles, and Richard Bauman. "'The Foundation of All Future Researches': Franz Boas, George Hunt, Native American Texts, and the Construction of Modernity." *American Quarterly* 51, no. 3 (1999): 479–528.

Bringhurst, Robert. *A Story as Sharp as a Knife: The Classical Haida Mythtellers and Their World*. Vancouver: Douglas & McIntyre, 1999.

Brock, Peggy. *The Many Voyages of Arthur Wellington Clah: A Tsimshian Man on the Pacific Northwest Coast* (Vancouver: University of British Columbia Press, 2011).

Brody, Hugh. *Maps and Dreams: Indians and the British Columbia Frontier*. Vancouver: Douglas & McIntyre, 1981.

Brooks, Peter. *Troubling Confessions: Speaking Guilt in Law and Literature*. Chicago: University of Chicago Press, 2000.

Brower, M. Brady. *Unruly Spirits: The Science of Psychic Phenomena in Modern France*. Springfield: University of Illinois Press, 2010.

Brown, Jennifer S. H. "'I Wish to Be as I See You': An Ojibwa-Methodist Encounter in Fur Trade Country, Rainy Lake, 1854–1855." *Arctic Anthropology* 24, no. 1 (1987): 19–31.

———. "Mission Indian Progress and Dependency: Ambiguous Images from Canadian Methodist Lantern Slides." *Arctic Anthropology* 18, no. 2 (1981): 17–27.

Bruchac, Margaret M. "Earthshapers and Placemakers: Algonkian Indian Stories and the Landscape." In *Indigenous Archaeologies: Decolonising Theory and Practice*, edited by Claire Smith and H. Martin Wobst, 52–74. New York: Routledge, 2005.

Bruner, Jason. "Keswick and the East African Revival: An Historiographical Reappraisal." *Religion Compass* 5, no. 9 (2011): 477–89.

Bryce, George. "Among the Mound Builders' Remains." *Manitoba Historical Society Transactions*, 1, no. 18 (May 28, 1885). http://www.mhs.mb.ca/docs/transactions/1/moundbuilders.shtml.

Buckner, Philip. "Parker, Robert." In *Dictionary of Canadian Biography*. University of Toronto / Université Laval, 2003–. Accessed November 8, 2015. http://www.biographi.ca/en/bio/parker_robert_9E.html.

Budd, Robert, and Roy Henry Vickers. *Raven Brings the Light*. Madeira Park, BC: Harbour, 2013.

Burge, H. M., Lord Bishop of Oxford. *The Doctrine of the Resurrection of the Body: Documents Relating to the Question of Heresy Raised against the Rev. H.D.A. Major, Ripon Hall, Oxford*. Oxford: A. R. Mowbray & Co., 1922.

Burkinshaw, Robert K. *Pilgrims in Lotus Land: Conservative Protestantism in British Columbia, 1917–1981*. Montreal: McGill-Queen's University Press, 1995.

Butler, Judith P. *Giving an Account of Oneself*. New York: Fordham University Press, 2005.

Bynum, Caroline Walker. *Christian Materiality: An Essay on Religion in Late Medieval Europe*. Cambridge, MA: Zone Books, 2011.

———. *Fragmentation and Redemption: Essays on Gender and the Human Body in Medieval Religion*. Cambridge, MA: Zone Books, 1992.

Byrne, Georgina. *Modern Spiritualism and the Church of England, 1850–1939*. Suffolk, UK: Boydell & Brewer, 2010.

Calloway, Colin G. *The Scratch of a Pen: 1763 and the Transformation of North America*. New York: Oxford University Press, 2006.

Campbell, Kenneth, and First Nations Education Council. *Persistence and Change: A History of the Ts'msyen Nation*. Prince Rupert, BC: Tsimshian Nation and School District 52, 2005.

Carter, Sarah. "'Daughters of British Blood' or 'Hordes of Men of Alien Race': The Homesteads-for-Women Campaign in Western Canada." *Great Plains Quarterly* 29, no. 3 (2009): 267–86.

Chamberlin, J. Edward. *The Banker and the Blackfoot: A Memoir of My Grandfather in Chinook Country*. Toronto: Knopf Canada, 2016.

———. *If This Is Your Land, Where Are Your Stories? Finding Common Ground*. New York: Random House, 2004.

Chapman, Mark D. *Ambassadors of Christ: Commemorating 150 Years of Theological Education in Cuddesdon, 1854–2004*. Aldershot, UK: Ashgate, 2004.

Chéroux, Clément. *The Perfect Medium: Photography and the Occult*. New Haven, CT: Yale University Press, 2005.

Child, Brenda J. *Boarding School Seasons: American Indian Families, 1900–1940*. Lincoln: University of Nebraska Press, 1998.

Cole, Douglas, and Ira Chaikin. *An Iron Hand upon the People: The Law against the Potlatch on the Northwest Coast*. Vancouver: Douglas & McIntyre, 1990.

Collison, William H. *In the Wake of the War Canoe: A Stirring Record of Forty Years' Successful Labour, Peril and Adventure amongst the Savage Indian*

Tribes of the Pacific Coast, and the Piratical Head-Hunting Haidas of the Queen Charlotte Islands, B.C. London: Seeley & Service, 1915.

Conservative Party of British Columbia., ed. *The Case of Kaien Island*. Victoria, BC, 1906.

Cooper, John M. "The Northern Algonquian Supreme Being." *Primitive Man* 6, nos. 3–4 (1933): 41–111.

Corbiere, Alan, and Crystal Migwans. "Animikii miinwaa Mishibizhiw: Narrative Images of the Thunderbird and the Underwater Panther." In *Before and after the Horizon: Anishinaabe Artists of the Great Lakes*, edited by David W. Penney and Gerald McMaster, 37–50. Washington, DC: National Museum of the American Indian, 2013.

Corntassel, Jeff, Chaw-win-is, and T'lakwadzi. "Indigenous Storytelling, Truth-Telling, and Community Approaches to Reconciliation." *ESC: English Studies in Canada* 35, no. 1 (2009): 137–59.

Corsiglia, John, and Gloria Sniveky. "Knowing Home: Nisga'a Traditional Knowledge and Wisdom Improve Environmental Decision Making." *Alternatives Journal* 23, no. 3 (1997): 22.

Coté, Charlotte. "Food Sovereignty, Food Hegemony, and the Revitalization of Indigenous Whaling Practices." In *The World of Indigenous North America*, edited by Robert Warrior, 239–62. New York: Routledge, 2014.

Coulthard, Glen Sean. *Red Skin, White Masks: Rejecting the Colonial Politics of Recognition*. Minneapolis: University of Minnesota Press, 2014.

Crosby, Thomas. *Up and Down the North Pacific Coast by Canoe and Mission Ship*. Toronto: Missionary Society of the Methodist Church, 1914.

Cruikshank, Julie. *The Social Life of Stories: Narrative and Knowledge in the Yukon Territory*. Lincoln: University of Nebraska Press, 2000.

Dane, Perry. "The Corporation Sole and the Encounter of Law and Church." In *Sacred Companies: Organizational Aspects of Religion and Religious Aspects of Organizations*, edited by Nicholas Jay Demerath, 50–61. New York: Oxford University Press, 1998.

———. "The Maps of Sovereignty: A Meditation." *Cardozo Law Review* 12, nos. 3–4 (1991): 959–1006.

Davis, Natalie Zemon. *Fiction in the Archives: Pardon Tales and Their Tellers in Sixteenth-Century France*. Stanford, CA: Stanford University Press, 1987.

Dawson, George Mercer. *To the Charlottes: George Dawson's 1878 Survey of the Queen Charlotte Islands*. Edited by Douglas Cole and Bradley John Lockner. Vancouver: University of British Columbia Press, 1993.

Dean, Joanna. *Religious Experience and the New Woman: The Life of Lily Dougall*. Bloomington: Indiana University Press, 2007.

de Beauvoir, Simone. *The Second Sex*. New York: Vintage Books, 1953.

Demers, Patricia, and Arok Wolvengrey. *The Beginning of Print Culture in Athabasca Country: A Facsimile Edition and Translation of a Prayer Book in Cree Syllabics by Father Émile Grouard, OMI, Prepared and Printed at Lac La Biche in 1883*. Translated by Naomi L. McIlwraith and Dorothy Thunder. Edmonton: University of Alberta Press, 2010.

Densmore, Frances. *Chippewa Customs*. Minneapolis: Minnesota Historical Society Press, 1929.

———. "A Minnesota Missionary Journey of 1893." *Minnesota History* 20, no. 3 (1939): 310–13.

Dougall, Lily. "God in Action." In *The Spirit: The Relation of God and Man, Considered from the Standpoint of Recent Philosophy and Science*, edited by Burnett Hillman Streeter, 25–67. New York: Macmillan, 1922.

Drummond, Anne. "Gender, Profession, and Principals: The Teachers of Quebec Protestant Academies, 1875–1900." *Historical Studies in Education* 2, no. 1 (1990): 59–71.

Duff, Wilson. *Histories, Territories and Laws of the Kitwancool*. Victoria: Royal British Columbia Museum, 1959.

Durkheim, Émile. *The Elementary Forms of Religious Life*. Oxford: Oxford University Press, 2001.

Du Vernet, Frederick H. *Out of a Scribe's Treasure: Brief Essays in Practical Religious Thinking*. Toronto: Ryerson, 1927.

———. *Spiritual Radio*. Mountain Lakes, NJ: Society of the Nazarene, 1925.

Du Vernet, Sylvia. *Portrait of a Personality: Archbishop Frederick Herbert DuVernet*. Toronto: Sylvia Du Vernet, 1987.

Edwards, Elizabeth. "Tracing Photography." In *Made to Be Seen: Perspectives on the History of Visual Anthropology*, edited by Marcus Banks and Jay Ruby, 159–89. Chicago: University of Chicago Press, 2011.

Edwards, Gail Elizabeth. "Creating Textual Communities: Anglican and Methodist Missionaries and Print Culture in British Columbia, 1858–1914." PhD diss., University of British Columbia, 2001.

Eisenstein, Elizabeth L. *The Printing Press as an Agent of Change*. Cambridge: Cambridge University Press, 1980.

Elden, Stuart. *The Birth of Territory*. Chicago: University of Chicago Press, 2013.

Ellis, Donald, Steven Clay Brown, and Bill Holm. *Tsimshian Treasures: The Remarkable Journey of the Dundas Collection*. Vancouver: Douglas & McIntyre, 2007.

Ely, Edmund F. *The Ojibwe Journals of Edmund F. Ely, 1833–1849*. Edited by Theresa M. Schenck. Lincoln: University of Nebraska Press, 2012.

Enemikeese. *The Indian Chief: An Account of the Labours, Losses, Sufferings, and

Oppression of Ke-Zig-Ko-E-Ne-Ne (David Sawyer), a Chief of the Ojibbeway Indians in Canada West. Toronto: Coles, 1974.

Engelke, Matthew. *God's Agents: Biblical Publicity in Contemporary England.* Berkeley: University of California Press, 2013.

——. *A Problem of Presence: Beyond Scripture in an African Church.* Berkeley: University of California Press, 2007.

Erdrich, Louise. *Books and Islands in Ojibwe Country.* Washington, DC: National Geographic, 2003.

——. *Love Medicine.* Rev. ed. New York: Harper Collins, 1993.

Erzen, Tanya. *Straight to Jesus: Sexual and Christian Conversions in the Ex-Gay Movement.* Berkeley: University of California Press, 2006.

Etherington, Norman. "The Missionary Writing Machine in Nineteenth-Century Kwazulu-Natal." In *Mixed Messages: Materiality, Textuality, Missions,* edited by Jamie S. Scott and Gareth Griffiths, 37–50. London: Palgrave Macmillan, 2005.

Eves, Richard. "'Black and White, a Significant Contrast': Race, Humanism and Missionary Photography in the Pacific." *Ethnic and Racial Studies* 29, no. 4 (2006): 725–48.

Ferguson, Douglas A. "Editor's Remarks." *Journal of Radio Studies* 14, no. 1 (2007): 91.

Field, Les. "Mapping Erasure: The Power of Nominative Cartography in the Past and Present of the Muwekma Ohlones of the San Francisco Bay Area." In *Recognition, Sovereignty Struggles, and Indigenous Rights in the United States: A Sourcebook,* edited by Jean M. O'Brien and Amy E. Den Ouden, 287–309. Chapel Hill: The University of North Carolina Press, 2013.

Foster, Hamar. "Letting Go the Bone: The Idea of Indian Title in British Columbia, 1849–1927." In *British Columbia and the Yukon,* ed. Hamar Foster and John McLaren, 28–86. Vol. 6 of *Essays in the History of Canadian Law.* Toronto: University of Toronto Press, 1995.

——. "We Are Not O'Meara's Children: Law, Lawyers, and the First Campaign for Aboriginal Title in British Columbia, 1908–28." In *Let Right Be Done: Aboriginal Title, the Calder Case, and the Future of Indigenous Rights,* edited by Hamar Foster, Heather Raven, and Jeremy Webber, 61–84. Vancouver: University of British Columbia Press, 2007.

Foucault, Michel. *The History of Sexuality.* Vol. 1, *An Introduction.* Vintage Books. New York: Random House, 1990.

Frazer, James George. *The Golden Bough: A Study in Magic and Religion, Taboo and the Perils of the Soul.* London: MacMillan, 1911.

Friedland, Martin L. *The University of Toronto: A History*. 2nd ed. Toronto: University of Toronto Press, 2013.

Galloway, Alexander R. *Protocol: How Control Exists after Decentralization*. Cambridge, MA: MIT Press, 2004.

Gamble, David Alexander, and David Vogt. "'You Don't Suppose the Dominion Government Wants to Cheat the Indians?': The Grand Trunk Pacific Railway and the Fort George Reserve, 1908–12." *BC Studies: The British Columbian Quarterly*, no. 166 (2010): 55–72.

Geary, Christraud M. "Missionary Photography: Private and Public Readings." *African Arts* 24, no. 4 (1991): 48–100.

Giesbrecht, Donovan. "Metis, Mennonites and the 'Unsettled Prairie,' 1874–1896." *Journal of Mennonite Studies* 19, no. 1 (2001): 103–11.

Gitelman, Lisa. *Always Already New: Media, History and the Data of Culture*. Cambridge, MA: MIT Press, 2008.

Gitelman, Lisa, and Geoffrey B. Pingree, eds. *New Media, 1740–1915*. Cambridge, MA: MIT Press, 2004.

Glover, Jeffrey, and Matt Cohen, eds. *Colonial Mediascapes: Sensory Worlds of the Early Americas*. Lincoln: University of Nebraska Press, 2014.

Graeber, David. "Exchange." In *Critical Terms for Media Studies*, edited by W. J. T. Mitchell and Mark B. N Hansen, 217–32. Chicago: Chicago University Press, 2010.

Gray, Charlotte. *The Massey Murder: A Maid, Her Master and the Trial That Shocked a Country*. New York: Harper Collins, 2013.

Greco, Monica. "On the Vitality of Vitalism." *Theory, Culture & Society* 22, no. 1 (2005): 15–27.

Griffith, R. Marie. *God's Daughters: Evangelical Women and the Power of Submission*. Berkeley: University of California Press, 2000.

Guedon, Marie-Françoise. "An Introduction to Tsimshian World View and Its Practitioners." In *The Tsimshian: Images of the Past, Views for the Present*, edited by Margaret Seguin Anderson, 137–59. Vancouver: University of British Columbia Press, 1984.

Guerlac, Suzanne. *Thinking in Time: An Introduction to Henri Bergson*. Ithaca, NY: Cornell University Press, 2006.

Hall, D. J. *From Treaties to Reserves: The Federal Government and Native Peoples in Territorial Alberta, 1870–1905*. Montreal: McGill-Queen's University Press, 2015.

Harding, Susan. *The Book of Jerry Falwell: Fundamentalist Language and Politics*. Princeton, NJ: Princeton University Press, 2001.

Harris, Cole. *Making Native Space: Colonialism, Resistance, and Reserves in*

British Columbia. Vancouver: University of British Columbia Press, 2002.

———. "Moving amid the Mountains, 1870–1930." *BC Studies: The British Columbian Quarterly*, no. 58 (1983): 3–39.

Harvey, Megan. "Story People: Stó:lō-State Relations and Indigenous Literacies in British Columbia, 1864–1874." *Journal of the Canadian Historical Association* 24, no. 1 (2013): 51–88.

Hatfield, Leonard F. *Simon Gibbons, First Eskimo Priest: The Life of a Unique Clergyman and Church Builder*. Hantsport, NS: Lancelot Press, 1987.

Hawkins, Sean. *Writing and Colonialism in Northern Ghana: The Encounter between the LoDagaa and "The World on Paper."* Toronto: University of Toronto Press, 2002.

Hayes, Alan Lauffer. *Anglicans in Canada: Controversies and Identity in Historical Perspective*. Chicago: University of Illinois Press, 2004.

Hayward, Rhodri. "Demonology, Neurology, and Medicine in Edwardian Britain." *Bulletin of the History of Medicine* 78, no. 1 (2004): 37–58.

Hedstrom, Matthew. *The Rise of Liberal Religion: Book Culture and American Spirituality in the Twentieth Century*. New York: Oxford University Press, 2013.

Hendershot, Heather. *Shaking the World for Jesus: Media and Conservative Evangelical Culture*. Chicago: University of Chicago Press, 2004.

Hillaire, Pauline. *A Totem Pole History: The Work of Lummi Carver Joe Hillaire*. Lincoln: University of Nebraska Press, 2013.

Hilmes, Michele, and Jason Loviglio, eds. *Radio Reader: Essays in the Cultural History of Radio*. New York: Routledge, 2002.

Hirt, Irène. "Mapping Dreams/Dreaming Maps: Bridging Indigenous and Western Geographical Knowledge." *Cartographica: The International Journal for Geographic Information and Geovisualization* 47, no. 2 (2012): 105–20.

Hofmeyr, Isabel. *Gandhi's Printing Press*. Cambridge, MA: Harvard University Press, 2013.

———. "Inventing the World: Transnationalism, Transmission and Christian Textualities." In *Mixed Messages: Materiality, Textuality, Missions*, edited by Jamie S. Scott and Gareth Griffiths, 19–36. New York: Palgrave Macmillan, 2005.

Holzkamm, Tim E., Victor P. Lytwyn, and Leo G. Waisberg. "Rainy River Sturgeon: An Ojibway Resource in the Fur Trade Economy." *Canadian Geographer / Le Géographe Canadien* 32, no. 3 (1988): 194–205.

Horton, Robert Animikii. "A Seventh Fire Spark: Preparing the Seventh Generation: What Are the Education Related Needs and Concerns of Students from Rainy River First Nations?" MA thesis, Lakehead University, Thunder Bay, 2011.

Hoskins, Janet A. "The Camera as Global Vampire? Tourism and Photography in Remote Areas." In *The Framed World: Tourism, Tourists and Photography*, edited by David Picard, 151–68. Hants, UK: Ashgate Publishers, 2009.

Hunter, Al. *Beautiful Razor: Love Poems and Other Lies*. Wiarton, ON: Kegedonce Press, 2012.

———. *Spirit Horses*. Wiarton, ON: Kegedonce Press, 2002.

Jackson, Gregory S. *The Word and Its Witness: The Spiritualization of American Realism*. Chicago: University of Chicago Press, 2009.

Jackson, Heather J. *Marginalia: Readers Writing in Books*. New Haven, CT: Yale University Press, 2002.

James, William. *A Pluralistic Universe: Hibbert Lectures at Manchester College on the Present Situation in Philosophy*. New York: Longmans, Green, and Company, 1909.

———. *The Principles of Psychology*. Vol. 1. New York: Holt, 1890.

———. *The Principles of Psychology*. Vol. 2. London: MacMillan, 1891.

———. *The Varieties of Religious Experience*. Cambridge, MA: Harvard University Press, 1985.

Jasanoff, Maya. *Liberty's Exiles: American Loyalists in the Revolutionary World*. New York: Knopf Doubleday, 2012.

Jensz, Felicity. "The Function of Inaugural Editorials in Missionary Periodicals." *Church History* 82, no. 2 (2013): 374–80.

Jensz, Felicity, and Hanna Acke, eds. *Missions and Media: The Politics of Missionary Periodicals in the Long Nineteenth Century*. Stuttgart, Ger.: Franz Steiner Verlag, 2013.

Johns, Adrian. *The Nature of the Book: Print and Knowledge in the Making*. Chicago: University of Chicago Press, 1998.

Johnson, Paul Christopher, Pamela E. Klassen, and Winnifred Fallers Sullivan. *Ekklesia: Three Inquiries in Church and State*. Chicago: University of Chicago Press, 2018.

Johnston, Anna. "British Missionary Publishing, Missionary Celebrity, and Empire." *Nineteenth-Century Prose* 32, no. 2 (2005): 20 43.

Johnston, Basil. *The Manitous: The Spiritual World of the Ojibway*. New York: HarperPerennial, 1996.

———. *Ojibway Heritage*. Toronto: McClelland and Stewart, 1976.

Kaplan, Louis. *The Strange Case of William Mumler, Spirit Photographer*. Minneapolis: University of Minnesota Press, 2008.

Karsten, Peter. *Between Law and Custom: "High" and "Low" Legal Cultures in the Lands of the British Diaspora—the United States, Canada, Australia, and New Zealand, 1600–1900*. Cambridge: Cambridge University Press, 2002.

Katerberg, William. *Modernity and the Dilemma of North American Anglican Identities, 1880–1950*. Montreal: McGill-Queen's University Press, 2001.

Keane, Webb. *Christian Moderns: Freedom and Fetish in the Mission Encounter*. Berkeley: University of California Press, 2007.

Kennedy, Rosanne, Lynne Bell, and Julia Emberley, eds. *Decolonising Testimony: On the Possibilities and Limits of Witnessing*. Humanities Research, vol. 15, no. 3. Canberra: Australian National University Press, 2009.

Kenyon, Walter Andrew. *Mounds of Sacred Earth: Burial Mounds of Ontario*. Toronto: Royal Ontario Museum, 1986.

King, Thomas. *The Truth about Stories: A Native Narrative*. Toronto: House of Anansi Press, 2003.

Kirk, Sylvia van. "From 'Marrying-In' to 'Marrying-Out': Changing Patterns of Aboriginal/Non-Aboriginal Marriage in Colonial Canada." *Frontiers: A Journal of Women's Studies* 23, no. 3 (2002): 1–11.

Klassen, Pamela E. "Christianity as a Polemical Concept." In *A Companion to the Anthropology of Religion*, edited by Janice Boddy and Michael Lambek, 344–62. London: Wiley-Blackwell, 2013.

———. "Fantasies of Sovereignty: Civic Secularism in Canada." *Critical Research on Religion* 3, no. 1 (2015): 41–56.

———. "God Keep Our Land: The Legal Ritual of the McKenna-McBride Royal Commission, 1913–1916." In *Religion and the Exercise of Public Authority*, edited by Benjamin L. Berger and Richard Moon, 79–93. Oxford: Hart Publishing, 2016.

———. "Mentality, Fundamentality and the Colonial Secular; or How Real Is Real Estate?" In *Transformations of Religion and the Public Sphere: Postsecular Publics*, edited by Rosi Braidotti, Bolette Blaagaard, and Eva Midden, 175–94. London: Palgrave Macmillan, 2014.

———. *Spirits of Protestantism: Medicine, Healing, and Liberal Christianity*. Berkeley: University of California Press, 2011.

Klassen, Pamela E., and Kathryn Lofton. "Material Witnesses: Women and the Mediation of Christianity." In *Media, Religion, and Gender: Key Issues and New Challenges*, edited by Mia Lövheim, 52–65. New York: Routledge, 2013.

Kloppenborg, John S. "James 1:2–15 and Hellenistic Psychagogy." *Novum Testamentum* 52, no. 1 (2010): 37–71.

Kortenaar, Neil ten. *Postcolonial Literature and the Impact of Literacy: Reading and Writing in African and Caribbean Fiction*. Cambridge: Cambridge University Press, 2011.

Kosek, Joseph Kip. *Acts of Conscience: Christian Nonviolence and Modern American Democracy*. New York: Columbia University Press, 2011.

Large, R. Geddes. *Prince Rupert: A Gateway to Alaska*. Vancouver: Mitchell Press, 1960.

Lass, William E. *Minnesota's Boundary with Canada: Its Evolution since 1783*. Saint Paul: Minnesota Historical Society, 1980.

Ledwon, Lenora. "Native American Life Stories and 'Authorship': Legal and Ethical Issues." *American Indian Quarterly* 21, no. 4 (1997): 579–93.

Lefebvre, Alexandre, and Melanie White. *Bergson, Politics, and Religion*. Durham, NC: Duke University Press, 2012.

Legget, Robert Ferguson. *Ottawa River Canals and the Defence of British North America*. Toronto: University of Toronto Press, 1988.

Leonard, Frank. *A Thousand Blunders: The Grand Trunk Pacific Railway and Northern British Columbia*. Vancouver: University of British Columbia Press, 1996.

Lewis, G. Malcolm. *Cartographic Encounters: Perspectives on Native American Mapmaking and Map Use*. Chicago: University of Chicago Press, 1998.

Lockhurst, Roger. *The Invention of Telepathy, 1870–1901*. Oxford: Oxford University Press, 2002.

Lofton, Kathryn. *Oprah: The Gospel of an Icon*. Berkeley: University of California Press, 2011.

Long, Kathryn T. "'Cameras 'Never Lie': The Role of Photography in Telling the Story of American Evangelical Missions." *Church History: Studies in Christianity and Culture* 72, no. 4 (2003): 820–51.

Longman, Mary. "Ancestors Rising: Aboriginal Art as Historical Testimonials." In *Decolonising Testimony: On the Possibilities and Limits of Witnessing*, edited by Rosanne Kennedy, Lynne Bell, and Julia Emberley, 97–106. Humanities Research, vol. 15, no. 3. Canberra: Australian National University Press, 2009.

Loo, Tina. "Dan Cranmer's Potlatch: Law as Coercion, Symbol, and Rhetoric in British Columbia, 1884–1951." *Canadian Historical Review* 73, no. 2 (1992): 125–65.

Lovisek, Joan A., Tim E. Holzkamm, and Leo G. Waisberg. "Fatal Errors: Ruth Landes and the Creation of the 'Atomistic Ojibwa.'" *Anthropologica* 39, nos. 1–2 (1997): 133–45.

Luckhurst, Roger. *The Invention of Telepathy, 1870–1901*. Oxford: Oxford University Press, 2002.

Lutz, John Sutton. *Makúk: A New History of Aboriginal-White Relations*. Vancouver: University of British Columbia Press, 2008.

Lux, Maureen Katherine. *Medicine That Walks: Disease, Medicine and*

Canadian Plains Native People, 1880–1940. Toronto: University of Toronto Press, 2001.

MacDonald, Joanne. "From Ceremonial Object to Curio: Object Transformation at Port Simpson and Metlakatla, British Columbia in the Nineteenth Century." *Canadian Journal of Native Studies* 10, no. 2 (1990): 193–217.

MacLean, J. Kennedy. "The Keswick Convention." *Quiver* 45, no. 9 (1910): 798–804.

Mainville, Sara J. "Manidoo Mazina'igan: An Anishinaabe Perspective of Treaty 3." MA thesis, University of Toronto, 2007.

Maitland, Frederic. "The Corporation Sole." *Law Quarterly Review* 16 (1900): 335–54.

———. "The Crown as Corporation." *Law Quarterly Review* 17 (1901): 131–46.

Mak, Bonnie. *How the Page Matters*. Toronto: University of Toronto Press, 2011.

Manktelow, Emily J. "The Rise and Demise of Missionary Wives." *Journal of Women's History* 26, no. 1 (2014): 135–59.

Marks, Lynne. "Leaving God Behind When They Crossed the Rocky Mountains: Exploring Unbelief in Turn-of-the-Century British Columbia." In *Household Counts: Canadian Households and Families in 1901*, edited by Peter Baskerville and Eric W. Sager, 371–404. Toronto: University of Toronto Press, 2007.

Marsden, Susan. "Adawx, Spanaxnox, and the Geopolitics of the Tsimshian." *BC Studies: The British Columbian Quarterly*, no. 135 (2002): 101–35.

Masuzawa, Tomoko. *The Invention of World Religions; Or, How European Universalism Was Preserved in the Language of Pluralism*. Chicago: University of Chicago Press, 2005.

Matthewman, Phyllis. *James B. McCullagh*. Heroes of the Cross. Grand Rapids, MI: Zondervan, 1957.

Matthews, Maureen. *Naamiwan's Drum: The Story of a Contested Repatriation of Anishinaabe Artefacts*. University of Toronto Press, 2017.

Mauss, Marcel. *The Gift: The Form and Reason for Exchange in Archaic Societies*. Translated by W. D. Hall. Oxford: Routledge, 2002.

Mawani, Renisa. *Colonial Proximities: Crossracial Encounters and Juridical Truths in British Columbia, 1871–1921*. Vancouver: University of British Columbia Press, 2010.

Maxwell, David. "Photography and the Religious Encounter: Ambiguity and Aesthetics in Missionary Representations of the Luba of South East Belgian Congo." *Comparative Studies in Society and History* 53, no. 1 (2011): 38–74.

May, Nicholas. "Feasting on the AAM of Heaven: The Christianization of the Nisga'a, 1860–1920." PhD diss., University of Toronto, 2013.

———. "Life of Niysyok: Exploring Nisga'a Religious Lives through Biography of a Personage." Paper presented at the Berkshire Conference on the History of Women, Toronto, May 24, 2014.

McCall, Sophie. *First Person Plural: Aboriginal Storytelling and the Ethics of Collaborative Authorship*. Vancouver: University of British Columbia Press, 2011.

McCann, Gillian. *Vanguard of the New Age: The Toronto Theosophical Society, 1891–1945*. Montreal: McGill-Queen's University Press, 2012.

McCullagh, James Benjamin. *The Aiyansh Mission: Naas River, British Columbia*. London: Church Missionary Society, 1907.

———. *The Indian Potlatch: Substance of a Paper Read before C.M.S. Annual Conference at Metlakatla, B.C., 1899*. Toronto: Women's Missionary Society of the Methodist Church, 1899.

McCullum, Hugh, and Karmel Taylor McCullum. *Caledonia: 100 Years Ahead*. Toronto: Anglican Book Centre, 1979.

McDonald, James A. "Bleeding Day and Night: The Construction of the Grand Trunk Pacific Railway across Tsimshian Reserve Lands." *Canadian Journal of Native Studies* 10, no. 1 (1990): 33–68.

McGowan, Katharine A. "'Until We Receive Just Treatment': The Fight against Conscription in the Naas Agency, British Columbia." *BC Studies: The British Columbian Quarterly*, no. 167 (2010): 47–70.

McKee, Stuart. "How Print Culture Came to Be Indigenous." *Visible Language* 44, no. 2 (2010): 161–86.

McKenzie, Donald Francis. *Oral Culture, Literacy and Print in Early New Zealand: The Treaty of Waitangi*. Wellington, NZ: Victoria University Press, 1985.

McLuhan, Marshall. *Understanding Media: The Extensions of Man*. Abingdon, UK: Routledge Classics, 2001.

McNab, David T. "The Administration of Treaty 3: The Location of the Boundaries of Treaty 3 Indian Reserves in Ontario, 1873–1915." In *As Long as the Sun Shines and Water Flows: A Reader in Canadian Native Studies*, edited by Ian A. L Getty and Antoine S. Lussier, 145–57. Vancouver: University of British Columbia Press, 1983.

McNally, Michael David. *Honoring Elders: Aging, Authority, and Ojibwe Religion*. New York: Columbia University Press, 2009.

McNeil, Kent. "Judicial Approaches to Self-Government since Calder: Searching for Doctrinal Coherence." In *Let Right Be Done: Aboriginal Title, the Calder Case, and the Future of Indigenous Rights*, edited by Hamar Foster,

Heather Raven, and Jeremy Webber, 129–54. Vancouver: University of British Columbia Press, 2007.

Meyer, Birgit. "Religious Sensations: Why Media, Aesthetics, and Power Matter in the Study of Contemporary Religion." In *Religion: Beyond a Concept*, edited by Hent de Vries, 704–23. New York: Fordham University Press, 2009.

———. *Translating the Devil: Religion and Modernity among the Ewe in Ghana*. Edinburgh: Edinburgh University Press, 1999.

Michel, Anthony P. "To Represent the Country in Egypt: Aboriginality, Britishness, Anglophone Canadian Identities, and the Nile Voyageur Contingent, 1884–1885." *Histoire Sociale / Social History* 39, no. 77 (2006): 45–77.

Middleton, Jesse Edgar. *The Municipality of Toronto: A History*. Vol. 3. Toronto: Dominion Publishing Company, 1923.

Miller, Bruce Granville. *Oral History on Trial: Recognizing Aboriginal Narratives in the Courts*. Vancouver: University of British Columbia Press, 2012.

Miller, James Rodger. *Shingwauk's Vision: A History of Native Residential Schools*. Toronto: University of Toronto Press, 1996.

Miller, Jay. *Tsimshian Culture: A Light through the Ages*. Lincoln: University of Nebraska Press, 2000.

———. "Tsimshian Ethno-Ethnohistory: A 'Real' Indigenous Chronology." *Ethnohistory* 45, no. 4 (1998): 657–74.

Miller, Robert J., Jacinta Ruru, Larissa Behrendt, and Tracey Lindberg. *Discovering Indigenous Lands: The Doctrine of Discovery in the English Colonies*. Oxford: Oxford University Press, 2012.

Milloy, John S. *A National Crime: The Canadian Government and the Residential School System, 1879 to 1986*. Winnipeg: University of Manitoba Press, 1999.

Mills, Antonia Curtze. *"Hang Onto These Words": Johnny David's Delgamuukw Evidence*. Toronto: University of Toronto Press, 2005.

Modern, John Lardas. *Secularism in Antebellum America*. Chicago: University of Chicago Press, 2011.

Moeran, Joseph William Wright. *McCullagh of Aiyansh*. London: Marshall Brothers, 1923.

Moreton-Robinson, Aileen. *The White Possessive*. Minneapolis: University of Minnesota Press, 2015.

Morgan, David. *Protestants and Pictures: Religion, Visual Culture and the Age of American Mass Production*. Oxford: Oxford University Press, 1999.

Morison, Odille. "Tsimshian Proverbs." *Journal of American Folklore* 2, no. 7 (1889): 285–86.

Morrison, Hugh. "'Impressions Which Will Never Be Lost': Missionary Periodicals for Protestant Children in Late-Nineteenth Century Canada and New Zealand." *Church History* 82, no. 2 (2013): 388–93.

Napoleon, Valerie Ruth. "Ayook: Gitksan Legal Order, Law, and Legal Theory." PhD diss., University of Victoria, 2009.

Nayar, Kamala Elizabeth. *The Punjabis in British Columbia: Location, Labour, First Nations, and Multiculturalism*. Montreal: McGill-Queen's University Press, 2012.

Nelles, H. V. *A Little History of Canada*. Toronto: Oxford University Press, 2004.

Neu, Dean. "'Presents' for the 'Indians': Land, Colonialism and Accounting in Canada." *Accounting, Organizations and Society* 25, no. 2 (2000): 163–84.

Neylan, Susan. *The Heavens Are Changing: Nineteenth-Century Protestant Missions and Tsimshian Christianity*. Montreal: McGill-Queen's University Press, 2002.

Niezen, Ronald. "Digital Identity: The Construction of Virtual Selfhood in the Indigenous Peoples' Movement." *Comparative Studies in Society and History* 47, no. 3 (2005): 532–51.

———. *The Rediscovered Self: Indigenous Identity and Cultural Justice*. Montreal: McGill-Queen's University Press, 2009.

———. *Spirit Wars: Native North American Religions in the Age of Nation Building*. Berkeley: University of California Press, 2000.

Nisga'a Tribal Council. *Nisga'a: People of the Nass River*. Vancouver: Douglas & McIntyre, 1993.

Nute, Grace Lee. *Rainy River Country: A Brief History of the Region Bordering Minnesota and Ontario*. St. Paul: Minnesota Historical Society Press, 1950.

Obarrio, Juan. "Postshamanism (1999)." *Cultural Studies Review* 13, no. 2 (2007): 166–89.

O'Brien, Jean M. *Firsting and Lasting: Writing Indians Out of Existence in New England*. Minneapolis: University of Minnesota Press, 2010.

O'Donnell, James J. *The "Confessions" of Augustine*. Oxford: Clarendon Press, 1992. Stoa Consortium. http://www.stoa.org/hippo/.

———. "Prolegomena." In *The "Confessions" of Saint Augustine*. Oxford: Clarendon Press, 1992. Stoa Consortium. http://www.stoa.org/hippo/comm.html.

O'Hara, James B. "The Modern Corporation Sole." *Dickason Law Review* 93 (1988): 23–39.

O'Neill, Kevin Lewis. "Writing Guatemala's Genocide: Truth and Reconciliation Commission Reports and Christianity." *Journal of Genocide Research* 7, no. 3 (2005): 331–49.

Owen, Alex. *The Darkened Room: Women, Power, and Spiritualism in Late Victorian England*. Chicago: University of Chicago Press, 1989.

Palmer, Mark. "Theorizing Indigital Geographic Information Networks." *Cartographica: The International Journal for Geographic Information and Geovisualization* 47, no. 2 (2012): 80–91.

Patterson, E. Palmer. *Mission on the Nass: The Evangelization of the Nishga (1860–1890)*. Waterloo, ON: Eulachon Press, 1982.

Perry, Adele. "The Autocracy of Love and the Legitimacy of Empire: Intimacy, Power and Scandal in Nineteenth-Century Metlakahtlah." *Gender & History* 16, no. 2 (2004): 261–88.

———. "Metropolitan Knowledge, Colonial Practice, and Indigenous Womanhood: Missions in Nineteenth-Century British Columbia." In *Contact Zones: Aboriginal and Settler Women in Canada's Colonial Past*, edited by Katie Pickles and Myra Rutherdale, 109–31. Vancouver: University of British Columbia Press, 2005.

———. *On the Edge of Empire: Gender, Race, and the Making of British Columbia, 1849–1871*. Toronto: University of Toronto Press, 2001.

———. "The State of Empire: Reproducing Colonialism in British Columbia, 1849–1871." *Journal of Colonialism and Colonial History* 2, no. 2 (2001). https://doi.org/10.1353/cch.2001.0028

Peters, John Durham. *Speaking into the Air: A History of the Idea of Communication*. Chicago: University of Chicago Press, 1999.

Phillips, Ruth B. "'Dispel All Darkness': Material Translations and Cross-Cultural Communication in Seventeenth-Century North America." *Art in Translation* 2, no. 2 (2010): 171–200.

———. "Things Anishinaabe: Art, Agency, and Exchange across Time." In *Before and after the Horizon: Anishinaabe Artists of the Great Lakes*, edited by David W. Penney and Gerald McMaster, 51–70. Washington, DC: National Museum of the American Indian, 2013.

Pinney, Christopher. *Camera Indica: The Social Life of Indian Photographs*. Chicago: University of Chicago Press, 1997.

Pinney, Christopher, and Nicolas Peterson. *Photography's Other Histories*. Durham, NC: Duke University Press, 2003.

Plas, Régine. "Psychology and Psychical Research in France around the End of the 19th Century." *History of the Human Sciences* 25, no. 2 (2012): 91–107.

Porter, Eric. "The Anglican Church and Native Education: Residential Schools and Assimilation." MA thesis, University of Toronto, 1981.

Price, Christine. "'A Very Conservative Radical': Reverend Robert Connell's Encounter with Marxism in the BC CCF." MA thesis, Simon Fraser University, 2006.

Pringle-Pattison, Andrew Seth. "Immanence and Transcendence." In *The Spirit: The Relation of God and Man, Considered from the Standpoint of Recent Philosophy and Science*, edited by Burnett Hillman Streeter, 1–24. New York: Macmillan, 1922.

Pyne, Stephanie. "Mapping Indigenous Perspectives in the Making of the Cybercartographic Atlas of the Lake Huron Treaty Relationship Process: A Performative Approach in a Reconciliation Context." *Cartographica: The International Journal for Geographic Information and Geovisualization* 47, no. 2 (2012): 92–104.

Raibmon, Paige Sylvia. *Authentic Indians: Episodes of Encounter from the Late-Nineteenth-Century Northwest Coast*. Durham, NC: Duke University Press, 2005.

Raj, Kapil. *Relocating Modern Science: Circulation and the Construction of Knowledge in South Asia and Europe, 1650–1900*. New York: Palgrave Macmillan, 2007.

Raunet, Daniel. *Without Surrender, without Consent: A History of the Nisga'a Land Claims*. Vancouver: Douglas & McIntyre, 1996.

Ray, Arthur. "Treaty 8: A British Columbian Anomaly." *BC Studies: The British Columbian Quarterly*, no. 123 (1999): 5–58.

Richet, Charles. *Thirty Years of Psychical Research*. New York: MacMillan, 1923.

Rivett, Sarah. *The Science of the Soul in Colonial New England*. Chapel Hill: University of North Carolina Press, 2011.

Robertson, Leslie. *Standing up with Ga'axsta'las: Jane Constance Cook and the Politics of Memory, Church, and Custom*. Vancouver: University of British Columbia Press, 2012.

Robertson, Michael. *Worshipping Walt: The Whitman Disciples*. Princeton, NJ: Princeton University Press, 2010.

Robinson, Eden. *The Sasquatch at Home: Traditional Protocols and Modern Storytelling*. Edmonton: University of Alberta Press, 2012.

———. *Son of a Trickster*. Toronto: Alfred A. Knopf, 2017.

Roth, Christopher F. "Goods, Names, and Selves: Rethinking the Tsimshian Potlatch." *American Ethnologist* 29, no. 1 (2002): 123–50.

Rowley, Owsley Robert. *The Anglican Episcopate of Canada and Newfoundland*. London: A. R Mowbray & Co., 1928.

Roy, Patricia E. *The Oriental Question: Consolidating a White Man's Province, 1914–41*. Vancouver: University of British Columbia Press, 2011.

Royce, Josiah. *The Problem of Christianity: Lectures*. New York: Macmillan, 1913.

Rugg, Linda Haverty. *Picturing Ourselves: Photography and Autobiography*. Chicago: University of Chicago Press, 1997.

Rutherdale, Myra. "Maternal Metaphors in the Northern Canadian Mission Field." In *Canadian Missionaries, Indigenous Peoples: Representing Religion at Home and Abroad*, edited by Alvyn Austin and Jamie S. Scott, 46–66. Toronto: University of Toronto Press, 2005.

———. *Women and the White Man's God: Gender and Race in the Canadian Mission Field*. Vancouver: University of British Columbia Press, 2003.

Ryan, Maureen. "Picturing Canada's Native Landscape: Colonial Expansion, National Identity, and the Image of a 'Dying Race.'" *RACAR: Revue d'Art Canadienne / Canadian Art Review* 17, no. 2 (1990): 138–49.

Sabine, Lorenzo. *Biographical Sketches of Loyalists of the American Revolution: With an Historical Essay*. Vol. 2. Boston: Little, Brown and Company, 1864.

Said, Edward W. *Culture and Imperialism*. New York: Vintage, 1994.

———. *On Late Style: Music and Literature against the Grain*. New York: Pantheon Books, 2006.

Sapir, E. "Nass River Terms of Relationship." *American Anthropologist* 22, no. 3 (July 9, 1920): 261–71.

Scherer, Matthew. *Beyond Church and State: Democracy, Secularism, and Conversion*. Cambridge: Cambridge University Press, 2013.

Schmidt, Leigh Eric. *Hearing Things: Religion, Illusion, and the American Enlightenment*. Cambridge, MA: Harvard University Press, 2000.

———. *Heaven's Bride: The Unprintable Life of Ida C. Craddock, American Mystic, Scholar, Sexologist, Martyr, and Madwoman*. New York: Basic Books, 2010.

Sconce, Jeffrey. *Haunted Media: Electronic Presence from Telegraphy to Television*. Durham, NC: Duke University Press, 2000.

Scott, Anne. "'Visible Incarnations of the Unseen': Henry Drummond and the Practice of Typological Exegesis." *British Journal for the History of Science* 37, no. 4 (2004): 435–54.

Scott, C. Anderson. "What Happened at Pentecost." In *The Spirit: The Relation of God and Man, Considered from the Standpoint of Recent Philosophy and Science*, edited by Burnett Hillman Streeter, 115–56. New York: Macmillan, 1922.

Semple, Rhonda. "Missionary Manhood: Professionalism, Belief and Masculinity in the Nineteenth-Century British Imperial Field." *Journal of Imperial and Commonwealth History* 36, no. 3 (2008): 397–415.

Simpson, Audra. *Mohawk Interruptus: Political Life across the Borders of Settler States*. Durham, NC: Duke University Press, 2014.

Simpson, Leanne. "Anticolonial Strategies for the Recovery and Maintenance of Indigenous Knowledge." *American Indian Quarterly* 28, no. 3 (2004): 373–84.

———. "Stories, Dreams, and Ceremonies—Anishinaabe Ways of Learning." *Tribal College* 11, no. 4 (2000): 26–29.

Smith, Harlan I. "Archeological Remains on the Coast of Northern British Columbia and Southern Alaska." *American Anthropologist* 11, no. 4 (1909): 595–600.

———. "The Man Petroglyph near Prince Rupert, or the Man Who Fell from Heaven." In *Essays in Anthropology: Presented to A. L Kroeber in Celebration of His Sixtieth Birthday, June 11, 1936*, edited by Robert Harry Lowie. Berkeley: University of California Press, 1936.

Smith, Jonathan Z. *Map Is Not Territory: Studies in the History of Religions*. Chicago: University of Chicago Press, 1993.

———. *Relating Religion: Essays in the Study of Religion*. Chicago: University of Chicago Press, 2004.

Smith, Keith D. *Strange Visitors: Documents in Indigenous-Settler Relations in Canada from 1876*. Toronto: University of Toronto Press, 2014.

Smith, Sidonie, and Julia Watson. *Reading Autobiography: A Guide for Interpreting Life Narratives*. Minneapolis: University of Minnesota Press, 2010.

Smith, T. Watson. "The Slave in Canada." *Collections of the Nova Scotia Historical Society* 10 (1899): 1–161.

Spray, William A. "Saunders, John." In *Dictionary of Canadian Biography*. University of Toronto / Université Laval, 2003–. Accessed November 8, 2015. http://www.biographi.ca/en/bio/saunders_john_6E.html.

Stearns, Mary Lee. *Haida Culture in Custody: The Masset Band*. Seattle: University of Washington Press, 1981.

Sterling, Christopher H. *Biographical Encyclopedia of American Radio*. New York: Routledge, 2013.

Sterritt, Neil. *Tribal Boundaries in the Nass Watershed*. Vancouver: University of British Columbia Press, 1998.

Stevens, Laura M. *The Poor Indians: British Missionaries, Native Americans, and Colonial Sensibility*. Philadelphia: University of Pennsylvania Press, 2004.

Stewart, Hilary. *Cedar: Tree of Life to the Northwest Coast Indians*. Vancouver: Douglas & McIntyre, 1995.

Stimson, Adrian. "Used and Abused." In *Decolonising Testimony: On the Possibilities and Limits of Witnessing*, edited by Rosanne Kennedy, Lynne Bell, and Julia Emberley, 71–80. Humanities Research, vol. 15, no. 3. Canberra: Australian National University Press, 2009.

Stolow, Jeremy. "Technology." In *Key Words in Religion, Media and Culture*, edited by David Morgan, 187–97. New York: Routledge, 2008.

Suzack, Cheryl. "The Transposition of Law and Literature in Delgamuukw and Monkey Beach." *South Atlantic Quarterly* 110, no. 2 (2011): 447–63.

TallBear, Kim. "An Indigenous Reflection on Working beyond the Human/Not Human." *GLQ: A Journal of Lesbian and Gay Studies* 21, nos. 2–3 (2015): 230–35.

Taves, Ann. *Fits, Trances, and Visions: Experiencing Religion and Explaining Experience from Wesley to James*. Princeton, NJ: Princeton University Press, 1999.

Taylor, Charles. *Modern Social Imaginaries*. Durham, NC: Duke University Press, 2004.

Taylor, Chloé. *The Culture of Confession from Augustine to Foucault*. New York: Taylor & Francis, 2008.

Tomalin, Marcus. *And He Knew Our Language: Missionary Linguistics on the Pacific Northwest Coast*. Amsterdam: John Benjamins Publishing, 2011.

Truth and Reconciliation Commission of Canada. *The Final Report of the Truth and Reconciliation Commission of Canada*. Vol. 1, *Canada's Residential Schools: The History, Part 1, Origins to 1939*. Montreal: McGill-Queen's University Press, 2016.

———. *The Final Report of the Truth and Reconciliation Commission of Canada*. Vol. 1, *Summary: Honouring the Truth, Reconciling for the Future*. Toronto: James Lorimer & Company, 2015.

Tuck, Eve, and K. Wayne Yang. "Decolonization Is Not a Metaphor." *Decolonization: Indigeneity, Education & Society* 1, no. 1 (2012): 1–40.

Turnbull, David, and Helen Watson. *Maps Are Territories: Science Is an Atlas: A Portfolio of Exhibits*. Chicago: University of Chicago Press, 1989.

Tusan, Michelle. "Gleaners in the Holy Land: Women and the Missionary Press in Victorian Britain." *Nineteenth Century Gender Studies* 6, no. 2 (2010).

Tylor, Edward Burnett. *Primitive Culture: Researches into the Development of Mythology, Philosophy, Religion, Art, and Custom*. London: J. Murray, 1871.

Umeek/E. Richard Atleo. *Principles of Tsawalk: An Indigenous Approach to Global Crisis*. Vancouver: University of British Columbia Press, 2011.

Usher, Jean. *William Duncan of Metlakatla: A Victorian Missionary in British Columbia*. Ottawa: National Museums of Canada, 1974.

Vecsey, Christopher. *Traditional Ojibwa Religion and Its Historical Changes*. Philadelphia, PA: American Philosophical Society, 1983.

Veer, Peter van der. *Imperial Encounters: Religion and Modernity in India and Britain*. Princeton, NJ: Princeton University Press, 2001.

Vickers, Patricia June. "Ayaawx (Ts'msyen Ancestral Law): The Power of Transformation." PhD diss., University of Victoria, 2008.

Vipond, Mary. *Listening In: The First Decade of Canadian Broadcasting, 1922–1932*. Montreal: McGill-Queen's University Press, 1992.

Vipond, Robert. *Making a Global City: How One Toronto School Embraced Diversity*. Toronto: University of Toronto Press, 2017.

Viswanathan, Gauri. *Outside the Fold: Conversion, Modernity, and Belief*. Princeton, NJ: Princeton University Press, 1998.

Waisberg, Leo G., and Tim E. Holzkamm. "'A Tendency to Discourage Them from Cultivating': Ojibwa Agriculture and Indian Affairs Administration in Northwestern Ontario." *Ethnohistory* 40, no. 2 (1993): 175–211.

Walker, Bruce Dudley. "The County of Missisquoi in the Eastern Townships of the Province of Quebec (1770s–1867)." MA thesis, McGill University, 1974.

Warner, Michael. "Publics and Counterpublics." *Public Culture* 14, no. 1 (2002): 49–90.

Watkinson, Stephen. "Life after Death: The Importance of Salmon Carcasses to British Columbia's Watersheds." *ARCTIC* 53, no. 1 (2000): 92–96.

Webber, Jeremy. *The Constitution of Canada: A Contextual Analysis*. London: Bloomsbury Publishing, 2015.

Wellcome, Sir Henry Solomon. *The Story of Metlakahtla*. London: Saxon & Co, 1887.

Westfall, William. *Founding Moment: Church, Society, and the Construction of Trinity College*. Montreal: McGill-Queen's University Press, 2002.

Wheeler, Winona. "The Journals and Voices of a Church of England Native Catechist: Askenootow (Charles Pratt), 1851–1884," In *Reading Beyond Words: Contexts for Native History*, edited by Jennifer S. H. Brown and Elizabeth Vibert. 237–61 Peterborough, ON: Broadview Press, 2003.

White, Bruce. *We Are at Home: Pictures of the Ojibwe People*. Minneapolis: Minnesota Historical Society, 2008.

White, Christopher G. *Unsettled Minds: Psychology and the American Search for Spiritual Assurance, 1830–1940*. Berkeley: University of California Press, 2009.

Wilson, Alan. *The Clergy Reserves of Upper Canada*. Canadian Historical Association Booklets 23. Ottawa: Canadian Historical Association, 1969.

Winks, Robin W. *The Blacks in Canada: A History*. Montreal: McGill-Queen's University Press, 1997.

Woods, Eric Taylor. "A Cultural Approach to a Canadian Tragedy: The Indian Residential Schools as a Sacred Enterprise." *International Journal of Politics, Culture, and Society* 26, no. 2 (2013): 173–87.

Index